LUDMILA ULITSKAYA

AND THE ART OF TOLERANCE

LUDMILA ULITSKAYA
AND THE ART OF TOLERANCE

ELIZABETH A. SKOMP

and

BENJAMIN M. SUTCLIFFE

THE UNIVERSITY OF WISCONSIN PRESS

The University of Wisconsin Press
1930 Monroe Street, 3rd Floor
Madison, Wisconsin 53711-2059
uwpress.wisc.edu

3 Henrietta Street, Covent Garden
London WC2E 8LU, United Kingdom
eurospanbookstore.com

Copyright © 2015
The Board of Regents of the University of Wisconsin System
All rights reserved. Except in the case of brief quotations embedded in critical articles and reviews, no part of this publication may be reproduced, stored in a retrieval system, transmitted in any format or by any means—digital, electronic, mechanical, photocopying, recording, or otherwise—or conveyed via the Internet or a website without written permission of the University of Wisconsin Press. Rights inquiries should be directed to rights@uwpress.wisc.edu.

Printed in the United States of America

Library of Congress Cataloging-in-Publication Data

Skomp, Elizabeth, author.
Ludmila Ulitskaya and the art of tolerance / Elizabeth A. Skomp and Benjamin M. Sutcliffe.
    pages   cm
Includes bibliographical references and index.
ISBN 978-0-299-30414-0 (pbk.: alk. paper)
ISBN 978-0-299-30413-3 (e-book)
1. Ulitskaia, Liudmila—Criticism and interpretation.
    I. Sutcliffe, Benjamin M., author. II. Title.
PG3489.2.L58Z87   2015
891.73'5—dc23
2014035271

For our parents

JOHN and ANN SKOMP
MJ SUTCLIFFE and CLAUD SUTCLIFFE

CONTENTS

LIST OF ILLUSTRATIONS
ix

FOREWORD:
INDIVISIBILITY AND THE THREADS THAT BIND
BY HELENA GOSCILO
xi

ACKNOWLEDGMENTS
xxv

AUTHORS' NOTES
xxix

INTRODUCTION:
MYTHS OF THE POST-SOVIET WRITER
3

1. REDEEMING THE BODY:
ULITSKAYA AND CORPOREALITY
32

2. IDEAS THAT BIND:
KINSHIP AS METAPHOR
68

3. AN OBSESSION WITH HISTORY:
ULITSKAYA'S INTELLIGENTSIA WRITES THE PAST
100

4. WRITING TOLERANCE:
MORALITY AND
ULITSKAYA'S THEOLOGY OF INCLUSION
130

CONCLUSION:
ULITSKAYA, INTELLIGENTSIA, AND
THE ETHICS OF THE ORDINARY
166

APPENDIX:
MAJOR WORKS BY ULITSKAYA, 1988–2013
173

NOTES
179

WORKS CITED
217

INDEX
237

ILLUSTRATIONS

Ulitskaya in Moscow near the beginning of her
   writing career   7
Ulitskaya inscribes a copy of *Daniel Stein, Interpreter*
   in Moscow, May 2012   101
Ulitskaya with Boris Akunin and Leonid Parfenov
   in Moscow, January 2011   134

FOREWORD: INDIVISIBILITY AND THE THREADS THAT BIND

HELENA GOSCILO

"Skreshchen'ia ruk, skreshchen'ia nog, Sud'by skreshchen'ia."
["Of crossed arms, crossed legs, and destinies that cross."]
Boris Pasternak,
"Zimniaia noch'," *Doktor Zhivago*
("Winter Night," *Doctor Zhivago*)

"Only connect!"
E. M. Forster,
Howards End

"Le moindre *mouvement* importe à toute *la nature*, la mer entière change *pour* une pierre."
["The least movement is of importance to all nature, the entire ocean is affected by a pebble."]
Blaise Pascal,
Pensées (Thoughts)

The Winning Author

For approximately the last decade, while Boris Akunin and Dar'ia Dontsova have ruled supreme over Russian pop fiction, Ludmila Ulitskaya has enjoyed fame as debatably the most popular author within the more prestigious but less lucrative category of literature.¹ With sales of several million volumes, bombarded by numerous invitations and accolades, Ulitskaya has received more international and Russian awards than any other contemporary Russian writer.² Her prose has been adapted for the small and large screen, translated into more than twenty-five languages, and acclaimed as the achievement of "a great writer" and "best-selling novelist." Indeed, her reputation and extraordinary status enable her to endorse fledgling writers, various projects, and special initiatives such as an educational series of vividly illustrated textbooks for children that promote diversity and tolerance while initiating them into the mysteries of the sciences and humanities. Ulitskaya's first publication, in fact, was a volume of children's stories (1982), and in the early 1990s she confided to me that if her literary efforts found no favor with the public she would abandon fiction to work for any organization that promoted children's well-being.³ More than once she has iterated her self-perception as a dilettante: "It's as if I'm a temporary writer. I'll write everything and then go and do something else."⁴

What accounts for Ulitskaya's remarkable success—not only with the Russian reading public at home and in the diaspora, but also with general readers in Europe and, to a lesser extent, in the United States? A reasonable answer might start with gender. Asked who is their favorite current Russian writer, women in Finland, Sweden, and Poland unhesitatingly name Ulitskaya, echoing the preference expressed by female émigrées and academics within Slavic studies in the United States.⁵ Men, no doubt, would respond differently. Though Ulitskaya explicitly dissociates herself from feminism, she may wish to ponder why specifically Russian male critics such as Mark Lipovetsky and the neo-Freudian Mikhail Zolotonosov have characterized her writing as neo-sentimentalist, thereby implicitly deprecating it.⁶ Other Slavists, such as Alexander Etkind, simply have bypassed her fiction, to focus on such figures as Vladimir Sorokin, Viktor Pelevin, and, among the younger generation, Dmitrii Bykov and former Omon officer Zakhar Prilepin, who all peculiarly mirror Vladimir Putin in their literary obsession with the broad sweep of Russia's past and envisioned future rather than life in its daily manifestations.⁷

In a patently hostile interview in 2011, the literary critic Lev Danilkin from the magazine *Afisha* demanded, "Why, instead of writing about the main thing, do you drown Big History [*sic*] in the individual, drab, and quotidian? Why drown Big Events in a wealth of personal things?"

He iterates his accusation later in the interview, dissatisfied with her frank response: "Strictly speaking, it's precisely the fate of the individual person that interests me. And the fate of governments is the domain of historians and political scientists."[8] Under Putin, apodictic pronouncements about history, grandiose claims that recall the primacy of huge canvasses under Stalin, and self-promotion are the order of the day, and these could hardly be more remote from Ulitskaya's sense of herself as an author. As she has stated, "My task is to pose questions, not solve them,"[9] and the questions absorbing her arise from human relationships in everyday circumstances; hence Western critics' emphasis on her psychological acumen and mastery of nuance in tracing thought processes and emotional shifts. Above all, what draws readers to her prose is their sense of the author behind the works, who projects a humane, down-to-earth, perceptive, and compassionate persona—one profoundly committed to the task of understanding, not judging, human behavior.[10]

Unlike Sorokin and Bykov, Ulitskaya personalizes history, preferring to narrate individual fates in close-up, which is why personal names appear in so many titles of her works: "Bronka" ("Bron'ka," 1989), "The Daughter of Bokhara" ("Doch' Bukhary," 1994), "Lialia's Home" ("Lialin dom," 1994), "Gulia" (1994), *Sonechka* (1992), *Medea and Her Children* (1996), *The Kukotskii Case* (2001), *Sincerely Yours, Shurik* (2003), and *Daniel Stein, Interpreter* (2006), among others. To appreciate how Ulitskaya's treatment of history differs from her male counterparts' one need only peruse the story "March 1953" ("Vtorogo marta togo goda").[11] The year at issue is 1953, and the memorable event that the story's conclusion references is Stalin's death on March 5, which in Tolstoyan fashion Ulitskaya links to the eleven-year-old schoolgirl Lily's rite of passage into womanhood—the onset of menstruation.[12] Both she and the unnamed Stalin, merely called "a dead person" (*mertvyi chelovek*), make a transition to "the next stage" of their lives. Contrasted to Stalin (whom the classmates tormenting Lily at school parallel in diluted miniature), Lily's fatally ill great-grandfather bonds with her by narrating episodes from the past that offer insight into human lives. As he puts it, in quintessentially Ulitskayan terms, "I'm not telling you 'this is bad, this is good.' I'm just telling you how it was."[13] Here, as in most of her stories and novels, memory preserved through narration ensures continuity—a notion already evident in one of her earliest ephemera—a brief essay about the fate of a piece of furniture over time.

Connection

The importance of continuity originates in connection—a fundamental principle of Ulitskaya's worldview from which several of her perennial concerns are inseparable. In a talk delivered in March 2003 at the Museum of Women in the Arts in Washington, DC, she elaborated on the multifaceted nature of what she called *sviazi* (ties, connections) among people and between humankind and nature. Unsurprisingly, in that context she cited Boris Pasternak's *Doctor Zhivago* as a genuine revelation, one that exerted a decisive influence on her perspective: "Pasternak convinced me at a young age that the world is woven from the most delicate threads." In literary creation, she declared, one has only to touch any thread in one's vicinity, and "it will lead one to the depths of the design, through the tension of passions, pain, sufferings, and love." When asked about the "message" she wished to relay to readers, she disavowed having any, and defined her own works as simply the part of her life "that had intersected with the numerous threads of other lives, thoughts, and images."[14] Accordingly, Daniel Stein's role of interpreting from one culture to another represents his efforts to spotlight and strengthen the threads linking individuals, groups, and cultures. Such universal connections carry moral responsibility, which is why Stein appears above all as a spiritual guide, not unlike Virgil leading Dante safely through the Inferno in *The Divine Comedy*.

In *Medea and Her Children* this interconnectedness is grounded in nature and geography. Inseparable from the Tauride coast of the Crimea ("For local people Medea Mendez had long been a part of the landscape"; "She could feel the goodness of this land through the soles of her feet"),[15] the eponymous protagonist integrates close and distant members of the Sinoply family, as well as friends and neighbors, into a multigenerational unit linked through the symbolic house that enables them to share their life experiences and that affirms their sense of belonging. The novel's conclusion comprises a paean to Medea's gift for forging these bonds over several eras: "It is a wonderful feeling, belonging to Medea's family, a family so large that you can't know all its members by sight, and they merge into a vista of things that happened, things that didn't, and things that are yet to come."[16]

Whereas after the implosion of the Soviet Union the concept of home as sanctuary virtually disappeared from Russian film, as Elena Stishova argued in 1993, it occupies a key place in Ulitskaya's fictional world.[17] For her, family, almost invariably troped as a hospitable, loving home, need not consist of blood relatives, as *Medea* and her early novella *Sonechka* testify. In the latter work, the monogamous wife and talented homemaker Sonechka treats the Polish Jasia—who negotiates her way through life by exchanging sex for various favors, manipulates her way into Sonechka's life, and sleeps with Sonechka's husband—as though she were her daughter. Whereas most individuals in Sonechka's orbit possess artistic gifts (painting, music, languages),[18] her particular talent is for life and the creation of a warm, generous environment based on the sort of unquestioning Christian values (i.e., those taught by Christ) that Ulitskaya prizes and steadfastly inscribes as a norm in her works.

Alterity

In urging connection those values foster acceptance of alterity, whatever form it may assume: ethnic and racial difference, which taps into Ulitskaya's sensitivity to Jewish issues, non-standard sexual orientations, or disparity in age between physically intimate partners. One of her earliest stories, titled "Lucky" ("Schastlivye"), describes how an elderly Jewish couple commemorates the death of their seven-year-old son, whom a passing car killed fifteen years ago. While the poignant, subdued narrative focuses on the oldsters' mode of coping with their unforgettable loss, the text makes a passing reference to the Holocaust, stating about the four daughters from Matthias's previous marriage, "the smoke from their bodies had long since dissipated over the pale fields of Poland."[19] Elsewhere Ulitskaya points out that Christ and his apostles were Jews, hence in a profound, non-ritualistic sense, Christian precepts are also Jewish. And *Daniel Stein, Interpreter*, with its ecumenical protagonist, who as a Jew survives the Holocaust and converts to Catholicism, implicitly celebrates nondenominational spirituality. Supremely aware of the hardships confronting Jews in Soviet Russia, Ulitskaya never privileges them as either sufferers or an exceptional people. Not sect, but humanitarian convictions translated into actions on behalf of just causes make for a righteous life. Jews, Catholics, and Orthodox all appear in her fiction, which articulates no partisanship or prejudice along religious or ethnic lines. Speaking of *Daniel Stein, Interpreter* in an interview, she insisted, in an echo of the Existentialists, "It's not important what we think about faith, about the problems of religious life. What's important is what we do."[20] In the same interview she pointed out that Russian schools need a course not on Orthodoxy but on religion examined from various cultural perspectives.[21] Such inclusiveness is one of Ulitskaya's salient features as both author and commentator on contemporary society.

At first glance sexual orientation may appear a rather troublesome category in Ulitskaya's works. For instance, Brian Baer in his excellent monograph *Other Russias* (2009) views her story "Darling" ("Golubchik") as an indictment of homosexuality.[22] Yet surely the story dramatizes the harrowing fate of homosexuals in Soviet Russia, where, under perpetual threat of arrest and incarceration, gays could be killed with impunity, for, as the narrative accurately explains, "the police weren't particularly interested in the murder of homosexuals."[23] Notably, Ulitskaya presents the long-lasting relationship between the adolescent Slava and his stepfather, Nikolai Romanovich, as one of love, not perverse promiscuity ("And how Nikolai Romanovich had loved him. How he had loved him . . .").[24] Though Ulitskaya seems naïve (if sympathetic) in her conviction that gayness can be "taught," her narrative shows awareness of Russia's gay celebrities, such as the pianist Sviatoslav Richter and the painter Konstantin Somov, who elicit not prejudicial criticism but admiration for their artistic brilliance.[25] Regrettably, her knee-jerk association of homosexuality with aesthetic refinement (Nikolai Romanovich teaches classics,[26] loves music, and worships beauty) betrays her superannuated notion of gayness, limited to the historical paradigm of Oscar Wilde, in whom Russian interest revived with a vengeance in the "no holds barred" 1990s.[27] "Darling" is problematic, not because Ulitskaya nurtures homophobic sentiments, but because she seems to have scant knowledge of homosexuality in contemporary praxis—its diversity and prevalence across social classes.

Heterosexuality, by contrast, is an area that she handles with self-assurance and subtlety. Perhaps the most memorable aspect of her portrayal of sexual congress is her penchant for dramatizing an unconventional scenario with which she is clearly familiar: spring-autumn sexual intimacy as a source of joy and pleasure, not as "unnatural" and warranting opprobrium. Uniquely, relationships between individuals dramatically disparate in age proliferate in her works and are impressively gender-neutral. So the thirteen-year-old Bronka bears several children fathered by sixty-nine-year-old Viktor Petrovich, a man who could be her grandfather and whom she loves with an exclusive and fully requited passion ("Bronka"); for several years Jasia becomes mistress to Robert Viktorovich, a sophisticated painter more than twice her age (*Sonechka*); Gulia enjoys and subsequently brags about what nowadays would be called a one-night stand with San, her best friend's son ("Gulia"), while attractive, middle-aged teacher Lialia becomes sexually enslaved to the handsome Kazia, her adolescent son's closest friend ("Lialia's Home" ["Lialin dom"]); and Shurik's compliant nature accounts for his readiness to gratify any number of significantly older women (*Sincerely Yours, Shurik*). Apart from Lialia's case, affection typically triggers these instances of sexual union, which Ulitskaya treats with taste and sympathy, never courting the frisson inexorably sparked by the presentation of an unconventional sexual pairing as scandalous. What many readers doubtless would deem sexual anomalies tend to be understated and assimilated into narratives of complex, often enigmatic relationships, for they instance the mystery of what draws people to one another rather than symptomatizing perversity.

Usually benefiting from her light touch, Ulitskaya's tranquil, matter-of-fact descriptions of such couplings spring from her conviction that body and emotions are of a piece—yet another instance of continuity/connection. And aesthetics is often what stimulates tender feelings and physical desire. Bronka finds Viktor Petrovich aristocratic in bearing and physically appealing; Jasia's young beauty inspires not only Robert Viktorovich's sexual ardor but also his art; Kazia's boyish beauty has everyone, including Lialia, in thrall. Aesthetics and emotions, in other words, lead naturally to sexual union, which Ulitskaya never casts in the key of *chernukha*,[28] prevalent in 1990s fiction and film, but depicts with restraint and sensitivity.

Discrepancies in couples' ages are not the only deviation from standard pairings. In "The Daughter of Bokhara," for instance, the beautiful Bokhara, abandoned by a husband who cannot cope with their offspring Mila's Down syndrome,[29] shortly before her death manages to arrange her daughter's marriage to Grigory, likewise a Down sufferer. "The Chosen People" ("Narod izbrannyi") focuses on the unlikely bond between the crippled, street-smart, hard-drinking Katia and Zinaida, a witless orphan with an adrenal glandular disorder incapable of taking care of herself; the two sustain each other psychologically.[30] And in *The Funeral Party* (*Veselye pokhorony*, 1997), as the painter Alik lies dying (a rite of passage frequently encountered in Ulitskaya's fiction), his wife, mistress, and the illegitimate daughter whom the latter bore Alik come together to celebrate his colorful life. In short, strange bedfellows (in both literal and figurative senses) constitute a norm in Ulitskaya's fiction, which narrates customarily unacknowledged lives and links.

The Intelligentsia

The collapse of the Soviet Union and the transition to Russia's version of a market economy spelled the demotion of the intelligentsia, which had enjoyed its privileged status and perquisites owing to Stalin. While Andrei Siniavskii famously dissociated himself from the post-Soviet intelligentsia on account of its moral compromise through political support of questionable governmental actions,[31] Ulitskaya, as the coauthors of the present study note, has retained faith in the group to which she has belonged throughout her life. Perhaps it would be more accurate to state that she places hope in some members of the intelligentsia, such as Mikhail Khodorkovsky, Akunin, her circle of friends and colleagues, and those who have taken risks by protesting against Putin's regime. As anyone conversant with current events knows, over the last decade she has undergone a gradual, reluctant politicization, though politics per se has never been at the core of her interests. At the same time, she is too astute to ignore the sea change undergone by a group that for two centuries prided itself on being "the conscience of the nation" and purportedly strove to protect the rights of the masses. In a recent interview, she justly observed, "the Russian intelligentsia has ceased to exist in the classic understanding of the word."[32]

Indeed, the sociopolitical and economic changes in Russia and the concomitant fragmentation have rendered the intelligentsia, if not obsolete, then certainly undefinable as a uniform, consistent entity. Accordingly, while the majority of Ulitskaya's characters belong to the intelligentsia, they hardly represent a unified "class" or adhere to a single set of convictions. Even her long fictional homage to the liberal intelligentsia of the 1960s, *The Big Green Tent* (*Zelenyi shater*, 2011), discriminates between those who dare to put their lives on the line when protesting against the state and those who, more temperately, exercise caution while remaining faithful to such goals as freedom of speech and civil liberties. In her speech when accepting the Austrian State Prize for European Literature (more precisely, for *The Big Green Tent*) on July 26, 2014, Ulitskaya dwelled at some length on the diversity of the *shestidesiatniki*—the 1960s intelligentsia, linked through the common cause of opposing a repressive government, primarily though not exclusively through "the power of the word."[33] Similarly, discrepancies today exist not only between writers and other *Kulturarbeiter* who, for whatever reason, ally themselves with Putin's policies and those who speak out against them, but also within those two factions. Ulitskaya's conviction that any improvements that may eventuate in Russian society depend on the intelligentsia (however heterogeneous and loosely defined) impresses me, unlike the coauthors of *Ludmila Ulitskaya and the Art of Tolerance*, as logical in light of her identification with that group and *faute de mieux*—the absence of any other significant and identifiable class protesting against Putin's authoritarian regime.[34]

Six years ago anyone reading a journalist's description of Ulitskaya as "a leading advocate for freedom of expression" would have assumed an error on *The Observer*'s part, for engagement in political activism only recently became a part of her life.[35] When asked by an interviewer in June 2013 what freedom means to her, she answered, "When I know the answer to that, I'll write a novel about it."[36] Yet the previous year, after a personal call from Akunin, Ulitskaya had accompanied the ten thousand participants in the "stroll for freedom" along Moscow's streets orchestrated by Akunin through his blog. Several years earlier, Akunin, himself a late convert to political agitation, had involved her and Boris Strugatskii in a published correspondence with the imprisoned Khodorkovsky, which yielded a collection titled *Mikhail Khodorkovsky: Articles, Dialogues, Interviews* (*Stat'i. Dialogi. Interv'iu*, 2010).[37] According to Akunin, whose veracity there is no reason to impugn, no other writers wished to exchange letters with the incarcerated "oligarch."[38] By 2011 the volume had undergone three editions. Convinced, along with Akunin and countless others, that the charges against Khodorkovsky were trumped up, and having attended his second trial, Ulitskaya has called him "an outstanding individual," explaining, "My support for Khodorkovsky primarily lies in how much money he spent on charitable enterprises"[39]—a reaction wholly in accord with Ulitskaya's longstanding devotion to charitable causes, particularly those benefiting children.

Preceding by several years Ulitskaya's belated and modest involvement in sociopolitical actions was her incorporation of "life texts" into her novels, whereby bona fide letters and other documents alternate with the fiction. This mélange is especially striking in *Daniel Stein, Interpreter*, though *The Kukotskii Case* paved the way; both works treat in semi-fictional fashion individuals who actually exist(ed). Above all, *Discarded Relics* (*Sviashchennyi musor*, 2012), with its atypical pronouncements ("Ludmila Ulitskaya's Rules of Life" ["Pravila zhizni Liudmily Ulitskoi"]), reminiscences, self-revelations, and thoughts about spiritual and religious issues, may justly be called a miscellany. Its major value is twofold: it makes plain what a fine line divides Ulitskaya's fiction from her essayistic voice and subject matter—a line that sometimes disappears; and it measures the extent to which she has become a public figure aware of the cultural authority she wields today.

Style

One of the most appealing facets of Ulitskaya's fiction for the general reader is its accessibility. Unencumbered by the stylistic mimicry and postmodernist devices that many find alienating in works by Sorokin and Pelevin, her prose is straightforward and transparent, firmly welded to the heritage of nineteenth-century realism. And, like Tolstoy, she adopts Pushkin's practice of beginning prose narratives *in medias res*. Natural-sounding dialogue and skillfully rendered, ample descriptions bring people and places to life, while irony, especially in her handling of situations that a different writer might infuse with vitriol, ridicule, or moral condemnation, cushions the reader by creating the illusion of a securely humane, balanced world. In fact, gentle irony (in the Horatian, not Juvenalian, register) is one of her signature stylistic traits and abets the impression of a wise and charitable vantage point acquired through experience.

Intent neither on shocking readers nor on avoiding what under Soviet censorship would have been impermissible scenes and topics, Ulitskaya manages to find tasteful solutions for potentially problematic phenomena, such as sexual explicitness, which continues to challenge Russian authors weaned on a hardy tradition of literary Puritanism, briefly followed by the knee-jerk reaction of a lurid, radical naturalism (*chernukha*).[40] Periphrasis and euphemism, both often combined with irony, permit Ulitskaya to refer to genitalia, a variety of sexual activities and positions, and what one might label bathroom phenomena. For instance, in "Lucky," as elsewhere, she resorts to euphemism by referring understatedly to baby Vladimir's penis as "his secret little cone";[41] or in "The Orlov-Sokolovs," when a couple married to two other people have sexual intercourse throughout the night, Ulitskaya writes, "The flesh wept bitterly and wordlessly until morning."[42] Narrating Tanya's loss of virginity during her sexual experimentation with her friend Boris, Ulitskaya describes the act of penetration as "the brief introduction, both figurative and literal, of something new."[43]

One need only imagine how Liudmila Petrushevskaia, the supreme practitioner of dysphemism, would have inscribed these moments to appreciate Ulitskaya's disarming discretion. Petrushevskaia's prose, in fact, offers a useful comparison to Ulitskaya's. Whereas Petrushevskaia is an existentialist for whom the world is an inhospitable realm rife with threats, disappointments, and disasters, Ulitskaya casts her eye on life's bounties. Both acknowledge betrayal as a human weakness and the potentially destructive nature of sexual appetite, but for Ulitskaya those drives tend to occur as exceptions in a world rich in love and human bonds that in Petrushevskaia's fiction seem utterly impossible. Illumination, promise, and fulfillment dwell in Ulitskaya's homes, where Petrushevskaia finds vicious conflict, desolation, and the desire to assert psychological power: for Ulitskaya, generations nurture; for Petrushevskaia, they vampirize. In short, many find Petrushevskaia's splendid fiction too lacerating for enjoyment, whereas Ulitskaya's more measured, warmer prose offers the reassurance purveyed by Woland in Mikhail Bulgakov's *Master and Margarita*: "Everything will be as it should; that's what the world rests on."[44] To a large extent the dramatic contrast in the fictional worlds of the two writers accounts for the discrepancy in their professional fates: by comparison with the slow recognition that has come to Petrushevskaia, who remained unpublished for decades and after more than thirty years has gained a reputation primarily among critics, Ulitskaya's ascent has been meteoric and primarily reader-based.

Evolution over a Quarter-Century

Whereas Ulitskaya started out as a short-story writer, with *Medea* she launched her series of novels, which, *The Funeral Party* aside, have grown steadily longer with the years. At the outset guided by Pushkin's two desiderata of brevity and precision (*kratkost' i tochnost'*), she rigorously expunged anything inessential from the narratives in *Poor Relatives* (*Bednye rodstvenniki*, 1994) and *Girls from Nine to Eleven* (*Devochki s deviati do odinnadtsati*, 1994), which still await a complete translation.[45] By contrast, her capacious novels of the last almost-twenty years are more leisurely, inclusive, and less strictly disciplined. Moreover, the condensed simplicity of her nineties' stories has ceded to more intricate narratives, into which she incorporates letters, diaries, poems, and other genres. Comprehensiveness has supplanted concision. If her early works made ample use of synecdoche and metonymy while focusing on individual situations, her novels tend to strive for a panoramic purview with a large cast of characters unfolding at a leisurely pace, which occasionally prompts critics' (in my view, inapposite) comparison with the works of Tolstoy.

Few writers, once they acquire fame, can resist writing directly about their beliefs, and the older Tolstoy, whom his numerous admirers considered an authority on "how to live," was no exception. Nor is Ulitskaya exempt from this temptation, judging by her recent volume, *Discarded Relics*. This compendium parallels the heterogeneous contents of her more recent novels. Encompassing information about her psychological state and her breast cancer, her travels, friends, family members, and her impressions of sundry people, events, and experiences, it also includes interviews and her ruminations on a host of topics. Anyone suspecting Ulitskaya of hubris on the basis of this collection should keep in mind that, as a writer whose fiction for more than two decades has narrated individual lives, here she merely has turned her authorial lens on herself. In that regard, as an impassioned believer in the interconnectedness of all beings, she demonstrates a consistency of viewpoint that, however, does not necessarily guarantee literary quality. And *Discarded Relics* belongs less to literature than to a *sui generis* miscellany or grab bag, united solely by the author's persona, with elements of autobiography, personal musings, and such indeterminate genres as sections of Dostoevsky's *Winter Notes on Summer Impressions* (*Zimnie zametki o letnikh vpechatleniiakh*, 1863) and *A Writer's Diary* (*Dnevnik pisatelia*, 1873-81). This salmagundi evokes a dinner prepared from what one happens to find in the refrigerator, and the volume's title suggests wry recognition of that fact.

Known principally as a fiction writer, Ulitskaya has authored half a dozen plays, with uneven success. Not unlike Petrushevskaia, who in *Three Girls in Blue* (*Tri devushki v golobom*, 1980) launched a dialogue with Chekhov's *Three Sisters* (*Tri sestry*, 1900), Ulitskaya has engaged Chekhov's *Cherry Orchard* (*Vishnevyi sad*, 1903-4) in her *Russian Jam* (*Russkoe varen'e*, 2008) and has voiced admiration for Chekhov as dramatist. Her notion of connection reverberates with his sense, attributed to a character in his gnomic story "The Student" (1894), that "'[t]he past [...] is tied to the present in an unbroken chain of events flowing one out of the other.' And he felt [that] he had just seen both ends of that chain: he had touched one end and the other had moved."[46] Chekhov's diachrony is Ulitskaya's synchrony. In her introduction to a recent collection of Chekhov's stories in translation, Cathy Popkin rhetorically asks, "Why read Chekhov's stories?" and answers, "Because they enlarge our capacity for understanding and awaken our compassion."[47] One can adduce precisely the same reasons for reading Ulitskaya's fiction, an activity for which the present volume serves as an invaluable and thought-provoking introduction.

ACKNOWLEDGMENTS

On a warm and sunny day in 2009 we decided to write the first monograph devoted to contemporary writer Ludmila Evgen'evna Ulitskaya. Thus began a massive project—over the next five years we exchanged e-mails, made phone calls, and met in person, usually once a year in the looming shadow of the annual convention of the Association for Slavic, East European and Eurasian Studies (ASEEES). While we had participated in several panels together, this was our first coauthored work. Meanwhile, Ulitskaya continued to publish, guaranteeing the relevance of our work (but also increasing its scope).

During our research we have benefited from the generosity of Ludmila Evgen'evna, who kindly agreed to be interviewed in person and by e-mail. We also express our thanks to Yulia Dobrovolskaya for help with procuring documents and photographs that have enormously enriched our manuscript. This book has benefited from many helpful colleagues at Sewanee: The University of the South, Miami University, and beyond. Edith Clowes, Jenne Powers, Helena Goscilo, and Yelena Furman gave insightful suggestions, as did Eliot Borenstein, Sibelan Forrester, and Karen Evans-Romaine. Iuliia Semikina, Il'ia Kukulin, Judith Kalb, Sharon Lubkemann Allen, Brian Baer, Maggie Levantovskaya, and Ellen Rutten shared their manuscripts with us. In 2010 part of this study was presented at the Everyday Life in Russia Workshop at Indiana University, where we received helpful comments, as also occurred at a number of ASEEES and AATSEEL panels. We have availed ourselves of the excellent assistance provided by the University of Illinois's Slavic Reference Service. Gwen Walker at University of Wisconsin Press has provided sustained support for our manuscript.

Likewise, Matthew Cosby, Adam Mehring, Marlyn Miller, and Nancy Zibman helped with the final stages of the project.

Colleagues present and past at the Havighurst Center for Russian and Post-Soviet Studies Faculty Research Seminar read and critiqued (sometimes pointedly!) most of the chapters. We thank Rad Borislavov, Vitaly Chernetsky, Karen Dawisha, Josh First, Venelin Ganev, Ted Holland, Scott Kenworthy, Neringa Klumbyte, Rebecca Mitchell, Ivan Ninenko, Steve Norris, Brigid O'Keeffe, Dan Prior, John Reuter, Dan Scarborough, Gulnaz Sharafutdinova, and Zara Torlone.

Not surprisingly, this project necessitated several trips to Moscow, where the staff at the Russian State Library (Lenin Library) and INION Library proved quite helpful. Elena Trofimova and Aleksandr Trofimov helped with logistics, hospitality, and an invigorating dose of skepticism.

Portions of this book appeared in a different form in *Russian Review*, *Slavic and East European Journal*, and the volume *Everyday Life in Russia: Subjectivities, Perspectives, and Lived Experience*. Photographs of Ulitskaya were provided by Ludmila Evgen'evna, Alexander Efremov, and RIA Novosti (Grigory Sysoyev).

The support and advice of colleagues and friends at Sewanee has proved enormously helpful throughout the development of this project. Cari Reynolds worked wonders locating hard-to-find resources on short notice. Tim Garner found a timely solution to any technical or logistical problem presented to him. Mark Preslar never failed to keep the energy level high and the atmosphere collegial within the Russian Department. Student assistants extraordinaire Sarah Lillibridge, Jesse Schupack, and Taylor Yost aided our work in a variety of ways. The students of Russian 354 (Gender in 20th- and 21st-Century Russian Literature and Culture) read Ulitskaya's work thoughtfully and challenged me to revisit familiar works with fresh eyes. Thanks are also due to the Office of the Dean of the College and Stephen R. Garrett. Beyond my home campus, Jehanne Gheith, Elena Koshkarova, Carol Apollonio, and Yvonne Howell all provided useful insights and materials. Liudmila Riabova and Anatoly Riabov provided valuable context and nuanced perspectives on contemporary Russia.

This project began during a pre-tenure sabbatical in 2009-10. Generous awards from Sewanee's University Research Grants Fund, a John B. Stephenson Faculty Fellowship from the Appalachian College Association, and the James P. Kennedy III Endowed Faculty Fellowship all enabled and enhanced my work on the project.

I owe special thanks to Emily Meade, Kimberly Katte, Eliza Stephenson, and Roxsana Patel for their unwavering friendship; to my parents, John and Ann Skomp, for a lifetime of love, nurture, and support; and especially to Martin Blackwell for his patience, kindness, and deep knowledge of Russian history. Vivien Alice Blackwell arrived in July 2013 and has made life infinitely richer and full of joy.

ELIZABETH SKOMP

Friends and comrades in Oxford provided moral support during this project's serpentine path to publication. In the Department of German, Russian, and East Asian Languages, Margaret Ziolkowski read drafts of chapters and has continued to be a wonderful mentor and exemplary colleague. Lolita Holmes, Juanita Schrodt, and Carolyn DeWitt resolved various conundrums (mainly of my own creation). Masha Stepanova and the staff at King Library procured obscure interlibrary loan requests. Research in Moscow and Oxford was greatly aided by support from the Philip and Elaina Hampton Fund for Faculty Research, a Summer Research Award, and a semester of leave through an Assigned Research Appointment. The College of Arts and Science also permitted several course releases, which helped this monograph appear in print earlier than it might have otherwise. Elizabeth Bergman, Mila Ganeva, Katie Gibson, Mariana Ivanova, Gael Montgomery, Deborah Lyons, Steve Nimis, and Nicole Thesz contributed good conversation, cold beer, and hot meals. Emily Rush and Kelly Tuttle provided cats, an explanation of ekphrasis, and the unique ritual of Arabic happy hour.

As always, Adam Zagelbaum lent a sympathetic ear. Family in Florida, Hawai'i, California, Washington, and (currently) the Caucasus never lost faith; my love and thanks go out to MJ Sutcliffe, Claud Sutcliffe, Brigid Mulloy, Ed Williams, Joanie Halverson, Christine Kukui Sutcliffe, Caroline Leilani Sutcliffe, Matt Sutcliffe, Christine Hatcher, and the memory of the inimitable Massey Sutcliffe. During the course of this project Theo Hatcher Sutcliffe made his appearance in the world, brightening all our lives.

BENJAMIN SUTCLIFFE

AUTHORS' NOTES

In the body of our monograph we refer to "Ludmila Ulitskaya," the most common transliteration of this writer's name in Anglophone materials. Notes and works cited follow the standard scholarly rendering: "Liudmila Ulitskaia." Per tradition in Slavic studies, we have used the modified Library of Congress system of transliteration for quotations, bibliographic information, and most character and author names. We have used conventional spelling for well-known figures such as Leo Tolstoy and Fyodor Dostoyevsky. Following a similar logic, we render characters' names as they appear in the best-known translations of Ulitskaya's work ("Jasia" instead of "Iasia," for example). All translations are our own unless otherwise noted.

LUDMILA ULITSKAYA

AND THE ART OF TOLERANCE

INTRODUCTION

MYTHS OF THE POST-SOVIET WRITER

In June 2006, Russian author Ludmila Ulitskaya was scheduled to read at the Moscow International Book Festival. Shortly before the event was to begin, the tent where she would soon appear discharged a wave of tall young men with closely cropped hair. At the center of the crowd was diminutive Eduard Limonov, onetime *enfant terrible* of Russian literature and now provocative leader of Russia's radical National Bolsheviks. As the tent began to fill again, the contrast between Limonov's group and Ulitskaya's could not have been more striking. The expectant members of Ulitskaya's audience included young couples and women ranging from teenagers to pensioners, a broad swath of the population that the author hopes to unite with her writing. As we explore in this introduction, Ulitskaya's readers and critics respond to conflicting yet often complementary agendas in her work; together they explain the surprising appeal of this writer.[1]

Ulitskaya is contemporary Russia's most significant author, bringing together intellectual and ordinary readers by modeling values imperative to preserving culture. Her ethical system comes from the intelligentsia, whose importance in Russia is mythological as well as literary and historical.[2] But she does not merely reiterate this group's age-old concerns; instead, Ulitskaya's singular approach acknowledges intellectual and moral traditions as a framework for conceptualizing contemporary culture. Her steadfast promotion of difference, manifest in the hybridity of characters who combine varying backgrounds and beliefs, affirms diversity and rejects monolithic forms of thought while avoiding superficial plurality. This constellation of concerns underlies Ulitskaya's persistent engagement with the past, which in turn critiques the creeping authoritarianism of the Putin era. Her first publications in the late 1980s and early 1990s depicted tolerance, sincerity, and positive actions in difficult times. These topics became more pronounced and elaborate in Ulitskaya's longer fictional works at the beginning of the twenty-first century and, more recently, in a shift away from fiction to documentary prose. At the same time, her works appropriate the humane realism that shaped Russian literature (and its readers) after Joseph Stalin's death in 1953; Ulitskaya's writing also borrows from the work of novelist and poet Boris Pasternak, who in turn draws on Fyodor Dostoevsky and Leo Tolstoy. Her plots focus on the late Soviet era, the time of her childhood and youth and a period of widespread interest for other contemporary authors as well. She thus continues Russian literature's longstanding use of a doubled approach to its subject matter: while Ulitskaya wrote during the nineties and the first decade of the twenty-first century, her style and content come from the 1950s and 1960s. Like many authors, Ulitskaya uses a post-1991 viewpoint to make sense of the traumas of recent history; what is unusual is how she inculcates intelligentsia ethics in contemporary readers even as her works critique the past. Concern with *intelligenty* and their values connects her post-Soviet perspective to narratives that focus on the USSR.

For Ulitskaya literature is inseparable from morality. Her assessment of past and present explores sincerity (*iskrennost'*) to connect these values. This key intelligentsia axiom is inherited from post-Stalinist culture, as Vladimir Pomerantsev posits in the 1953 essay "On Sincerity in Literature" ("Ob iskrennosti v literature"). Attacking the artificiality of socialist realism, Pomerantsev called for works that would depict reality in an honest way through "events in the personal lives of people," a trope of Russian literature Ulitskaya expresses by privileging the individual instead of the state.[3] In this respect her oeuvre reveals a focus that became increasingly prominent in late Soviet and post-Soviet prose and that manifests itself as a "new sincerity" in Russian literature of the twenty-first century. Ulitskaya's works follow a moral master plot in which characters struggle to retain their principles in an ethically deformed society. Individual integrity, however, must likewise promote collective tolerance, a complicated negotiation of self and society that Ulitskaya accomplishes through personalizing history and presenting it from a liberal, post-Soviet intelligentsia viewpoint. Her artistic and journalistic works (*publitsistika*) underscore a need to accommodate the manifold ideas, ethnicities, and bodies that were overlooked or attacked during the Soviet era. This stance is also evident through a focus on the periphery, whether literal or metaphorical, with special attention to Crimea as a site of intersecting ethnic and religious identities. Among Ulitskaya's distinguishing authorial characteristics is a positive outlook that sets her apart from other contemporary writers. She provides a hopeful diagnosis that, while critical of Russia's present path, offers an alternative both to the dominant apocalyptic predictions about its future and the often hectoring tone of her intellectual predecessors.[4]

Ulitskaya, a crucial, complex, and sometimes contradictory figure, has received little attention from Anglophone scholars. This critical lacuna is particularly striking given how the discussions of Stalinism, the body, and lived experience that inform her works are of increasing interest to Slavists in North America and elsewhere. Though English-language translations and criticism of Ulitskaya's works date from the 1990s, our study is the first full-length monograph on the author. Several scholars have addressed her work from specific perspectives. Edith Clowes examines her connection to imagined geography and Russian identity; Benjamin Sutcliffe focuses on Ulitskaya, women's prose, and everyday life.[5] There is also a Hungarian-language volume edited by Edit Gilbert, as well as a number of Anglophone articles, including Margarita Levantovskaya's excellent piece on Ulitskaya's novel *Daniel Stein, Interpreter*. A few dissertations center on Ulitskaya, though most are comparative in nature. In its examination of this important writer, our book thus fills a key gap in studies of contemporary Russian society and literature.[6]

Ulitskaya is deeply concerned by the present and future as well as the past. The author laments the "catastrophic fall" of culture taking place worldwide, an ongoing crisis stemming from consumption and gratification instead of constructive action and responsibility. Maintaining that in post-1991 Russia consumerism and poverty are linked, she decries capitalism's irresponsibility and shortsightedness. From this viewpoint, materialistic culture leads to a rehabilitation of the Soviet past as frustrated Russians revolt against the new ideology of capitalism. Such antipathy is ironic in light of her commercial success. Acknowledging the realities of consumer culture in today's Russia, we examine Ulitskaya as a phenomenon whose name critic Nikolai Aleksandrov labels a "guarantee of popularity."[7] Helena Goscilo and Vlad Strukov note a disturbing feature of contemporary Russian culture: a focus on image and superficiality that makes celebrity and glamour markers of the Putin era. Ulitskaya represents an alternative, as she incorporates intelligentsia values into an anti-commercial message that nonetheless implicitly links sincerity and sales. Such an approach is not unique to Ulitskaya: in a discussion of Eksmo, her former publisher, Aleksandrov notes its paradoxically savvy focus on mass literature combined with a careful selection of "serious" writers who are both "popular" and "accessible."[8]

It is impossible to ignore the relationship between consumer culture and this author's career. Ulitskaya's rise to prominence in the 1990s coincided with the decline of "serious" literature and the ascendancy of pulp fiction and glossy magazines. Indeed, two decades ago robust sales and literary quality were seen as incompatible, a scenario she helped change through a traditional style that conveys reassuring values in an era of gloom and chaos.[9] Ulitskaya disavows interest in selling her work, claiming that a few dozen readers excitedly devouring her books would be more meaningful to her than a profitable marketing strategy. Her stature thus reiterates Russia's enduring axiom that good literature needs no justification.[10]

However, her quality writing has garnered unexpected benefits, even beyond the nation's borders. In 2005, a representative of the Education Commission of the Moscow City Duma argued that the country's literature was a more reputable brand abroad than either Russian politics or economics. This reification of writing is anathema to Ulitskaya's intelligentsia values, yet is a central (albeit unintended) aspect of her career: she inscribes herself into the Russian canon while lamenting the decline of "good" prose, a concern that influences her depictions of late Soviet culture from a post-1991 perspective.[11]

Creating Ulitskaya: Literature and the Anti-Market Author

Ulitskaya's upbringing, which tellingly resembles those of her characters, connects her post-1991 oeuvre to the Soviet era that dominates her plots. She was born in 1943 in the village of Davlekanovo near Ufa to a Moscow family firmly rooted in the Jewish secular intelligentsia. Her parents had been evacuated from the capital, fearing a Nazi attack with dire consequences for any Jews captured by the Germans. For its part the Soviet state also persecuted the family: before and after the war her grandfathers spent time in labor camps.[12] Ulitskaya's father was a biochemist and her mother an agricultural engineer; they divorced while their daughter was still in school. The author has also noted tensions between her mother and grandmother—indeed, the strong-willed older generation, with its

Ulitskaya in Moscow near the beginning of her writing career. (Ludmila Ulitskaya)

values forged before 1917, has a pronounced presence in her writing. Ulitskaya underscores how her grandmother literally and morally sustained the family: in the Stalin era she had an illegal private business sewing bras and underwear on the Singer machine she had received as a wedding gift in 1917. Ulitskaya graduated from Moscow State University in 1967 and worked as a geneticist at the Institute of General Genetics from 1968 to 1970. Like her predecessor I. Grekova (pseudonym of Elena Venttsel'), Ulitskaya came to literature with a scientific and academic background that has strongly influenced her writing.[13]

In 1970 Ulitskaya was forced to leave her position with the Institute of General Genetics after she was caught distributing underground literature (*samizdat*). In lamenting the relations between science and state, Ulitskaya gives another version of why she left, explaining that she was fired for not voting to condemn dissidents. Regardless of the reason, the stress of the event contributed to her mother's death.[14] Ulitskaya came to realize that even the natural sciences were controlled by the government, a view that informs several of her works and contributes to her insistence on the dichotomy between embattled intellectual and governing regime. She then worked for the Jewish Chamber Theatre as head of the literary section (1970–1982), acquiring the feel for drama evident in the plays she would publish much later. Ulitskaya has been married three times; her first husband was a physicist, the second a geneticist, and her current spouse is the artist Andrei Krasulin. During her second marriage she had two sons, one of whose experiences with life in New York shaped several of her narratives.[15]

In the 1980s Ulitskaya authored children's books, an interest that later reappears in a series she edited that is devoted to instilling tolerance (*tolerantnost'*) in young readers. During perestroika she penned a play and several screenplays for feature and animated films. In 1989 she published her first short story, "Bronka," which addresses the themes of sexuality, family, and Soviet history that are amplified in the novella *Sonechka*. In 1996 her novel *Medea and Her Children* was published in the thick journal *New World* (*Novyi mir*); however, many of Ulitskaya's longer works would later be issued as separate volumes.[16] Toward the end of the 1990s Ulitskaya garnered a host of honors, among them the Prix Médicis for *Sonechka* (France, 1996), the Penne Prize (Italy, 1997), and the Prize Giuseppe Acerbi (Italy, 1998). In 2001 Ulitskaya was the first woman to win the Russian Booker Prize, the nation's most prestigious literary award. She received it for *The Kukotskii Case*, which was later made into a TV miniseries. Her *Daniel Stein, Interpreter* was awarded the Big Book (*Bol'shaia kniga*) prize for 2007. Such distinctions clearly convey acclaim by Western and Russian intellectuals, yet Ulitskaya is also widely read by the general public; her books are issued in high print runs exceptional for the depressed post-Soviet book market.[17]

Ulitskaya has become a best-selling writer, identified by her characteristic morality, straightforward style, and commercial success, not to mention her willingness to engage with the "eternal questions" that form the backbone of Russian literature. Profitability presumably transfers to books she edits and introduces, and bookstores stock them under her name to ensure sales.[18] Ulitskaya nevertheless lambastes the book market that has furthered her fame. This excoriation is far from surprising, given that the opposition between consumption and integrity is a leitmotif of the embattled post-Soviet intelligentsia. Indeed, as Katerina Clark points out, suspicion of consumerism united intellectuals and the socialist state they so hated; in many ways, the intelligentsia and the regime were interdependent and shared a surprising number of cultural values. After 1991 this symbiosis dissolved, leaving Ulitskaya to trumpet liberal intelligentsia values in an era that strongly challenged their relevance. While her works define intellectuals by differentiating them from the regime, Ulitskaya's own comments rely on the common antipathy for the market economy harbored by the Soviet government and *intelligenty*. Kenosis by capitalism forms a cornerstone of Ulitskaya's worldview and comprises part of her mythology of the intelligentsia.[19]

Ulitskaya's Intertextual Intelligentsia

The post-Soviet intelligentsia for its part is indisputably in a state of crisis. The group sees itself as embodying the best traits of society: pursuit of knowledge; a firm sense of moral imperative; conscience; independence; belief in enlightening society (and thus improving humanity); autonomy from both the state and the common people (*narod*); self-sacrifice; and lack of concern for material conditions. In the 1990s, however, dramatic decreases in state support, widespread poverty, and loss of cultural prestige destroyed intellectuals' status. Several different but overlapping theories, often composed by intellectuals themselves, explain this plight. According to one, only the "true" (morally uncompromised) *intelligenty* survived the turbulent Yeltsin years, which were marred by massive theft of state resources by those with political power or the means to buy it. Another narrative defines intellectuals in terms of marginality and defeat.[20] Ulitskaya ascribes such failure to the laudable but doomed efforts of dissidents Aleksandr Solzhenitsyn and Andrei Sakharov: to be an *intelligent* means striving to better society yet consistently failing. Her novel *The Big Green Tent* illustrates this bleak characterization as it depicts the gloomy fate of friends who grow up to become political and cultural opponents of the Soviet state. Some are forced to collude with the regime; others emigrate or commit suicide. By focusing on the characters' lives in the era of Stagnation (1964-1984), the narrative shows the collapse of the private existence Ulitskaya upholds as the site of moral value and potential change. The late Boris Dubin has identified another quandary for *intelligenty*: while in the past the intelligentsia was oriented toward youth, in the post-Soviet era it is the provenance of the aging, who are less able to ensure its perpetuation.[21]

Literature is of paramount importance for both Ulitskaya and her intellectual readers, especially given the turbulent state of post-1991 Russian society and its writers' attempts to understand the Soviet past. Critics call on the novel in particular to portray (and thus presumably explain) the tragedies of twentieth-century history, which Ulitskaya's liberal intelligentsia views as an ordeal of death and imprisonment. Literature is a civilizing counterpart to both this brutality and what sociologist Lev Gudkov identifies as the violence of everyday life. However, Ulitskaya worries that, at the moment when they are most needed, books are being replaced by new technology. She implies that such a shift will bring catastrophe, given that literature is the artistic rendering of what joins humanity to its world.[22] Her view recalls Wolfgang Iser's meditation on culture as something that must be constantly engaged instead of taken for granted. For Ulitskaya culture is the only guarantor of human survival, and literature is its central component and primary means of expression. Reading conveys the core values of positive action, sincerity, and tolerance that the intelligentsia traditionally has protected, first from the Soviet state and now from callous consumerism.[23]

Literature helps these ethics survive in a hostile world. *The Big Green Tent* opens with an epigraph from a 1952 letter that Pasternak wrote to author and former Gulag prisoner Varlam Shalamov. Pasternak urges: "Do not take comfort in the injustice of the times. Their moral injustice does not make us right; their inhumanity by itself is not enough for us who disagree with them to be men." This excerpt from the writers' correspondence underscores Pasternak's optimism and the duties of the two authors as members of the intelligentsia—living in an immoral era does not make the individual who opposes it righteous, just as larger problems do not excuse our own errors. As Guy de Mallac argues, Pasternak worried that Soviet culture had destroyed "natural values," including the sincerity and morality that Ulitskaya also finds essential.

Indeed, her corpus is an extended version of this concern and the need to respond in an ethical manner; literature must always take the side of rectitude and individual responsibility, no matter how trying the context.[24] She thus gives authors a paradoxical mandate. Ulitskaya sadly notes that it is a delusion to assume that reading changes lives, yet both she and the intelligentsia passionately believe in this transformative quality. Her screenplay for the film *A Woman for All* (*Zhenshchina dlia vsekh*, 1991) portrays middle-aged *intelligentka* Anna giving a neighbor books in hopes of guiding him; similarly, a critic asserts that when librarians place the appropriate reading in children's hands, positive behavior and morals appear of their own accord. Ulitskaya sees literature as vital to helping the right values survive.[25]

With these assumptions, it is no surprise that the author's prose and drama contain many instances of intertextuality. Sometimes these references to other literary works are allusions to Ulitskaya's own narratives. In *The Big Green Tent*, some of the main characters visit the grave of modernist poet Maksimilian Voloshin in Crimea. His widow tells them that they can spend the night with her acquaintance, a dentist's widow who is the protagonist of the novel *Medea and Her Children*. This connection underscores the kinship between positive characters, a trait of pre-1917 literature that authors such as Pasternak used as well. Ulitskaya's allusions refer the reader to both her own narratives and their literary inspirations; intertextuality is unified by concern for common intelligentsia ethics and literature as the best way to illustrate how they weathered the turbulent Soviet era. Medea, the central figure in Ulitskaya's novel, resembles the poet Voloshin by evoking a past untainted by the Communist state.[26]

The author's use of intertextuality resonates with Russian literary tradition, which, as Andrew Wachtel observes, developed at a frenetic pace. It thus relied on appropriation of precursors, a supportive process that for Iser means that the memory of a work is its representation by other authors. Intertextuality is a basic pattern for cultural memory, the depiction of the past that the Russian intelligentsia has long held to be its purview. Ulitskaya accesses a wide range of intertexts, from folklore and hagiography to women's prose of the 1980s and 1990s (a debt she does not acknowledge). Most of her references come from the nineteenth and early twentieth centuries, an era untainted by the Soviet belief that literature must serve ideology. Alluding to such prerevolutionary writing constitutes a basic function of intertextuality: legitimating the author who references the previous work.[27] As Harold Bloom famously notes, intertextuality comes with a sense of indebtedness, which in turn fuels the anxiety of influence many writers feel toward their predecessors. Sandra Gilbert and Susan Gubar, however, point out that Bloom's model is a patriarchal one that should be revised in the case of a woman writer, who "must confront precursors who are almost exclusively male, and therefore significantly different from her." Our analysis later in this introduction highlights Ulitskaya's contrasting approach to (largely male) literary predecessors and her more recent precursors in women's prose. Discussing the stage adaptation of *Sonechka*, a novella with deep roots in the Russian classics, Ulitskaya was worried by the responsibility involved in citing nineteenth-century literature. Such intertexts complicate her narrative: appropriation of the literary masters is not to be undertaken lightly in the culturally charged realm of Russian letters.[28]

Intertextuality guides the author's introduction to the short-story collection *People of Our Tsar* (*Liudi nashego tsaria*, 2005). The title itself comes from nineteenth-century prosaist Nikolai Leskov, who provides some of Russian literature's most colorful depictions of provincial life. In citing Leskov, Ulitskaya comments that individual identity stems from the act of compiling: "Beginning in youth you make great efforts to collect and build your 'I' from others' incidental gestures, thoughts, and feelings that you have picked up. Finally it seems that you are ready to become complete." This fragile sense of self is a compendium of references, analogous to Iser's idea that intertextuality shapes the identity of a given work. Intertextuality defines both book and reader. Those who have read the same works can access the common ideas that unite Russian literature, and those who have not are alien to Ulitskaya, even if bound by ties of ethnicity and family. In a memoir she laments how in childhood she could not communicate with her father's Talmudist friends; while she respected these clearly learned men, the future writer was unable to find common ground with those who did not know nineteenth-century luminaries such as Tolstoy, Dostoevsky, and Pushkin.[29]

Intelligenty, as Dubin notes, incorporate prerevolutionary literature into their identity. Intelligentsia culture is a humane entity at odds with the recent and brutal past; in *The Big Green Tent*, literature teacher Viktor Iul'evich Shengeli inspires his students, who will later become opponents of the state. He observes to himself that Ivan Bunin, Aleksandr Kuprin, and Anton Chekhov could not have imagined the lack of privacy in the postwar USSR when they penned their narratives of love and adultery. Shengeli tries to make sense of Stalinist society in light of these pre-1917 and émigré authors. Ulitskaya has a more complex task: in describing Viktor Iul'evich from a twenty-first-century viewpoint, she must make both this Soviet teacher and the writers he mentions relevant for her readers in contemporary Russia. She does so by using literature as a transhistorical way of presenting the positive ethics of the intelligentsia, ethics that connect her post-1991 publishing career and the Soviet experience she portrays. Ulitskaya thus continues the intelligentsia's reliance on writing to convey those aspects of culture that it most esteems. Her own role in Russian literature, however, has sometimes been a source of contention.[30]

Tradition through a Contemporary Lens: Ulitskaya and Russian Literature

Ulitskaya engenders contradictory reactions that, when examined together, explain her wide-ranging appeal. Some critics complain that her works are for the defeated intelligentsia (presumably vanquished by the market forces Ulitskaya fears), yet others praise her as writing for the common reader.[31] One critic hints at an underlying reason for the latter opinion: Ulitskaya, like Chekhov, attempts to understand instead of judging. In adopting this approach, she also avoids the accusations of moralizing leveled at so many of her intelligentsia predecessors. Ulitskaya's stance, shaped by her interest in difference and suspicion of universalizing truths, creates characters whose tragedies are envisioned against the background of an uncaring state. In *The Big Green Tent*, Mikha, one of the childhood friends influenced by Shengeli, later becomes a poet disillusioned by Soviet society's dishonesty and cynicism. He kills himself after being pressured to cooperate with the KGB. In jumping to his death, Mikha exemplifies the fate of the talented and conscientious at the hands of a regime that values only the loyal and mediocre. The pathos of this moment is grounded in the novel's descriptions of everyday life, a key concern of Chekhov. In Ulitskaya's image of the era of Stagnation, this background underscores the moral dilemma that Mikha can resolve only through suicide.[32]

The evocation of Chekhov and morality brings to light another dichotomy in her reception: tradition and postmodernism. Mikhail Zolotonosov, who identifies a number of patterns in reviews of Ulitskaya's works, argues that she repackages the classic novel for the consumer.

Many characterize her writing as traditional, seeing in it emulation of the vaunted nineteenth-century narrative. This similarity itself is hardly noteworthy; as Wachtel's observations on intertextuality imply, the past hundred-odd years of writing are themselves largely the reworking of themes and styles from the 1800s.[33] For Ulitskaya the enduring values of the great novel are the same ones she professes: compassion, sincerity, and concern with the individual as opposed to the state. More interesting is the appearance of these concerns through what Gary Saul Morson terms the triumph of everyday truth over abstract idealism.[34]

Ulitskaya explains that she enjoys her favorite authors both as reader and writer, singling out Pushkin, Tolstoy, Bunin, Pasternak, and Joseph Brodsky. It is the nineteenth century in particular that shapes her works from the 1990s. *Medea and Her Children*, for example, adopts Tolstoy's *Anna Karenina* as a foreboding intertext. Ulitskaya's novel describes the intergenerational loves and tragedies of a network of relatives and friends who gather each summer at the Crimean home of protagonist Medea. In a dream, Medea sees her deceased husband hammering at something, a vision that evokes Anna's recurring dream before her suicide. Soon afterwards, Medea uncovers evidence of her spouse's infidelity; unlike Tolstoy's heroine, by the end of the novel Medea exchanges resentment for forgiveness. In several instances Ulitskaya titles her narratives with clear references to literary predecessors. *Medea and Her Children* is the most prominent case: as we assert in chapter 2, the novel's kind protagonist has little in common with her murderous classical namesake (aside from their husbands' betrayal). Such multilayered references place Ulitskaya within the type of literary tradition Bloom discusses while revealing another function of her intertextuality: a ludic independence that emphasizes control over what she writes.[35]

Critics insistently define Ulitskaya's writings by their resemblance (or dissimilarity) to nineteenth-century prose. One maps Ulitskaya's evolution from *Sonechka*, with its heroine's love of classical literature, to *The Big Green Tent*'s presentation of late Soviet culture. This description astutely argues for intertextuality (whether literary or cultural) as a way to chart the author's development. Another critic is less charitable, accusing Ulitskaya of lying about Tolstoy's personal life when she discusses him in her memoir *Discarded Relics*. The critic then alleges that she fails to appreciate the profundity of *Anna Karenina* and unjustly critiques the war in Chechnya.[36] Connecting nineteenth-century writing to post-Soviet events is bizarre yet telling: this flawed logic posits that bad readers make bad citizens. Misuse of the classics is tantamount to disloyalty, and the latter increasingly provokes ostracism and punishment in Putin's Russia. As a contemporary author who describes the past, Ulitskaya cannot forget that the relationship between literature and culture is complex and perilous, rendering even intertextuality controversial.

Engaging with the nineteenth century fulfills yet another function of Ulitskaya's intertextuality: eliding the influence of socialist realism. In an image rich in symbolism of literature's ritualistic role, an undertaker in *The Big Green Tent* notes that he has buried authors from futurist poet Vladimir Mayakovsky to Pasternak. The years in between these deaths encompass most of the Stalin era, which Ulitskaya and the liberal intelligentsia understandably dismiss as devoid of good writing and antithetical to their values. Instead, the author looks to Pushkin, Russia's most revered literary figure. This choice is predictable, given the many Russian writers who have appropriated his oeuvre; Pushkin and Ulitskaya share a tendency to blur the line between literature and history. In *The Big Green Tent*, when Shengeli teaches Pushkin's play *Boris Godunov*, he comments on the murky nature of the past and hints at a more recent ruler with blood on his hands: Stalin. Once again, Ulitskaya as post-1991 author deftly combines references to the darkest days of the USSR with nineteenth-century literature; *Boris Godunov* compellingly depicts power struggles in medieval Russia to critique oppression throughout history.[37]

Some, such as Zolotonosov, link Ulitskaya's love for the classics with a "neosentimentalism" that emphasizes feelings through a style that calls to mind the nineteenth century.[38] This assessment is more distracting than accurate. Ulitskaya clearly favors the realist narrative's prominence of emotion (common to the sentimentalist and Romantic narrative as well). The problem, however, lies in neosentimentalism's implicit division of literature into female traits (feelings) and male characteristics (ideas); Zolotonosov's phrasing replicates the platitudes long used to dismiss women writers. Ironically enough, the neosentimental label also obscures the interconnection of emotions, daily existence, and morality that manifests Ulitskaya's values in her early works, and that for Morson comprises the ideational legacy of the classic Russian novel.[39]

Critics are more justified in linking Ulitskaya to another aspect of nineteenth-century prose: the family chronicle. Oddly enough, this celebrated genre still lacks sustained theoretical treatment from Slavists. Robert Stephens, describing kinship and fiction in American literature, lists several factors that also define Ulitskaya's novels: multiple generations representing the past; long-lasting effects of familial conflict;

lineage and doom as inheritance. Examining *Medea and Her Children*, Irina Savkina succinctly characterizes the family chronicle as making kinship into a fortress against the hostile forces of history. The related antagonism between family and state runs through twentieth-century Russian literature and constitutes one of the basic divisions between public and private life. Leonid Bakhnov thus incorrectly disqualifies *Medea and Her Children* as a family chronicle based on its non-linear narrative and narratorial subjectivity.[40] The first claim has more merit than the second; the latter's narrowness would decimate the ranks of the "classic" family chronicle, which include Sergei Aksakov's *Family Chronicle* (*Semeinaia khronika*) and, in a gloomier vein, Dostoevsky's *Demons* (*Besy*). As examined in chapter 2, Ulitskaya's contribution to the family chronicle is a profound element of ambivalence that is especially evident in her longer works, in which the influence of the state poisons positive familial ethics.[41]

Ulitskaya cites several other literary influences, none tarnished by association with socialist realism. (She argues that Soviet literature was a doomed enterprise, failing at the great tasks it set for itself.) As with the author's presumed neosentimentalism, the actual similarities are less interesting than the aura they impart, which legitimates her place in Russian literature as a whole and not merely its post-1991 instantiation. For instance, Ulitskaya has acknowledged her affinity for modernist poet Osip Mandel'shtam, whose literary sophistication and hatred of Stalin led to his death. She calls Vladimir Nabokov, an author whom she discovered as a university student, an ideal prose writer; one critic compares her to this master of style, whose dismissal of all things Soviet was more aesthetic than moral.[42] Drawn to Nabokov's capacity for translating the inexpressible into literary form, Ulitskaya also lauds his dual interest in art and science. Curiously, *Discarded Relics* contains an entire chapter on reading Nabokov's novel *The Gift* (*Dar*), which itself engages with Nikolai Chernyshevsky's nineteenth-century utopian novel *What Is to Be Done?* (*Chto delat'?*). Ulitskaya asserts that Nabokov in his writing "made a break, in part shocking the Russian reader: with his almost alchemical art he freed his native literature from its inherent tinge of painful religiosity, unfounded messianism, social unrest with a hint of hysteria, feeling of eternal guilt mixed with didacticism, and created an almost crystalline, transparent 'higher' literature, with a non-Russian degree of estrangement of the author from his text." This perceptive praise signals the contradictions involved in discussing the authors who have influenced one's own writing. Despite her oeuvre's clear connection of literature to morality, Ulitskaya praises Nabokov for moving Russian letters beyond this pairing. Likewise, while her style is more akin to realism, both she and Nabokov have a modernist's respect for the word as art, a similarity that ultimately renders their differences less important.[43]

At times a particular narrative shapes her use of literature, as when *The Big Green Tent* draws from Pasternak's *Doctor Zhivago*. For Ulitskaya, this work—especially Yuri Zhivago's death scene—exemplifies the interconnectedness of human life as well as prose. She explains her affinity for the chance, unrecognized encounter as a source for understanding the correlation between life and literature. Like the many relations that link human beings to the world and to each other, Ulitskaya states, "a book that is read accumulates the same connections: all who have read it are, in a special way, connected to one another by [their] relationship to the book's characters, reflections on their fates and the circumstances of their lives. Such accumulations of connections are found in great musical works and in paintings and sculptures," but are most distinct in literature. As we observe in chapter 3, both Ulitskaya and Pasternak depict the sincerity of the post-1953 intelligentsia, critique the state for brutal indifference to the individual, and question the sweeping social projects that justify this callousness.[44]

Some critics make the unconvincing argument that Ulitskaya is a postmodernist. This assertion relies on her use of allusions and intertextuality, two devices that were also key to Nabokov and Pasternak and, as Wachtel reminds us, mark every literary era's appropriation of its predecessor. Jasmina Vojvodić notes that Ulitskaya's prose lacks the grimness of many postmodernists.[45] More importantly, her works extol the intelligentsia as exemplars of embattled humanism, a scenario that advances the belief in progress and rationality that postmodernists gleefully dismantle. Ulitskaya positions herself as a preserver of culture, not its destroyer.[46]

A more legitimate link is with the writers of the 1960s (*shestidesiatniki*), who defined urban intellectual culture in the post-Thaw era. Given her background and criticism of the Soviet state, it is not surprising that Ulitskaya refers to herself as a "junior member" of this group (*mladshaia shestidesiatnitsa*) and identifies with these authors instead of those who appeared after 1991. In terms of her writing career (though not her biological age) she is far too young to be their contemporary, yet in theme and style Ulitskaya resembles authors Iurii Trifonov and Solzhenitsyn. Trifonov and Ulitskaya share a concern with the morality of the intelligentsia (expressed through sincerity), the relationship between the individual and history, fascination with everyday life, and Moscow as emblematic of the Soviet experience. Her work resembles Solzhenitsyn's in exploring the darker realities of Soviet history and experience, voicing suspicion of both Communist and consumer culture, and exhibiting considerable overlap between fiction and *publitsistika*. Trifonov, Solzhenitsyn, and Ulitskaya all spring from the mythologized milieu of the well-educated reader.[47] In *The Big Green Tent*, the narrator observes how literature, in the suffocating atmosphere of the Brezhnev era, went from teaching about life to replacing it. The written word became more meaningful than its referent, a utopian assessment that says less about late Soviet reality than about how intellectuals perceived it. This transubstantiation builds on the intelligentsia assumption that ultimately there is no distinction between literature and history, and that both must be interpreted by the thinking class. Ulitskaya views the present status of this imperative as uncertain, as shown in her provocative remark that Putin's 2012 reelection means readers failed to internalize the lessons of *Gulag Archipelago* (*Arkhipelag GULag*). We examine the intelligentsia's representation of literature and history in greater depth in chapter 3.[48]

Trifonov, Solzhenitsyn, and Ulitskaya also promulgate the cult of sincerity, a bedrock value of the intellectual class. Pomerantsev reveals *iskrennost'* (sincerity) to be a lens for viewing the trauma of the (Stalinist) past, which Ulitskaya sees as the most troubling era of Soviet/Russian history. In contemporary Russia, as Mark Lipovetsky and Alexander Etkind observe, literature views history as violence. Sincerity has a crucial role for Ulitskaya, who uses this *shestidesiatnik* ideal to counteract bloodshed by using *iskrennost'* to evaluate the national legacy as well as individual behavior. As with her promotion of tolerance, sincerity is embodied through the day-to-day actions of her characters. The result is novels with a strong ethical base, a selling point for the demoralized post-Soviet reader of serious literature.[49]

Ulitskaya and Women's Prose: A Reluctant Inheritance

Ulitskaya is much less enthusiastic about another important context for her oeuvre: women's prose (*zhenskaia proza*), prominent from the late 1980s to the early 1990s and thus contemporaneous with her first major publications. Both her fiction and non-fiction take up themes earlier established by *zhenskaia proza*: sexuality, family, intelligentsia, the need for personal responsibility, and a state vacillating between negligence and oppression of all its citizens and women in particular. These topics emerge through the representation of everyday life (*byt*), a cultural arena shared by women's prose and the *shestidesiatniki*. As Helena Goscilo notes, Ulitskaya's depictions of the body traumatized by society recall the battered female body in Liudmila Petrushevskaia's works, where corporeality conjoins personal and familial history.[50]

These two authors also contribute to the Moscow text, that group of writings about Russia's capital. Petrushevskaia's treatment of the city is more mystical and less focused on explicit history, yet both writers illustrate how Moscow shapes individuals at the level of daily life. As Tat'iana Kazarina discerns, without Petrushevskaia's legitimation of *byt* as a serious topic for mainstream prose Ulitskaya's portrayal of the quotidian would be more controversial.[51] The two authors also engage in ekphrasis, providing comments on the visual and aural arts in the form of prose and drama. Ulitskaya supports Petrushevskaia's diagnosis of social ills as brutal but correct, seeing her as a dramatist in all respects. Indeed, after winning the Booker Prize, Ulitskaya noted that Petrushevskaia should have received it for her novel *Number One or In the Gardens of Other Possibilities* (*Nomer Odin, ili V sadakh drugikh vozmozhnostei*).[52]

The vicissitudes of male sexuality were an easy target for women's prose, and Petrushevskaia's gallery of types is unmatched in this regard. As with many aspects of *zhenskaia proza*, this attack on masculinity followed the logic of 1990s culture, amassing overwhelming evidence to document sexual violence, unfaithfulness, and other faults.[53] Nina Sadur capitalized on such sentiment in her *skaz*-influenced vignette "Worm-Eaten Sonny" ("Chervivyi synok"), where the narrator wishes that women could abuse and destroy all males. At times women's prose argued that lack of freedom was the culprit: it was impossible to be a strong, independent man in oppressive Soviet society. Such a trite formulation exonerated the weak male and ignored the ways in which both genders supported the state and its policies. Ulitskaya builds on these previous depictions of sexuality; as we examine in chapter 1, her images are for the most part more varied and optimistic than those in *zhenskaia proza*.[54]

Illness is a key theme in women's writing that also shapes Ulitskaya's oeuvre. In the novel *The Kukotskii Case*, which portrays the gradual disintegration of an intelligentsia family, daughter Tanya realizes that her life has been forever altered when she sees her friend Toma's mother dying from an illegal abortion. The girl comes to live with protagonist Pavel Alekseevich and his kin, initiating a series of events that radically change all involved. What Tanya does not know is that years later she will die a similar death, disregarded by an overworked medical staff and a doctor too drunk to appear for his shift.[55] Not surprisingly, the hospital is another inherited locus for Ulitskaya that loomed large in *zhenskaia proza*. Goscilo argues that it is a female chronotope originating in part from the male-oriented realm of prose about Soviet labor camps: both literary trends privilege introspection and a strict segregation of the sexes that presupposes lack of autonomy. To Ulitskaya such separation heralds disaster, for the hospital combines isolation with a debasement of the body it purportedly serves.[56]

Homosexuality is another theme where women's prose shapes Ulitskaya's writing. The author's discussion of gays and lesbians is both positive and innovative in presenting sympathetic queer characters, a phenomenon still new in Russian prose and quite important in the increasingly homophobic Putin years. However, these personages embody a problematic trope of *zhenskaia proza*, which described a culture where male homosexuality was illegal until 1993: for women authors, queerness was an index of social injustice rather than one aspect of a complete personality. This distorting conception comes with a plea for sympathy. Homosexuality, victimization, and marginalization intertwine to create a message of tolerance grounded in the limiting late Soviet idea that gays are both symptom and victim of an oppressive state and decaying society. Petrushevskaia is the most prominent example of this tendency: her prose associates gay men with rape, self-destruction, or both. While it is laudable that Ulitskaya presents any sort of positive depiction of homosexuality, in chapter 4 we show that the parameters within which she does so renders these characters two-dimensional.[57]

As with other aspects of the body, beauty is a topic that Ulitskaya inherits from *zhenskaia proza*. Tat'iana Tolstaia and other women authors connected physical attraction to corruption and artifice. This trope surfaces in Ulitskaya's oeuvre, as we note in chapter 1. It is evident in her screenplay for the film *The Liberty Sisters* (*Sestrichki Liberti*, 1990), where she depicts the unsuccessful transformation of twins Liuba and Vera, whom sophisticated gay artist Sergei tries to remake as Style Moderne muses. The two women become a living example of ekphrasis as life and art blend on the pages of the script; however, Sergei cannot eradicate their greed and duplicity, which ultimately causes Vera's suicide after Liuba flees to Italy with her sister's lover. The moral is evident: nothing of aesthetic or ethical value can exist in a society that scorns both of these. Ulitskaya wrote the screenplay during perestroika, at the height of *zhenskaia proza* and its attack on beauty and established gender roles.[58]

Though she acknowledges her persistent interest in female fates, Ulitskaya denies that this literary movement has shaped her work; in fact, she has called women's prose an "anti-female term." Ulitskaya is similarly dismissive of feminism, which in her view paradoxically demands both equality and special privileges. Ironically enough, such authorial disavowal was voiced by most writers associated with women's prose during perestroika and the early Yeltsin years. Societal prejudice, hostile critics, and a suspicion of "alien" Western conceptions such as feminism caused Petrushevskaia and others to distance themselves from a literary trend seemingly marginalized by its gender. At the same time, as Goscilo notes, culture urged women to move from the public to private sphere and return to the putatively natural roles of homemaker and mother.[59]

The complicated relationship with women's prose is the strongest current in criticism of Ulitskaya. Praise of her writing often relies on a trope inherited from perestroika-era responses to *zhenskaia proza*: Ulitskaya's emphasis on ideas and meaningful existence (*bytie*) elevates her from this suspect category.[60] Detractors also echo commentary prevalent in the Gorbachev years, arguing that her status as woman or her excessively physiological subject matter bars Ulitskaya from the rarefied realm of serious literature and thus assuming that women's prose is antithetical to the classics of the nineteenth century. (One simply states that her characters are ruled by their vaginas.) Both sets of critics violate a maxim crucial to Ulitskaya's oeuvre: body, soul, and intellect are bound together and cannot be understood in isolation.[61]

There are, however, substantial differences between Ulitskaya's works and women's prose. First, just as *zhenskaia proza* itself evolved from the work of Grekova, Natal'ia Baranskaia, and other women writers in the 1960s and 1970s, Ulitskaya expands and changes the themes that writers such as Petrushevskaia had established in the late 1980s and early 1990s; we discuss these innovations in chapters 1 and 2. Likewise, Ulitskaya's narratives do not operate in the atmosphere of crisis that enveloped *zhenskaia proza*. Appearing during the last years of the USSR, such writing understandably focused on the quickly collapsing society around it. Portraying contemporary life was the priority, whereas Ulitskaya focuses on a Soviet past that clearly is already a part of history (however unsettling and contested that period may be). Ulitskaya's main topics—tolerance, sincerity, positive actions—emerge through her sympathetic depiction of the intelligentsia, a group assailed by Petrushevskaia and Tolstaia as hopeless, cynical, and corrupted either by the state or personal greed. Finally, as Ulitskaya moved from the short story to longer genres, her works accrued a scope and range of theme much broader than that of *zhenskaia proza*, which was rooted above all in the minute and myriad problems of daily life.[62]

Literature, Culture, and Crisis in Contemporary Russia

Ulitskaya's inherited contexts from late Soviet culture exist within the stratification of high and low literature in contemporary Russia. This distinction is not a new one. There was, for instance, a hunger for potboiler detective fiction, first between 1905 and 1908, then during the 1920s (the reign of the "Red Pinkerton"), before it vanished during Stalinism and then reemerged after 1953.[63] What distinguishes the post-Soviet context is the catastrophic confluences of the 1990s, when state subsidies for (approved) authors dramatically decreased, book distribution was disrupted, cheap translations of foreign literature—classic and lowbrow alike—flooded the market, previously banned (high culture) authors became passé, and pirated videos competed with print culture. At the same time, incomes dropped precipitously and spending on books likewise decreased. Against this backdrop, during the Putin and Medvedev years Ulitskaya has seen literature's freedom from censorship as proof that the printed word is considered less important than media such as television.[64]

For Ulitskaya, who consistently speaks on behalf of the liberal intelligentsia, these developments are disastrous. Today's readers, she complains, have distanced themselves from fiction and are far removed from those in *The Big Green Tent* who lauded fiction as more real than life. Nonetheless Ulitskaya hesitates to attribute too great an importance to literature in the context of human history, citing seminal texts such as the Vedas, the Bible, the Gospels, and Marx's *Capital* but adding her opinion that no literary fiction falls into this category.[65] She longs for an ecology of reading, which would protect society from literary pollutants and, at the same time, assure the survival of quality literature. As we explore in chapter 3, Ulitskaya consistently assumes unity of thought among reader, writer, and intelligentsia as she formulates a diagnosis and cure for Russia's cultural ills. Part of her authorial persona is claiming the right to practice social prophecy as well as craft good prose.[66]

Ulitskaya's own worth, however, is subject to debate. Critics disagree over her place within the division between high and low literature. Some, linking her with the discredited category of women's prose and its alleged naturalism, accuse her of writing for the mass reader. Lev Danilkin, for instance, decries her works as resembling the Latin American *telenovelas* ubiquitous on Russian television in the 1990s.[67] Supporters claim Ulitskaya as an impressive author whose writings will not suffer the ephemeral popularity (and subsequent oblivion) inevitable for less serious works. This second group argues that Ulitskaya continues the nation's great literary tradition, an assertion that relies heavily on her connections to nineteenth-century prose. Indeed, her emergence helped counter fears that the novel—Russia's most prestigious genre—had died along with socialism. Ulitskaya, for her part, has remarked that literary criticism in Russia today has become detached from the act of reading.[68]

While her comments in interviews and her memoir link her to the *shestidesiatniki*, Ulitskaya is also connected to several other contemporary Russian writers in theme and prominence. She reads the work of philologist-turned-best-selling author Boris Akunin, whose highbrow mysteries, set in the nineteenth century, subtly critique Russia's mythologies of imperial grandeur.[69] In her public image, she contrasts starkly with National Bolshevik leader Limonov: both, however, use literary success to spotlight their scorn for the Putin regime. For Wachtel, Limonov's transformation from exiled author to political gadfly exemplifies one path chosen by Russian writers who wish to remain visible in an altered cultural landscape. An author can either skillfully adapt representations of the past to the tastes of contemporary readers, or offend these same tastes and solidify notoriety (and publicity). While Ulitskaya's public and literary persona more closely resembles that of Akunin, for conservatives her statements are as provocative and scandalous as those of Limonov.[70]

On a more fundamental level, Ulitskaya's humanist worldview, critique of the state, and interest in the past ally her with Dmitrii Bykov. He, like Ulitskaya, often attacks the nation's drift towards authoritarianism; both authors took part in the May 2012 protest march through central Moscow organized by Akunin. The two likewise share a horror of how the government strives to deform the public perception of history. In the novel *Justification* (*Opravdanie*), Bykov gives a grotesque view of Stalinism, in which repression creates a stronger nation based on those tenacious enough to survive. Both Bykov and Ulitskaya believe the twentieth century to be defined by the individual resisting regimes whose utopian plans create dystopian reality.[71] By contrast, author Dina Rubina is less direct in her appraisal: in the novel *On the Bright Side of the Street* (*Na solnechnoi storone ulitsy*) she implicitly endorses tolerance for cultural difference by depicting the vibrant nature of multiethnic Tashkent. Aside from a shared emphasis on *tolerantnost'*, critics note other similarities between Rubina and Ulitskaya: both authors are ethnic Jews, and Rubina's works foreground this heritage alongside women's concerns and everyday life.[72]

Success at home and abroad has made Ulitskaya one of Russia's cultural exports. In this sense she is different from Rubina (who resides in Israel) and literary exiles such as Nabokov or Solzhenitsyn. Despite her familiarity with the West, Ulitskaya speaks to the world and its Russian diaspora as an author whose intercultural worldview remains rooted in Moscow as the center of post-Soviet life. Her works' critique of Soviet culture and history underscore this connection; writing links readers to a past they may abhor but cannot deny as a formative part of the present. For her, literature unites Russian readers wherever they may be, and writing creates a new geography that supersedes physical borders and distance.[73]

Readers and Translators: Conveying the Ethics of the Intelligentsia

Ulitskaya sees the intelligentsia as the moral force in post-Soviet society, albeit one whose voice is too often ignored. While situated in the specific context of Russia after socialism, *intelligenty* share the same values as their counterparts across the world: good reading and the right actions transcend nationality and, for that matter, the decades separating Ulitskaya's literary career from the events and lives she depicts. Regardless of origin or time, Ulitskaya's implied reader has positive ethics molded by literature. In fact, the author sees herself as the sum of the books she has read and acknowledges the considerable influence of literature on her development as a person.[74]

The trope of the translator conjoins Ulitskaya's writing and life. One of her sons works as a simultaneous interpreter, but this biographical detail is not the principal reason why translators recur in her oeuvre. Ol'ga, the main female character in *The Big Green Tent*, works with

French, Spanish, and Italian texts. Knowledge of another language fosters the tolerance Ulitskaya prizes as a core value of this group; in Olga's case, it contributes to seeing worldviews other than those of her parents, who are members of the Party elite. In a parallel move, the author stresses culturally diverse border zones such as Crimea over Russia's more chauvinist center (Moscow); translation is a linguistic manifestation of the attraction to liminality that Clowes observes in Ulitskaya's works.[75] The image of the translator implicates the sacred as well as the secular. *Daniel Stein, Interpreter*, a novel that explores the repercussions of the Holocaust and how to bridge the gaps between different faiths and ethnicities, begins by citing the New Testament: "I thank my God, I speak with tongues more than ye all: Yet in the church I had rather speak five words with my understanding, that by my voice I might teach others also, than ten thousand words in an unknown tongue." This quotation from 1 Corinthians refers to a shift from many languages to a single one that promotes universal comprehension. *Daniel Stein* focuses on its polyglot protagonist, a Polish-Jewish convert to Catholicism who immigrates to the Holy Land to reconcile Christianity, Judaism, and Islam. A priest and monk, Daniel is a translator of God's word, an intermediary between heaven and earth. As his last name (Stein) suggests, he is the firm foundation of Ulitskaya's conception of Christianity as a faith that should promote understanding.[76]

In his thoughtful study of Russian Jews in the twentieth century, Yuri Slezkine points out that textual interpretation and cultural mediation were important skills for this group. Daniel exemplifies both abilities—he is able to transmit and explain those crucial elements of culture that Ulitskaya believes will help humanity survive. We explore this character in greater depth in chapter 4, revealing that the translator is more dependent on corrupting political context than Ulitskaya would admit.[77] Wachtel describes how those in the USSR sometimes "corrected" the material they were translating from minority languages into Russian, recalling Edward Said's observation of the same practice in Europeans who worked with allegedly primitive Middle Eastern texts. In the Soviet Union the relationship between translation and cultural imperialism was inherited from nineteenth-century conceptions of Russian as the omnipotent language of a culture that, as Dostoevsky believed, could unite the world. Ulitskaya's image of translation is contaminated by this legacy and the concomitant assumption that the intelligentsia should make others' ideas comprehensible, possibly distorting them in the process.[78]

Critics and scholars disagree about the significance of Ulitskaya's multiethnic and transnational agenda. As Levantovskaya observes, such themes create a literal and metaphorical exchange of people and ideas. Likewise, emigration is bound to tolerance in works such as *Daniel Stein, Interpreter* and the novel *The Funeral Party*, which portrays the lives of friends and lovers in the United States during the last years of perestroika. Literature of the Russian diaspora yields rich intertexts for Ulitskaya and provides another overlap with Nabokov; similarly, two characters from *The Funeral Party* encounter Brodsky in New York (a city that figures prominently in many works about Soviet exiles).[79] This glimpse of a renowned poet underscores Ulitskaya's axiom that good readers transcend temporal and geographical distances: her image of the intelligentsia is one that crosses borders yet also implies the unique genius of Russian culture. As Adrian Wanner aptly notes, diaspora authors' consciousness is always connected to the country they have left; while Ulitskaya has not moved away from Russia, her oeuvre often portrays the complicated identities of those who have left or will, yet remain connected to their former homeland by the cultural ties of literature.[80]

Some have accused Ulitskaya, presumably due to her Jewish heritage, of being a future emigrant herself, though Ulitskaya eschews the possibility and claims that "all [her] receptors are oriented toward Russia." Critics' vitriol reveals the mixture of envy, wounded national pride, and xenophobia that surrounds debates over leaving Russia. One liberal critic, while sharply attacking Ulitskaya's ideas on religion, praises her "humane" treatment of emigrants. The discussions concerning fiction reaffirm literature's place as an arena for debate, despite the changed conditions of post-1991 society. Ulitskaya's multifaceted status as author remarking on past and present is inseparable from her visibility in the public sphere; her writing and persona use the values of the intelligentsia to cement fiction and reality.[81]

Ulitskaya's Imagined Intelligentsia: Idealism and Despair

Ulitskaya speaks for the humane intelligentsia, the part of the educated class that supports a liberal, tolerant, civil society for Russia. Her close friends formed her primary audience when she first began to write. As her career progressed, this circle expanded, yet the author still describes her ideal readers as people of her own age: women in the provinces, pensioners who save their money to buy her works. All have an educated background and the Western-influenced values this presumably entails; thus for Ulitskaya shared attitudes create a constant that runs from her first publications to the appearance of her latest works. Ulitskaya's readership is by no means limited by Russia's borders; in fact, she observes that "the same people" come to see her everywhere. She argues that globalization's commonalities across cultures can yield positive results, namely a single language with the power to counterbalance consumerism. Such communication ideally will express the ethics central to Ulitskaya's writing, which itself strives to bridge the gap between different faiths and ethnicities and overcome the trauma of Soviet history. These morals, evident in her earlier works through depictions of body and family, later play a more explicit role: ethics constitute an overarching plot that unites her narratives.[82]

The promotion of unity recalls the inclusive humanism of those who inspired Ulitskaya, including dissident author Iulii Daniel', priest Aleksandr Men', and activist Sakharov. All these *shestidesiatniki* embraced the morally righteous honesty that opposed the falsehood dominating Soviet culture. Ulitskaya identifies the latter two—and the more conservative Solzhenitsyn—as decisive figures who molded the generation also influenced by Trifonov's literary depictions of how past and present shape morality. Further, her views of these three reveal a fascinating caveat to her view of the intelligentsia. She sees Solzhenitsyn as a great man who outlived his importance and views Sakharov as a failure because he did not achieve his grand goals: the scope of his liberal, progressive agenda was too broad. Men', on the other hand, had more modest aims and did not attempt to transform the world: "he didn't destroy the old, didn't undertake something new, but showed the individual the possibilities slumbering within him."[83] Society, she implies, must abandon large-scale plans and instead focus on changes at the personal level. As her novels suggest, those who attempt to advance history will be crushed by it. Grandiose schemes for wholesale improvement smack of the abstractions Morson derides and may provoke horrific repression like that of the Soviet era. By contrast, real progress happens at the level of everyday behavior; the intellectual class succeeds in living rightly but fails in its plans to remake society. This central problem of the intelligentsia recurs throughout Ulitskaya's oeuvre.

Clark identifies two other troubling attributes of the intelligentsia, both central to Ulitskaya's mythology. *Intelligenty* define themselves as the conscience of the nation and its defenders against the country's greatest threat: the *narod* (and, by extension, the authoritarian regime that engendered its development). Whether embodied in *Homo sovieticus* or the post-1991 market economy, the masses oppose the "real" values of Russia (as identified, of course, by the intelligentsia).[84] Ulitskaya posits that the intelligentsia is better educated than the *narod*—in both morality and erudition—and must save the lower orders from their own innate destructiveness. This elitist formulation is an intellectual axiom that precedes and outlasts the Soviet era; Irina Paperno argues that *intelligenty*, through the interweaving of literature and history, envision themselves as a community that survived totalitarianism thanks to shared ideas. Ulitskaya's image of the intelligentsia is less a function of reality than how she imagines it: she sees intellectuals as good readers and moral individuals who persevere despite antagonism from the state and common people. As we explore in chapter 3, Ulitskaya's writing actually reveals a more ambiguous and troubling picture.[85]

Intellectual and moral affinities bind the intelligentsia together, just as mythologization of the past defines both the intelligentsia and this author's depiction of it. Many of the concerns she addresses in her literary and journalistic works reflect the preoccupations of intellectuals in the post-Soviet period, including emigration, the fate of literature, and the survival of the thinking class itself. The last problem entails perennial development of thought: for Ulitskaya, questioning one's own assumptions is essential to being a morally vibrant, cogent individual. This constant challenging extends to given truths, such as the ossified Marxism underlying Soviet ideology or the collusive Orthodoxy of the Putin era. As we note in chapter 4, other tenets remain unquestioned; for instance, Ulitskaya's definition of the intelligentsia as a priori liberal excludes such key figures as author Aleksandr Prokhanov or village prose writer Valentin Rasputin.[86]

Despite the intelligentsia's disputed status and current travails, Ulitskaya and other writers assume its time-honored burden: critiquing the past. Ulitskaya's reassessment of Soviet history is inseparable from recent debates over textbooks (especially their treatment of Stalinism). Such arguments go hand in hand with the Kremlin's forceful attempts to impose a dominant historical narrative on educators (and others) across the nation.[87] A broader controversy involves divergent assessments of "worthy" subjects in the Soviet period. Danilkin takes Ulitskaya to task for neglecting to discuss the space program in *The Big Green Tent*, claiming that her omission replaces the glory of the USSR with a handful of malcontent dissidents. Ulitskaya retorts that the trial of Daniel' and Andrei Siniavskii was more significant, a liberal assertion that elevates human rights over technological state prowess. Here and elsewhere she attacks the longing for the Soviet past that results in either whitewashing of repression or its transformation into a consumer good (evident in the hammer and sickle T-shirts worn around the world). These unsavory alternatives reflect two of Ulitskaya's fears: nostalgia for Stalinism and the dominance of commodity culture.[88]

The intelligentsia has long claimed the right to interpret the present as well as the past; Ulitskaya's innovation is to envision Russia's plight in terms of genetic degeneration and crisis. Part of the cultural decline she identifies comes from globalization and consumerism, but Ulitskaya also views these social problems as originating with the *narod* and the younger generation (particularly adolescents). Her most damning assessment, elaborated in *The Big Green Tent*, is that Russia is a larval society, devoid of members with moral maturity.[89] This characterization, which we examine in greater depth in chapter 3, is consonant with the sense of genetic apocalypse that Serguei Oushakine observes in Russians' worries over falling birthrates, increased morbidity, and an influx of immigrants from other former Soviet states.[90]

Though she eschews didactic literature, Ulitskaya presents herself and her works as a cure for what plagues Russia.[91] In both writing and philanthropy, she regards the irregular and ailing body as a manifestation of sincerity and the antithesis to the seamless physicality prized by Soviet culture. Her literary corpus attempts to rehumanize the disabled and elderly, an effort she literalizes in hospital-based charitable endeavors that resemble her other social projects, including the Good Book (*Khoroshaia kniga*) initiative and her editing of a series of children's books about tolerance. The healing mandate that informs her work in hospitals has a metaphorical resonance in the tolerance texts; the latter suggest that the rifts existing between people of different beliefs and backgrounds may be overcome through understanding. Such a view is evident in the oft-quoted final paragraph of *Medea and Her Children*, with its vision of inclusive kinship and the human family, both of which have managed to outlive Soviet trauma. Ulitskaya, like her positive characters, attempts to model the values of the intelligentsia through actions in everyday life.[92]

The author sees her writing and social projects as an attempt to repair past damage and safeguard the future. The optimism underlying this effort is a positive alternative to the ordeal and rupture Mark Lipovetsky and Alexander Etkind identify as endemic to post-Soviet literature. It likewise opposes the patriotism of despair that, Oushakine argues, negatively unites Russians by construing loss as national identity.[93] For Ulitskaya ethical action brings people together: the author's narratives may be read as a single text that stretches from the last years of Stalinism to the beginning of perestroika. Her publications present a constant set of themes, which appear in miniature form in her early (and shorter) works, then expand to dominate her later novels. Responding rightly through crisis and uncertainty, her characters remain a moral constant against the backdrop of change; the values that her first stories link to flesh and family later shape mind, soul, and faith. Ulitskaya thus provides a narrative of stability otherwise absent from Russia's history. Taken together, her works link past and present through the positive ethics of the intelligentsia. While in chapter 4 a portion of our analysis points out the limits and contradictions of this author, we do so in order to better understand Ulitskaya's extraordinary contributions to Russian literature and culture.[94]

Our study analyzes Ulitskaya's works through a focus on tolerance, sincerity, and other liberal intelligentsia values, beginning with their depiction through the body. We introduce major themes in different chapters, returning to these topics to show how their development and interconnections run throughout the author's work. This approach thus reflects Ulitskaya's own wariness of boundaries and strict categorization. Summaries of the author's major works follow the conclusion. In chapter 1 we examine physicality and Ulitskaya's innovative corporeal reading of history. Analogous to the prescriptive ideal of the uniform Soviet body that Lilya Kaganovsky deconstructs, Ulitskaya presents beauty as problematic. She likewise counters the grim visions of the Gorbachev and Yeltsin eras offered by Petrushevskaia and film director Aleksei Balabanov. Instead, she sympathetically depicts irregularity through such varied forms as catatonic, ailing, or handicapped bodies as well as holy fools (*iurodivye*). The author's diverse images of sexuality and humanization of gay characters are strikingly new in Russian literature. In her rehabilitative, pluralistic approach to corporeality, Ulitskaya recasts both male and female identity, creates a sincerity of the body, and reminds the reader of her conviction that flesh is the foundation for community.

In the second chapter we chart the functioning of individuals within the family, a key theme that Goscilo and Yana Hashamova observe in contemporary culture. Building on an unacknowledged debt to women writers such as Petrushevskaia, Ulitskaya expands the portrayal of female roles (mothers, daughters, and sisters) and, to a much lesser degree, male roles. In redefining kinship, Ulitskaya proposes new familial models based not on blood ties but on shared ideals. These families of affinity sharply contrast with the oppressive Great Family, a problematic paradigm in Soviet culture that continues in Putin's cult of the strong ruler.

In the final two chapters we focus more on Ulitskaya's later works, whose longer length and more developed discussion of ethics expand on the need for tolerance, sincerity, and positive actions implied in her earlier and shorter narratives. Chapter 3 analyzes Ulitskaya's depiction of the intelligentsia and its uses (and abuses) of what Wachtel labels the vexed relationship between literature and history. The intelligentsia's multifaceted mandate, according to Ulitskaya, is to uphold ethical standards, guide society, and engage in documentation by narrating the past. Her personalization of the Soviet experience rewrites large-scale narratives on the level of everyday life. This attention to the varieties of individual experience promotes tolerance, the central principle that underpins all her work.

Chapter 4 is an examination of the broader implications of Ulitskaya's inclusive, ecumenical stance (inherited from, among others, the scholar Dmitrii Likhachev). Ulitskaya, a secular Jew who converted to Russian Orthodoxy, critiques the corrupt collaboration of Church and state. Drawing on Isaiah Berlin, we map her religious and philosophical positions and the unexpected ways in which she links Christianity and tolerance. Ulitskaya's fiction, commentaries and social projects—her words and deeds—together create a unifying ethical worldview. This stance also legitimates the role of the intelligentsia, which struggles to navigate between a capricious market economy and increasingly restrictive government policies.

The conclusion explores Ulitskaya's turn from author to public figure and memoirist, a change that resonates with what Irina Kaspe views as the rise of documentary prose in contemporary culture. Against this backdrop, Ulitskaya's ethics, actions, and writing will continue to make her a distinct and significant voice in Russia.

1

REDEEMING THE BODY

ULITSKAYA AND CORPOREALITY

I got food poisoning from eating something ridiculous. I've been ill for a day and a half and experienced a whole gamut of emotions: first puzzlement—after all, I eat absolutely anything and never suffer any consequences—then irritation at myself—why on earth do I eat absolutely anything, after all, the tomato juice which I unreflectingly chucked into the dinner had been standing on the buffet for who knows how many days. [. . .] I realized that I was expelling all the nightmare I have been gulping down all these last months of reading, the painful reading of all those books about the destruction of the Jews during the Second World War, all the tomes of medieval history, the history of the Crusades and the earlier history of the Church councils, the fathers of the Church from St. Augustine to St. John Chrysostomos, all the anti-Semitic opuses written by highly enlightened and terribly holy men. I puked out all the Jewish and non-Jewish encyclopedias I have read over the last few months, the whole Jewish Question which had poisoned me more powerfully than any tomato juice.[1]

Writing in the summer of 2006, the autobiographical narrator of *Daniel Stein, Interpreter* viscerally experiences the oneness of body and spirit that unites the works of Ludmila Ulitskaya. Researching the roots of anti-Semitism, she is overpowered by the toxic legacy of intolerance. Sickness of the flesh is inseparable from ailments of the soul, and the horror of religious and ethnic hatred contaminates both. Ulitskaya engages the physical form in three ways: attacking the ideal Soviet physique; depicting aspects of corporeality (*telesnost'*) shunned by society; and presenting new markers of gender identity. Her texts dismember the Soviet body, laying bare an obvious yet overlooked truth: it is the physical form, in all its varied manifestations, that makes us human. The ethics of the spirit appear in the flesh, and *telesnost'* creates a sincerity that parallels the values Ulitskaya ascribes to the liberal intelligentsia. Her holistic approach insists that the erotic belongs equally to the intellectual and physiological spheres as she argues for a tolerance that encompasses both.[2]

By beginning our analysis with the body we acknowledge what Judith Butler famously theorized as its preeminent role in defining gender and meaning. *Telesnost'* supersedes dichotomies; Ulitskaya's vision of corporeality refuses to privilege mind over body and portrays the latter as central to understanding subjectivity. For Elizabeth Grosz, the body is "the crucial term, the site of contestation, in a series of economic, political, sexual, and intellectual struggles." In this vein Ulitskaya's writing illuminates the centrality of the physical entity by showing how it illustrates an individual's struggle to live a moral life despite the tragedies of the Soviet past. *Telesnost'* is a fundamental part of the author's unique combination of history and the personal.[3]

Depictions of the flesh also influence literary reception. As we note in the introduction, some critics have seen Ulitskaya's writing as "neosentimentalism," a feminized depiction of body and emotion that privileges sympathy for characters. Ellen Rutten observes that emphasis on feelings (*chuvstvitel'nost'*) was a cornerstone of Sentimentalist authors; late eighteenth-century writers such as Nikolai Karamzin and Aleksandr Radishchev saw the body as honest, while the mind could be duplicitous. This characterization surfaces in Ulitskaya's works through her consistent linking of corporeality and sincerity. While early responses to her works focused on neosentimentalism, this trope in criticism mainly disappeared as her later and longer works more explicitly addressed history, ethics, and the great ideas prized by Russian prose. Mikhail Zolotonosov claims that her novel *Sincerely Yours, Shurik* critiques the same sentimentalism Ulitskaya had previously inculcated in readers. The narrative, which details its sensitive protagonist's loveless sexual entanglements, departs from the union of body and emotion that Zolotonosov espies in classical Russian literature.[4]

Corporeality's contested presence in writing comes from its role in history. Helena Goscilo and Andrea Lanoux outline how the body in Russian culture has a multilayered mythology that obscures physical reality. Ulitskaya, a post-1991 author writing mostly about the Soviet era, responds to the earlier period's conceptions of *telesnost'*. Revolutionary rhetoric ushered in the New Man. Molding and melding body and (secular) soul, this effort tried to erase the longstanding division between these two halves.[5] Stalinism, the backdrop to the beginning of most of Ulitskaya's works, privileged the firm, youthful body in hypertrophied dimensions. Bared muscles and ample (covered) bosoms loomed on the screen as virile men and their buxom lovers enchanted moviegoers; the malnourished and deformed bodies of war, famine, and Gulag vanished behind the overly robust masculine and feminine forms.[6]

During the Thaw and the Brezhnev period physicality evoked a scarred, sagging, and imperfect world. Works such as Iurii Trifonov's *The Exchange* (*Obmen*) embody the muddled morality of middle age via dumpy matrons and their pudgy husbands.[7] Perestroika subsequently revealed the human form as suffering from all that ailed the USSR. The film *Little Vera* (*Malen'kaia Vera*) scandalously co-opted corporeality to convey existence enlivened only by drunken brawls and sexual misadventures, while authors such as Liudmila Petrushevskaia yoked physicality to violence, poverty, and other formerly taboo subjects. This era, and particularly women's prose, demolished a tenet of earlier Russian culture: corporeal suffering strengthens the soul and connotes loyalty to the Great Family, the dominant metaphor of allegiance that Katerina Clark connects to the state. The perestroika body, exemplified in *chernukha* (literature of crime and slime), was above all a traumatized presence undermining previous assumptions that the flesh reflected the values of a healthy society.[8]

The collapse of the USSR tied *telesnost'* to a nation plummeting into despair and chaos. The hard bodies of gangsters on the big and small screen vied for popularity with the alcoholic idyll of the film *Peculiarities of the National Hunt* (*Osobennosti natsional'noi okhoty*). For women, the new status quo linked the flesh to homemaking, connubial bliss, and ending the precipitous decline in the ethnic Russian population. While concern over falling birthrates (versus large families in the non-European republics) had marked Soviet discourse, the intensified debate over national survival in the 1990s gave the reproductive body new urgency, especially in light of prostitution and mail-order marriage to foreigners. Corporeality became a striking symptom of the "patriotism of despair" that Serguei Oushakine ascribes to the Yeltsin years.[9] The gay body added to post-Soviet anxieties. Even after the 1993 decriminalization of homosexuality, representations of queerness were more metaphorical than direct. These depictions envisioned homosexuality as both the cause and result of alienation, binding it to the decadent West and a concomitant undermining of Russian masculinity. However, as we note in the introduction and chapter 4, Ulitskaya sharply deviates from this script: she depicts queerness through the intelligentsia value of forbearance, a connection that resonates uneasily in her writing.[10]

In the era of Vladimir Putin and his protégé Dmitrii Medvedev, supposedly only healthy, heterosexual *telesnost'* can redeem Russia. In this climate homosexuality has become increasingly marginalized and (re)criminalized, linked to anti-Western polemics as tensions with the United States and Europe rise. Clearly the body is at the forefront of Russia's reassertion of itself as superpower. The nationalist masculine revenge film *Brother 2* (*Brat 2*) and the impressive, frequently photographed physique of Putin himself promised security and a new respect after a decade of perceived national humiliation.[11] For women the mystery novels of Dar'ia Dontsova and the glamour literature of Oksana Robski implied that sexuality could lead to love and marriage with a New Russian; as Eliot Borenstein argues, the beginning of the new century devalued sex and violence (unless in the national interest) in favor of tranquil domesticity. In this restrictive context the imperfect body was an impediment to be hidden or corrected, much as it had been concealed in the USSR for more overtly ideological reasons.[12]

The Kukotskii Case: Corporeality, Maternity, and Ways of Seeing

Ulitskaya's novel *The Kukotskii Case* is primarily concerned with corporeality as it describes the slow disintegration of the Kukotskii clan headed by gynecologist Pavel Alekseevich. Beginning during the Great Patriotic War, the novel's plot depicts first the expansion and then the collapse of Pavel Alekseevich's family over the next four decades. He marries Elena and adopts her daughter Tanya and then Toma, the child of their impoverished janitor (*dvornikha*). Husband and wife have a bitter argument over Pavel Alekseevich's attempts to legalize abortion in the postwar era, and their marriage never recovers. Family members drift apart, Tanya and Toma each marry, and the USSR itself fundamentally changes and eventually collapses. Throughout the plot, the work presents ways of seeing, perceiving, and experiencing the physical world, especially in connection with the female body. This focus is the basis of the narrative's broader concerns: preoccupation with *telesnost'* leads to the biologization of motherhood, the consideration of who may raise questions about the maternal body, and a redrawing of familial relationships. By focusing on several depictions in the novel, in this chapter we introduce the reader to the complex revisions of corporeality throughout Ulitskaya's prose, plays, and nonfiction.

Pavel Alekseevich initially appears in *The Kukotskii Case* not only as a figure of authority, but as an almost saintly image endowed with a special capacity for bringing life into the world and arbitrating questions related to birth and pregnancy. When Elena, Pavel Alekseevich's future wife, regains consciousness after a hysterectomy, she experiences a strong sensation that someone will soon reveal to her a "definitive truth that is more important than life itself"; she then sees for the first time the man who has saved her. As we discuss later, this connection between Elena, intuition, and non-rational visions comes to dominate her life in the last part of *The Kukotskii Case*. Two brief clips from Iurii Grymov's 2005 miniseries based on the novel continue the doctor's veneration: as Elena first glimpses Pavel Alekseevich, the light around his head creates the effect of a nimbus; similarly, the deeply religious household servant Vasilisa believes she sees his face in an icon. This image resonates with the early portion of the novel's treatment of Pavel Alekseevich as emblematizing the intelligentsia, a class whose humane values contrast with the everyday brutality of first Leninism, then Stalinism and the Great Patriotic War.[13]

Part of Pavel Alekseevich's authority resides in a special gift he possesses: an "internal vision" (*vnutrividenie*) that links explicitly to his long fascination with the female (and particularly maternal) form. His ability to see into women's bodies—to perceive the illness that they themselves cannot—translates into his indisputable knowledge of what is best for them. It also compensates for a concern not offered by another authority: the Stalinist state, which through military blunders and indifference places Elena and millions like her in danger as they live in evacuation (or, even worse, under occupation). Pavel Alekseevich saves Elena's life but in the process removes her womb, thus excluding her from the procreation demanded of women. While she will survive, this character is now marginal to a society that mandates childbearing to compensate for population loss. However, precisely because her body no longer fits the norms of Soviet culture, Elena becomes more important to Ulitskaya's oeuvre, which attempts to rehumanize those neglected by society because of their *telesnost'*.[14]

Elena illustrates that what might initially appear to be a reduction of women to their reproductive organs is, in fact, a more complicated question as *The Kukotskii Case* connects procreation, the state, autonomy, and *telesnost'*. In her key discussion of motherhood and the body, Marianne Hirsch asserts that "maternity, inasmuch as it is represented as biological, poses the question of the body as pointedly as is possible. [...] The perspective of the maternal makes it difficult simply to reject the notion of biology and forces us to engage both the meaning of the body and the risks of what has been characterized as essentialist." Motherhood (*materinstvo*) as physical process cannot be considered without the social implications embodied in Elena's altered role after her surgery. While the narrated experience of *materinstvo* is sometimes absent, incomplete, or unreliable, it is crucial to human experience and thus for Ulitskaya warrants readers' attention. To oversimplify or ignore it is to risk construing the mother as a mere childbearing vessel.[15] This negative depiction is striking within a text that privileges issues of birth, reproduction, and fertility, not to mention the special position traditionally accorded to the mother in Russian literature and culture. Indeed, the reader witnesses the eventual inadequacy, disappearance, death, or madness of nearly every biological mother in Ulitskaya's novel; more often than not, another individual appears to be better suited to the maternal role.

It is ironic that the text's most authoritative voice on issues concerning the day-to-day lives of mothers and children is that of Kukotskii, whose work with embryology and gynecology involves examination of the fetus and little or no contact with children after they enter the world. This focus is foreshadowed by a gift Pavel Alekseevich receives as a youth: "His father gave Pavlik a small brass microscope with 50x magnification. All objects incapable of being spread on a microscope slide ceased to interest the boy. In the world that didn't fit into the microscope's field of vision, he noticed only what coincided with the amazing pictures observed through the binocular. For example, the design on a tablecloth caught his eye, since it reminded him of the structure of cross-striated musculature." The gift of the microscope symbolizes the Kukotskii family's longstanding connection between masculinity, intellect, and acquiring information about the world. What begins as the observations of a curious adolescent later becomes the scientist's myopic attention to the biological. Pavel Alekseevich's obsession with the female body renders it a purely medical object and reveals a restrictive focus that overlooks social relationships and human concerns. His proximity to issues of birth and maternity thus indicates that he is still removed from their quotidian reality. This constitutes an emphasis on theory instead of practice, a scenario that Ulitskaya's texts criticize for leading to the subordination of individual lives to abstract principles.[16]

The novel shows how the doctor's attention to children signals a shift in his philosophy. Kukotskii's adoption of Tanya immediately after his marriage to Elena marks a turning point in his interaction with those he helps bring into the world. In saving Elena's life during the war, he enacts a trope inherited from women's prose: namely, a male controls the destiny of future mothers. His authority is reinforced by an abstract duty—Pavel Alekseevich's mission to reform the postwar Soviet health system as it relates to mothers and children. A dismal demographic situation frames Kukotskii's professional activity: a lack of men, low birth rate, high infant mortality, and poverty plague the USSR. Much of his work deals with the consequences and complications resulting from illegal abortions, an ironic result given that, as Goscilo and Lanoux assert, "[a]bortion became criminalized in 1936 so that women could expand the 'small family' according to the blueprint devised by the patriarch of the 'Big Family.'" Ulitskaya sees the prohibition on terminating pregnancies as invidious to women, restricting freedom even as it proved counterproductive to the Stalinist goal of increasing the population. Kukotskii advocates for repealing the ban, realizing that illegal terminations of pregnancy harm women's health and that decriminalization of abortion is necessary to preserve the well-being of the next generation.[17]

The Kukotskii Case binds the right to speak (*pravo golosa*) on this topic to dire familial consequences. In the argument that initiates the collapse of their marriage, Elena discovers a new, cold side of her husband. The couple argue about Toma's mother, who died because of a botched abortion. When Elena compares terminating pregnancy to murder, "Pavel Alekseevich's face hardened and Elena understood why his subordinates were so afraid of him. She had never seen him this way. 'You don't have the right to speak [*pravo golosa*]. You don't have that organ. You aren't a woman. Since you can't get pregnant, don't dare to judge,' he said angrily. All their family happiness, light and unconstrained, their chosenness, closeness, the unbounded nature of their trust—all was destroyed in a single moment. But he, it seemed, had not understood."[18] Pavel Alekseevich, who removed Elena's womb to save her, now uses this fact to disqualify her from judging other potential mothers. He realizes neither the hurt he has caused nor that he has forever altered a previously harmonious marriage. Following this conversation, Kukotskii forbids Tanya to go to the funeral for Toma's mother and Elena protests: "'And why do you think you have the right to speak [*pravo golosa*]'? Meek and not vengeful, she dealt a crushing blow. And she herself did not know how it came about . . . 'After all, you are not Tanya's father.'" Kukotskii robs Elena of her right to speak; she uses the same phrase to verbally deprive him of his paternity. In initiating this fateful exchange, Pavel Alekseevich demonstrates an inability to look beyond restrictive semantic distinctions, and his powers of seeing are correspondingly limited in their reliance on the literal. This stems from his status as male medical authority, a power that Elena shows to be ultimately illusory: no man, however experienced in gynecology, can be a mother. The passage shows another problem in Pavel Alekseevich's thinking—he is fixated only on the corporeal, a mistake that ignores the union between body and soul in this novel.[19]

The Kukotskii Case implies that women as well as men must participate in discussions of reproductive health, or else both sides ultimately will suffer. This assertion is underscored by another parallel that unites husband and wife. Special sight is not unique to Pavel Alekseevich alone: Elena also possesses this gift. Their abilities are differentiated— Kukotskii's sight grants him a transparent view of "living matter," yet Elena acquires access to another type of existence. While her husband's ability relates to the physical and material, Elena's gift extends to the intangible and the ideal. Kukotskii sees conditions as they are; his wife envisions an alternate world of things as they might or should be. Elena's special sight figures in the second part of the novel, in an extended oneiric narrative in which she is "reborn" as the "New One" (*Noven'kaia*) and wanders through a desolate landscape. This portion of the narrative comes from her senility, which is the direct result of her traumatizing argument with Pavel Alekseevich. In the dream, Elena/the New One witnesses a woman giving birth to eight children. The most troubling aspect of this birth is that the children are born without umbilical cords—there is nothing anchoring them to the mother, and they fly away. The scene at once reflects Elena's anxiety over her collapsing marriage and her growing detachment from her own daughter. This part of the novel relies on allegorical images removed from everyday life; such portrayals are unusual in Ulitskaya's corpus and underscore the extent to which Elena's thoughts have diverged from those of Pavel Alekseevich.[20]

The question of the right to speak is another reason for the shifts between the main part of the novel and segments from Elena's journals. Her entries present a maternal plot that contrasts with the male/medical one articulated by Kukotskii. The trajectory that Elena voices, however, is incomplete and unstable. Though Elena is granted the textual "right" to express herself in the first person, she repeatedly undermines her own narrative ability and her maternal connection to Tanya. While the journal is initially lucid, it gradually becomes less cohesive and comprehensible, eventually exhibiting clear signs of Elena's memory loss and linguistic deterioration. This depiction does not imply that Pavel Alekseevich's more rational approach is correct; in fact, the latter portions of the novel show that his attempts to improve the lives of his family have failed.[21]

Tanya undergoes a less dramatic but intriguing change. Later in *The Kukotskii Case*, she moves from viewing herself primarily as a daughter to identifying herself as a mother—extensive description of her pregnancy expresses her maternal experience. It is the first such portrayal in a narrative that is devoted to the topic but previously dominated by Pavel Alekseevich's scientific and detached commentary. Tanya's detailed, cogent reflections on the physical and emotional changes she experiences also contrast sharply with Elena's irrational narration about motherhood and her confused claim about her daughter's birth: "Tanya will give birth to Tanechka." This statement signals the claustrophobic chaos that increasingly marks the family's life. Tanya for her part displays a mixture of the intuition and reason initially exhibited by Elena and Kukotskii respectively when she considers her pregnancy neither a joy nor an affliction, but simply an "interesting occurrence." Ultimately, it is Tanya's daughter, Zhenia, who achieves a balance of the characteristics and worldview she has inherited from Elena, Pavel Alekseevich, and her mother; she combines acceptance of the body with care for her family and a scientific perception of the world. Similarly, critic Lev Pirogov views Zhenia as a positive embodiment of the traits of her forebears. She proves that the corporeal and intellectual can coexist, a hope that runs throughout Ulitskaya's writing.[22]

Dismantling the Ideal, Redeeming the Irregular

As *The Kukotskii Case* shows, Ulitskaya's treatment of *telesnost'* alternates between introducing new paradigms and reworking old patterns. One significant shift is her works' suspicion of physical beauty, that hallmark of Stalinism. Questioning the relationship between appearance and essence has a long history in Russian literature, and during perestroika it contributed to women authors' attack on culturally mandated feminine allure. Ulitskaya deems both male and female beauty potentially problematic, if not a harbinger of outright disaster: the outwardly attractive form may conceal moral deficiencies or character flaws.

Beauty signals danger. In the story "Singing Masha" ("Pevchaia Masha"), it accompanies mistrust and a grave distortion of Christianity. When Orthodox Ivan and Masha marry, the groom is tall, dark-eyed, and handsome, yet his gaze becomes that of an angry icon after he mistakenly decides his wife is unfaithful. He beats their son, which Masha at first interprets as a sign of affection. Later rumors assert that Ivan has hanged himself—neither physical beauty nor a successful career in the Church can save him from groundless suspicions and sorrow. These problems are inseparable from the story's treatment of gender relations; Ivan's mistrust of his wife, like Pavel Alekseevich's assertion of the right to speak for mothers, comes from a problematic male assertion of authority. Just as Kukotskii erroneously believes his medical insight justifies deciding the fates of women and their fetuses, Ivan's religiosity is fundamentally flawed because it deems the husband morally pure and the wife susceptible to temptation. These two narratives show that the problem is not science or Orthodoxy, but how these two characters distort these systems. After a long absence from home, Ivan gives his wife a custom-made double icon depicting Ivan the Warrior and Mary Magdalene, emblematizing his retrograde notion of their respective identities. When Ivan's return prompts a resurgence of sexual passion in Masha, he views her as an unrepentant sinner and claims the couple's children are illegitimate. After their marriage is annulled at his request, Masha reregisters the children under her own name "as if no male had taken part in their birth." Masha's identity is bifurcated into supposed sexual promiscuity (Mary Magdalene) and sacred maternity (Mother of God). Negative characters such as Ivan insist on divisions that isolate individuals from one another, often reiterating rigid religious or political ideologies at the same time.[23]

As "Singing Masha" suggests, beauty can conceal inner turmoil. The story "The Daughter of Bokhara" critiques handsome Dima, who resembles a Russian warrior. He brings his Uzbek bride Alya to postwar Moscow but abandons her after she gives birth to Mila, a girl with Down syndrome. For Dima, love is incompatible with the imperfection he sees when he looks at his child. Bokhara, as the neighbors derisively nickname Alya, is left to raise their daughter. As Ivan shows in "Singing Masha," male beauty is misleading, accompanied by a pride and rigidity incompatible with family life and, in the case of Dima, a duplicity that violates the intelligentsia's emphasis on sincerity. While Alya is attractive, it is her inner strength and Mila's childlike goodness that shape the narrative and prove more lasting than Dima's handsomeness. Indeed, the author uses him to reject the idea that appearance and character create a unified whole, an incorrect assumption that guided how the Soviet state envisioned its citizens.[24]

There is a curious corollary to Ulitskaya's wary treatment of the attractive: the fine-tuned physicality of the trained performer. In the story "Lialia's Home," middle-aged mother Lialia has an affair with teenage neighbor Kazia, who is a born beauty from Central Asia: "The boy was magnificent. In him his father's crude darkness smoothed to a Persian brown, and his slightly swarthy skin was stretched so tightly on his forehead and cheekbones that there appeared to be not quite enough of it. He already had a man's height but his bones had not yet become coarse, and his hands with their long fingers were of a truly regal breeding."[25] Kazia, still a high school student, already performs with the circus. Like Alya, he is an exotic outsider in Moscow, but in contrast to her portrayal, we are never privy to his emotions. Kazia remains little more than a mute vehicle for satisfying Lialia's desire, a narrative strategy that implies the limitations of the well-trained body. He has a personal philosophy that subordinates the mental to *telesnost'*; this mindset proves to be correct, though not in the way he anticipates. Many years after his simultaneous affairs with Lialia and her daughter, the narrator mentions Kazia's service in a brutal Asian war (presumably Afghanistan) and his present work as a butcher. He now inhabits a purely physical realm devoted to destroying bodies instead of perfecting them. Kazia's fate reveals that corporeality, whether male or female, is subject to a distorting state ideology that renders physicality mute and subservient. Likewise, characters who ascribe too great an importance to *telesnost'* isolate the flesh from its spiritual and ethical dimensions.[26]

Some portrayals of the acrobatic body are more ambivalent. In the novel *The Funeral Party*, friends, lovers, and acquaintances of the dying painter Alik gather at his New York loft. His first wife, Irina Pirozhkova, is a former acrobat who once worked as an exotic dancer to pay for law school in the United States. Like Alik, with whom she had a child, Irina moves between American culture and the Russophone diaspora, a role for which her tightrope training prepared her well. She initially envisions the talented body as a route to freedom, much as artist Alik sees creativity as an alternative to government control. Irina defects during a visit to Boston, despite appreciating that physical prowess grants her privileges unthinkable for most Soviets during the Brezhnev years. In fleeing the USSR Irina acknowledges that liberty can only come with changing her country—otherwise, her *telesnost'* will be the property of the same state that distinguishes her and Kazia from the less talented. The novel is not a simplistic endorsement of American "freedom" over Soviet repression; instead, it shows that Irina and Alik are in control of their talents, whether these are physical or creative. In the USSR the acrobatic body, like its artistic and intellectual counterparts, is subject to coercion and appropriation by the government. For Ulitskaya, the physical beauty of the human form is destroyed when corporeality must serve the needs of the Soviet Union. Subordinating the body to a higher power creates a fissure between appearance and reality that threatens the *iskrennost'* prized by the intelligentsia; Ulitskaya's innovative images of how the state co-opts the talented body reveal that sincerity may be compromised on a corporeal as well as intellectual level.[27]

Beauty is clearly problematic, yet a darker fate awaits characters whose physicality does not fit the government's needs and expectations. The handicapped or irregular body defies prescriptive Soviet norms. Pioneering disability studies theorist Simi Linton has noted the consequences of medicalizing the differently abled: instead of challenging the institutions that perpetuate their marginalization, such a perspective "casts human variation as deviance from the norm, as pathological condition, as deficit, and, significantly, as an individual burden and personal tragedy." Rolf Hellebust and Keith Livers maintain that the image of the ideal human form served as metaphor for a healthy collective, especially during the Stalinist period.[28] Departure from this norm, even if involuntary, evinced disharmony and otherness, traits that could signal the ultimate flaw: disloyalty. However, difference did not always lead to marginalization in the Soviet context; Lilya Kaganovsky addresses the fetishized damaged male body, which implies selfless sacrifice in Stalinist literature and film. Ulitskaya, however, eschews the heroically disfigured form and instead shows the humble power of the "ordinary" irregular body (not the state's secular saints or martyrs). The prominence of such physicality in her texts has elicited some negative critical reaction, such as Lev Kuklin's harsh dismissal of her characters as "magnets for tragedies and defects" and "biological losers."[29]

Often the Soviet government itself has abused the body. In "The Foundling" ("Podkidysh"), the mannish janitor Bekerikha exemplifies this maltreatment. When little Victoria tells her twin sister that this frightening woman is Gayane's real mother, she scares Gayane into a comatose state. The narrator, however, makes clear that Bekerikha is the real victim. At the end of the story she dies of a heart attack, having served a sentence in the Gulag because of her German ancestry and survived the deaths of her husband, mother, sister, and three-year-old daughter. Wartime repression turned this formerly gifted nurse into a terrifying creature whose body, like her mind, bears the marks of her suffering. The twinned evils of Stalinism and fascism deform Bekerikha, underscoring the many parallels Ulitskaya sees in these totalitarian systems.[30]

Sincerely Yours, Shurik discusses how the state scorns the disabled. The novel highlights the treacherous nature of Soviet body myths as ill-starred Shurik, a sensitive intellectual raised exclusively by women, moves from one love affair to another during the 1960s to 1980s. After a childhood bout of polio, Valeriia, Shurik's supervisor at the Lenin Library, can walk only with the aid of a cane or brace. This condition dramatically worsens after she attempts to have a child with Shurik. Valeriia, presented to the reader as one of the protagonist's most sympathetic lovers, is well aware that she is not alone in her disability. For Ulitskaya, she is part of the "unfortunate tribe of Soviet people, a generation of the armless, legless, burnt and physically disfigured, completely crippled by the war, but dwelling in an environment of plaster and bronze workers with powerful arms and peasant women with strong legs." While Valeriia's handicap stems from debilitating illness, not abuse by the government, she and others like her are surrounded by representations of the bodies they should have but cannot. The result is a feeling of inadequacy—the handicapped individual cannot live up to the impossible standards the state sets for *telesnost'*. This awareness helps Valeriia formulate a theory about bodily disability, "which gradually cripples the soul. She observed unfortunate, suffering, embittered people, demanding of those around them, envying, and she couldn't bear this form of spiritual deformity. She wanted to be whole [*polnotsennoi*]." Valeriia realizes that the handicapped internalize the state's demand for "normal" bodies, a scenario that leads to strife and conflict instead of solidarity and compassion. As is sometimes the case with Ulitskaya's passages containing important social commentary, the idea that Valeriia voices borders on the didacticism the author eschews. Indeed, in this significant but heavy-handed formulation, the reader concludes that Soviet society's mandate for an ideal form leads to unreasonable expectations and subsequent self-loathing: the disabled become persecutors of one another and victims of rigid cultural expectations.[31]

Valeriia critiques an uncaring system that has created an irreconcilable rift between the ideal and the real. In contrast, the story "The Chosen People" more subtly argues that disabled bodies serve a higher purpose, precisely because they have been scorned by state and society. After the death of her mother, overweight Zinaida begs for alms outside a church, but her basic knowledge of Christianity is so limited that she describes the Mother of God as "Mother of her daughter." Indigent and lame Katia the Redhead befriends Zinaida and attempts to instruct her. Rather than begging without thought, Katia has developed a theory that distinguishes between scroungers and "real" beggars: "A true beggar is one of God's people and serves the Lord." These are the "'chosen people'" who manifest meekness, humility, and take only what they need to survive. All three virtues are rooted in *telesnost'* and a view of Christianity that stresses good deeds over dogma, a crucial tenet we explore in chapter 4.[32]

For Ulitskaya, the beggars exemplify Christianity. Katia makes this clear with her belief that irregular bodies are the product of divine intent. After seeing the nun Evdokiia, with "no legs nor arms nor human voice," she "realize[s] why the Lord puts [. . .] the weak, the freaks, and the cripples on the earth . . . for comparison, as an example, or for consolation." The irregular body elicits a variety of reactions: reflection and self-examination, seeing the disabled person as virtuous, or gratitude for one's own (comparatively) comfortable existence. Even as this range of external viewpoints may involve the misreading of disability, the multiplicity of responses links the imperfections of the flesh to introspection and subtly threatens the monolithic certainty of Soviet corporeality. Considering others' problems promotes both compassion and the reexamination of our lives that Ulitskaya defines as key to development. The irregular body thus aids the contemplation and tolerance the author upholds as essential traits of the intelligentsia.[33]

These two practices guide the portrayal of the title character in "The Daughter of Bokhara." Developmentally disabled Mila has empathy, sensitivity, and an appreciation for beauty that distinguishes her from the family's crude neighbors. She is, however, marked by otherness: she has a non-Russian mother; she is not male (as family tradition would prefer); and she suffers from Down syndrome and is described as a "defective" baby expected to die at an early age. The different responses of Mila's parents to her condition are telling. At first Dima, who is a doctor, attempts to understand his daughter's disease; however, he eventually leaves her and Alya. The emphasis on perfection and others' opinions, Ulitskaya suggests, can lead the morally weak astray. Alya, by contrast, does not see her happy and placid daughter's "deficiency" and apparently is immune to the mockery they face. Knowing she will die soon, Alya teaches her daughter life skills and plans her marriage to developmentally disabled Grigory. Even though husband and wife are scorned and misunderstood, the narrator describes their union as a "good marriage" marked by tranquility and independence from the hostile world around them, which has been poisoned by the demand for physical perfection that Valeriia laments. Mila and Grigory, unaware of what the world expects from them, are untainted by envy or resentment. The couple's quiet existence is more harmonious than that of most families we examine in chapter 2.[34]

Irregular bodies defy easy conceptualization. Idealized *telesnost'* shares certain characteristics, such as resemblance to stylized images (Dima looks like a warrior, while Ivan's face recalls an image from an icon). However, handicapped characters depart from the norm in a host of surprisingly dissimilar ways, evincing the combined individuality, plurality, and simplicity Ulitskaya valorizes. She foregrounds a particularly striking manifestation of these values via the holy fool, a woman who combines physical limitations with spiritual overtones and the mocking of established social patterns. In his seminal study of Russian folk culture, Andrei Siniavskii outlines how such figures evoked fear, laughter, and "acted on a profound religious assumption: that contempt for one's own person and dignity serves the glory of God."[35] Degradation of the flesh to serve the soul, a vital trope in Orthodoxy, also recalls Kaganovsky's discussion of those who mortified their bodies for the secular heavenly kingdom—however, Ulitskaya's characters do not serve any dominant ideology. The *iurodivaia* is new to neither Russian culture nor literature after 1991. For the holy fool the link between human and God occurs through *telesnost'* more than spirit, an assertion echoing the earthy theology that appears in "The Chosen People" and is key to Ulitskaya's writing.[36]

Traits of the holy fool are present in a number of her characters, but not all of Ulitskaya's holy fools are equally sympathetic: scheming Toma in "A Gift Not Made by Hands" ("Dar nerukotvornyi") seems to lack the kindness and humility that mark Ulitskaya's *iurodivaia*. A group of enthusiastic new Young Pioneers comes to visit the armless protagonist, who gained fame for using her feet to sew a portrait of Stalin. This act literalizes the subordination of the body to the state, yet Toma cleverly exploits it to receive a private apartment. Shocking the girls with her cynicism and obscenities, she orders them to leave and then gives the bottle purchased with their money to an elderly friend. Toma is capable of benevolence as well as cruelty, demonstrating an ambivalence that is characteristic of the holy fool, whose alternation between kindness and aggression critiques the hypocrisy of an immoral society. Her physical appearance solidifies this status: "By the window stood a trestle bed, and lying on it was what appeared to be a big little girl, covered up to the waist by a thick blanket. She sat up and put her big feet on the floor. It looked as if her dress had wings on the shoulders, but no arms could be seen under these empty wings. When she walked around the room it seemed that she was small, scrawny, and reminded you of a duck, because her stride was a little off-balance with her legs facing almost completely out; the arches of her feet were unusually wide, and her toes were large, fat, and placed far apart from each other."[37]

Toma's physical handicap comes from a deformed body (missing arms, duck-like walk) but has hints of spirituality (the presence of wings). She elicits the unsettling, paradoxical feelings that are the essence of the *iurodivaia*: repugnance and respect. Toma inhabits the margins of the Great Family, which first rewarded her with the apartment and then abandoned her. Like crude Katia the Redhead, Toma is the victim of an uncaring society yet helps and pities those who are still less fortunate. Ulitskaya shies away from extolling such figures, but she ultimately characterizes them as more compassionate and righteous than many of the able-bodied. Likewise, the irregular body and its behaviors cause readers to reflect on—and perhaps improve—their own lives.

The holy fool is most explicit in Ulitskaya's play *Seven Saints from Briukho*. Dusia and Mania Gorelia are *iurodivye* who have long despised each other. Dusia inspires Timosha, a deserter from the newly formed Red Army, to become a holy fool. Near the conclusion of the play, he realizes that Mania is none other than Dusia's long-lost runaway fiancé. The narrative contrasts the holy fool with the brutal first decade of the Soviet state: after the Bolsheviks shoot Dusia, Mania, and their disciples, Timosha sees seven crowns floating into heaven.[38] Ulitskaya notes that her play falls within a long literary tradition that begins with Aleksandr Pushkin and continues with the holy fools depicted by Fyodor Dostoevsky and Andrei Platonov. These predecessors contextualize a character type whose unusual physicality is the most striking feature; this depiction implies that the playwright sees no distinction between the literary, spiritual, and corporeal. In transforming Mania from Dusia's male lover into a woman, Ulitskaya creates one of the few positive transgendered characters in Russian literature, a remarkable step given the nation's enduring distrust of "sexual minorities." She thus also adds a new dimension to the literal and textual body of the holy fool, blurring biological lines as well as destroying social conventions. At the level of history, Dusia and Mania, like Toma, critique the cruelty of the USSR; *Seven Saints* relates such malice to the conjoined perils of atheism and violence. The Red Army's executions occur after the villagers refuse to surrender their icon, which according to local legend saved a merchant wounded in the belly (*briukho*). The epilogue reveals that a different part of the body now gives the area its name—the village has been renamed Rogovsk, after the Red Army executioner whose name suggests the Satanic horns of the Soviet state.[39]

Briukho and its martyrs wed the irregular body to holiness and the oppression of both by the Bolsheviks; their trauma challenges the ideal Soviet body and its gloriously mangled counterpart that Kaganovsky depicts. Characters show how *telesnost'* itself is a source of significance: virtues such as compassion and humility mean nothing without the body. The holy fool resists the secondary status accorded corporeality and its place in an unjust world, implying a need to look beyond the sacral image of the *iurodivaia* to discover its physical presence. As the author's handicapped characters demonstrate, the suffering flesh deserves recognition for its own pain in addition to religious and social significance.

Rehumanizing the Body: Illness and Aging

Ulitskaya's works highlight the theme of the ailing body—the normally healthy physical form altered by malady. Indeed, illness is one of Russian literature's favorite topics, yet its recent prominence in women's prose garnered acrimony for purportedly debasing flesh and soul, miring the didactic mission of writing in a cesspool of naturalism.[40] Such charges have also been leveled at Ulitskaya: one critic complains that she devotes too much detail to sickness, while another speculates that such emphases come from her background in biology. Both rely on the unfounded but prevalent assumption that writing is the realm of the ideational, not the corporeal. These opinions fail to consider the basic axiom that, as we argue below, for Ulitskaya the body needs no "higher" justification.[41]

Concern with the ailing body holds biographical significance for the author. In her memoir *Discarded Relics* Ulitskaya remarks on the new way she began to think of corporeality after being treated for breast cancer and having a mastectomy: "And why am I writing all this? The point is that I need to establish a new relationship with my body, first of all with my breasts. At the end of my seventh decade, having been feeling guilty for the most varied of reasons, I sharply sensed that I was guilty before my own body [*pered svoim telom*]. It is strange that, having all my life treated my blameless body with indifference, even brutality, I was so late in realizing this!"[42] Ulitskaya has taken *telesnost'* for granted, ignoring its needs as she focused on those of the heart and mind. It is appropriate that she repents in written form, apologizing to her body and, in so doing, closing the gap between the mental and physical that has marked her life. As our discussion of physicality makes clear, *telesnost'* is not merely the corporeal shell of the soul—it has significance in its own right. Even as the narrator of *Discarded Relics* admits that she is guilty of exploiting *telesnost'*, it continues to aid her: accessing a trope common to narratives of illness and recovery, Ulitskaya credits her ailing body with giving her increased clarity. As she explains, recovering from breast cancer granted her the ability to enjoy life in its minor and grand manifestations and liberated her from approaching existence with a checklist mentality.[43]

Illness—whether linked to self-transformation or not—influences Ulitskaya's characters. In *Medea and Her Children* the protagonist humanizes medicine through her work as a nurse, just as she brings together relatives and friends who spend the summer at her Crimean home. The novel depicts how a malady precipitates and then concludes a marriage: when Medea meets her future husband Samuel he shyly stutters that he is being treated for a "nervous i-illness"; he then ends up caring for his future wife when she comes down with the flu. Years later, attending to him after cancer surgery, she becomes a servant of his body as her husband slowly starves because of a disrupted digestive system: "Samuel at first turned away squeamishly, embarrassed at the exposing of this unpleasant physiology, but then he detected that Medea was not having to make the slightest effort to conceal revulsion, and that she was much more concerned about the inflamed edge of the wound or a delay in the outpouring of porridge which had only slightly changed its appearance than about the unpleasant smell coming from the wound."[44] The ailing body is natural, free from the material corruption and spiritual emptiness that cling to it in the works of authors such as Petrushevskaia.

Telesnost' is no longer an indicator of *chernukha* or its antipode—the physical utopia of young, healthy bodies that Stalinism showcased. Instead, it signals virtue rooted in the individual: Medea regards her husband's pain as a sign of his Christian meekness, despite the fact that he has rediscovered the Judaism of his youth. As with Ulitskaya's image of the holy fool, corporeal suffering is not an impediment to spirituality but an expression of it, regardless of the faith one professes. Soul and body are bound by everyday life, in which positive characters live rightly despite an array of problems large and small.[45]

The body in pain manifests sincerity. At times it points to emotional strife: in *The Kukotskii Case*, the hurt that Elena feels toward Pavel Alekseevich after their argument over abortion resembles a tumor—neither growing nor shrinking, its malevolent presence wounds flesh and soul. Pavel Alekseevich states that everyone in the family but Tanya has some sort of mental illness, a sign of the deepening divide between them. In reaching this conclusion, he as a doctor realizes that his plans to help women have succeeded (he helped legalize abortion), but his own family has suffered as a result. The rational male authority has been discredited, another legacy of *zhenskaia proza*. Though *telesnost'* in women's prose often manifests intractable social problems, its function is different here: corporeality hints at a solution, as Elena shows when she forgives Pavel Alekseevich from within her catatonic state. The body excuses what the mind cannot, evincing a fundamental human kindness that parallels the promulgation of tolerance we examine in chapter 4.[46]

In Russian literature the flesh cannot lie. This imperative is one reason why Ulitskaya's corporeality continues the long tradition of using illness to critique the state. Aleksandr Solzhenitsyn's *Cancer Ward* (*Rakovyi korpus*) famously describes the disease as a symbol and, in some cases, a direct result of Stalinism's corruption of the collective body.[47] What Ulitskaya contributes to this disturbing cavalcade of images is the depiction of totalitarianism as a sickness that particularly deforms the female body. Literature addressing this period previously focused on male characters, such as Solzhenitsyn's scientists and the denizens of Trifonov's *House on the Embankment*. Pavel Alekseevich, however, diagnoses the era with the necessarily specific gaze of the gynecologist. Pleading with a high-ranking functionary to decriminalize abortion, the doctor brings him a jar containing the deformed uterus of a woman who tried to terminate her pregnancy by inserting an onion into her womb. This image effectively conveys the dangers of illegal abortion while showing how the state reductively considers women units for increasing the population. In the context of Stalin's pronatalist policies, Kukotskii's action is just as foolhardy as that of his friend Il'ia Gol'dberg, who is sent to the camps for reporting the Red Army's mass rapes of German women. Both Pavel Alekseevich and Gol'dberg risk their careers and freedom to decry the Great Family's victimization of the female body, a taboo topic that exposes brutality at the level of *telesnost'* and history.[48]

At times the body revolts against the state. During the Civil War, Samuel in *Medea and Her Children* is in charge of requisitioning grain from the peasants and shooting those who resist. He describes how he avoids murdering a family: "We lined the three of them up, the Red Army soldiers facing them with their rifles. Well, then the women and little children raised such a shriek that something struck me in the head and I fell down. I'd had something like an epileptic seizure. After that, of course, I remember nothing. They put me in the cart, right there on top of the grain, and took me back to the city. I was told that I turned black, and my arms and legs were like sticks, completely rigid." Samuel's body becomes a parodic exaggeration of the unbending, obedient physicality the Bolsheviks demand from their soldiers. Fortunately, this literalized metaphor saves Medea's future husband from taking part in the execution that presumably occurs without him. As in *Seven Saints from Briukho*, Ulitskaya characterizes the Civil War in strikingly physical terms, linking the Soviet state to mass violence even before the rise of Stalinism.[49]

Given the prominence of the body in pain, it is no surprise that doctors are important in these works. Ulitskaya links biology, one of medicine's foundations, with the writer's craft: both investigate the human condition. In *The Kukotskii Case* Pavel Alekseevich complicates the image of the physician as the novel depicts the gradual implosion of his family from the Stalin to the Yeltsin years. Modeled on the famous surgeon Sergei Spasokukotskii, as a gynecologist he constantly operates on the boundary between masculine (surgery) and feminine (midwifery). He is likewise part of the Stalinist medical elite in *The Kukotskii Case*, where the token woman bureaucrat is described in overwhelmingly masculine terms; as we discussed earlier, his gendered status is one reason for the disagreement over abortion that destroys his marriage.[50]

Pavel Alekseevich reveals the moral limits of the doctor's power. Irina Zherebkina astutely observes that it is Elena who motivates the plot, though the gynecologist gives the novel its title—while he begins the narrative, she survives him. Within her senile state she remains morally pure in a way that Kukotskii cannot be. As a doctor he is a *de facto* arbiter of life and death, yet the text questions his judgment on the central issue of abortion. The work clearly upholds his unstinting (and dangerous) efforts to decriminalize the procedure. Denying reproductive freedom, the narrator remarks, not only is oppressive but relegates women to the status of animals, for "isn't this the essential boundary between human and animal, the ability and right to go beyond the bounds of biological law and create progeny because of one's own wish and not the will of natural rhythms?" Ulitskaya's omniscient narrator, appropriating the discourse used by Pavel Alekseevich, frames his argument using the irrefutable vocabulary of science. Likewise, the narrator opines, it is bitterly ironic how, after the (re)legalization of abortion in 1955, the government that has killed millions has given women the right to terminate their pregnancies. In this sense Pavel Alekseevich's actions are clearly positive, granting female citizens a corporeal voice within the Great Family. This is the same *pravo golosa* he and Elena deny each other. It also has broader implications: Russian culture has long examined Stalinism by noting who could speak and who was silenced. Elena's opposition to abortion, however, suggests a second and more disturbing view. This negative standpoint, shared by servant Vasilisa with her medieval theology, identifies Pavel Alekseevich as a murderer, a characterization reinforced by the aborted fetuses his wife sees in her catatonic state.[51] The doctor cannot transform irreproachable public service into helping his family, and this failure undermines his authority to determine the fate of the unborn. Pavel Alekseevich's ambiguity substantially expands the characterization of doctors, a prominent category that women's prose earlier populated with extremes: either the devoted professionals of I. Grekova's writing or the callous butchers depicted by Petrushevskaia and Marina Palei.[52]

For Ulitskaya illness can create togetherness in addition to alienation, as *The Funeral Party* masterfully illustrates. One critic mistakenly (and unfavorably) compares this narrative to Tolstoy's *Death of Ivan Ilyich* (*Smert' Ivana Il'icha*). The works are diametrically opposed—while Tolstoy sees death as bringing about realization of a life wrongly lived, Ulitskaya's novel envisions it as a celebration of memory. As the sociable painter Alik dies, friends, former and present lovers, and chance acquaintances gather in his Chelsea loft. His wake exemplifies the bond between sickness, friends, and a community that stretches across the globe:[53]

People came and went from the table carrying plates and glasses, coming together in groups and moving away again. There had never been such a mixture of people. Alik's musician friends came, along with several people whom no one had seen before; it wasn't clear where he had picked them up or how they had learnt of his death. The Paraguayan [street musicians] stood in a phalanx, led by their leader with his dark-pink scar and craggy, handsome face. A Columbia University professor talked animatedly to the driver of the garbage-collection truck. Berman fancied Gioia, but pressures of work meant he hadn't touched a woman for over two years and he wasn't sure if he should let the genie out of the bottle now. If he had known what Alik knew he certainly wouldn't have contemplated it, for not only was she a virgin, she was also the scion of a noble Roman family which was mentioned by Tacitus.[54]

Alik's wake, a variegated tableau at the heart of both the narrative and its film adaptation, is a motley celebration of the man illness has taken and the humanity that remains. It is a fitting recognition of an artist who refused to believe in boundaries between the spirit and the flesh. Accordingly, *telesnost'* plays a large role as the guests eat, drink, and in several cases make love. Music is central to this scene as the Paraguayans who have been performing outside the apartment join the wake; their rhythms underscore an eroticism that Alik's former lover Valentina discovers to be like nothing she has experienced.[55]

Death is placed at the center of life, pairing loss with new beginnings, whether they are the conception of children or simply friendships. Before he dies, Alik takes "pleasure in the half-naked women clinging to him from morning to night" and their life-affirming bodily presence, which comforts while quietly emphasizing the central place of sexuality in everyday life. The celebration following his funeral continues this logic. Flesh, mind, and spirit are inseparable for Ulitskaya, recalling Grosz's call to recognize corporeality as more than a conduit to higher meaning. *Telesnost'* and spirituality are inviolably linked; the ailing body reaffirms the primacy of the physical in human existence, as *Discarded Relics* illustrates after the author's mastectomy. Its humble needs and imperfect forms convey a sincerity rooted in the flesh. The body likewise has the potential to create communities of compassion and forgiveness, virtues central to Ulitskaya's worldview.[56]

The elderly also play an important role in Ulitskaya's narratives. Often Soviet culture elided the aging as well as the ailing body; both were marginalized by a cult of (healthy) youth, meager disability pensions, and lack of accessible public transportation. In a society presumably marching toward a brighter future, older citizens were dismissed as remnants of the past or presented as exemplars of how to suffer for the state, whether at the front or in the camps. When Ulitskaya began to publish in the 1990s, the aged were Russia's most vulnerable population, lacking the skills, energy, and mindset to adapt to the cataclysm following perestroika. The film *Brother* (*Brat*) depicts the elderly as weak and completely demoralized, capable only of carping at the society that discarded them. The Great Family's collapse humiliated the very members credited with its construction and defense.[57]

As with her illustrations of illness, Ulitskaya humanizes the aging body, but with a stronger emphasis on history: these characters influence the present while preserving the past. Ulitskaya's autobiography illuminates one reason for this approach—the author recalls that her grandmother played a central role in holding the family together while she was alive.[58] The positive older personage is an established figure in Russian literature, as Solzhenitsyn's Matryona exemplifies. A basic attribute of these characters is their ability to survive. Given the litany of destroyed lives in works such as *The Big Green Tent* and *Daniel Stein, Interpreter*, defying death is itself notable, especially when conjoined with preserving one's personal ethics. For Ulitskaya's religious elderly—be they Jewish, Christian, or Muslim—transmitting the culture of the past is a moral imperative. In the story "March 1953," Aaron tells his great-granddaughter Lily about the heroes of ancient Judaism as a counterweight to the state's intolerance. Sitting next to him, she draws strength from his presence: "And Aaron would tell her of Daniel, or Gideon, of legendary heroes of the past and fair virgins, of wise men and czars with obscure names, all of them long-dead members of their tribe, until Lily was firmly persuaded that her great-grandfather, himself so ancient, must have known and personally remembered some of them at least."[59]

Aaron is the physical and cultural link between the Jews' past and their uncertain present during the last year of Stalinism. Making Lily realize that she, like these figures from ancient Israel, is part of the same "tribe," he voices a crucial but subtle counterargument against state claims about rootless cosmopolitans who lack loyalty or homeland. Jewish culture, Judaism, and the elderly body are inseparably bound together. Esfir' in the play *My Grandson Veniamin* hopes to fulfill a function similar to Aaron's—she is one of the few Jews to escape the Nazi massacre in Bobruisk. It is no coincidence that Aaron and Esfir' have weathered the calamities of Stalinism and fascism. At times Ulitskaya's narratives use elderly lives to compare these two systems; aged survivors form a kinship where suffering brings wisdom that opposes the brutal ignorance of the Great Family and similar regimes of intolerance.[60]

Ulitskaya depicts aging as normal for both individual and culture, a significant assertion in light of the 1990s rhetoric that characterized Russia as a dying nation. *The Kukotskii Case* ends with the birth of Zhenia's son and Elena's interminable decline, while Aaron dies the same day as Lily's first period begins (and very shortly before Stalin's demise). As with *The Funeral Party*'s image of Alik's wake and the new relationships that follow, death gives rise to new phases of life and is an integral part of existence.[61]

Social interactions that revolve around *telesnost'* and the aging body can also unite people, as *The Kukotskii Case* makes clear through several ritualized images of bathing that together comprise a corporeal narrative embedded within the novel. The first of these moments occurs early in the plot when Pavel Alekseevich, after the operation that has saved Elena, brings her, little Tanya, and Vasilisa warm water for washing. This seemingly simple gesture is a luxurious rarity amidst the grime and cold of wartime evacuation. Many years later, after the birth of her own daughter, Zhenia, Tanya bathes Elena: "Her mother's scrawniness was painful, and the issue was not her light weight—Tanya herself did not make it to the fifty kilo mark. From Elena's shoulders and forearms hung empty folds of skin, and it came to Tanya, in the face of her mother's nakedness, that the human skeleton is gloomy and sexless, and it is only the bits of interspersed fatty meat that create a woman's charm and a man's strength, and even the very difference between man and woman.... Of her mother's former femininity there remained only her pale breasts and the slight shadow of her almost hairless privates." This scene is a counterpart to the male gaze that is the province of Pavel Alekseevich as doctor. He first sees Elena's body on the operating table as he performs the surgery that saves her life but removes her uterus, a process that reiterates male agency and female powerlessness. In the passage above, however, one woman regards another; daughter Tanya sees her mother's difficult life inscribed on the body. Elena's almost sexless form evokes compassion, not repulsion.[62]

Tanya makes an even more striking discovery when she accompanies Vasilisa to the *bania*. In this communal context of female nakedness, Tanya sees Vasilisa's distended womb, an organ that was unneeded during a life of caring for others' children. Tanya's thoughts while looking at the bodies of Elena and Vasilisa qualify her attempts to escape their fate. Rebellion has been replaced by recognition of others' sacrifice, yet this realization still exists alongside gratitude that the daughter herself has avoided such a life. *The Kukotskii Case* embraces female physicality in all its imperfection, and the sadness that we see through Tanya's eyes comes from the suffering she perceives through *telesnost'*—the body does not cause sorrow, but speaks for those who cannot otherwise voice their pain. Corporeality becomes its own subject and, as Grosz asserts, helps the spirit express itself, effectively reversing the traditional mind/body dichotomy.[63]

In the final bathing scene in the novel, Zhenia washes Elena, who has survived Pavel Alekseevich (and Tanya) and is living out her last years with Toma and her husband. It is only in the humid privacy of the bath that Elena speaks, pairing true communication with corporeal needs and the compassion they elicit. This consideration unites Zhenia, Tanya, and Elena herself, suggesting a positive history transmitted from one generation to the next via caring for the older body. *Telesnost'* evokes sincerity and tolerance, values opposing the ideals that deformed the literal and metaphorical flesh of Soviet citizens.[64]

This contrast is even starker in *The Big Green Tent* as underground artist Muratov draws pictures of old women bathing in the village where he has taken refuge from the police. While he is used to their wrinkled faces, in the *bania* "[t]heir wrists and feet looked larger and even more deformed. Beaten by working with the land, gnarled like the roots of old trees, fingers and toes had taken on the color of the dirt they had dug in for decades." The legacy of collectivization and neglect of the countryside is inscribed on the body, with the state more directly implicated than in *The Kukotskii Case*. Ulitskaya transforms the rhetoric of women's prose, which connected deformed female bodies with government indifference and brutality. In *The Big Green Tent*, the female form is simultaneously revealed and aestheticized—it is more than an index of societal problems. When Muratov's drawings are exhibited in Cologne, he is arrested in the USSR for pornography, a charge revealing that the Soviet government strives to control both *telesnost'* and its representation. *The Big Green Tent* engages in corporeal ekphrasis: the body is first depicted in visual form (Muratov's artwork), then takes on a second life through written depiction (the narrative in which he appears). Ulitskaya's images of the aging body are extraordinary. In portraying it in a vulnerable moment—naked, inspected by those younger and healthier—she forces readers to acknowledge the *telesnost'* of the elderly as a testament to survival and sacrifices made for successive generations. As with Solzhenitsyn's Matryona, the elderly body acts as social commentary; however, for Ulitskaya it holds significance in its own right as well as indicating struggle and oppression.[65]

Ulitskaya is unique in portraying the erotic aging female body, a theme Russian culture often elides with wizened widows and stern grandmothers. Such women use sexless corporeality to prove their long service to family and state. By contrast, Alexandra, Medea's carnally precocious sister, continues her favorite activity well into her fifties, challenging the dictum that female sexuality withers after middle age, if not childbirth. Her husband responds with gratitude: "What he most appreciated in intimate relations with his wife was the very fact that they occurred at all, and in the depths of his simple soul at first supposed that his demands could only be a source of vexation to his noble wife. It was some time before Alexandra succeeded in getting him more or less attuned to the extracting of modest and muted matrimonial joys." Not only does Alexandra have sex, but it is she, with her rich experience, who takes on the role of teacher. Sexuality is normalized as a fact of life for all, not merely the virile and nubile figures who dominate Soviet and post-1991 conceptions of carnality.[66]

The eponymous protagonist of the story "Gulia" shares Alexandra's appetites, but they play a less crucial role. Gulia's crafty seduction of middle-aged Shurik embodies the holiday spirit enlivening the winter of her years. Her erotic nature starkly contrasts with the staid grandmothers in the works of earlier authors such as Natal'ia Baranskaia, for whom lack of sex is yet another aspect of a life forfeited for others.[67] Gulia's liaison with a much younger man is deemphasized within a biography that includes arrest, exile, marriages, and numerous romantic escapades. Her brief affair signals that such events are, as with Alik's death in *The Funeral Party*, a natural component of existence that is important to old and young alike. Such nuanced images of the elderly are a welcome respite from the "patriotism of despair" Oushakine espies lurking beneath the rhetoric of post-Soviet Russia as infirm and helpless.[68]

Telesnost' and sexuality are inseparable from the commentary on culture and history uniting Ulitskaya's oeuvre; this connection appears in characters' physiological and mental ways of apprehending the world. Some female personages experience catatonic states, displaying external indicators (muteness and aging) of internal suffering. In a trope borrowed from women's prose, this group demonstrates the physical impact of psychological trauma.[69] The body ceases to interact with reality, recalling Julia Kristeva's discussion of the "depressive affect" that ensures survival by providing a buffer between the hostile world and psychic self-destruction. In Ulitskaya's corpus, however, the division comes from irreconcilable conflict between a woman's sense of self and how those in her family perceive this identity.[70]

In the story "Someone Else's Children" ("Chuzhie deti"), Armenian Margarita gives birth to twins Gayane and Victoria after many years in a childless marriage with older Sergo. Her husband, away at the front, imagines himself a cuckold; he is unaware of the birthmark both he and the twins share. Drying the twins after their bath, "[h]e did not pay attention to the tea-colored birthmark emblazoned on their little buttocks. And the only person who could have poked him in his flat rear, in the very middle of the birthmark in the form of an overturned crown, was his poor wife Margarita, who continued to sit in her armchair and talk to the husband she so loved." As a result of his accusations, Margarita has fallen into depression, imagines conversations with her husband, ages dramatically, and must be cared for like a child. Only she could point out the birthmark that proves the children are his, a feature whose evident symbolism (the overturned crown) references both Sergo's fears of his wife's infidelity and the rupture of a previously solid marriage. Sergo is a poor reader of the body, overlooking the evidence of his paternity as he attempts to bring Margarita out of the helpless despondency his unfounded suspicions provoked. Kazarina notes that the shocks, insights, and revelations experienced by Ulitskaya's heroines are seen as "illness, eccentricity, and folly," yet catatonic states are "those moments when a person [has] direct contact with the unseen underpinnings of existence."[71]

As *The Funeral Party* and *The Kukotskii Case* demonstrate, often moments associated with death and dementia are the most significant in a work. Throughout Ulitskaya's oeuvre catatonic states are an extreme and destructive form of corporeal sincerity through which the body expresses with shocking honesty the soul's torment. In "Lialia's Home," the protagonist's horror at the sight of her daughter having sex with her own (much younger) lover Kazia induces a muteness that resembles Margarita's condition; Lialia's contemplation of a walled-in kitchen window visually recalls her now-vanished sexual freedom. After emerging from her state of shock, Lialia exhibits an extreme sympathy and sensitivity for all living things and even inanimate household objects.

This maudlin sensibility, markedly different from her previous self-interest and adultery, suggests a parody of the devoted and penitent woman.[72]

For Lialia and Margarita shock provokes catatonia. By contrast, in *The Kukotskii Case* it is the argument about the ethics of abortion that eventually prompts Elena's mental deterioration. However, in all three cases women suffer a blow to a central and valorized part of their gendered identity. As noted above, Pavel Alekseevich and Elena disagree over who may speak on issues of maternity. Kukotskii initially advocates for mothers, enacting the scenario Hirsch depicts: "To speak for the mother [. . .] is at once to give voice to her discourse *and* to silence and marginalize her." Much earlier Pavel Alekseevich asserts his claim to debate such questions: he severs ties with his mother when he criticizes her for having another child at a relatively advanced age. Later in the novel, Elena neither fully emerges from her catatonic state nor forgives her husband in the primary narrative. Such transformations can occur only across generations, a situation conveyed by Zhenia's more balanced life and Elena's unifying vision of relatives before her death. As we explore in chapter 2, family for Ulitskaya is transhistorical, outlasting individuals and even the seemingly immutable Soviet state.[73]

Beyond Shock and Scandal: Rewriting Sexuality

Catatonic characters are one way of addressing prescribed female behavior; innovative images of sexuality are another. Ulitskaya departs from the taboo-shattering epatage of women's prose and *chernukha*, despite certain critics' assertions to the contrary. Echoing charges earlier leveled at women's prose, some misread Ulitskaya's depiction of sexuality as bestializing human nature or catering to a mass readership.[74] Unlike Petrushevskaia's lacerating narratives, Ulitskaya rejects the idea of eroticism as dangerous, dirty, and demeaning. Instead, she rehumanizes the female body by examining and presenting it at every stage, from newly born (the twins in "Someone Else's Children") to late in life ("Gulia"). Ulitskaya contextualizes female sexuality within a wide-ranging portrayal of corporeality that assumes less restrictive gender roles.

To this end Ulitskaya conjoins female sexuality and self-awareness; as one critic succinctly notes, knowing the body means knowing the world. "March 1953" depicts physical transitions as natural—while Lily's ailing great-grandfather suffers from the tumor growing within him, she struggles with the bewildering signs of puberty. Aaron has accepted his illness and the inevitability of death, but the protagonist is much less comfortable: "She was eleven years old. Her armpits ached and her nipples itched incessantly. From time to time a wave of disgust would break over her at all the little changes taking place in her body, the swellings and the coarse dark hairs, the pustules on her forehead; her very soul protested blindly at all these disagreeable, impure things. [...] Only by snuggling up to her great-grandfather, who smelled of camphor and old paper, could she be delivered from the malaise that tormented her." The narrator lists with both compassion and mock horror the changes occurring to the protagonist as physicality renders Lily a stranger in her own body. Ulitskaya vividly portrays the end of childhood, a narrative moment that coincides chronologically with a similar point in her own life (both author and character were eleven in March 1953). For Lily the beginning of puberty is a time of corporeal chaos assuaged only by Aaron's presence, which offers reassuring smells, a sense of stability, and tales from the past. As is often the case with the older generation, Aaron is a bulwark against the hostile Soviet present. Adding to Lily's unease are the taunts she receives from the bully Bodrik, whom Lily beats when he attacks her. This frightening event, the onset of menstruation, and Aaron's decline all anticipate the death of Stalin. The last event will have implications for decades to come—Ulitskaya personalizes history by stressing its corporeal effects on individuals who respond to events beyond their control.[75]

Another story in the same collection, "Chicken Pox" ("Vetrianaia ospa"), has a more limited scope. During late Stalinism Lily's friends engage in make-believe games (including a mock wedding) and tentative discussions of sex. Tanya Kolyvanova, the lone girl from a poor family and a relative of armless Toma in "A Gift Not Made by Hands," has more practical know-how than the others—her experience diverges from Soviet Victorianism and the "hygienically correct upbringing" of the others. In scenes new to Russian prose, the girls imitate coitus, instruct one another in masturbation, and simulate giving birth. Since no boys are present, some of the friends take on the role of groom and father, an understated reminder of the segregated world of childhood even as it tries to comprehend the rituals of adulthood. Later most of the girls come down with chicken pox, a physical manifestation of the knowledge gained. It is no coincidence that Tanya and Lily, who are not infected, are the only members of the group previously aware of the basics of intercourse. The narrative emphasizes changes in friendship and new knowledge more than the actions themselves; for Ulitskaya, the erotic (or, in this case, its precursor) cannot be divorced from its social context.[76]

Contradicting the foreboding accounts of women's prose, the author describes early sexual experience as multivalent. Though the author maintains that sex is "a gift from God" that warrants respect, her endorsement of good deeds over dogma extends to the erotic: restrictions on sex are less meaningful (and viable) than responsible action. "Bronka," Ulitskaya's first published story for adults, portrays a thirteen-year-old girl from Birobidzhan who after moving to Moscow mysteriously becomes pregnant and eventually bears four illegitimate children. Her humble nature and lack of shame underscore her innocence by evoking the Mother of God, and the reader once again realizes that for Ulitskaya a character's Jewishness does not preclude portrayal in Christian terms. These depictions run throughout the author's oeuvre, shaping in a much more explicit way works such as *Daniel Stein, Interpreter*. Decades later Bronka narrates her experience to childhood acquaintance Irina, and the transformation from object (of ridicule) to subject shocks her listener: "[y]esterday's little tart, the laughing stock of the whole neighbourhood, had no business having such deep, complicated feelings." This narrative provides a rare glimpse of the intelligentsia (Irina) reassessing its relations with the common people (Bronka and her impoverished mother). Bronka reveals the identity of her children's father—photographer-neighbor Viktor Popov—and explains that his cultured gentility provided her a refuge from the coarseness of postwar life. Indeed, he, like *Sonechka*'s Robert Viktorovich, lessens the privation and tedium of Stalinism by hinting at a vibrant artistic tradition driven underground. In the montage photographs that Bronka shows Irina, she and Viktor are coevals, while in reality they were thirteen and sixty-nine. In addition, Bronka's claim that she seduced Viktor mitigates the taboo nature of their relationship.[77]

There are no explicitly described erotic encounters in "Bronka," yet in Ulitskaya's works photography is often linked to what Laura Mulvey describes as (male) visual pleasure. Aside from Popov's photographs, his relationship with the protagonist is a disembodied one: we see the product (four sons) but not the process. Coitus is less important than the mysteries of a love that enlivens its drab Soviet backdrop. Likewise, eroticism is depicted via layers of representation that show it to be an inextricable part of culture. Bronka presents a more nuanced picture of teenage sexuality than antecedents in women's prose such as Mon'ka in

Palei's "Cabiria from the Bypass" ("Kabiriia s Obvodnogo kanala"), who suffers from uncontrolled eroticism and suicide attempts. Ulitskaya's protagonist, in contrast, derives meaning, stability, and lasting satisfaction from her affair with Popov: the author's images of sexuality are more closely connected with human relationships than the isolating despair that perestroika pairs with carnality.[78]

The Kukotskii Case extends the depiction of nascent sexuality by connecting it with self-exploration suggestive of scientific inquiry. One critic thus errs in alleging the novel celebrates the flesh alone. While *telesnost'* is a central focus, erotic themes are inextricable from the depiction of the Kukotskiis' decline as the USSR itself moves through its last decades.[79] Sexual discovery is the purview of Tanya; her first exposure to the aroused male body occurs in the office of womanizer Professor Gansovskii. She narrowly escapes rape, and though the situation horrifies her, seeing Gansovskii's penis "[makes] an impression" and spurs her interest. She calmly divests herself of her virginity on a nighttime walk when she interrupts a young man in the midst of an unsuccessful suicide attempt. After the event, when the post-coital conversation proves to be uninteresting, she simply leaves. This holistic view of a first sexual encounter is a welcome contrast to the violence, pregnancy, and hopelessness stemming from many such moments in women's prose. Tanya's subsequent carnal experiences display a similarly matter-of-fact detachment, but they lack the overtones of authoritative coldness attached to Pavel Alekseevich's use of science; Tanya is discovering the erotic on her own terms, not deciding the fates of others. After a few years of this new life, she begins a sexual relationship with Gena Gol'dberg and then his twin Vitalik, stating that for her there is no difference between them. Downplaying emotional affinity (and monogamy) meets with a negative male response: not surprisingly, the Gol'dberg brothers bristle when viewed as interchangeable. In Tanya's worldview, however, neither brother should be jealous, since such emotions have no place alongside what for her are the uncomplicated pleasures of sex. Her mindset as a teenager is almost utopian, as it divorces the physical act of love from its consequences.[80]

Inventive images of heterosexuality are a mainstay of Ulitskaya's prose and drama. Her first novella, *Sonechka*, illustrates the relationship between an aging artist, his forbearing wife, and the young mistress who becomes an unlikely but central part of their family as they live together from late Stalinism through the Brezhnev years. The work presents contrasting approaches to the erotic that together suggest the author's philosophy of the body. The first of these involves desire and books and echoes Ulitskaya's own readerly biography: in her memoir she describes reading as an intimate act and characterizes her adolescent discovery of Pasternak and other writers as "constructed according to the principles of a romance novel." Similarly, when Robert Viktorovich first sees his future wife, reading and erotic representation are inseparable. Serving out his exile in the Urals, he ventures into Sverdlovsk, where Sonechka is living in wartime evacuation. Already impressed by the provincial library's collection of French volumes, he observes Sonechka, "looking at her pure forehead and smiling inwardly at her marvelous resemblance to a patient, gentle young camel, and thinking, *She even has the coloring: that swarthy, sad, umber tint, and the pinkishness, the warmth.*"[81] Establishing a key pattern, the former avant-garde painter recreates Sonechka according to his own image of her, a portrayal that reflects his travels earlier in life. She is a representation, but not only because of Robert Viktorovich. From childhood, reading habits have rendered her passive in both an intellectual and erotic sense. At fourteen she lost her virginity to a "brutal young Onegin," a classmate ironically likened to the more cultured hero of Pushkin's famous novel in verse. After she meets Robert Viktorovich, literature blinds her to the intent of the man who soon will propose to her: "Sonechka, meanwhile, placid soul that she was—cocooned by the thousand volumes of her reading, lulled by the hazy murmurings of the Greek myths, the hypnotically shrill recorder fluting of the Middle Ages, the misty windswept yearning of Ibsen, the minutely detailed tedium of Balzac, the astral music of Dante, the siren song of the piercing voices of Rilke and Novalis, seduced by the moralistic despair of the great Russian writers calling out to the heart of heaven itself—this placid soul had no awareness that her great moment was at hand, preoccupied as she was by the question of whether she was taking rather a risk in allowing a reader to borrow books that she was only allowed to issue for use in the reading room."[82]

Sexuality is constructed by reading. This link has weighty cultural implications for a woman already tied to Pushkin's Tat'iana Larina because of her unfortunate first erotic experience: both heroines allow their initial expectations for romance to be shaped by the books they have read, and both are gravely mistaken. Familiarity with the great minds of Russia and the West has not empowered Sonechka. She is a submissive, suggestible reader who lacks the autonomy Robert Viktorovich has as a male artist who integrates literature into a wide-ranging knowledge of the world.

Only with the next generation does *Sonechka* privilege the connections between female eroticism and independence. As with her namesake in *The Kukotskii Case*, teenage Tanya's first sexual encounters with friends are positive experiments: "For Tanya the most interesting thing was a new awareness of her body. She discovered that every part of it, her fingers, her breasts, her stomach, her back, responded differently to touch and had the ability to allow all manner of delightful sensations to be elicited, and the shared experimentation gave [. . .] them no end of pleasure." Thanks to further practice, they "mastered every aspect of the physical side of love without in the process experiencing the least emotion beyond the bounds of a friendly and practical partnership." While this series of experiments also establishes a pattern that *The Kukotskii Case* follows, the narratives quickly diverge. In *Sonechka*, Tanya's "heart crie[s] out for some higher communion, a conjoining, a fusion, a reciprocity beyond all bounds," and she becomes platonically attached to Jasia, who has a disturbingly different outlook forged by her life in a Stalinist orphanage. Motivated by calculating pragmatism rather than honest interest, Jasia uses sex as currency with men, "having at an early age mastered an inexpensive technique for settling her debts to them." Her relationship with Robert Viktorovich means a stable home for the Polish waif but a crushing realization for Tanya; Jasia's corporeal insincerity reveals that sexuality can be a means to an end as well as manifesting the *iskrennost'* Ulitskaya prizes. This truth remains forever alien to Tanya, who has never been forced to barter with her body in order to survive.[83]

Sincerely Yours, Shurik also foregrounds sex, but despite the dizzying number of couplings it contains, the novel is avowedly non-erotic. Shurik's role with women is described repeatedly as consoler; female desire and satisfaction elide male needs. Indeed, only coitus can ease the physical and moral suffering of characters such as handicapped Valeriia, who "felt completely free only in bed, when the damned crutches were completely unneeded, and there, she knew, her disability disappeared, and she became whole—oh, more than a whole woman! She flew, soared, levitated."[84] This clichéd metaphor illustrates the escape from ordinary physicality that lovemaking provides for Valeriia, who has been crippled by childhood polio. Here Ulitskaya appropriates the flight motif French feminists have long viewed as "the emblem of women's writing" (at least in the West); the liberation born of carnal fulfillment symbolizes transcendence of constraining roles and stresses the union of the material and spiritual. Valeriia's feeling is a positive alternative to the catatonia of Margarita, Lialia, and Elena.[85]

Shurik is not so fortunate. In contrast to the usual representation of Don Juan, he strives not to debauch and destroy, but only to comfort and ease suffering. However, constant sublimation of his desires creates a false relationship with *telesnost'*. In this sense he resembles Jasia: his sexuality becomes a form of insincerity, leaving him the servant of others' bodies without admitting the wishes of his own. Jasia's experiences are more traumatic, just as her use of sexuality is calculated instead of reactive. For both characters, however, the erotic is a cumbersome duty instead of the pleasant discovery Tanya enjoys. One of Shurik's lovers, the manipulative and psychologically damaged Svetlana, sews him a coat; the narrator compares it with Nikolai Gogol's story "The Overcoat" ("Shinel'"). The intertext suggests a loose parallel between Svetlana and the humble clerk Akaky Akakievich, yet it is clearly Shurik who is the victim in their relationship.[86]

Ulitskaya's depictions of heterosexual males are not particularly innovative when compared with her other images of the body. A number of characters recall those found earlier in women's prose, for instance, the predacious misanthrope (Shurik the Spider in "Poor, Happy Kolyvanova" ["Bednaia, schastlivaia Kolyvanova"]), the self-destructive genius (Tanya's would-be boyfriend in "The Body of a Beauty" ["Telo krasavitsy"]), or the brutal drunk (Vas'ka in "The Ladder" ["Pristavnaia lestnitsa"]).[87] However, the precedent of *zhenskaia proza* allows Ulitskaya to move beyond dismantling Soviet male sexuality and produce a more complex examination of men and the erotic. In the autobiographical "A Terrifying Story on the Road" ("Strashnaia dorozhnaia istoriia"), the narrator must take the train back to Moscow from the Caucasus after a plane is hijacked. When the Georgian men who have helped the narrator board the train lead her to their compartment, she knows they will assault her if she falls asleep. Like Scheherazade, she tells story after story, distracting them as the group drinks. Considering her situation, she notes: "They were not rapists, just normal Georgian men, who from childhood know that there is one way to relate to Georgian women and to Russian women a different one. We have, alas, a bad reputation!" Ulitskaya's fictionalized counterpart realizes that her present crisis is the result of ethnic and gendered stereotypes perpetuated by both sexes. She does not justify the men's (potential) actions, but contextualizes them in a history of misunderstanding between Russians and Georgians. Her seemingly banal analysis is in fact quite insightful; it considers the age-old mythologies of gender that Goscilo and Lanoux outline and, in doing so, transcends the offensive national stereotypes that dominate Soviet and post-1991 culture. The Georgian men later reveal that they knew she was lying about many of her stories, but give her children some of the tangerines they are smuggling. The narrator's role thus oscillates between two extremes: potential sexual victim and maternal figure, a simplistic schema anomalous for this author.[88]

Several more unusual images of the male heterosexual appear in Ulitskaya's works. The first is the reluctant seducer, who tries to resist but then has an affair with a much younger female character. In "Bronka" and *Sonechka* men have sex with women at least thirty years younger, yet the narrative does not censure them. Viktor Popov bears a striking resemblance to Robert Viktorovich in *Sonechka*, who sleeps with his daughter's closest friend. Jasia does not bear a child as a result, yet she becomes a permanent part of Robert Viktorovich's family, just as Popov and Bronka are able to continue having sex unnoticed despite the communal apartment's close quarters. The actions of Popov and Robert Viktorovich recall Petrushevskaia's rapists and seducers, yet "Bronka" and *Sonechka* treat their misdeeds not as a crime but as a mystery of the body. In the first work, we only learn the details from Bronka's viewpoint, since Popov died many decades ago. Robert Viktorovich's guilt before his wife, the narrator of *Sonechka* hints, is less important than the other relationship destroyed by the affair: the passionate friendship between Jasia and his daughter. The male heterosexual in Ulitskaya's works is more nuanced than his predecessor in women's prose—the multifaceted treatment of often immoral characters suggests a search for comprehension instead of invective. While the author does not applaud her male miscreants, she shows that recognition of all aspects of sexuality is crucial to understanding life.[89]

Ulitskaya humanizes *telesnost'*; it is more than the loyal servant of the state (as Stalinism would have had it) or a metonym of the abused populace (the body in *chernukha*). The physical form, these narratives imply, is not merely a springboard to loftier plans or an indication of how such ideas have failed. Ulitskaya's works avoid the post-Soviet corporeality of despair. Instead, they assess the body as a dynamic part of the human experience, in particular as a source of the sincerity and tolerance the author extols. Her writing redirects attention to the fundamental role of the flesh, the raw material that both supports and delimits higher aspirations. That the body makes us human is an obvious statement nonetheless neglected by idea-oriented Russian literature. Ulitskaya implies that harnessing *telesnost'* as the engine of ideology is at times almost as invidious as ideology itself. Indeed, her narratives are populated by those who have been physically and morally misshapen by fascism and Communism, two systems that view corporeality as a human resource for the state.

Interactions between bodies are also important. Such relations transcend the sexual or physiological brutality Eliot Borenstein decries in the *telesnost'* of "overkill." Ulitskaya guides the reader to recognize how deteriorating, imperfect, or sexually "deviant" corporeality forges ties between people as it elicits compassion and models humility. Physical needs and failings, her narratives imply, connect individuals in a positive and meaningful manner that opposes the ersatz affinities of the Great Family. The body is a natural part of life; ignoring it is both futile and self-destructive.

2

IDEAS THAT BIND

KINSHIP AS METAPHOR

In May 2003, after reading the novel *Medea and Her Children*, an inquisitive radio interviewer tried to guess which of the work's numerous ethnic groups represents Ludmila Ulitskaya's own roots. The author's response was telling: "[I]f I were to choose a homeland in a geographical sense, I would choose Crimea. . . . [Since] I started going there [in] the 1950s, it's evident that the undertone of some ethnic paradise has been preserved. Russians, Tatars, Ukrainians, Greeks, Bulgarians, [. . .] Krymchaks, Jews, Estonians, Armenians, and many, many other peoples. And they got along well with one another, it was a good family structure. It was a spot where the ideas of Soviet internationalism lay on good ground. This, of course, was all exploded, the Father of the Peoples destroyed all this."[1]

Ulitskaya enumerates the different groups and faiths that populated Crimea before Stalinist deportations and Nazi ethnic cleansing; it is notable that the peninsula attracts her as an ideal homeland for reasons that differ sharply from Vladimir Putin's claims that the region belongs to ethnic Russians. She then adds that universal values must stand above national ones, invoking one of her central beliefs: the diverse human family, based on shared convictions, is more legitimate than state or ethnic loyalties. It is no surprise that this conversation was broadcast on pro-Western Radio Liberty (*Radio Svoboda*); for Ulitskaya, the need for a more inclusive concept of kinship is inseparable from the liberal intelligentsia message of tolerance and understanding that underlies her oeuvre. In a broader sense, she credits training in genetics for her awareness of the connections that exist among all living beings; as with Ulitskaya's conceptions of the body, a background in the biological sciences shapes her writing about kinship.[2]

Ulitskaya's emphasis on the family is striking even within a literary tradition that has long used kinship to impart ideas, whether about relations between individuals or national identity. It is impossible to discuss kinship without building on the questions of physicality and gender that we raise in chapter 1. Her prose and plays treat consanguinity in moral as well as physical terms, repeatedly underscoring how similar ethical responses are more significant than blood ties and draw together characters from divergent backgrounds.[3] While her approach contains the broad scale and philosophy beloved by Russian letters, Ulitskaya's works also show how these larger concerns operate in everyday life via family and the body, through fathers and sons and, more often, mothers and daughters. Indeed, the author focuses on the female to the extent that some male relations are oddly absent. This gap, a break with the nineteenth-century prose that informs her writing, conveys embedded cultural concerns and implies that Ulitskaya is more connected to the legacy of Russian women's prose than she admits. At the same time, her focus on multiethnic kinship demonstrates how family has the potential to transcend and transform tradition as well as respond to it. Given the increasingly aggressive and xenophobic tone under Putin, this hopeful image is a crucial development in Russian literature.

The past casts a long shadow over Ulitskaya's image of kinship. One critic, discussing *Daniel Stein, Interpreter*, recalls author Vasilii Aksenov's comment that the record of a family is the history of a nation.[4] Prose written after 1953 repeatedly reinforced this link, itself rooted in the foundational family idea (*mysl' semeinaia*) that runs throughout the literature of the nineteenth century, most prominently in the writing of Leo Tolstoy. Dramatic changes in the Russian family are the backdrop to Ulitskaya's writing. Most plots of the author's longer works begin in late Stalinism and continue into the Khrushchev and Brezhnev eras, when cultural interest gravitated from public to private life. Serguei Oushakine observes a pervasive "rhetoric of kinship" after 1991 and the prominent and repeated use of family to make sense of the recent past.[5]

The tragedies of the twentieth century directed attention to intimacy and private life since, as Irina Savkina notes, novels dealing with kinship presuppose enmity between the home and the hostile forces of history. From the 1930s to the early 1950s biological or emotional connections were valued only to the degree that they served the state. In her seminal discussion of Stalinism's idea of the Great Family, Katerina Clark describes how the era "focused on the primordial attachments of kinship and projected them as the dominant symbol for social allegiance."[6] The epic war melodrama *The Fall of Berlin* (*Padenie Berlina*) illustrates how the public integrates the private into a universal, ideological network of kinship: at the end of the film, steelworker-turned-soldier Alesha reunites with his love Natasha at the same moment that the Father of the Peoples celebrates victory over fascism. The state, in the formulation of Michael Herzfeld, continuously invokes "kin, family, and body to lend immediacy to its pronouncements." Imagined closeness legitimates oppression.[7]

The Thaw revealed a more ambiguous set of relations beyond the Stalinist Great Family. I. Grekova's story "Summer in the City" ("Letom v gorode") portrays a mother's pain when, discovering her daughter is to have an abortion, she recalls her own unsuccessful attempt during Stalinism to terminate the pregnancy that led to her daughter's birth. Familial tragedies recur, the work implies, and the state offers limited help. Kinship became a means of expressing loss, whether literal or symbolic, even as changes in family life influenced representation of the home.[8] Helena Goscilo and Yana Hashamova, for example, map how the disappearance of actual fathers (whether during collectivization, the terror, or ensuing war) was mirrored in culture; after 1953, Stalin was no longer an adequate paternal substitute. During the Brezhnev years films such as *Autumn Marathon* (*Osennii marafon*) depicted families that were physically whole yet emotionally dead, even as the blockbuster *Moscow Does Not Believe in Tears* (*Moskva slezam ne verit*) sought to persuade women that nothing was more important than a good man.[9]

Thaw and Stagnation culture assumed that, significant problems notwithstanding, the government supported the family. The advent of perestroika negated this precept, as Liudmila Petrushevskaia showed in the novella *Our Crowd*, where a mother tricks hard-drinking friends into adopting her son before she dies. The state received an even grimmer characterization, as Seth Graham avers: films such as *Repentance* (*Pokaianie*) assailed Stalinism as a poison contaminating kinship from one generation to the next. By the end of the 1980s the myth of the Great Family had completely imploded.[10] The first post-Soviet decade witnessed a steep decline in most families' standard of living. On a symbolic level, prostitution became a national humiliation, and Russian men seemed emasculated by social tumult. Two films by Aleksei Balabanov envisioned how this chaos influenced the reinterpretation of kinship. In 1997 *Brother* showed a young Chechen war veteran apprenticed to his sinister male sibling in crime-ridden Petersburg. Three years later, *Brother 2* enacted a revenge scenario: the protagonist wreaks havoc on Ukrainian mafiosi, corrupt American businessmen, and sundry other enemies of the homeland. Hot-headed Danila discovers that he belongs to a Great Family comprised of the ethnic Russians who, at the beginning of the Putin regime, hoped to regain their literal and metaphorical prowess.[11]

The new president personified masculine vigor for a nation desperately in search of a paternal figure. Andrei Zviagintsev's film *The Return* (*Vozvrashchenie*) vividly parallels this quest via two young brothers whose reunion with their long-absent father provokes a painful passage into adulthood. As Oushakine observes, Putin-era culture fixated on extended kinship, which promised to replace the disarray of the Gorbachev and Yeltsin years with a presumably more stable order. Against this background Ulitskaya's familial narratives contributed to her success, reflecting readers' hope that biological connections could minimize the confusion of a rapidly changing society. The author, however, relies on a different remedy: responsibility, sincerity, and tolerance, all of which bring people together. It is these positive values that shape kinship, in the process bridging the distance between the Soviet themes she emphasizes and her post-1991 portrayals of them.[12]

Ulitskaya's Metaphors of Family

The family is a prominent constant in Ulitskaya's works, with members often described through the compelling corporeal images we investigate in chapter 1. Relatives' interactions, however, have an ethical dimension that endows consanguinity with metaphorical as well as physical meaning.[13] Not surprisingly, in her works the correct values of kinship strongly contrast with those the Soviet (and post-1991) state promotes. To borrow from American feminists, for Ulitskaya "the familial is political," as was evident when she criticized Aleksandr Solzhenitsyn for believing the fate of the nation supersedes that of one's relatives. Kinship is a concept that embraces humanity as a whole yet must privilege the home.[14]

The connection between family and the outside world is a source of tension in Ulitskaya's works. In *Medea and Her Children*, the protagonist's nephew, Georgii, visits the Crimean graveyard where Medea's mother and husband are buried. He travels at the beginning of a summer that will culminate in the death of one family member while reminding Medea of how her sister and deceased husband had an affair decades ago. Georgii's observations in the cemetery illuminate several interrelated themes that guide both the novel and Ulitskaya's narratives: "The graveyard sloped up from the road. Above was the ruined Tatar section with what remained of the mosque. The eastern slope was Christian, but after the deportation of the Tatars, Christian burials had begun to creep over onto Tatar territory, as if even the dead were involved in depriving them of their land. All the Sinoply forebears had been laid to rest in the old Theodosia cemetery, but by this time it was closed and in part even demolished, and Medea had buried her Jewish husband here with an easy mind, a good distance from her mother. Red-headed Matilda, a good Christian in every respect, was zealously Orthodox, had no time for Muslims, feared the Jews, and had an aversion for Catholics. Her views on sundry Buddhists, Taoists, and the like are not known, if indeed she had ever heard of them."[15] Georgii has come to the cemetery to clean around the tombstones but is unsurprised to find that his aunt has already done so. Her care is evident even in this place — just as she keeps strict order in the kitchen, Medea tends to the small corner of the world that belongs to her kin. There is a deeper significance to her care for Samuel's grave. First, it implies forgiveness of his adultery. Likewise, with the careful planning, respect for others, and common sense passed down through her relatives, she has reached a compromise with the intractable Jewish question, burying her husband far from her kind but anti-Semitic mother. This detail is telling for both Medea and Ulitskaya; it implies that the large conflicts that have distorted the twentieth century can be mitigated, if not resolved, on a personal level by individual actions. Finally, her attention to Samuel's last resting place is a connection to the past, just as elderly Medea herself personifies a bygone era for her younger relatives.

The cemetery, however, has been changed by forces beyond Medea's control. After Stalin's 1944 deportation of the Tatars, Christians began to encroach; the graveyard is an all-too-literal metaphor for the lost multiethnic Crimea Medea knew as a child and that Ulitskaya extols in her Radio Liberty interview. The work's conclusion returns to this topic, which recurs in expanded form in her novel *The Big Green Tent* and implicates Putin's 2014 aggression, a series of actions focusing on alleged Russian victimization and ignoring the Tatar tragedy. The headstone of Samuel, Medea's husband, is another testament to the violent state: while the monument mentions Samuel's Communist Party membership and army service, the reader is not yet aware that during the Civil War he served in a detachment that executed peasants accused of hoarding grain. Samuel's confession of this detail to Medea was a catalyst for their unlikely marriage, and now his widow has found a way to modify this memory: "Medea had amended the symbolism of the five-pointed Soviet star, silvering not only it but also the point of the obelisk to which it was attached, with the result that it acquired a sixth, inverted ray and looked more like the Christmas star as depicted on pre-Soviet greeting cards and also hinted at more ancient associations."[16]

Medea has respected her husband's wishes for his gravestone yet changed it to reflect their own marriage: Samuel was raised in the Jewish tradition to which he returned shortly before his death, while Medea's simple Christianity, passed down by her Greek Orthodox ancestors, guides her during a life that spans most of the Soviet period. The unobtrusive alteration to Samuel's final resting place signals her philosophy, which places family and ethics above all other loyalty. Such muted righteousness is not new to Russian literature, as one critic reminds the reader when comparing Medea to the old women populating village prose. However, Ulitskaya's Medea does not harbor the narrow-minded ideology that sometimes contaminates such characters. Instead, she has reclaimed this small portion of the cemetery from the massive violence inflicted on Crimea, first by the Axis occupation and then by Stalin's brutal reprisals. The graveyard becomes a symbol of survival as well as a locus of loss and, in its own modest way, illuminates how kinship functions in Ulitskaya's writing. At its best, the author shows, family creates a system of mutual support built on the tolerance, understanding, and sincerity that Medea models. These bulwarks, however, are constantly under attack from the same larger pressures that have changed the cemetery.[17]

Focusing on the metaphors of kinship stresses continuity, which leads to an emphasis on biological rather than spousal roles within the family: wives are significant because they are mothers, while husbands (when present) are important as fathers. However, to build on our discussion in chapter 1, procreation involves transmitting morals as well as genes. Indeed, Medea shows that nurturing is not limited to raising one's own offspring; the childless protagonist unites a number of subplots involving her relatives. Privileging progenitors over spouses affirms stability as the crux of kinship, and connecting past with present is likewise one of Ulitskaya's key concerns for a culture in chaos. Her emphasis on metaphorical as well as genetic relatives, along with portrayals of families that span multiple decades, evokes nineteenth-century representatioins of both positive and negative generational succession.[18]

Appropriating a trope from Petrushevskaia and, more fundamentally, Iurii Trifonov, Ulitskaya illustrates that a family may be intact—with both parents and children present—yet hollow. *The Kukotskii Case* centers on this idea as relations between Elena and Pavel Alekseevich deteriorate despite their best intentions. Ulitskaya asserts that families may be examined scientifically, making this novel a complex and ultimately discouraging case study of the intertwined implications of kinship and corporeality.[19] After their arguments over abortion and paternity, Elena constantly carries her hurt within her; Pavel Alekseevich has adopted Tanya and takes Toma into his home, yet the family seems to empty rather than expand. Relatives have their own neuroses, as Pavel Alekseevich acknowledges when he laments a domestic atmosphere akin to a "[b]ig insane asylum." The Kukotskiis do not, as Savkina suggests, begin to fall apart when Toma joins them—the true moment of rupture occurs with the parents' fateful disagreement over terminating pregnancy and the hurtful words they exchange. The critic does, however, make the apt observation that everyone abandons the family in his or her particular way: Pavel Alekseevich drinks, Elena falls into a catatonic state, and Toma is more concerned with plants than human beings. Together these attitudes justify Ulitskaya's claim that *The Kukotskii Case* is a narrative about approaching death.[20]

During the last New Year celebration the Kukotskiis will experience together, the relatives form a disturbing scene as they sit down at the table: "It was the strangest family holiday that could be imagined. Aside from Tanya and [her boyfriend] Sergei [. . .] each person present suffered from an acute alienation from everyone else and a deep feeling of loneliness. It was as if the natural bonds of kinship had come undone, gotten tangled up and distorted: Pavel Alekseevich's wife had long ago become his child, and his daughter had during the last three weeks unexpectedly become the head of the family." This mournful group is far removed from the gatherings of friends, relatives, and the likeminded that appear in Ulitskaya's other longer works.[21] In coming together, the Kukotskiis reaffirm their alienation from one another. Tanya has emerged as the most stable member of the clan, possibly because she no longer lives at home. However, in the following year she dies during childbirth and Elena continues her slow decline. This gradual dissolution echoes the darker moments of the traditional family saga, where the plot chronicles the destruction—not preservation—of kinship. Despite the argument over abortion, Pavel Alekseevich's drinking, and other fault-lines indicated in the novel, Ulitskaya presents the deterioration of the Kukotskiis as a mystery; as the author comments, it is a rare talent to be able to keep a family together.[22]

Some narratives provide more original images of family, as is the case with *Sonechka*. After discovering her husband's affair with Jasia, Sonechka still invites the orphan to move with them to their new apartment. Their unconventional home life continues until the day Robert Viktorovich dies in the arms of Jasia, who eventually emigrates with Sonechka's help. Establishing the pattern subsequently evident in *The Kukotskii Case*, in this novella kinship is not primarily biological: Jasia is adopted (as are Tanya and Toma in the later novel). One critic is entirely incorrect when labeling Ulitskaya the "anti-Turgenev": in fact, both authors depict the family as positive but not ideal. Stylized and perfect images of kinship signal falsity in Ulitskaya's writing, unless evoked when remembering those who have died.[23]

Indeed, at times art provides a false image of family, which is surprising at first glance, given Ulitskaya's cavalcade of creative characters. At issue is idealization, not the medium in which it takes place. In *Medea and Her Children*, Alexandra's first husband, Alexei Kirillovich, is charmed by the sight of his wife nursing their child. This portrayal has an earlier and more problematic referent—in *Sonechka*, returning home from work during the family's period of exile, Robert Viktorovich sees an idyllic image of his wife and young daughter: "[E]ach evening Robert would open his front door and see Sonechka in the living fire-breathing light of the oil lamp, wreathed in an uneven flickering nimbus, sitting in their only chair, which he had refashioned into an armchair. Firmly attached to the pointed end of her pillowlike breast was the little grayish head, soft and shaggy as a tennis ball, of his baby. In the mildest way imaginable, the whole picture would shimmer and pulsate, with waves of uneven light, with waves of the unseen warm milk, and with other invisible currents that left him unable to move or close the door."[24]

The force of this domestic scene overwhelms the artist. Envisioning kinship as a function of the maternal body, Robert Viktorovich transforms the details of this setting as he subordinates physical reality to his vision of what should be. As when he first meets her in the library, Sonechka is less an individual than a subject fashioned by her artist husband. Indeed, this tranquil scene combines two of the novella's recurring tropes: Sonechka as creature of the hearth and Robert Viktorovich's creation.²⁵ Both will be compromised when he begins his long affair with Jasia. Sonechka herself adds to this false image of home through the books she reads at the beginning and end of her life. Hoping to experience the warm domesticity of the nineteenth-century heroine, she instead brings to mind Anton Chekhov's deluded Darling (Dushechka) in the eponymous story. As N. A. Baksaraeva notes, the fact that Sonechka is Jewish (while Dushechka is Russian Orthodox) suggests that theology is less important than personal behavior, a core tenet of Ulitskaya's works. At the conclusion of the *povest'*, Sonechka again finds solace, and the narrative switches to present tense to summarize her life as a widow: "Each spring she goes over to the Vostryakovo Cemetery and plants white flowers on [Robert Viktorovich's] grave, but they never take root. In the evenings, she perches a pair of lightweight Swiss spectacles on her nose shaped like a pear and plunges into blissful depths, returning to the shady avenues of Bunin or flinging herself headlong once more into the torrents of spring."²⁶

Sonechka tends the grave of her unfaithful husband and again immerses herself in the literature that has protected and deformed her life. The reference to her nose returns the reader to the novella's first portrayal of the heroine, provided by her uncharitable elder brother Efrem, who "never tired of repeating, 'All that reading has given Sonechka a butt like a chair and a nose like a pear.'" This recurring detail shows how images—both others' and her own—have limited Sonechka, robbing her of meaningful control over her actions or the objective ability to perceive life. Substituting image for reality invites disaster in Ulitskaya's corpus, as when Sonechka and Robert Viktorovich are fooled by their fantasies of family and this delusion leaves the widowed mother alone in her final years.²⁷

Problems come from outside as well as inside the family. The state is a damning illustration of false kinship, exemplifying what Herzfeld notes as a tendency to exploit familial images. In "A Gift Not Made by Hands," Pioneer initiates view a museum exhibit of surreal gifts to the Father of the Peoples, including a carpet that an Uzbek woman wove from her hair and the portrait of the leader that Toma Kolyvanova sewed with her feet. Both objects underscore the corporeal nature of obedience to the Great Family, a fact not lost on the girls and one that for Ulitskaya reveals how Stalinism manipulates at the level of kinship as well as physicality. Having pledged their loyalty to the state, in body and mind they feel that they are now "completely different people, proud and ready for a great feat." In this work and others in the cycle *Girls* (*Devochki*), the characters' childhood imitates the strict hierarchy of Stalinism as they sense sharp but unspoken differences in privilege.[28] Handicapped Toma, whose body bewilders and shames the girls, shows that adulation for the ideological patriarch can be deployed for personal gain (in Toma's case, the reasonable but self-serving claim to a private apartment). The Soviet model of kinship is one of shifting loyalties yet constant subordination to the state and its ideas (at least in public); Toma can only improve her life because of the largesse of those more powerful in the Great Family.[29]

The false kinship of ideology is an even stronger force in some of Ulitskaya's later works, and it is particularly invidious in the lives of characters in *Daniel Stein, Interpreter*. The novel's plot portrays Daniel Stein, a Polish Jew who survives the Holocaust, converts to Catholicism, and emigrates to Israel. In this work Rita Kovač, a Jew involved in the ghetto escape that Daniel organized, embodies the perils of ideological kinship. She switches her allegiance from family to Stalinism and, many decades later, to Anglicanism. Her daughter Ewa is shocked when Rita observes that with this final shift she has found true belonging; for her mother, bonds to children, lovers, and friends are less meaningful than zeal for causes secular and sacred.[30] Extremist Judaism presents another model of the false family, reiterating the novel's attempt to depict the shortcomings of both Jews and Christians. As with Stalinism (and Russian ethnic superiority), Judaism conceals problems beneath a veneer of presumed unity. Gershon Shimes, a radical Jew imprisoned in the USSR, helps the fanatic Baruch Goldstein, who was killed in 1994 after attacking Arabs at a mosque. (Goldstein, like many of the novel's minor characters, is a figure taken directly from the sad annals of Arab-Israeli relations.) Gershon's son Bin'omin, who must identify the body, later commits suicide. This second death, which has implications for the novel's protagonist, portrays Jews as capable of intolerance. The warmth and humanity of figures such as Aaron in "March 1953" have nothing to do with the paranoia and violence Ulitskaya identifies in Israel's extremists. The portion of *Daniel Stein* that focuses on the Holy Land critiques Shimes, Goldstein, and other radicals, who destroy their own families (and those of their victims) in their deluded pursuit of righteousness. Grave consequences follow from exchanging the biological family for one based on exclusionary ideology. This displacement assumes a basic subordination of flesh to dogma, a position Ulitskaya condemns as deeply mistaken.[31]

Instead, the author illustrates how true kinship comes from a family of affinity, where members choose to be unified by shared values. As in the false variants of kinship, genetics are less important than ideas, which may be abstract (ecumenism, tolerance) but appear through characters living rightly from moment to moment. These positive metaphors of family advance the concepts that are upheld throughout Ulitskaya's narratives and that underlie our analysis; in doing so, they reflect the values of the intelligentsia that we discuss in chapters 3 and 4. *The Funeral Party* provides what at first seems an unlikely backdrop for the family of affinity. The lovers, fellow artists, and acquaintances who gather as Alik is dying include few relatives in the conventional sense, yet their togetherness comforts the ailing artist: "Alik sprawled in his chair. Around him were his friends, shouting, laughing and drinking. It was as though he wasn't there, yet they were all focused on him and he felt this. He enjoyed the everydayness of life; like a hunter, he had spent his life chasing after mirages of form and colour, but now he knew there had been nothing better than these senseless parties where people were united by wine, friendship and cheerfulness in this studio with no table, where they laid a makeshift tabletop on trestles."[32]

Alik draws strength from his friends, relatives, and lovers, realizing their importance. For Ulitskaya this awareness occurs via the "everydayness of life" that bolsters the family of affinity: the artist knows that those around him are joined by the compassion and respect that bring them to him as he weakens. The body—and its impending death—motivate this extraordinary illustration of kinship. Alik has exchanged the solitary life of the painter for community; some of his friends tellingly sit beneath his reworking of the Last Supper. This painting and Alik's comment convey that gatherings during a key moment in life are doubly significant because of plot and the people involved. The assembled crowd is so diverse that one critic describes the variegated characters as a new version of Noah's ark. Irina, the artist's former wife, supplies a secular metaphor for the scene: Alik's friends are a vision of a Russia that never was.[33] More specifically, the Chelsea loft, with its wine, parties, and "makeshift tabletop on trestles" recalls the evenings in apartments and dachas that shape the memories of youth for Ulitskaya's generation. New York becomes a referent to days and nights spent in and around Moscow and Leningrad, the capitals of *shestidesiatnik* culture. What binds these places together is a sense of togetherness that continues even after Alik's death. As we discuss in chapter 1, his wake creates a utopian realm in which Jewish doctors and Russian Orthodox artists converse and where African-Americans, whites, and Paraguayan street musicians commune. The posthumous celebration begins with the body but expands to create the family of affinity central to Alik and Ulitskaya, an environment in which no combination is shocking, yet where communication and understanding are more important than diversity for its own sake.[34]

Like Alik, Medea values kinship in various forms. She retains this conviction despite a bewildering series of divorces, new marriages, and affairs among her relatives and their friends. *Medea and Her Children* is no saccharine paean to the ties that bind: infidelities lead to Masha's suicide and Medea's refusal to speak with her sister for almost twenty-five years. The novel's concluding paragraph, however, lauds the family of affinity as a multiethnic group formed by choice and shared values: "It is a wonderful feeling, belonging to Medea's family, a family so large that you can't know all its members by sight, and they merge into a vista of things that happened, things that didn't, and things that are yet to come." The protagonist herself has died, but the "feeling" of family remains and emanates from Medea's quotidian kindness, which literally and metaphorically keeps kin and home together. In her insightful study Svetlana Timina summarizes this axiom when she describes Medea's loosely defined clan as linked by shared moral responses in difficult times. The willingness to live and let live—and the tolerance consequently implied—are the main criteria for joining this family.[35] Even the reader can participate, drawn in by the last line of the novel. Through this model Medea demonstrates how a home built on kindness can survive the tragedies of the twentieth century; the narrative, which spans roughly eighty years, shows the ultimately positive characteristics of human nature. The family of affinity is a constant that outlasts the Soviet state and, presumably, the chaos following it.[36]

Some of Ulitskaya's works explicitly envision family as based on tolerance and positive actions. The most prominent example is *Daniel Stein*, which links the family of affinity to religion's beneficial aspects as its protagonist argues that faith is omnipresent and constitutes a spiritual kinship that includes almost everyone. For Daniel belief is a call to unity, not a false barrier promoting exclusion (or worse). The message reiterates that of the final paragraph of *Medea and Her Children*: humanity is one large family whose members should recognize their kinship. As we explore in chapter 4, belonging, tolerance, and faith are interlinked. The family of affinity is built on choice and a shared positive response to the dilemmas of the quotidian, counterbalancing the 1990s sense of apocalypse and the increasingly intolerant early years of the twenty-first century. Her characters' refutation of state in favor of clan critiques not only the Great Family of Stalin but also its reformulation under Putin and Medvedev; for Ulitskaya, kinship allows the reader to see more clearly the problems of a government that professes unity yet promotes discord.

Mothers, Fathers, Grandparents: Ambivalence, Affinity, and Absence

At the center of the family of affinity is the mother, a complex figure who in this author's writing overshadows fathers and grandparents. This character is inseparable from corporeality; in this chapter we draw attention to how Ulitskaya's fictional mothers exist alongside the nation's persistent portrayal in feminine and often maternal terms. As Goscilo and Lanoux note, this depiction glorifies the "amorphous, sacred, essential, life-giving force that is 'Mother Russia.'" Several of Ulitskaya's characters challenge these attributes, embodying the absence, ambivalence, agency, and communication that Elizabeth Podnieks and Andrea O'Reilly ascribe to mothers.[37] Questioning traditional representations of motherhood and presenting alternatives, Ulitskaya links corporeal sincerity to maternity that is chosen, not mandated. Despite this depiction, motherhood is inevitable for female characters in many Ulitskaya texts; indeed, the author admits that she once believed a woman had to have a child to be fulfilled but later concluded motherhood should be a choice.[38]

Maternal feelings are not a given for Ulitskaya's characters, who, in a trope inherited from women's prose, often worry about these sentiments (or their absence). She argues in her memoir *Discarded Relics* that maternal happiness is stronger than its paternal equivalent: "Giving birth to children is the privilege of women, although it is impossible without the participation of men. But women experience the happiness of maternity much more sharply and markedly than a man is capable of experiencing fatherhood." Ulitskaya, drawing on her background in genetics, argues for a basic biological distinction between the genders. This view in part accounts for the imbalance in parental roles portrayed in her works but does not address the question of maternal ambivalence or inadequacy. *The Kukotskii Case* is a telling narrative in this context. The novel initially approaches motherhood from a biological perspective, as Pavel Alekseevich argues for decriminalizing abortion. However, it quickly becomes evident that the work's discussion has implications for conceptions of kinship and society as well.[39] While the esteemed surgeon interprets motherhood and kinship on a national scale, Elena is more involved with the fate of her family, yet the results of her concern are far from ideal. The difficult relationship with her own child (Tanya) is paralleled by an unwillingness to serve as adopted Toma's substitute mother. Elena exhibits a barely hidden hostility toward her, blaming the orphan for the argument over abortion and the marital rift that takes place soon after Toma moves in with the Kukotskiis. Notably, Pavel Alekseevich and Elena become Toma's guardians, not her adoptive parents. Elena cannot envision herself as the mother of an "unlikeable [*malosimpatichnoi*] girl" and is relieved by the semantic distance guardianship implies. Toma, on the other hand, wishes that Kukotskii were her "real" father (but voices no desire to have Elena as a parent).[40]

Despite Elena's antipathy, Toma displays a preference for the family one chooses as opposed to kinship based solely on genes; indeed, her materially disadvantaged life improves dramatically with the death of her biological mother, destitute janitor Lizaveta. The novel never depicts Toma as a nurturing or even caring person, qualities she presumably lacks because of her difficult early childhood. Tanya, however, becomes closely connected with maternity. When she moves from rebellious daughter to seeing herself as a mother, the narrator's description of pregnancy privileges Tanya's experience. As an adult her definition of family is flexible and deals with choice as much as biology, which strikingly differs from the experience of her mother. Elena's mental decline is itself a comment on motherhood and how it links generations. As we note in chapter 1, after learning of Tanya's pregnancy, Elena tells Kukotskii that Tanya will give birth "to Tanechka"; when Pavel Alekseevich later announces that Tanya now has a daughter named Zhenia, Elena responds that it was *she* who gave birth. The maternal confusion of corporeal and familial relationships is further reinforced in the way Elena addresses her husband. Though she has called him "P-A" for many years, the term eventually becomes the monosyllabic "pa." Elena's mistaking Pavel Alekseevich for her own father echoes an actual similarity between them; both men endured risk and persecution in pursuit of their beliefs, whether related to medicine or Tolstoyism. Such repetition within a family is a hallmark less characteristic of Ulitskaya than of Petrushevskaia, whose works recall the regressive families that populate the darker novels of the nineteenth century. The concern with motherhood and kinship, however, also situates Ulitskaya within Soviet culture's fears that the bloodshed of Stalinism and the Great Patriotic War weakened the bonds of the family, a rhetoric amplified by the demographic crises between 1960 and the present. Ulitskaya, who was a child in the late 1940s and began her literary career some forty years later, integrates these concerns into her post-Soviet narratives' depiction of late Stalinism.[41]

The end of *The Kukotskii Case* expands the themes of maternity, repetition, and kinship with attention to Zhenia, whose given name, Evgeniia, has evident symbolism; as a descendant of geneticist Gol'dberg and the granddaughter (though not biological) of Pavel Alekseevich, she represents the idea of noble birth and heritage. As we note in chapter 1, she represents a more balanced view of the body. In terms of kinship, Zhenia emblematizes Ulitskaya's hope for her family and, by extension, a nation that has survived the traumas of the Soviet era. As a young woman expecting her first child, Zhenia visits the Kukotskii apartment where Toma and elderly Elena now live. In a brief moment of lucidity, Elena tells her granddaughter not to be angry with Toma, because she is an orphan. Zhenia's response—that each of them is an orphan— seems to call all family bonds into question. However, as Zhenia goes into labor, Elena has a redemptive vision in the moments before dying. She sees a group of people on a balcony, including her grandparents, the servant Vasilisa, her parents, and a couple in the center who represent Zhenia and her husband. The woman, who also resembles Tanya, holds a baby: "In this newborn comes together all the happiness in the world, all the light, all the meaning. As if on a sunlit day another sun has risen . . . this newborn will belong to them all—and they to him. And Elena Georgievna cries from complete happiness and while doing so is a little surprised, because at the same time she feels the salty sweetness of tears and her own complete weightlessness [*svoiu bestelesnost'*]." Elena is overjoyed at the vision of the newborn, who lights up the world as Elena herself prepares to depart it. Joy and sadness mix as she awaits death, metaphorically passing life on to the next generation. Following the paradigm illustrated in Alik's last days, death and renewal are connected, integrated into an authorial philosophy where both are a normal and central part of existence. The final scene in *The Kukotskii Case* reconciles literal and metaphorical kinship: the child belongs not merely to Elena's family, but to a larger community that encompasses all of humanity.[42]

In linking the corporeal and spiritual to a redemptive vision of kinship, the novel also echoes *Medea and Her Children*. The inclusive family motivating Medea's narrative could not differ more sharply from that of the classical heroine from whom the protagonist takes her name.

As Tat'iana Rovenskaia and Anja Grothe point out, Ulitskaya's Medea acts in precisely the opposite way. Her biological childlessness contrasts with several telling facts: her position as a nurse on a maternity ward, the way she meets her husband (while working at a sanatorium specializing in fertility problems), and her unflinching acceptance of mothering duties.[43] Medea first assumes such a role in caring for younger siblings after the death of her parents and continues to do so in various ways throughout her life. She likewise enjoys comparing her clan's physical traits, passed down from generation to generation. At the beginning of the novel, the narrator remarks on this activity: "Many years later the childless Medea would gather her numerous nephews and nieces, grandnephews and grandnieces together in her Crimean home and subject them to quiet, unscientific observation. It was assumed that she loved them all dearly, although what kind of love a childless woman has for other people's children is uncertain. At all events, she took a lively interest in them, and this grew even stronger when she was old."[44]

Gathering relatives together motivates the plot of *Medea and Her Children*. This narrative structure in turn answers the question of how a childless woman can care for others' offspring, elaborating how Medea serves as surrogate nurturer, protector, and disciplinarian. In the process it demonstrates Ulitskaya's belief that ethics (not genetics) are paramount for raising children. *Medea and Her Children* asserts that the protagonist's positive behavior and strict morals define both her life and those of her relatives. The undertones of self-sacrifice in Medea's maternal duties add luster to her muted righteousness.

Lack of genetic progeny (despite Medea's wishes) foregrounds asceticism, endurance, and grief, while her sister Alexandra's fertility signals a carefree nature and uncomplicated moral code. Throughout the novel approaches to sexuality and nurturing differentiate the two sisters. In fact, Medea supervises the birth of Alexandra's first child, Sergei, and the protagonist's interactions with her nephew suggest surrogacy: during "the first month of little Sergei's life, [Medea] vicariously experienced to the full the motherhood that would never be hers. Sometimes it seemed to her that her own breasts were filling with milk. She returned to Theodosia with a sense of profound inner emptiness and loss." The reader cannot help but think that Medea would have made a better mother than Alexandra, an idea that again validates the preeminence of behavior over biology. Years later, on the way to visit her sister-in-law, Medea ponders Samuel's infidelity with Alexandra and briefly laments her childlessness: "She had been degraded by her husband, betrayed by her sister, abused by fate itself, which had denied her children while the child fathered by her husband, the child that by rights was hers, had been placed in her sister's relaxed and fun-loving body." Only weeping with Alexandra over Masha's tragic suicide will eventually bring the sisters together.[45]

At times expectations about kinship roles influence (and warp) family dynamics. In *Daniel Stein, Interpreter* Ewa sees her mother Rita not as an individual, but instead judges her by what the relationship between a mother and daughter should be. This abstract notion of family complicates matters further, given that Rita herself justifies placing her children in an orphanage to pursue the Bolshevik cause by asserting that this choice will eventually allow them to "live in a just society." The narrative condemns her sacrifice of biological kinship to the utopian dreams of the Great Family. Likewise, both mother and daughter substitute the reality of family life for idealized conceptions, a scenario that never bodes well in Ulitskaya's oeuvre. By contrast, Ewa considers her friend and confidante Ester Gantman a substitute mother and aunt, as when the older woman reveals some of the untold family history Ewa craves. It is significant that Ester addresses Ewa as "child." Ester's own lack of children emphasizes that their kinship is one of affinity—both have been shaped by the Holocaust and its lingering aftershocks. Unsurprisingly, the maternal figure Ewa has chosen herself is more comforting than her actual mother. Ester likewise lacks the ideological fervor that taints Rita and distorts her relations with others. Ewa tells Ester, "Only with you have I formed a link which sustains me and makes me stronger and wiser." The resulting more inclusive definition of motherhood subtly extends to her son's boyfriend, Enrique, who has become a relative of sorts. Given this shift away from the biological family, it makes sense that the novel problematizes certain hierarchical familial relationships. When Rita converts to Anglicanism, she claims, "I sinned in that I did not respect my parents." Notably, she does not view surrendering her children to an orphanage in terms of guilt. She instead situates culpability in a lack of consideration for her forebears; in this way Rita also implicitly reproaches Ewa for the daughter's failure to understand her mother's choices.[46]

Ewa's experience as Rita's unloved child directly shapes the expectation for her own maternal duties. She is thus disappointed by perceived failures, not least because her circumstances do not coincide with the dream of a "real family" she has held since childhood. The novel traces this gap to the character's past, recalling Oushakine's idea that consanguinity is a geobiographical document that creates a history of its members based on collective experience. In Ulitskaya's writing, the assertion of kinship—whether through biological ancestry or the family of affinity—is an imperfect attempt to respond to the trauma inflicted by the state, be it Stalinist or Nazi. In the larger context of post-Soviet chaos, it is a search for meaning and order, comforts that Putin's regime is all too willing to provide in exchange for limits on freedom.[47]

Ulitskaya also links maternity to creativity as well as trauma and manipulation. It is in this vein that a very different image of motherhood structures "Diana," the first segment of the novella *Women's Lies* (*Skvoznaia liniia*). Prevarication, the thread implied by the Russian title, unites the individual stories of the text and complicates the intelligentsia precept that sincerity must govern behavior. When narrator Zhenia and vivacious Irish émigrée Irene meet on vacation in Crimea, the latter relates her fantastic, tragic, and partially fictional autobiography, which includes the deaths of four (imaginary) children. Zhenia feels duped and hurt when the lies are exposed, yet these are not the overarching falsehoods of the state that Ulitskaya and Aleksandr Solzhenitsyn decry. The story Irene tells is a feminine counterpart to Popov's photographic idealization of the affair with Bronka in the eponymous story. In both works literature comments on the arts (including the art of prevarication), and kinship is defined by creativity as well as corporeality.[48]

Ulitskaya refuses to condemn Irene and the other dissimulators in the novella, in part because life itself lies to the narrator as she struggles amid the tumult and failed dreams of 1990s Russia. The untruths the characters tell are the deceits that some people—most often women—need to formulate and embellish existence, "if only for a minute to create the illusion of what one dreams of, as though it had all come true." At a basic level this statement reiterates the purpose of literature. However, Ulitskaya reworks this commonplace as an innovative message, a move signaled by her identification of this book as her "truest" (*samaia pravdivaia*) but also her most playful. The solution to this paradox lies in the author's conception of maternity. The relationship between motherhood and female creativity is a complex one, as the discussion of Penelope and Odysseus in the introduction to the novella suggests. Evoking this foundational epic makes prevarication a transhistorical phenomenon, as old as the civilizations that depict it. While the narrator defines Odysseus as a liar of literally epic proportions, his wife does not have such talent: "Penelope ended up with nothing. There she had sat, recycling her yarn, weaving and unpicking, and her lying, like her handiwork, was as well formed as it was duplicitous. Yet for all her best efforts over those years, she has been allotted no place as prominent as that of her husband or her cousin [Helen of Troy]. She was lacking in some special feminine gift of mendacity. And yet the fibbing of woman, unlike the pragmatic lying of man, is a highly rewarding topic. Women do everything differently: alternative thinking, feeling, suffering—and lying."[49]

Unfortunate Penelope must compensate for Odysseus's absence by deceiving her suitors, yet she cannot even do this effectively. In this added misfortune, the narrator observes, she is distinct from those adults and girls whose accounts comprise the bulk of *Women's Lies*: female characters for whom prevarications become a creative act. This view has a number of implications for gender roles, echoing Helene Deutsch's foundational assertion that "[t]he urge to intellectual and artistic creation and the productivity of motherhood spring from common sources, and it seems very natural that one should be capable of replacing the other." Irene, unlike Penelope, succeeds in this substitution. By relating an alternative biography, she replaces in a narrative sense the children she does not have in a physical one. Motherhood thus can be a function of imagination as well as body; creativity is part of the rich experience of body and kinship that informs Ulitskaya's fiction.[50]

In *Women's Lies*, Zhenia's uncertainty about maternity spurs her search for a model of literary or lived motherhood. She settles on *Anna Karenina* to compare her own personal problems with the "real drama of a real woman." As an *intelligentka*, however, Zhenia should recall that Anna's maternal instincts are anything but a positive model and that her inability to distinguish between perception and reality leads to suicide. In "Diana," what is taken for experience triumphs over fiction—after first hearing Irene's compelling story, Zhenia eschews Tolstoy's heroine, who now seems outmoded, irrelevant, and bland. Later, after the revelation of Irene's deceit, Zhenia ultimately develops her own intuitive source of maternal authority, one that, fortunately for all involved, is more stable and viable than Anna's. In the process, Ulitskaya and her character engage in an intertextuality that emphasizes the intelligentsia's connections to literature as a palliative measure in troubled times.[51]

Ulitskaya shows that definitions of motherhood may be positive or harmful; as with the family of affinity, characters such as Medea who choose maternal roles are often more nurturing than biological mothers.

They build kinship with a humble, quotidian morality that is more viable than a search for perfection. The social conventions of the maternal, however, constantly complicate and threaten to deform this key role; such pressures make imagination a necessity for those who must enliven their drab reality. Valorized lies are a rare instance in which Ulitskaya qualifies her demand for *iskrennost'*: in this sense, mothers reveal the tensions between the high expectations for the intelligentsia and the practicalities of daily life.

In striking contrast to their focus on the maternal, Ulitskaya's works relegate fathers to the margins. Often this parent is absent, replaced by an adoptive figure or even a surrogate, an unrelated male with overtones of authority. The last of these three categories, recalling Ulitskaya's emphasis on metaphorical families, contains both positive and negative substitutes whose actions reflect issues that mark the author's body of writing as a whole. The missing or miscreant father is a holdover from women's prose, in which Petrushevskaia supplies the most notorious examples: in *Our Crowd* the father must be fooled into caring for his child, while *The Time: Night* depicts several generations of women living in a family bereft of any positive or permanent male presence. Petrushevskaia for her part inherited the absent father from the prose of Grekova and Natal'ia Baranskaia. Baranskaia's *A Week Like Any Other* (*Nedelia kak nedelia*) presents Ol'ga's apathetic husband as a good spouse by default; while reluctant to do housework, he is sober, loves their children, and, most importantly, has not abandoned them.[52]

In Ulitskaya's fiction one of the few present and positive biological fathers is Boris, the second husband of Tanya in "The Body of a Beauty," a short story in the collection *People of Our Tsar*. The narrator fleetingly describes him, mainly in contrast to Tanya's previous husband, jealous and abusive Serezha. Boris is blind, and his disability makes him similar to Ulitskaya's many sympathetic handicapped characters. Lack of sight confirms that he is attracted by something deeper than the physical charm that has caused boys and men to pester Tanya since she was an adolescent: "Their marriage turned out to be very happy. Son Boria was born a year later. When they walked down the street, they were so beautiful that people paid attention. But only the attentive person guessed that the broad-shouldered man was blind. After giving birth Tanya put on a lot of weight, and her body stopped provoking intense interest from young men. It belonged to her blind husband."[53] As with disabled Mila and Grigory in "The Daughter of Bokhara," the good marriage is a mystery impenetrable to all but husband and wife.

For Ulitskaya, their union is the best that a couple can hope for; they neither envy others nor mistrust each other. At the beginning of their lives together, Boris and Tanya seem exceptional to those around them, but eventually their appearance more closely resembles what they have always longed to be: ordinary, caring spouses and parents.

Pavel Alekseevich, the adoptive father of Tanya and then Toma in *The Kukotskii Case*, is Ulitskaya's most prominent paternal figure. Presented as intelligent and compassionate, soon after his fateful argument with Elena he begins drinking heavily to avoid meetings denouncing his "cosmopolitan" colleagues. Later he blames himself for not being able to save Tanya the way he had earlier intervened to keep his wife from dying—Pavel Alekseevich concludes he has not lived up to his own exacting standards. In this context he is defeated both as father and *intelligent*: as we examine more fully in chapter 4, failing to embody one's professed values is a sin all too prevalent among Ulitskaya's intellectuals. Kukotskii's shortcomings, however, arise from a genuine desire to help others (another intelligentsia axiom). His latent alcoholism surfaces when he tries to avoid meetings to denounce Jewish coworkers, and the argument that destroys his marriage comes from his support of reproductive rights.[54]

The role of the father is more straightforward in *Sincerely Yours, Shurik*, Ulitskaya's weakest novel and one undistinguished by subtlety. Shurik's misadventures with women come as no surprise given his upbringing. After Aleksandr Sigizmundovich is hit by a car, unmarried Vera becomes a widow, and their illegitimate son is left without a father. Growing up as a male only child in a markedly female environment, Shurik experiences a series of role reversals that make him simultaneously son, father, and mother as Vera grows more dependent on him. Shurik has paternal feelings for her throughout the narrative, sentiments that keep them tied to each other in a manner detrimental to both. He does not, however, fulfill this fatherly role for his ward, Mariia, the daughter of a friend. Through a series of misadventures, Shurik becomes a father-figure for this talented yet troubled future ballerina. The young teenager eyes Shurik as a potential husband, which understandably makes him nervous about the incestuous undertones of the situation. Paternal roles—whether actual or presumed—are unstable and shifting in these narratives.[55]

The surrogate father is an especially mutable character. In Ulitskaya's works this paternal image is removed from the family and has important political or intellectual status. This type of replacement figure is an unsurprising presence in the USSR where, as different characters observe, all citizens are orphans because of a past that has been lost or distorted. *Medea and Her Children*'s athletic Valerii Butonov, raised by a single mother, has disillusioning encounters with three surrogate fathers. This first of these is gymnastics coach Nikolai Vasilievich: "He took a lot of trouble with Valerii, and his straightforward way of calling him 'my son' was very meaningful and important to the boy. Valerii looked for shared features with his idol: he was glad their hair was the same color and their greyish-blue eyes similar; he narrowed his eyes the way Nikolai Vasilievich did, imitated the rolling, springing way he walked, and even bought himself white handkerchiefs like the ones Nikolai Vasilievich had."[56]

Butonov looks for similarities and mimics the movement and even sartorial style of the coach, who is a clear paternal influence on the teenager. Following the youth's realization that one of his competitions was fixed, he abandons gymnastics and joins the circus college. Here another surrogate father, Anton Ivanovich, initiates him into a rarified world where Butonov again discovers that the corruption of Soviet life limits his potential. It becomes clear that he is only a son if he performs well in an uneven contest whose outcome has been fixed beforehand. Ivan, his last mentor, teaches him about physical therapy and the East, all the while working for the KGB. Together these images imply that a more abstract surrogate father—the Soviet government as head of the Great Family—is to blame. It is no coincidence that Butonov's loss of faith occurs because of the state's appropriation of his body for ideological purposes. Indeed, it reiterates a vital problem Ulitskaya ascribes to Russian culture: when co-opted by the state, *telesnost'* becomes an obstacle to sincerity. The philosophy of the corporeal that we examine in chapter 1 is inseparable from images of the family; both are susceptible to manipulation.[57]

Ulitskaya provides a more extreme example of connections between father, state, and corrupting paternal surrogate in the story "The Writer's Daughter" ("Pisatel'skaia doch'"), where Masha meets her biological father only once. Active in the purges, he commits suicide after one of his victims confronts him. We learn nothing about his role in Stalinism. Instead, the reader sees the opulent apartment he and his ex-wife have been given; as with Butonov, the state rewards its loyal progeny. For Masha Communism takes the place of her father, and its ideology continues to harm her even after she gladly moves to the decadent West.

Political dogmatism, however, is no substitute for biological parents, as Masha belatedly realizes. Before she eventually takes her own life, the protagonist characterizes Stalinism as an inherited disease spread by the father. Ideology interpreted as paternal curse, a theme of perestroika culture, reworks Clark's idea that political maturity is passed from the mentors/fathers to the initiates/sons in Soviet culture. For Ulitskaya, stable kinship is incompatible with philosophies of hate and their troubled legacies. Enmity, whether based on political convictions or petty grievances, is detrimental to the overarching human family.[58]

Positive surrogate fathers are rare and usually unsuccessful. In the story "The Great Teacher" ("Velikii uchitel'"), Leonid Sergeevich, an adherent of theosophy, befriends working-class Gena and promises to introduce him to a learned scholar of Rudolf Steiner. When Gena realizes that the esteemed disciple is his despised neighbor Kupelis, he is mortified. "Instead of Dr. Steiner, with his handsome [. . .] face, with his silk bow-tie, slightly rumpled dress coat, it turned out to be this disgusting tadpole," whose bodily noises Gena abhors. The protagonist hides in shame, abandoning the studies that gave his life meaning. Gena cannot reconcile the image of his spiritual father with the everyday unpleasantness of those in his *kommunalka*. Here the issue is not Leonid Sergeevich but his "son," who refuses to recognize that the beautiful abstraction of anthroposophy can exist within the banal realm of the communal apartment. It is telling that this failed surrogate relationship is one involving an *intelligent* who attempts to instruct a member of the common people—as we explore in chapter 3, interactions between the two groups are always fraught in Ulitskaya's oeuvre.[59]

Daniel Stein depicts two surrogate fathers who are more effective. These characters' presence reflects the novel's belief that literature can instill positive ethics, thus counterbalancing the invective and hatred conveyed by the totalitarian state. Hilda, whose father worked as a Nazi rocket scientist, comes to Israel hoping to atone for national and familial guilt. Daniel, not surprisingly, becomes her father's replacement: he advises her in matters of the heart and spirit. Daniel is the novel's philosophical paterfamilias, giving advice to parishioners and even to Pope John Paul II. Unlike the false father of the Great Family, Daniel includes and comforts rather than excluding and punishing. Hilda's second surrogate father, Professor Neuhaus, is more intriguing. The aged expert on Judaica thrills her with his lectures, which assert the underlying unity between the chosen people and gentiles. Hilda copies down his thoughts and conveys them to the reader, in the process replacing her biological father with an ideational surrogate who helps her come to terms with her status as a German Christian in Israel.[60] Hilda's literal and metaphorical *Bildung* parallels Daniel's narrative of moral development, the heart of the novel's attempt to reconcile the sundered family of Judaism and Christianity. The reader is also included in this kinship of tolerance. As with the conclusion of *Medea and Her Children*, the structure of the novel expands outward to accommodate all those with similar ethics; these values themselves come from the act of reading Ulitskaya's narrative of tolerance. In *Daniel Stein* ideas literally supplant family, yet in a positive manner grounded in daily life and the belief that all faiths should promote unity. Ulitskaya's works are uneasy when depicting the rare biological father or his adoptive counterpart—as with the treatment of kinship as a whole, her writing is more comfortable when it joins the paternal figure to a discernible system of values.[61]

This conjunction of kinship and morality makes grandparents less problematic than fathers. These older characters' representation is another indication of how ethics, kinship, and corporeality interact in Ulitskaya's works. Their roles in the family are largely a function of age, which connects them to prerevolutionary humane values that their own sons and daughters often lack. Most of these elderly characters are positive, in contrast to the notoriously manipulative and unstable grandmother Anna Andrianovna of Petrushevskaia's *The Time: Night*. Ulitskaya presents two types of grandparents who raise children. Some compensate for absent or inadequate parents. Others attempt to atone for their own mistakes by taking advantage of a second chance at child-rearing. Upbringing (*vospitanie*) is a significant component of this theme, recalling Ulitskaya's nuanced representation of motherhood. She underscores the stakes of *vospitanie* by indicating that, though children are not responsible for the sins of their parents, the inverse might be true. *Sincerely Yours, Shurik* portrays how the pedagogue Elizaveta Ivanovna tries to take an active role in raising her grandson (much more so than does Vera, Shurik's mother). In the absence of a father figure, this grandmother also assumes the "masculine" role in *vospitanie*. The fact that Vera does not participate is not a tragedy, according to Elizaveta Ivanovna, because each person is ultimately responsible for his or her own development: "Cain and Abel had the same parents. Why was one meek and kind, and the other a murderer? Each person is the fruit of *vospitanie* [*plod vospitaniia*], but the main educator [*vospitatel'*] of a person is himself! And a pedagogue opens the necessary valves of the personality but closes the unnecessary ones."⁶²

Elizaveta Ivanovna, using the word *plod*, connects upbringing to both the abstract (the fruits of one's labors) and the physical (flesh). Shurik's subsequent failure to shape the course of his life validates her idea: he is influenced by how he was raised, which contributes to his endless sexual misadventures. However, his fate questions the latitude Elizaveta Ivanovna allowed Vera in raising him — neither he nor his mother could serve as *vospitateli*. On a more troubling level, the grandmother's intelligentsia discourse of upbringing has made Shurik an ethical person yet one whose strong morals bring misfortune to himself and others. Part of this problem stems from the corporeal insincerity we discuss in chapter 1: Shurik has a surfeit of values but a lack of honesty in recognizing his own sexual desire. This deficit is the legacy of Elizaveta Ivanovna's well-meaning pedagogical theories, theories that attempted to compensate for Vera's lack of parenting skills. Shurik embodies the connections between *telesnost'*, kinship, and intelligentsia ethics, yet his life shows that these three elements are not always harmonious. As in *The Kukotskii Case*, good intentions sometimes lead to calamity. Though she abdicated responsibility for her son, Vera comes to view raising Shurik's talented "daughter" Mariia as her destiny, even claiming that she loved Shurik less as a child than she does Mariia. Her devastation when she must surrender Mariia to the child's biological mother masks the root problem: Vera's second try at *vospitanie* is less atonement for neglect of Shurik's upbringing than a final attempt to vicariously realize her own aspirations, artistic and otherwise. Ulitskaya frowns on such sublimation, portraying Vera as delusional, egotistical, and ultimately self-destructive. Problems ensue when *vospitanie* is motivated by anything other than love and good intentions.⁶³

Ideology sometimes plays an explicit role in *vospitanie* and points to a sharp generational divide. Conflicting models of parenting clash in "March 1953" as Lily is reared by older relatives. Her great-grandfather Aaron steeps Lily in religious stories, while her secular scientist grandmother Bela pragmatically focuses on surviving Stalinism, a system personified by Lily's father's role as a Gulag warden. The ethical disparities between these generations are striking, and Ulitskaya's sympathies (predictably) lie with the elderly relatives. Bela and her husband Alex are contemporaries of Ulitskaya's own grandparents, whose now-vanished generation interests the author more than that of her parents. The elderly body is imbued with meaning by its formative role in kinship and inculcating values that oppose those of the Great Family.[64]

At times catastrophe engenders new familial responsibilities for the older generation: in *Medea and Her Children*, Masha's maternal grandparents take her in after both her parents perish in an automobile accident. The tragedies continue, as Masha must be rescued from her grandmother Vera Ivanovna when the latter begins to torment her innocent granddaughter by blaming Masha for her mother's death. Clowes sees Vera Ivanovna, strikingly anomalous in Ulitskaya's fiction, as a "northern" character who evokes "ethnic Russian selfhood and contemporary Russian chauvinism" as well as bearing the psychological scars of the 1930s. She is both victim and tormentor, portraying the distorted kinship roles inherent in the Great Family. When Alexandra and her husband Ivan Isaevich welcome Masha, they embody the opposite: the warm, inclusive view of family long espoused by Medea and her sister-in-law Elena. Their home is crowded: "But then again, as far as the love prescribed by the doctor was concerned, things could not have been better: Alexandra's heart was simply overflowing with prayerful gratitude that Masha's life had been spared by a miracle and that she was well and living in her home. None of her own children seemed to her at that moment as dearly loved as this fragile, grey-eyed little girl who didn't seem at all like the rest of them."[65]

Alexandra and Ivan Isaevich show that love is a solid foundation for kinship, a fact that cannot be overstated given emotionally empty families such as the Kukotskiis. Kindness leads to Masha and Nike's closeness, an intimacy later poisoned by their simultaneous affairs with Butonov, which in turn contributes to Masha's suicide. The result is an intergenerational ambivalence that complicates the representation of kinship in this family chronicle but underscores the paramount importance of empathy and tolerance; what destroys Masha is certainly not the comfort she receives as a traumatized child. Indeed, after Masha's death, the family is reconciled, and Medea's clan ultimately overcomes the tragedies that threaten it. Parents and grandparents constitute a crucial barrier against the vicious Great Family, which all too easily eradicates or deforms its smaller biological counterpart. The elderly are protected by values formed before the advent of Bolshevism; the mercy, contemplation, and caring they manifest constitute powerful examples for younger members of the family. Parents—and the children they raise—must struggle to maintain their own morality in an era where the state is all too willing to serve as *vospitatel'*.

Ulitskaya and Her Children: Sisters, Brothers, Rivals

Younger family members in Ulitskaya's works challenge the myth of idyllic childhood that Andrew Wachtel sees dominating Russian literature. Children likewise guide her appropriation of the family chronicle, which depicts the uneven battle between relatives and a more powerful (and malevolent) world. Ulitskaya's contribution to this genre is a nuanced understanding of how offspring both benefit and suffer from kinship. Sisters thus have a highly significant presence in Ulitskaya's texts. Within a literary tradition that typically has emphasized connections among fathers, sons, and brothers rather than mothers, daughters, and sisters, Ulitskaya focuses on the latter constellation of familial bonds. This shift evinces yet another facet of her unacknowledged debt to women's prose, which legitimated gynocentric plots in literature.[66] The author's attention to sororal scenarios shows how these sisters share important affinities, yet such likenesses are often rooted in destructive rivalries with high stakes: identity, sexuality, or parental love. In some cases interactions between female siblings take on unusual forms as Ulitskaya reworks Old Testament narratives to illustrate the values linked to kinship and the larger human family that unite her work. These religious allusions likewise imply the ties that bind Jews and Christians, two groups Ulitskaya hopes to reconcile by emphasizing their shared theological ancestry. Though she critiques Russian Orthodoxy, Ulitskaya also claims that literature could not exist without religious themes: Christianity functions as a cultural base and primer, she asserts, even for nonbelievers.[67]

One example of this Biblical undergirding in Ulitskaya's works is the pair of twins Victoria and Gayane in the *Girls* cycle. "Someone Else's Children" and "The Foundling" are two closely connected stories that present these identical twins, born fifteen minutes apart but on different days. Though they do not clash in the womb, from the first lines of the latter text Victoria's "struggle to be born" suggests that the sisters are a feminized variant of Jacob and Esau. Indeed, Gayane and Victoria compete almost from the moment of their birth. Later Victoria, the younger twin, dominates the docile Gayane (who, like Esau, is easily fooled) and even "steals" her identity to manipulate her sister, claiming that she too is named Gayane.[68] "The Foundling" further elucidates the rivalrous nature of the twins' relationship. Victoria imagines various narratives of her sister's disappearance, envisioning Gayane as an abandoned baby who turns up in their courtyard. When Victoria invokes another Biblical story and rephrases Cain by stating that she is not her sister's keeper, she "wasn't quoting. It's just that her whole little life wanted to become a quotation, and it floundered, not finding the proper context." As in *Women's Lies*, here prevarication is a function of gender and responding to one's problems (even at a very early age). For Ulitskaya the first half of life consists of internalizing laws and axioms and then testing these rules for oneself. Ethics must be experienced through body and family, not mandated by state or church. However, she also asserts that "sacred texts demand a new reading and a renewed understanding"; her rewriting of Biblical stories is thus not parody or literary revision but an attempt to gain a deeper understanding of them through the contemplation she values. Family life, the first set of social interactions a person experiences, is a key arena for engaging and modifying Christian teachings. Appropriating such scriptural narratives personalizes tradition and indicates the close relationship between fiction and theology that runs throughout Ulitskaya's oeuvre.[69]

When Victoria spins tales in "The Foundling," refashioning familiar folk narratives and devising new plots, she defines herself in relation to her sister—in Ulitskaya's works female siblings are presented in opposition to one another. Gayane, in contrast to her twin, "was the silent observer, storing in her memory other people's ribbons, brooches, insignificant events and dropped words. Her favorite amusement until the age of ten was preparing 'little secrets,' that is, arrangements of leaves, flowers, candy wrappers, and pieces of foil under a piece of glass. Even in the summer, at their dacha, where the girls had a lot more freedom, Gayane preferred this solitary and sedentary amusement best of all, while Victoria rode on her bike, swung on the swings and played ball with the proper (from [nanny] Fenya's point of view) children from the neighbouring dachas."[70] The twins differ in personality and habit. Gayane's interiority and behavioral resemblance to their mother suggests that Victoria's antics compensate for a mother-daughter affinity she does not share. The similarities between Margarita and Gayane are another example of Ulitskaya's proclivity to represent daughters' repetition of maternal behavior, a pattern inherited from *zhenskaia proza* (but without the sense of doom that authors such as Petrushevskaia added). Maturity, identity, and the growing pains that accompany the transition into young adulthood are key to the *Girls* cycle in which the twins appear, and Victoria's storytelling encapsulates her search for self. While Inessa Tsiporkina identifies the characters' playacting in these stories as preparation for their futures as women, Victoria's tales indicate a more immediate move toward independence instead of biological predestination.[71]

Just as the narratives featuring Victoria and Gayane begin with allusions to Jacob and Esau and Cain and Abel, in *Medea and Her Children* the ties between Medea and Alexandra loosely recast the legend of Leah and Rachel: both sisters are sexually involved with Medea's husband. Alexandra's infidelity with Samuel (which Medea discovers only after his death) understandably weakens the sibling bond. This scenario prefigures that of Nike and Masha—cousins who are raised as sisters—just as the secret liaison of Samuel and Alexandra anticipates the later love triangle involving Nike, Butonov, and Masha. As we discuss above, Masha comes to live with Nike and Alexandra after her parents are killed, and the subsequent relationship between adolescent Nike and Masha has a maternal tinge: "Nike now felt herself the matriarch of a large family consisting of her daughter Masha and lots of doll granddaughters. Many years later, after Katya had been born, Nike confessed to Alexandra that she must have used up the first flush of her maternal feelings on her cousin, because she never felt for her own children a comparable all-consuming love, the taking of another person so completely into her heart as she did in the first years Masha lived in their house."[72]

Alexandra and Nike's love saves Masha's life and minimizes her suffering after her parents' death and grandmother's accusations. However, Nike, like Alexandra, has a limited capacity for maternal love, and this shortage of feelings signifies a corresponding deficiency in character. Motherhood for Ulitskaya is only mutable to a degree before she condemns it; expectations can only be transformed within the limits of the author's own upbringing in Soviet culture. In *Medea and Her Children* the lack of "maternal feelings" aggravates strained sororal relations that lead to catastrophe when Masha and Nike realize that they share a lover. The betrayal the younger "sister" feels is compounded by her earlier sense of Nike as both sibling and parent.

This feeling is intensified by how Masha misconceives their relations. While unwilling to share Butonov with Nike, Masha for a time imagines their triangle in terms that recast (and try to redeem) it in light of cultural tradition: "And now Butonov had joined them together in some sacramental way, like Jacob marrying two sisters. They could have been called comrades-in-arms. Jacob entered the tents, took the sisters, took their handmaidens, and they were one family. And what after all is jealousy but another form of covetousness? You can't possess another person. Well then, let it be: everybody would be brothers and sisters, husbands and wives. She smiled to herself, thinking about utopian Chernyshevsky and the grand brothel in one or other of the dreams of his heroine in *What Is to Be Done?*" This passage illustrates the association between body, family, and text. Drawing on her intelligentsia upbringing and poet's creativity, Masha's vision of herself, Nike, and Butonov moves between the Hebrew Bible and a scenario that alludes to Nikolai Chernyshevsky's nineteenth-century novel *What Is to Be Done?* The combination of two antagonistic cultural traditions (Biblical and utopian socialist) underscores Masha's misreading of the situation. Likewise, if Medea and Alexandra respectively parallel Leah and Rachel, Masha's profoundly mistaken musings suggest that the comparison resonates across generations but yields destruction instead of harmony. Though an avowed advocate of tolerance, Ulitskaya echoes women writers of the late Soviet era when depicting how unbridled permissiveness has dire consequences. In a corporeal sense, lack of sexual restraint can have devastating results for individual and family when the lines between sister and rival blur.[73]

Sibling roles influence Ulitskaya's portrayal of marriage as well. In *Medea and Her Children*, Masha describes a "special relatedness" to her husband Alik through the word *Geschwister*, "meaning brother and sister, but the German conjoining [has] some hidden additional meaning." The novel privileges sibling ties and, in this case, even suggests that a brother-sister bond is stronger than the one between spouses. This link between them cannot, however, ensure fidelity. What dooms Alik and Masha's marriage is its easy reformulation into other relationships at the expense of the core values that should unite husband and wife; as with the family of affinity, shared responsibility and ethics must connect individuals. The fate of their union shows that Ulitskaya, despite her disavowal of literary didacticism, here and elsewhere uses narratives to instruct readers, whether at the level of family or nation.[74]

Ulitskaya focuses most prominently on relations involving mothers and daughters; fathers and brothers are less common and more problematic in her work. The absence of the paternal figure, as Goscilo and Hashamova note, is not surprising given the decimation of Russia's male population during the twentieth century. The dearth of male siblings signals that this loss is symbolically transmitted through generations, recalling the female families recognizable to readers from the works of perestroika-era women authors. Medea, for instance, lost first her father, mother, and then her brothers, one of whom was killed by the Reds during the Civil War, while another died because of the Whites; during the Great Patriotic War a third was killed by the Soviets and a fourth by the fascists. The only brother Medea knows as an adult is Fyodor, a Stalinist functionary in Tashkent and the most dubious of her relatives. As the relations among Alexandra, Medea, Nike, and Masha reveal, this novel is a female-dominated narrative; men at times contribute to the problems inherited through the family along with the more valued lineage of tolerance and kindness that Medea represents.[75]

The most prominent brother in Ulitskaya's writing is Rostislav, a New Russian in the play *Russian Jam*. The plot concludes as he buys his family's dacha from an unscrupulous handyman and then destroys it to make room for a lucrative development. A clear allusion to Ermolai Lopakhin from *The Cherry Orchard* (*Vishnevyi sad*), Rostislav is a more malevolent force than Chekhov's pragmatic but humane character; unlike Lopakhin, he has at best marginal sympathy for those who raised him. This play provides one of Ulitskaya's few images of the post-Soviet businessman. He spouts 1990s clichés, alternating them with trite socialist sayings rendered degrading in the context of Yeltsin-era capitalism. When his family complains about the dacha's plumbing, he retorts: "What catastrophe? What are you talking about? Everything is great! The economy is taking off! Investment is coming! Debts are being written off! Taxes are being lowered! And, moreover, to each according to his need, from each according to his ability! Well that, of course, is only in our one single family [*v nashei otdel'no vziatoi sem'e*]."[76] Rostislav mockingly reverses one of the foundational phrases of Soviet culture, further ironizing at the expense of the departed regime by comparing its (failed) attempt to build socialism in one country to his dysfunctional family. Such cynical discourse signals that for him kinship is, at best, secondary to increasing personal wealth. However, as with his prototype Lopakhin, this character's power is exacerbated by his intelligentsia relatives' inertia and gullibility. The male sibling in Ulitskaya's works, little more than a schematic representation, is anomalous for the author, who usually invests even minor characters with more psychological depth. This incongruity reaffirms the marginal place they inhabit in a narrative concerned with the matrilineal and matriarchal.

Ulitskaya continues Russian literature's tendency to see the family as a metaphorical as well as biological structure. Works such as *Daniel Stein* show the danger of using kinship to exclude; instead, the narratives urge readers to strive for understanding and tolerance in ethnicity, faith, and ideas. These virtues, crucial to the intelligentsia and part of Ulitskaya's overall message, form the basis for families of affinity: members choose to belong to a common group marked by ethical responses to life in difficult times. Blood ties are less important than their ideational potential, a stance that qualifies the author's treatment of corporeality that we discuss in chapter 1. However, as the emphasis on mothers and daughters demonstrates, kinship is meaningless without the *telesnost'* that supports it.

Ulitskaya's images of the family fall between two twentieth-century extremes. The Stalinist Great Family masked oppression and coercion by using kinship to naturalize exploitative relations. Its antipode, the family depicted by Petrushevskaia and other women writers during perestroika, used consanguinity to assail the material and spiritual corruption of the Great Family's legacy. Neither of these representations allowed a viable network of relations outside of their polarized worldviews. Ulitskaya's innovation is to link the family to values that transcend the two extremes, promoting tolerance and reconciliation that allow for continuity between generations.

3

AN OBSESSION WITH HISTORY

ULITSKAYA'S INTELLIGENTSIA
WRITES THE PAST

On a sunny day in May 2012, an unusual crowd of protesters gathered near the monument to poet Aleksandr Pushkin in central Moscow. The group, which eventually numbered close to ten thousand, walked calmly through the capital's streets, protesting Vladimir Putin's crackdown on the mass rallies that had shaken the city in the past half year. This event was different from its predecessors: instead of irate youths there were middle-aged women, retired people, and other members of the intelligentsia. The rally was a "test stroll," organized by author and opposition figure Boris Akunin to assert the public's right to gather without permission from the state. Among those in attendance was Ludmila Ulitskaya, drawn by the confluence of conscience and literature that is a hallmark of her prose, plays, and non-fiction. The protest's point of departure reinforces this connection: a statue of Russia's most revered writer, who himself had little love for oppression. The staid yet determined marchers embodied Ulitskaya's hopes for a population that, with the guidance of the intellectual class, can learn from literature's lessons of the past.[1]

Ulitskaya is, to borrow Andrew Wachtel's phrase, "obsessed with the idea of history." This condition, while symptomatic of post-Soviet writing, has been a constant throughout Russian literature at least since Nikolai Karamzin. Nor is Ulitskaya exceptional in arguing that the past offers warnings that only the intelligentsia is intellectually and ethically capable of heeding. This claim is an inherited discourse in her writing, built on a literary and historiographical rejection of orthodox Soviet conceptions. What is original is the lesson she gleans from these two stances: Ulitskaya's fictional record of the twentieth century originates

Ulitskaya inscribes a copy of *Daniel Stein, Interpreter* at the May 2012 "test stroll" in Moscow. (Alexander Efremov)

in a call for tolerance that underlies her work as a whole and contributes to her success as an author. In the process she conveys a strong focus on *byt*, body, and kinship, and together these themes create a domestication of history. Along with developing conceptions of corporeality that we explore in chapter 1, this section examines in greater depth the values and problems of *intelligenty* as a key image of the family of affinity we discuss in chapter 2.[2]

In Isaiah Berlin's famous analysis, the Russian intelligentsia believes in objective truth, a hidden meaning within culture that only intellectuals can uncover. Ulitskaya shares this view but fears that with the diminished role of *intelligenty* such knowledge may be lost forever—her worries connect the mission of the group to shaping the future in light of the past. This scenario of ontological apocalypse posits writing as a last source of hope.[3] Ulitskaya's heavy emphasis on the painful moments of the twentieth century is the latest manifestation of a national tendency for "serious" authors to create their own versions of history, a trend that, as Margaret Ziolkowski notes, has led some Russians to misread fiction as fact.[4]

The intelligentsia's interpretation of events varies greatly according to ideology. Ulitskaya, however, has a specific and subjective definition of *intelligenty*, exemplified by the sensitive poet Mikha in *The Big Green Tent* and humanist monk Daniel Stein in *Daniel Stein, Interpreter*. Such characters model sincerity and Western, liberal mores, signaling that this group is well-educated, shaped by prerevolutionary values that preclude totalitarianism and instead reflect ethical behavior. Some readers viewed them (and Ulitskaya) as traitors for displaying behavior more concerned with conscience than furthering national glory.[5] Our approach to Ulitskaya's reading of history does not diminish the real and indisputable death, torture, imprisonment, exile, and harassment of intellectuals before the collapse of socialism and their impoverishment and marginalization afterwards. There is, however, a need to critique the self-produced sacral image of the group, a depiction passed down from late Soviet culture and the Yeltsin years; this self-representation binds Ulitskaya's post-1991 texts to themes and plots dealing with the USSR. Examining the intelligentsia in a critical light is crucial to understanding this author's writing, given that her works assert the unique ability of these progressive thinkers to diagnose and cure the ailments of past and present.[6]

Idealization of the intelligentsia recalls Dmitrii Likhachev's impassioned defense of the group. In a 1993 letter to a literary journal the esteemed scholar and advocate of democracy lauds *intelligenty* for incarnating the best traditions of Russian history and argues that those who scorn them denigrate the intelligentsia's valor in the face of state persecution.[7] In this way he tried to sway public opinion during one of the darker periods in recent Russian history. However, there is a need for close examination of Likhachev's assertion, which builds on assumptions crucial to the image of the post-1991 intelligentsia and how Ulitskaya depicts such characters in her portrayal of the Soviet era. By defining them as virtuous (and tormented) individuals, Likhachev creates a paradigm for post-Soviet intellectuals, one inherited from previous martyrologies stretching from the saint's life to socialist realism. He asserts that the intelligentsia is best explained by looking at those who personify its values, a formulation that recalls the positive heroes of Stalinism as well as the Orthodox tradition the state spurned. Likhachev's choice of venue—the canonical liberal thick journal *New World* (*Novyi mir*)—reveals enduring faith in intelligentsia discourse. This hope, however, was mistaken: in the 1990s the readership of such magazines shrank precipitously. Ulitskaya, following Likhachev's dictum, portrays characters whose actions evince the essence of the intelligentsia, in the process creating a mythology that counters what she decries as morally reprehensible Soviet falsehoods. Among her fictional works, *The Big Green Tent* functions most directly as an apologia for the late Soviet intelligentsia. *Discarded Relics* continues her praise of the *intelligenty* in a memoir profiling members of her grandparents' generation—for her, kinship is inseparable from the ideals of the thinking class.[8]

Ulitskaya succinctly defines an *intelligent* as one who follows a specific code of moral behavior. This bond between identity and action echoes traditional conceptions of the intelligentsia as guided by sincerity, ethics, and knowledge that benefits the *narod*. All these lead, as Irina Paperno explains, to "an overwhelming sense of the historical significance of one's personal life." For the intelligentsia history, ethics, and self-presentation are intertwined, a situation that also shapes Ulitskaya's portrayal of families of affinity, which are based on ethics more than blood ties. While many of these characteristics come from nineteenth-century culture, the socialist period added a "double bind of privilege and martyrdom" that contrasted sharply with pre-1917 intellectuals' often literal position on the margins or in exile. The Soviet state for its part strove to associate the group with suspect convictions and a lack of political engagement—and, as several conservative critics we cite unwittingly reveal, the government succeeded in this task.[9]

Various types of *intelligenty* appear in Ulitskaya's prose. The "classic" intelligentsia includes characters involved in scientific or other academic inquiry, above all the Jewish wunderkind. Among these characters are Alik, Masha's husband (*Medea and Her Children*) and Alex, Ewa's husband (*Daniel Stein, Interpreter*). Members of the creative professions are also important, including painter Alik in *The Funeral Party* as well as the doomed poets Masha (*Medea and Her Children*) and Mikha (*The Big Green Tent*). The older generation provides prominent and positive personages: Medea exemplifies their moral acuity and sincerity. As we describe in chapters 1 and 2, Ulitskaya persistently endows grandparents in her works with a humane and ethical approach to life. This older value system is inseparable from the intellectual pedigree we outline here; it aided an intelligentsia that matured before the intrusion of the Soviet state.

The false intelligentsia also figures in Ulitskaya's works. Aleksandr Solzhenitsyn labels this group "smatterers" (*obrazovanshchina*): those who have the intellect but not the ethics of the intelligentsia. Some live in relative luxury because of colluding with the government. Novelist Eleonora in "The Writer's Daughter," the mother of troubled Communist Masha, has been rewarded extravagantly for serving the state: "There was a home like none anyone had. There were bookshelves with sliding glass panels, gilded spines, albums, papers, many with the defunct letter 'yat' [. . .] and nanny Dusia, squat, with a wart and a worn apron around her stomach, and a mother [. . .], a writer, laureate of the Stalin Prize, with mouselike eyes, a spiteful, smart, and passionate woman. We'll call her Eleonora. Her major novel, dedicated to a partisan girl who died at the hands of the fascists, was included in the school curriculum and compositions and essays were written about it."[10]

This luxurious apartment is rich in objects, including pre-1917 books, manuscripts, Dusia and the owner herself. Material wealth implicates those associated with it; in a parodic reworking of Marxist theory, Ulitskaya reveals how under socialism state patronage reduces people to the status of things while objects become more important. Eleonora for her part is so closely connected to the regime that her novel is read by children across the USSR. Likewise, her estranged husband actively participated in the purges. In *Discarded Relics* Ulitskaya notes that Eleonora is based on Stalinist poet Margarita Aliger, who was the mother of a childhood friend. The character's apartment, dacha at Peredelkino, and chauffeur are all dubious material comforts; they reiterate her corruption by characterizing this *intelligentka* in ways that emphasize the world of things instead of the ideas or morality that the intelligentsia embraces. Eleonora clearly fails to live up to the standards of Likhachev and Ulitskaya. Compromising ethics—especially for political or personal rewards—is immoral.[11]

The author also portrays inaction as antithetical yet endemic to the intellectual caste. The protagonist's intelligentsia family in *Sincerely Yours, Shurik* cannot realize its potential: despite great musical promise, Shurik's father Aleksandr Sigizmundovich ends up as an accompanist, while his mother Vera works as a secretary in a theater after failing to make her mark as an actress. Ulitskaya's frequent comments in support of intellectuals show no concern over their stymied plans, yet her intelligentsia characters seldom achieve the success their abilities suggest is within their reach. The seeming contradiction between the defense of the thinking class and portrayal of its shortcomings is in part a realistic element common to the author's fiction and nonfiction works; indeed, the intelligentsia as a group has been concerned about its inertia and superfluity since the nineteenth century.[12]

As we note in the introduction, during the post-Soviet period the intellectual class has been greatly diminished, and its very survival remains a contentious topic. While Clark acknowledges that an intelligentsia of sorts still exists today, she is not hopeful about its future in part because of its reliance on "print-based culture," which itself has dramatically transformed in recent decades.[13] After 1991 this group felt itself under siege in a new way, as evident in Ulitskaya's warnings about the mass culture of consumerism, whose pernicious avarice replaces enduring values with material objects and irresponsibility. Other critics variously attributed the intelligentsia's decline to market forces, as well as disintegration of the state that had served as a central opponent and, through generous funding, often a partial enabler of *intelligenty*. Another reason was the intelligentsia's failure to anticipate how the *narod* would react after Communism. The final factor is especially telling, as it posits that the common people and intellectuals fundamentally disagree. Against this unwelcoming background and a lament about the declining importance of the written word due to "the structure of contemporary culture," Ulitskaya reiterates the age-old intelligentsia plea for good literature as a tool to instill consciousness in the common people. Worthy writing must make sense of history, a task that only intellectuals can manage.[14]

Rewriting the Past: The Intelligentsia and Trauma

Mark Lipovetsky and Alexander Etkind identify the task of reassessing history as one of the core concerns of literature in the post-Soviet period. The tendency of contemporary authors to engage with the (Soviet) past, these scholars note, unites postmodernist writers as well as those, like Ulitskaya, who embrace a more traditional aesthetic. Her plots, which take place in the USSR but were authored after 1991, are part of a larger trend in contemporary Russian writing. Themes of sadness, loss, and trauma are common in these works regardless of style and mode. Discussion of history directly leads to critique of contemporary society. Etkind asserts that writers such as Viktor Pelevin, Vladimir Sorokin, and Dmitrii Bykov respond "not to an abstract 'trauma of modernization' but to the post-Soviet situation of recent catastrophe and present obliviousness." This notion of social criticism motivates Ulitskaya's revisiting of the Soviet past, an act intended to combat the apathy and complacency of today's readership. Reassessment of history is not limited to literature, as Putin's machinations in Ukraine make all too evident. Likewise, recent textbook debates have called into question inherited Soviet narratives about major events (especially the Great Patriotic War) as well as the content of historical texts and the right to authorship. Description of the past is increasingly ideologized during the Putin era; sometimes entire historical periods are condemned, as has happened recently with conservatives' attacks on the Khrushchev era.[15]

The Thaw's current ambivalent image repeats a tendency evident earlier, as in the film *Moscow Does Not Believe in Tears*, which portrays duplicity among 1950s liberals. Some recent discussions have highlighted the era's failures in order to attack perestroika's liberal politics, which began as emulation of the Thaw. Others have emphasized the positive aspects of society after Stalin: increased freedom, hope for socialism, and the prominence of a voice countering the state's. Denis Kozlov observes a conservative view in the early Yeltsin years that scorns the "confusion and instability" of the *shestidesiatniki* and criticizes them for their "civic cowardice and opportunism, for presumed absenteeism from true political action in favor of sociability, reading, movie-going, romantic travel, poetry recitals, and guitar singing." This deeply flawed opinion has become more pronounced under Putin.[16]

Kozlov's biting characterization of a supposedly self-involved generation that destroyed the USSR illuminates one cause of Ulitskaya's interest in the Thaw. The starting point of *The Big Green Tent*—the death of Stalin and the nascent Khrushchev era—is a crucial moment. Clark and Boris Dubin identify this era as a time of renewed vitality for the thinking caste: the intelligentsia established a niche within Soviet society, especially among the future *shestidesiatniki*, while refusing to acknowledge the role many of its older members had played during Stalinism.[17] Ulitskaya wrote *The Big Green Tent* in great part to rehabilitate this generation, whose opposition to the government is often faulted for post-Soviet chaos. Instead, the novel reveals, it is a cruel and calculating state that is to blame as it destroys or drives out the most talented, those who could have positively influenced their society then and later. *The Big Green Tent* follows a group of dissidents from their school days under Stalin to the Yeltsin era. While the narrative chronicles the decline of the intelligentsia, Ulitskaya's comments and the work's subject indicate that she retains hope in intellectuals' ideals after 1991 precisely because the group has shrunk significantly as a social stratum. This optimism initially appears as a pyrrhic form of persistence: Soviet thinkers opposing the state unwittingly enacted their own demise by wishing for an end to the oppressive regime. For Ulitskaya, however, a diminished intelligentsia means a return to purer principles. The thinning of the *intelligenty*—the persistent scapegoat of Soviet history—thus acquired a Darwinian tinge. Those who managed to retain their intelligentsia identity (i.e., morality and sincerity) in the post-perestroika period became the standard-bearers for their class. Intellectuals' attenuation as a physical presence ensured their continuity as moral arbiters of the embattled national past. Mikhail Edel'shtein echoes this assertion in his discussion of *The Big Green Tent* as both a "history textbook" and a "monument to departed friends"; the second description links the intelligentsia to the family of affinity that appears throughout Ulitskaya's fiction.[18]

Two intelligentsia authors—Aleksandr Solzhenitsyn and Iurii Trifonov—typify the melding of history and literature in late Soviet writing and signal how Ulitskaya responds to this era. Ulitskaya observes that when *The Gulag Archipelago* began circulating as *samizdat*, it forced society to see the "truth" in history. *The Big Green Tent*, a novel intimately shaped by the nexus of underground literature, the intelligentsia, and the USSR, relates the difficulties caused when a copy of Solzhenitsyn's opus makes its way to the KGB.[19] Trifonov, who consistently links the past and private life, is more influential than Solzhenitsyn for Ulitskaya. In this sense Rosalind Marsh may be incorrect when she posits that Ulitskaya's focus on internal values would have been attacked during the Soviet era: Trifonov, drawing on the legacy of Solzhenitsyn, legitimated these topics in works such as *House on the Embankment* (*Dom na naberezhnoi*). Geography provides another affinity—Ulitskaya and Trifonov are major contributors to the Moscow text in Russian literature. In *The Big Green Tent*, thanks to teacher Viktor Iul'evich Shengeli, the future dissidents learn about the history of the capital's intelligentsia via excursions through the city streets: "On Wednesdays Viktor Iul'evich dragged his lovers of Russian writing [. . .] through Moscow and took them, playing on his flute, out of an impoverished and painful time into a place where thinking reigned [*rabotala mysl'*], where freedom lived, as well as music and various arts. Right here is where it all resided! Behind these windows! [. . .] The renaming of the Moscow streets grated on Viktor Iul'evich's ears and he constantly referred to them by their old [pre-1917] names with the children."[20]

Viktor Iul'evich combines the status of surrogate father, instructor, and *intelligent* as he molds the future generation. These outings familiarize the boys with the topoi of the intellectual caste; Shengeli introduces his pupils to Moscow's cultural geography in an attempt to inoculate them against the capital's overbearing, "impoverished and painful" Stalinist presence. This image understandably is more striking than those found in Trifonov's works, which obliquely critique the totalitarian capital through nostalgia for a time before urban expansion and renovation. Longing for a departed past appears in Trifonov's prose through images of everyday life, the third commonality between his writing and Ulitskaya's. Trifonov's legitimation of *byt* shaped the *shestidesiatniki*, influenced women's prose, and set the stage for Ulitskaya's blending of the family, quotidian, history, and literature.[21]

Ulitskaya, Solzhenitsyn, and Trifonov uphold literature as documentation, which is a continuum between autobiography at one end and fiction emphasizing history at the other. Works such as *Daniel Stein, Interpreter* and the autobiographical sections of *The People of Our Tsar* appeal to the "real" nature of narrated facts, yet historical events appear in all of Ulitskaya's works. Accuracy is not the issue; instead, she lays claim to the sense of deeper truth that Berlin sees the intelligentsia appropriating and that Dubin calls an obsession with *iskrennost'*. Post-Stalinist authors conjoined these concerns to sincerity in literature, particularly documentary genres. What distinguishes Ulitskaya is her goal in conjoining fiction and history: she urges readers to understand the people whose ethnicity, ideas, and bodies make them outcasts in Russian society.[22] A generation earlier Trifonov had employed a domestic focus in his critique of Stalinism. Ulitskaya expands this idea, addressing not only the politically repressed, but also those whose religion, body, or sexuality was unacceptable. Exploiting Russian literature's malleable relationship with history, Ulitskaya's intellectuals act out the tragedy of principled humanity in a barbaric era.

Taking the Past Personally:
Reading the Body, Ethnicity, and History

For Ulitskaya, brutality is the precursor to narrative. Several of her novels, including *Sincerely Yours, Shurik*; *The Kukotskii Case*; and *Daniel Stein, Interpreter*, share temporal origins in late Stalinism; *Medea and Her Children* and *The Funeral Party* address roughly the same time frame, and *The Big Green Tent* focuses on the Thaw and Stagnation periods. Most of her long works have an overarching master plot that charts individuals' coming of age along with the slow disintegration of their families and friendships.[23] The movement of history is yoked to kinship, the dominant framework through which Ulitskaya depicts the past. As outlined in chapter 2, she tends to approach the past through the family, and shared ideals are more likely than blood relationships to determine meaningful bonds; as we explain at the end of the present chapter, this trait is inherited partially from Boris Pasternak's *Doctor Zhivago*. While her works assert the primacy of ethics, Ulitskaya also believes in what Alexei Yurchak describes as the value of comprehending society through lived experience and distilling meaning from everyday life.[24]

In her study of Soviet memoirs, Paperno asserts that their authors found the intelligentsia to be stronger than consanguinity as a foundation for "identity and authorship." Ulitskaya revises this model; in her works, kinship of ideas is the fundamental basis for the construction of community. The *intelligenty* are a special family of affinity, joined by ethics, education, and moral behavior in difficult times. Indeed, *The Big Green Tent* illustrates how at the beginning of the Brezhnev era, shared concern for others, revulsion for Stalinism, and love of reading bring intellectuals together in a way that biological kinship cannot. Ol'ga's experience in the same novel confirms this assertion, as she transforms from a loyal Soviet citizen reared by the false intelligentsia to a full-fledged opponent of the regime, in the process marrying dissident Il'ia. Antonina Naumovna, Ol'ga's doctrinaire mother, is an editor who resembles Eleonora in "The Writer's Daughter." Both have large apartments, a host of special privileges, and truly believe in the success of Soviet society. Learning that Ol'ga has been expelled from university, Antonina Naumovna is horrified: "Olia, a good girl, had gotten mixed up with corrupting influences [*tletvornogo vliianiia*] in that university and, when one of the university instructors, a hidden anti-Soviet and, it goes without saying, enemy of the people, had been imprisoned for libel published abroad, [O'lga] had signed, along with certain of her classmates—fools who had been led astray—a letter in his defense." The third-person narrator gives a skillful, *skaz*-like rendering of the Soviet clichés Antonina Ivanovna parrots as she condemns the "corrupting influences" and "libel published abroad" that have caused her previously "good" daughter's expulsion. In doing so, Ol'ga's mother ironically justifies those such as Viktor Iul'evich, who train the younger generation to resist the government contamination of culture implicit in her discourse. For her part, Ol'ga, acting on the values Ulitskaya upholds, distances herself from a biological family implicated in state repression—ultimately ethics take precedence over blood ties.[25]

Reading is a formative influence in Ol'ga's transformation and a prerequisite for membership in Ulitskaya's intelligentsia; indeed, Dubin observes that books have lives that parallel and comment on those of their owners. The printed word is important because of its material existence and the morals it conveys. In *Discarded Relics*, Ulitskaya notes how her paternal grandfather, while imprisoned in the Lubyanka, lovingly created the cover for a volume of Anatole France. Several tomes in *The Big Green Tent* have adventures that implicate those who read them. Mikha and his friends lose a briefcase containing an early *samizdat* copy of *1984*; the poet's later reading of George Orwell's novel confirms his realization that the Soviet revolution has failed. Ulitskaya sees this dystopia as a model for literature, noting that Orwell was more prescient than any historian or philosopher in combining literature and history through a critique of iniquity. Books possess a physical gravitas that solidifies the metaphorical weight of the intelligentsia, which has produced, read, and tried to protect them from the predacious Soviet state. *The Big Green Tent* demonstrates how this love of the written word is an integral part of daily life: for intellectuals, there can be no boundary between *byt* and the realm of ideas.[26]

Describing the adventurous lives of books literalizes Ulitskaya's idea that fiction and society are interdependent. However, her innovation comes from another connection: joining the physical form to history and thus compelling the reader to use *telesnost'* to interpret the past through everyday life. *Byt*, body, reading, and history are interlinked—one cannot exist without the others. Female corporeality is transhistorical, characterizing Stalinism (as we examine in chapter 1) and Ulitskaya's depiction of the Thaw and Brezhnev years. For instance, in *The Kukotskii Case* when Pavel Alekseevich's daughter Tanya discovers her sexuality, the narrator notes that she has no idea that during this time young people all across the globe are doing the same. *Medea and Her Children* elaborates on this sexual revolution and its consequences. The novel's imperturbable protagonist quietly observes the romantic adventures of the relatives who come to stay at her Crimean home: "The young mothers with babies or toddlers usually arrived at the beginning of the season; their working husbands didn't stay long, a couple of weeks, rarely a month. Friends of some sort would come, rent a bed in the Lower Village, and at night they would come secretly to the house, moaning and crying out on the other side of Medea's wall. Then those mothers separated from one husband and married another. The new husbands brought up old children and fathered new ones; the stepbrothers and stepsisters visited each other, and then the ex-husbands came back with their new wives and new children to spend the holidays together with the older ones."[27]

History comes from family. Both involve the cycle of marriage, birth, divorce, and remarriage, a chain of events that the novel depicts as an inevitable, sometimes chaotic process that marks a generation's place in time. The kinship and *telesnost'* of Medea's relatives give a new meaning to one critic's observation that coming to understand the body (whether one's own or that of others) means knowing the world. It is through corporeality and consanguinity that Ulitskaya conveys the harmony and trauma of the past, in the process reminding readers how physicality denotes and delimits an individual's place in society. This is especially true of the author's less fortunate characters, whose lives have often been literally deformed by the state. What Paperno refers to as the human document allows history to be understood at the level of scars and deformities accrued through the brutal twentieth century, a powerful lesson for a contemporary Russia intent on glorifying its dark past and the misguided present.[28]

Members of the intelligentsia claim the right to chronicle history even as they experience it, making the past simultaneously lived experience and a matter of preservation. To borrow a prominent phrase from *The Kukotskii Case*, only they have the right to speak (*pravo golosa*) about history. This assumption, as Paperno demonstrates, has long been within intellectuals' "historical self-consciousness," which she defines as "the sense of self derived from the coincidence of personal life and world history." Ulitskaya's oeuvre thus reflects a persistent intellectual concern. In a trope inherited from Aleksandr Herzen's *My Past and Thoughts* (*Byloe i dumy*), authors of memoirs and diaries (as well as many of Ulitskaya's characters) "import catastrophic historicism that contributes both to a strong sense of self and a sense of community to which one belongs—'the intelligentsia.'" Intellectuals experience the events of this "catastrophic historicism" firsthand and, in narrating them, use the past's calamities as justification for their elitist stance: only *intelligenty* can make sense of Russia's bloody and chaotic legacy. In a cynical parody of this notion in *The Big Green Tent*, Il'ia's KGB interrogator, who claims to have an interest in contemporary history, tries to convince him that truth about the past is best preserved in the archives of the secret police. Such an idea renders the state responsible for recording history, a terrifying prospect for the liberal intelligentsia.[29]

Ulitskaya's *intelligenty* likewise hold themselves responsible for educating others. In *Daniel Stein, Interpreter*, intellectual Pawel Kociński chastises Ewa for her desire "not to know about the past in order to maintain [...] equilibrium in the present [...]. [If] we conspire to erase the past from our memories and shield our children's minds from the horrors of those years, we will be failing in our duty to the future." To this end, Pawel composes a first-person history of Yiddish-speaking people in Eastern Europe to document more accurately the culture destroyed by totalitarianism. For Ulitskaya, *intelligenty* such as Pawel must preserve what the state—whether fascist or Stalinist—attempts to erase. In like manner, her attacks on Putin's rehabilitation of Soviet culture assert that eliding the wrongs of history violates the intelligentsia's duties of upholding sincerity, educating the common people, and conveying the truth of the past.[30]

Pawel's choice of subject in his project sheds light on an intriguing aspect of Ulitskaya's characterization of the intelligentsia: her persistent and multilayered connection of intellectuals to another mistrusted minority in Russia—Jews. Given the prominent role played by Jewish intellectuals (and Ulitskaya's own ethnic background), this association by itself is unsurprising. Critic Mikhail Gorelik, for instance, argues that the words "*intelligent*" and "Jew" are effectively synonyms. However, as throughout Ulitskaya's corpus, a common trope of post-Stalinist culture undergoes a series of shifts to become original. At the most basic level, the *intelligent*/Jew is the object of hostility, as when Mikha (*The Big Green Tent*) unwisely shares a *samizdat* novel by Iulii Daniel' with his colleague. The latter calls Mikha an ungrateful "kike" (*zhidovskaia morda*) and denounces him, causing Mikha to lose his teaching position at a school for deaf-mutes. Ulitskaya herself has been the object of similar vitriol and attacked as a putative future emigrant (viz., disloyal Jew).[31]

In Ulitskaya's works both Russian Jews and the intelligentsia see the common people as a frightening and unknowable mass, prone to either spontaneous violence or participation in prolonged attacks (the Holocaust and Stalinist terror). The result is a constant feeling of marginality and estrangement within one's native land.[32] Professor Neuhaus, who voices many of the key ideas in *Daniel Stein, Interpreter*, illuminates another set of similarities between Jews and *intelligenty*.

> The immense vitality of Judaism, the great faith of a small people, lost among hundreds of other tribes of the Middle East, of Judaism which has given birth to two of the greatest world religions, is founded on two principles. One of these is restrictive. The behavior of a Jew is strictly regulated [...]. Such is the Talmud, a comprehensive set of laws for good, correct behavior.

> So then, what is the second principle I mentioned? It is the principle of complete and totally unfettered freedom of thought. The Jews were given a sacred text on which they have been working for centuries. [...] In this area, the Jews were afforded a fantastic freedom unheard of in any other religion. There is effectively a total absence of prohibitions on intellectual investigation. Everything is open to discussion and there is no dogma.[33]

As we note in chapter 2, Neuhaus is a positive surrogate father for Daniel's parishioner Hilda, a role that adds to the weight his opinions carry in the novel. The professor maintains that the ethical and hermeneutic strengths of Jews come from their holy texts and have helped them survive among alien groups, a scenario that strongly resembles Ulitskaya's conception of the besieged intelligentsia. Jews have two sources of resilience. The first, he posits, is the codification of proper behavior, while the second is freedom of thought stimulated by a strong tradition of interpretation. Both of these claims — as opposed to their complex reality — evoke Ulitskaya's characterizations of her positive intellectual characters; hinting at this, in a critique of the relationship between intelligentsia and the state, she claims that the first group is governed by a set of ethics and cannot steal (unlike the government). The author's prose suggests that Jews and *intelligenty* have more in common than they may realize. Ultimately the two groups' similarities rely upon perceived intellectual rigor and ostracism by others. Professor Neuhaus argues that Jews are characterized by a constant attempt to better themselves mentally, a worldview that parallels Ulitskaya's hopeful assertion that crisis is a healthy condition because it forces constant questioning of assumptions.[34]

A number of the writer's *intelligenty* defend Russia's Jewish minority, whether openly or tacitly. Viktor Iul'evich, for instance, lays bare Ulitskaya's tenets concerning prejudice, ethnicity, and class. Anti-Semitism bothers the beloved literature teacher, himself part Jewish, "most of all aesthetically: ugly people, dressed in ugly clothes, behaving in an ugly way." His assessment ascribes hatred of Jews to the uncultured, whose unattractive garments match their distasteful thoughts and base actions. For Viktor Iul'evich, anti-Semitism precludes sophistication, an assessment that is obviously false in Russian culture (particularly before 1953). The teacher, like his creator, nonetheless decries anti-Semitism as anathema to *intelligenty*.[35]

The thinking caste to which Viktor Iul'evich belongs is itself under threat. For the last two decades the intelligentsia has undergone massive change, as optimists maintain, and may now be a matter of interest only to historians, as Vladislav Zubok and others contend. Such disagreement suggests the lingering presence of *intelligenty* and the values of discussion and inquiry Likhachev and others ascribe to it. At the beginning of "A Happy Incident" ("Schastlivyi sluchai") in *Women's Lies*, Zhenia notes that in the new market economy, "Many people [in the intelligentsia] began to drown. Some of them drowned, some learned how to swim, and there were those who in the shaken-up world found their bearings and made a splash [*poshel v bol'shoe plavanie*]." Zhenia falls into the middle category; though she adapts to the chaos of the 1990s, she neither prospers nor ever fully accepts life after socialism.[36] We learn less about Zhenia's life during the Yeltsin years than we do about her acquaintances and relatives during late socialism, a fact that underscores this character's (and author's) interest in the latter era. The single most detailed picture of post-Soviet intellectuals in Ulitskaya's work places the blame for their decline squarely on the individuals themselves. In the play *Russian Jam* a bumbling intelligentsia clan lives at a dacha slated for destruction, recalling, as we have noted earlier, Chekhov's *Cherry Orchard*. Elena is an impractical middle-aged woman who has passed up a decent job in Moscow. Her brother, the New Russian Rostislav, plans to develop the land where the dacha now stands and calls the family "superfluous people," an indictment that conflates the privilege, inertia, and ineptitude attributed to the intelligentsia in the early years of the USSR. The family loses their ancestral home not because of lawless capitalism but due to their own moral bankruptcy, a state Likhachev and Ulitskaya find antithetical to intelligentsia sincerity. For Andrei Arkhangel'skii, the play depicts one big, unhappy clan and insinuates that intellectuals have failed to create an alternative to the mythologized Great Family that dominated the Soviet era.[37] The plot reveals this state of affairs to be only one source of the family's crisis. In *Russian Jam* the seeds of doom are not planted but grafted: the grandfather earned a dacha and a Stalin Prize for his work to create a new gooseberry called the Dawn of Communism. This adroit reference brings to mind Chekhov's story "Gooseberries" ("Kryzhovnik"), which depicts a foolish landowner refusing to admit his incompetence. In Ulitskaya's play, by contrast, the country house's original occupant is guilty of a much graver crime. During Stalinism he persecuted other geneticists and thus committed the ultimate sin—attacking his fellow *intelligenty*.[38]

Russian Jam presents Ulitskaya's most complex set of intertexts as it portrays the intelligentsia. One character, Natal'ia Ivanovna, comments that Chekhov's portrayal of family is overly ironic, a quip that directs audience attention to her own dysfunctional kin. Another relative wants to sell cherry jam (even the container harboring a dead mouse) for a hundred dollars a jar. The intermission reduces characters to a set of meaningless sounds, effectively exaggerating Chekhov's combination of estranged individuals and their verbal idiosyncrasies. Ulitskaya confesses to having disliked the playwright until she realized that he was creating a theatre of the absurd, a scenario that fits her critique of this shiftless group of *intelligenty*. *Russian Jam* is a less nuanced and ambivalent work than *The Cherry Orchard*, and the audience is left with the conclusion that this family's lax ethics and squabbling are more to blame for their problems than a quickly changing society.[39]

As a rule, however, Ulitskaya portrays intellectuals as a marginalized group that has remained morally pure in the face of constant pressure from the state and market forces; for her, those who survived the Yeltsin years are the hope of both intelligentsia and the nation as a whole. Despite striking evidence that *intelligenty* and government have always had a symbiotic antagonism, Ulitskaya assumes that this segment of the population advocates Western-style civil society and tolerance.[40] As we discuss at the beginning of the chapter, such a selective definition disqualifies prominent figures such as writer Valentin Rasputin (not to mention the bombastic politician Vladimir Zhirinovsky). Likewise, although some of her characters combine intelligentsia values with business sense, for Ulitskaya intellectuals must choose noble poverty over commercialization, a choice she herself faced when penning a screenplay of questionable artistic value during the Yeltsin era.[41]

As *The Big Green Tent* asserts, late Soviet dissidents are the moral predecessors to and inspiration for today's embattled intelligentsia. This ethical legacy is a powerful connection between Ulitskaya as a post-1991 author and her Soviet-era subjects. These dissidents, she claims, need no defense, since their selfless dedication is evident to everyone.[42] However, as a number of critics contend, such an assumption is at best naïve. In the 1990s, Masha Gessen observes, the apathy of the apolitical *narod* was the enemy. Now disinterest has turned to hostility, in which "dissident" and "intellectual" are often synonymous with "Russophobe." In *The Big Green Tent* KGB investigator Chibikov offers a sinister counterbalance to liberal rhetoric. Threatening to arrest dissident Il'ia, the official notes that even the Decembrists—the model of prerevolutionary intelligentsia for Soviet thinkers—chose to denounce their fellow conspirators rather than lie to the state. Through this allusion Ulitskaya implies that, à la Dostoevsky's Grand Inquisitor, the powerful subvert reason in order to confuse and manipulate the moral individual.[43]

Given the backlash against the thinking class, the 1991 coup that is a focal point of *The Funeral Party* was a rare moment of glory when the intelligentsia and the *narod* stood together to defend reform (and thus unwittingly hasten the collapse of Soviet society). As we note in chapter 1, this novel, Ulitskaya's only long work to focus on perestroika, recalls the informal gatherings that marked the culture of the *shestidesiatniki*. One such moment occurs on a fateful day in August. In a scene of central importance, émigrés, former defectors, and visitors from the USSR sit in Alik's sweltering loft, watching on television as Soviets come together to claim their democratic future: "Something incomprehensible was happening: a twitching marionette popped up, a bathhouse superintendent, a moustached man with a face like a dog, half-devils, half-people, phantasmagoria from the dream sequence in *Evgeny Onegin*, and the tanks. Troops were entering Moscow. Huge tanks were sliding through the streets of the city, and it was unclear who was fighting whom." Even during this moment of togetherness, Alik's intelligentsia friends are horrified by the appearance of the coup leaders, apparently taken straight from the ranks of the "bathhouse superintendent" and those whose animal-like features recall the worst aspects of the *narod*. This moment foretells the alienation and hostility that lie ahead, as the author herself notes, when the intelligentsia will be relegated to poverty while both the common people and *intelligenty* try to survive the Yeltsin era. The enthusiasm of 1991 gave way to defeat, implying that intellectuals too participated in the patriotism of despair as national identity devolved into a rhetoric of loss. This malaise produced a backlash against liberal thinkers and their discredited democratic ideology. Misunderstanding and hatred resonate in Ulitskaya's narratives, which from a post-Soviet standpoint depict the differences between *narod* and intelligentsia as a core feature of culture in the USSR.[44]

Antagonism and Devotion: Writing the *Intelligentsia* and the *Narod*

While sympathetic portrayals of the *narod* appear in the author's prose, the majority reflect intelligentsia wariness and the common people's reciprocal scorn for the thinking class. In a trope inherited from women's prose in particular and post-1953 literature in general, communal apartment neighbors are especially reviled (whether as anti-Semites or as thieves). Likewise, at the dacha the incompetent intelligentsia family in *Russian Jam* is cheated by Semyon, the Jew-hating handyman.[45] Some of Ulitskaya's supporters also contribute to the bifurcation between intellectuals and the masses, accepting this division as axiomatic. One praises the author for appearing at a festival in Boldino, noting that writers have long journeyed into the provinces to meet their readers. The location of this particular venue—one of Pushkin's places of exile—links Ulitskaya to a tradition that pairs intelligentsia/center/author with *narod*/periphery/reader, a rhetoric that assumes the former must educate the latter. Such a theory underlies Ulitskaya's laudable but failed project to supply books to far-flung libraries that literally and metaphorically seek knowledge from Moscow, the geographical and intellectual capital.[46]

Two loci exemplify the *narod* in Ulitskaya's works. The first is the *elektrichka* (or its double, the third-class train car). In the autobiographical story "Moscow-Podrezkovo, 1992" ("Moskva-Podrezkovo, 1992") the narrator rides a commuter train in one of the darkest years of the Yeltsin era. While purchasing her ticket at the station, she is astounded by a homeless woman: "A dream of Fellini, one of Salvador Dali's visions: by the doors to the ticket counter, sitting on a trash can, painted with a silver that had long ago started fading, swinging its dirty, bare feet that did not reach the floor, was a figure from a fantasy—a poor old woman in a light-brown raincoat that was silver with grease. Her thick gray hair waved in the slight breeze, and her face was painted silver, her nose with a thicker layer, her cheeks with a thinner one . . ."[47]

This is the piteous nightmare of the common people, driven mad by the poverty and hopelessness of an uncaring society that has discarded the less fortunate. The narrator, whose car is being repaired, is shocked by the train station, which in the 1990s was a living spectacle of the trauma and chaos of the Yeltsin period. On the *elektrichka* the narrator listens to a drunken man rant about the impending redemption of Russia, which will come at the expense of all foreigners: "'We'll gather our strength—and cut them all up. It will be a great time!' His eyes had a gleam like those of Pugachev." Later he utters another commonplace, cursing the laziness of the common people. The comparison with rebel and folk hero Emel'ian Pugachev recalls Pushkin's *The Captain's Daughter* (*Kapitanskaia dochka*), a historical novel that portrays a bloody rebellion by blending historiography and fiction. Pushkin's work and

Ulitskaya's story attribute a fundamental alterity to the *narod*: its elemental, spontaneous passion, which has the potential for violence or kindness, is foreign to the intelligentsia. Another intertext is Venedikt Erofeev's *Moscow to the End of the Line* (*Moskva-Petushki*), whose alcoholic intellectual narrator seeks understanding from the common people and instead is murdered. Though in Ulitskaya's story the result is not nearly as dramatic, the moral is the same: the *narod* is intractable, unknowable, and hostile.[48]

The labor camp is also linked with the common folk and, predictably, more starkly emphasizes its potential for brutality. In *The Big Green Tent*, while Mikha serves a prison sentence for helping deported Crimean Tatars, a camp official joyfully crushes his glasses. The dissident observes that for such people all political prisoners (i.e., intellectuals) look alike; the camp criminals for their part enjoy destroying idealistic thinkers. Continuing a trope from intelligentsia accounts of the Gulag, in *The Big Green Tent* the thinking class becomes the persecuted moral minority in a bestial wasteland. This scenario is not limited to the camps, a lesson Mikha and his friends learned as teenagers when battling neighborhood bullies. More broadly, in the 1980s human rights leader Ludmila Alexeyeva praised dissidents as isolated "cells of humanity," implying that the *narod* by contrast is an undifferentiated and apathetic mass. As Ulitskaya's autobiographical narrator finds on the train, the common people outnumber—and do not heed—the intellectual.[49]

Ulitskaya does not mince words over some Russians' low level of morality and responsibility. In a contentious assertion, she links the growth of Western religion to civilization while maintaining that Orthodoxy has stunted culture. Likewise, in *The Big Green Tent* Vinberg, a German Jew who was in the Gulag for twenty years after fleeing Nazism, characterizes his adopted homeland as infantile. Discussing the USSR, he complains: "'A childish country,' he said to his wife, whom he had acquired in the camp hospital. 'A childish country! Culture blocks natural reactions in adults but not in children. And when there is no culture, there is no blocking. There is a cult of the father, obedience, and at same the time unregulated childish aggression.'" Physical brutality, family, and the state are interconnected: the USSR has its Father of the Peoples, Vinberg maintains, but no check on its immaturity and violence. By implication, the Soviet Union has yet to develop to a European level, a woeful state of affairs Ulitskaya also ascribes to the Russian Federation. Her image of a juvenile and uncultured nation, a portrayal that characterizes the *narod* in corporeal terms, continues (liberal) intelligentsia assumptions that the common people need intellectuals' moral guidance if Russia is to make progress.[50]

Ulitskaya likewise depicts the *narod* through the cultural intertext of folklore. This is a common feature of high culture's image of the common people; Russian literature has long incorporated folkloric motifs. One of Ulitskaya's heroes, dissident intellectual Andrei Siniavskii, became familiar with the folktale during research expeditions and his time in labor camps. For him the wondertale in particular is radiant in both literal and symbolic senses: "Its images are incandescent: golden locks, golden plumes, golden scales, golden manes, golden roofs [. . .] an iridescent blaze of colors." For Siniavskii and Ulitskaya, the *narod* is capable of creating narratives of astounding beauty. However, as we explain in chapter 1, seemingly wondrous beauty often accompanies cruelty, like that of abusive husband Finist in Ulitskaya's story "Finist the Bright Falcon" ("Finist Iasnyi Sokol"). Unlike in the wondertale, the protagonist neither magically transforms nor brings happiness to his beloved.[51]

Death is sometimes depicted via the rituals of folklore. In the film *A Woman for All*, boisterous working-class Mariia sings folk songs from the North; later the *pesni* accompany her funeral. Intellectual neighbor Anna, who earlier has scolded Mariia, realizes by the end of the film that Mariia represents the kindness and simplicity that are the best aspects of the *narod*. Hagiographic aspects accompany death in two linked stories whose titles themselves evoke saints' lives: "They Lived Long . . ." ("Oni zhili dolgo . . ."), ". . . And died on the same day" (". . . i umerli v odin den'"). In "They Lived Long . . ." the daughter of the deceased explains that her parents were virgins when they married; they are to share the same grave, and a double rainbow appears during their funeral. Ulitskaya, who observes that from an early age she respected death, uses sacred topoi to draw attention to those who lived humbly but ethically. As with Medea, they need no grand monument or elaborate posthumous praise; instead, their grateful relatives recognize their quiet but moral lives. The intertext of the saint's life (*zhitie*) is fitting for Ulitskaya's selective appropriation of Orthodox theology, which we address in chapter 4: *zhitiia* have long blended Church doctrine and popular belief. Ulitskaya's use of this genre, like her portrayal of folklore as a whole, implies that the intelligentsia has the right to use and modify art forms of the common people.[52]

When the thinking caste tries to mold the *narod* itself, results range from simple bungling to utter disaster. In *The Kukotskii Case*, Zhenia dislikes Toma's apartment (once the home of Pavel Alekseevich and Elena) for its stink of poverty and *kommunalka*. Her real concern is Toma's callous approach to caring for Elena, Toma's adoptive mother. As we noted in chapter 1, Toma has failed to absorb the Kukotskii family's intelligentsia values: tolerance for others, sincerity, and self-sacrifice. This is in part due to Elena's muted antipathy for her. However, for Ulitskaya the underlying conclusion is that intellectuals and the *narod* cannot mix; such association is precluded by the different sets of values that are for her more meaningful than other ties. Zhenia's dislike of Toma underscores the permanent and unbridgeable gap between the intelligentsia and the *narod*, and the concomitant quiet call for cultural segregation questions the status of the thinking class.[53]

Several recurring events shape Ulitskaya's works. Together, these episodes historicize the author's axiom that intellectuals and the common people are fundamentally different, with the *narod* constantly threatening to engulf and destroy the intelligentsia. This catastrophic scenario fits the siege mentality of the post-Soviet thinking class, not to mention the heightened popular distrust of liberal intellectuals by the *narod* and the state alike during the Putin and Medvedev years. In *The Kukotskii Case*, Tanya and Toma narrowly escape being crushed by the crowd at Stalin's funeral. *The Big Green Tent* describes this event, which occurred when Ulitskaya was ten years old, in greater detail. This time it is future dissident Il'ia who avoids being trampled. He sees the masses as "human cobblestones," an elemental and dehumanizing image that attacks unthinking support for the Great Leader, acknowledges the engulfment of bystanders from the intelligentsia and other groups, and critiques its horrifying consequences: decades of repressions and then the deaths of 1,500 citizens who perish trying to view his body. The symbolism is clear—the Father of the Peoples created a society where fear and power eclipsed all rational and ethical behavior. What remains is the adulation of authority and unchecked violence that Vinberg laments.[54]

A second repeated scene opposes the elemental flood of support for Stalinism and its legacy. In *The Big Green Tent* Mikha describes for Voice of America how in August 1968 a small group of dissidents unfurled a banner on Red Square to protest the invasion of Czechoslovakia. The story "The Carpathians, Uzhgorod" ("Karpaty, Uzhgorod") illustrates the same event, in which the dissident Natal'ia Gorbanevskaia, Ulitskaya's mentor, participated: "[M]y friend Natasha [Gorbanevskaia] had already been arrested. She had gone out onto Red Square with a stroller, in which her three-month-old son Os'ka slept, together with seven people who were just as crazy, and a small poster: 'For your freedom and ours.' And she spent five years in a prison psychiatric hospital." Gorbanevskaia, the autobiographical narrator observes, was "crazy" to believe her protest would have any actual result. The short demonstration on Red Square, which led to arrests and reprisals, was one of the most visible events of the opposition movement before 1985. It encapsulates the author's vision of the dissidents as embodying individual responsibility, morality, and selfless service to an ungrateful nation; as Ulitskaya wrote in a eulogy for her mentor, who died in November 2013, "It was she who saved the honor of our fatherland." Gorbanevskaia and others may have had no hope of changing events, but the moral code of the intelligentsia compelled them to act. In contrast, the *narod* in Ulitskaya's writing acts like the crowd at Stalin's funeral—it surges without thinking, manipulated by the same state Gorbanevskaia was imprisoned for defying. These juxtaposed images, and those we examine below, insinuate that a few wise and ethical individuals must guide the herd, which otherwise may destroy itself in an unthinking stampede.[55]

Ulitskaya's intelligentsia sees the behavior of the common people as a problem exacerbated by twentieth-century history. In *The Kukotskii Case*, during a drunken conversation with Pavel Alekseevich, dissident scientist Il'ia Gol'dberg asserts that the Soviet gene pool was decimated by a series of factors, ranging from the defeat of the White Army to the purges, collectivization, and destruction of an entire generation of young men in the Great Patriotic War. Over the course of these travails, he asserts, Soviets began to change at a genetic level: "[W]hich qualities gave an individual greater chances of survival? Intelligence? Talent? Honesty? A sense of one's own dignity? Moral fortitude? No! All these qualities inhibited survival. The carriers of these qualities either left the country or were carefully destroyed. And which qualities helped individual survival? Caution. Secretiveness. The ability to be hypocritical. Moral flexibility. Lack of a sense of one's own dignity. In general, any distinctive quality made a person noticeable and immediately put him in danger. The boring [*seryi*], mediocre, average student, so to speak, ended up in an advantageous position."[56]

Because of emigration, imprisonment, or execution of the capable, those most likely to survive in the USSR were people who escaped notice: the stealthy, unexceptional, and immoral. These nonentities then passed on their inferior traits and harmful ethics to successive generations, creating a demographic crisis in which the *narod* perpetuates genetic decay. When Gol'dberg publishes these findings in the West, his sons are badly beaten by KGB thugs. Their fate, a way of threatening Gol'dberg himself, hints that the USSR's leadership sees his unsanctioned research as credible: the Soviet Union has deformed the national body along with the *telesnost'* of those whom it repressed. Teacher Viktor Iul'evich and his friend Misha Kolesnik expand on this topic in *The Big Green Tent*, using insects as analogy—many people in Soviet society, like certain larvae, never completely mature. However, they are capable of reproducing, and those they spawn also fail to develop fully. This topic has familial as well as social resonance for Ulitskaya, whose paternal grandfather was a demographer who wrote a dissertation and book between periods of imprisonment for alleged Zionism. Together with her image of history as acting on the female body, this genetic interpretation of the Soviet era sets Ulitskaya apart from contemporary authors dealing with the past.[57]

For Ulitskaya, *intelligenty* are far from effective in influencing this foreboding history. Beginning with *The Kukotskii Case*, all of her longer narratives question the intelligentsia's ability to transform thought into action. In *The Big Green Tent* Viktor Iul'evich plans to research and write a book about Russian childhood based on his observations of students. His musings about Pasternak's *Childhood of Luvers* (*Detstvo Liuvers*) as the only book in Russian literature that describes a girl's development quickly become ironic. After all, it is Viktor Iul'evich who robs Katia (a classmate of Sania, Il'ia, and Mikha) of her childhood by impregnating her while she is still a schoolgirl. Though Ulitskaya credits Pasternak for "[throwing] off the sedateness of the nineteenth century" and writing his innovative *Childhood of Luvers*, she critiques his reticent descriptions of the body and menstruation. Viktor Iul'evich's focus on moral awakening as a significant component of maturation prompts readers to reexamine his own ethical development, given his relationship with Katia. Interestingly, the narrator withholds judgment of the teacher's romance and even suggests that the couple's eventual marriage neutralizes the teacher's impropriety. This depiction is consonant with the nuanced portrayal of May-December romances in "Bronka" and *Sonechka*; in all three works the narrative is more concerned with the lasting effects of these mismatched unions than their nefariousness, and the relationships provide a framework for contact between a young woman coming of age and the intelligentsia of an earlier generation.[58]

More serious than Viktor Iul'evich's relationship with a schoolgirl is his failure to complete his book; in fact, Il'ia later ponders the failure of the entire group to complete anything. Such portrayals suggest that

Ulitskaya views dissidents as idealists rather than as individuals guiding the common people and becoming agents of real change. The inability to act is the lingering tragedy of the late Soviet intelligentsia, caught between its own inertia, an oppressive state, and an indifferent *narod*. This situation likewise qualifies Ulitskaya's assertion that those *intelligenty* who retained their principles in the turbulent 1990s represent the purest of the thinking class—her prose and plays imply they remain isolated and ineffective despite their honorable intentions.[59]

Moral development (or its absence) shapes history. It is no coincidence that *The Big Green Tent*'s Mikha, while leaping to his death, mutters "Imago"; this final utterance implies that he can surpass the larval stage of development only by dying. *The Big Green Tent* has scant faith in those who remain: the *narod*, which, failing to reach moral maturity, degrades as each generation is less ethical than its predecessor.[60] Viewing the intelligentsia and the common people as antagonistic forces in history relies on a contradiction at the heart of Russian culture. First, Ulitskaya's fictional images of these two groups' interactions show them to be inherently divergent, with the *narod* unwilling to follow the better example set by intellectuals (and *intelligenty* apparently in no need of outside guidance). However, the traumatic specter of the common people's deformation of history necessitates intervention by the intelligentsia, which must persevere in its doomed attempt to save the less-educated from ignorance, brutality, and self-destruction. Ultimately, Ulitskaya's writing is more about the thinking class's intentions than its actions, as *intelligenty* try to make sense of a surrounding world that is at best uninterested in their conclusions. For this reason her most effective intellectuals are those, such as humble Medea, who offer modest, personal goals instead of sweeping change, and who treat the common people with compassion.

Redeeming History in *The Big Green Tent*: Art and the Intelligentsia

Art supplies one means of acting at the individual level. Creativity, like critique, has long been arrogated as the domain of the intelligentsia, and Ulitskaya's works continue this tradition. In *The Big Green Tent*, for example, poetry is a privileged means for intellectual expression during the Thaw and Stagnation eras. Alexeyeva recalls that in those periods, a "passion for poetry became the sign of the times. Poetry took over the hearts of people who had had no particular interest in poetry or in literature generally before and would have none later. Moreover, a heightened need for self-expression, awakened in a society that had come out of its paralysis, made many put pen to paper." Verse was the privileged medium of post-1953 culture; in contrast to the novel, it appeared more sincere and less implicated by socialist realism's (mis)appropriation of literature.[61]

Russian literary heritage occupies an important role in *The Big Green Tent*, with poems by modernist Mikhail Kuzmin and nineteenth-century greats Pushkin and Petr Viazemskii acting as intertexts. Aged intellectual Anna Aleksandrovna and young Mikha discuss the Decembrists as representatives of an idealized historical past that has the potential to redeem the country. (Their conversation foreshadows the KGB's attempt to pervert the image of this group when coercing Il'ia to work with them.) Anna Aleksandrovna, born before 1917, is the moral and artistic authority who shows Mikha the book *Notes of the Decembrists* (*Zapiski dekabristov*). Anna Aleksandrovna typifies Ulitskaya's valorized older generation as she explains: "The history we have in Russia is, without any doubt, awful, but that time [in the early 1800s] was not the very worst. There was a place for noble action and dignity, and a sense of honesty. Are your hands clean?" Her closing question hints at morality as well as hygiene. She, like Viktor Iul'evich with his excursions through cultural Moscow, wants to show Mikha that Stalinism is not a permanent condition. The Decembrists' pursuit of sincerity, merit, and a sense of honor make them an attractive alternative and a (doomed) model for aspiring *intelligenty*. These embedded authors and works in *The Big Green Tent* serve multiple functions, including what Zubok identifies as "an attempt to reassert the ethos of the prerevolutionary intelligentsia in the realm of literature" and history as well.[62]

Siniavskii locates a similar reconstructive impulse as central to *samizdat*, which sought to establish itself as a direct descendant of Silver Age works (thus conveniently bypassing Soviet corruption). Contemporary verse also appears in *The Big Green Tent* and has an analogous function: the lines of Gorbanevskaia, Pasternak, Eduard Limonov, and Joseph Brodsky all find places in the novel, as do the stanzas of beleaguered Mikha, who situates himself firmly within this literary tradition. Mikha maintains that true poetry can only be written in Russian—for that reason he refuses to consider emigration, which presumably would rob his language of its potent cultural context. Mikha's reluctance to leave places him within the Romantic milieu of such poet-patriots as the Decembrists, a parallel that signals Anna Aleksandrovna's influence and underscores how the artist is doomed by love for an ungrateful nation oppressed by tyranny. On another level, the intelligentsia's search for a usable artistic past and its accompanying selective treatment of history ironically recall the refusal of many Russians to acknowledge Stalin's crimes; in both cases a group ignores its ties to a brutal period that profoundly shaped art and culture.[63]

The Big Green Tent uses Viktor Iul'evich's words to address more broadly the function of literature and its salvatory power. In averring that fiction is a "more exact science" than history, Shengeli adds that "what a great writer says will become historical truth" and thus underscores the intelligentsia's power to literally and metaphorically author as well as interpret history. For Viktor Iul'evich literature is a tool for survival that serves to inoculate readers against the "abominations" and "oppressive elements" in life, a summary that encapsulates the conception of *slovesnost'* guiding Ulitskaya's oeuvre. The narrator, however, hints that Shengeli may be mistaken in his optimism, a doubt justified later by the unenviable fates of his former students (and of Viktor Iul'evich himself). The implications for Ulitskaya and the intelligentsia are evident: confidence in the protective or redemptive nature of art must be tempered by acknowledging reality.[64]

Doctor Zhivago, itself a novel about the tragedy of intellectuals, is the most significant intertext in *The Big Green Tent*. As Alexander Gershchenkron asserts, Pasternak saw his masterpiece as praise for an intelligentsia that, while vanquished by the Soviet era, could rise again. Ulitskaya's use of *Doctor Zhivago* optimistically asserts something similar: great literature and moral instruction survived Stalinism to create a crucial link between present and past. Pasternak's narrative greatly influenced both the post-Stalinist thinking class and the ways this group conceived of its own identity and history. His biography also illustrates the complicated position of an *intelligent* in relation to the Soviet state, torn between convictions and a wish to publish. The publication history of *Doctor Zhivago* itself enters Ulitskaya's text when Katia brings Viktor Iul'evich the manuscript from the hands of her grandmother, who happens to be a friend of the great author. While Ulitskaya was finishing *The Big Green Tent*, she read documents about Pasternak's vilification by the Soviet literary establishment as part of her research; this experience once again shows the blurred lines between fiction and history.[65]

Ulitskaya's narrative shares many affinities with Pasternak's: both incorporate poetry, prominently employ coincidences, portray creativity as mainly masculine, and contain a rambling plot that both mimics and modifies the nineteenth-century novel.[66] The two narratives begin and end with a death, laying claim in between to a broad section of Soviet and Russian history. Both also show *byt* to be a network of connections that reveal characters' fates, ideals, and the conditions that stymie them—as Christopher Barnes notes, for Pasternak the everyday contains eternal truths. Most importantly, the novels exhibit parallel systems of intelligentsia ethics, including the sincerity that Ellen Rutten connects to the Thaw. Indeed, in these works morality guides culture. In *Doctor Zhivago* Yuri's uncle Nikolai Nikolaevich argues for the centrality of Christianity in history; the values he espouses, including the need for "spiritual equipment," "love of one's neighbor," "the idea of free personality and the idea of life as sacrifice," are also the ideals of Pasternak, Ulitskaya, and the intellectuals in *The Big Green Tent*. Such humanistic freethinking causes Nikolai Nikolaevich to leave the Orthodox Church, thus distinguishing the intelligentsia from ecclesiastical as well as Bolshevik authorities; from his viewpoint (and Ulitskaya's) both entities discourage personal ethics and individualism. Though Nikolai Nikolaevich identifies these two concepts as "the basic ideals of modern man—without them he is unthinkable," they are later misused by the state. In both works the reader concludes that the intelligentsia must uphold these virtues and diagnose the errors of the Soviet experience.[67]

What elevates human life, according to Nikolai Nikolaevich, is "an inward music: the irresistible power of unarmed truth, the powerful attraction of its example." Truth and morality become synonymous in the idealized intelligentsia worldview; indeed, Ulitskaya's memoir links all art to freedom. In *The Big Green Tent* music acts as a central metaphor when Sania studies music theory. (His plans to become a concert pianist are ruined when working-class bullies injure his hand.) It is no accident that he meets and works with a professor named Iurii Andreevich, who, like his namesake Yuri Zhivago, recognizes the significance of music both within aesthetics and in the entire creative process of life. Zhivago describes inspiration as a phenomenon in which language, "the home and receptacle of beauty and meaning, itself begins to think and speak for man and turns wholly into music, not in terms of sonority but in terms of the impetuousness and power of its inward flow." This characterization, with its echoes of the Romantic organicism prized by Pushkin and other poet-heroes of the intelligentsia, suggests that art is both created by and beyond the individual. As de Mallac avers, for Pasternak art is where the values of history are perfected. *Doctor Zhivago*'s pairing of music and language as part of artistic inspiration parallels

Mikha's argument for the primacy of poetry and Sania's conviction that music is the highest form of expression.[68] Elsewhere Ulitskaya suggests that this art form is a means of resistance—both the saxophonist Sergei in *The Kukotskii Case* and the proto-bard Alesha Peterburg, Tanya's boyfriend in *Sonechka*, are bohemian characters who embody freedom of thought through their musical opposition to the Soviet regime. After Mikha's suicide, Iurii Andreevich advises Sania that Bach's *Well-Tempered Clavier* is an ideal restorative for body and soul. Bach's dying words, "Ende Gut—Alles Gut," give *The Big Green Tent*'s final chapter its title; they suggest the healing power of art, partially redeeming the late Soviet period despite the suffering and failures of the thinking class. Ulitskaya's photographer and painter characters underscore the holistic nature of ekphrasis as one art form comments on another: just as literature and history are inseparable, so are literature and art. In accordance with intelligentsia mythology, the creative and perceptive can be saved by beauty—if they are fortunate.[69]

Both *The Big Green Tent* and *Doctor Zhivago* map the uneasy relationship between the abstract and the mundane. Barnes observes how Zhivago understands history as an everyday yet sacred phenomenon, a richness of the ordinary that Ulitskaya shares; indeed, it underlies her repeated depictions of key events through *byt*, body, and family. *The Big Green Tent* recalls de Mallac's characterization of *Doctor Zhivago*'s illustration of history, which resembles an impressionist painting whose individual lines coalesce into a subtle, harmonious whole. Both novels portray the thinking class as the victims of history. Zhivago is a predominantly passive protagonist who, despite his observations and theories, is at the mercy of larger forces. He views cultural change as imperceptible. It is "eternally growing, ceaselessly changing history, the life of society moving invisibly in its incessant transformations," which explains his conviction that "[o]nly the familiar transformed by genius is truly great." As Yuri reflects on the revolution, he asserts that he has been enriched as an artist through his difficult experiences, a statement that guides *The Big Green Tent* as well. The beneficence of trauma reinforces Lipovetsky and Etkind's hypothesis that the intelligentsia requires catastrophe to justify its continued existence. Ulitskaya for her part both draws from and condemns the legacy of the violent twentieth century, whose brutality (in which the *narod* is complicit) necessitates a mindful thinking class.[70]

In *The Big Green Tent* art, history, and *intelligenty* intersect in the trial of authors Iulii Daniel' and Siniavskii as well as the depiction of underground literature. Discussing Daniel', Ulitskaya argues for a rewriting of the Soviet past, in which the letters Daniel' wrote from prison would become the history of the entire country. Analogously, one critic has suggested that Siniavskii is the model in *The Big Green Tent* for Ol'ga's professor, who is expelled from the university.[71] These two assertions share a common basis: challenging repression in the present and rejecting distortion of the past. Real concern for culture, the novel implies, is expressed through opposition to the state. In this vein we first see the colorful Artur Korolev, a *samizdat* bookbinder. He exposes Ol'ga to a new definition of the intelligentsia, one that eschews the corruption of Ol'ga's mother and her odiously official prose. Artur, like Mikha, demonstrates that sincerity and ethical behavior are the prerequisites for a true love of literature, a moral leitmotif that connects the novel to Ulitskaya's writing as a whole. Ol'ga gradually becomes alienated from the false intelligentsia and joins the dissidents; learning of her repressed religious relatives further complicates Ol'ga's relations with society. In this sense her dream of the green tent and reconciliation is, like the incorporation of Bach's dying words, an assurance that with death all differences will be overcome.[72]

At the end of *The Big Green Tent*, Sania ponders what sustains art. He surmises that "all culture is like a complete sphere [*zavershennyi shar*]." This idea, with its references to wholeness and fragility, justifies the intelligentsia's drive to safeguard the best of what the world has produced. Sania's concept of culture and Ulitskaya's assumption of intellectuals' responsibility for it recall the central message of Aleksandr Sokurov's *Russian Ark* (*Russkii kovcheg*).[73] Both the film and *The Big Green Tent* urge conservation in the face of unceasing chaos—only art, these works conclude, can save humanity from itself. The liberty that Sania sees art bringing, however, is questionable: Soviet dissident O. Altaev (the pseudonym of Vladimir Kormer) argues that the intelligentsia, because it is implicated in the state's crimes, cannot be free. Solzhenitsyn agrees with this gloomy assessment, citing the corruption of major artistic figures by the USSR's government. Ulitskaya's more optimistic thesis relies on a basic intelligentsia axiom: art must bring liberty because the spiritual world overcomes material problems. This scenario is rooted in Russian culture's assumption that the realm of meaning (*bytie*) ultimately will vanquish banal *byt*.[74]

Literature encompasses such meaning. Writing, as Paperno and others have noted, creates kinship through connections based on a shared appreciation of intellectual principles and the narratives that model them. While individual thinkers such as Viktor Iul'evich and

Pavel Alekseevich may fail, those who survive will carry on art's mission. Unlike the fallible morals of the characters Ulitskaya portrays, literature itself promises permanence, transcendence, and morality. The author thus expresses hope for the intelligentsia via the texts it continues to create and consume. The group's claim on what Wachtel notes as the parallel processes of writing history and fiction is not merely self-legitimation; as chroniclers and writers, intellectuals uphold the ethical imperative to save Russian culture.

4

WRITING TOLERANCE

MORALITY AND
ULITSKAYA'S THEOLOGY OF INCLUSION

In 2007 Ludmila Ulitskaya visited the Siberian city of Khanty-Mansiisk as part of a children's literature festival. The local response to Ulitskaya was at times hostile: the author lamented how an "entire troop," including a school director and "representatives of the Orthodox Church" came to the presentation of the literary series she edits, which is designed to instill tolerance in young readers. Foreshadowing Russia's more draconian anti-gay legislation of 2013, opponents accused Ulitskaya of "propagandizing" the "mortal sin" of homosexuality and reserved special anger for a volume on families that includes a same-sex partnership. Ulitskaya matter-of-factly responded that the book was nothing more than a reflection of reality; further, she commented that such hostile reaction served as proof of the pressing need for the books in the series.[1]

The controversy did not end when Ulitskaya returned to Moscow. Another complaint appeared in a 2009 letter from members of a parents' council in Khanty-Mansiisk protesting the school curriculum's inclusion of the same controversial book, Vera Timenchik's *Our Family and Others' (Sem'ia u nas i u drugikh)*. The missive accused the text of "propagandizing homosexuality, rejecting true family values and a healthy way of life" and instilling in children a "positive relationship to [gay marriage] as to something completely normal." A response from the local Department of Education confirmed that the "ambiguous perception of the context" of individual books in the series had caused the suspension of the tolerance project in the region's educational institutions. At the same time, these officials acknowledged the importance of developing *tolerantnost'* among children and adolescents.[2]

The events in Khanty-Mansiisk illustrate Russia's vexed relationship with tolerance and point to that topic's privileged place in Ulitskaya's worldview. *Tolerantnost'*, along with concerns about religion and the state, unites her prose, plays, and non-fiction and is one of the organizing principles of our study, which maps its appearance in body, family, the intelligentsia, religion, and ethics. This virtue connotes accepting divergent thoughts, heritage, and actions while holding self and other to high standards of sincerity and responsibility (both central to the liberal intelligentsia). For Ulitskaya it shapes daily life, reflecting the conviction that deeds are more reliable than dogma. Tolerance offers a powerful way to examine the Soviet past through the post-1991 context of Ulitskaya's literary career—*tolerantnost'* is crucial for her in light of contemporary xenophobia, racism, and the cult of a strong central state. Such alarming trends have inverted the USSR's prominent friendship of peoples, an idea promoted alongside the myth of the Great Family. These developments reveal the Soviet mode of community to have been founded on hierarchy and oppression instead of equality and affinity. While the weakening of this coercive kinship under Gorbachev ushered in new freedoms, it also reinvigorated hate speech and contributed to the emergence of ultraconservative groups.[3]

It is unclear whether such harsh views have become more common, yet they—along with the accompanying violence—have dramatically increased in visibility since the collapse of the USSR. In the twenty-first century, skinhead activity, the Moscow theater hostage crisis, suicide bombings, the Beslan tragedy, attacks on migrant workers, and anti-Ukrainian demonstrations have alternately motivated and responded to increasing tensions within and beyond Russia's borders. The end of the multiethnic Soviet empire created a vacuum that, alongside impoverishment and disenchantment with mismanaged democracy, allowed underlying conservative values to seep into public discourse. There are several reasons for the heightened prominence of xenophobia, including the Yeltsin-era perception of national humiliation and possible state collapse, population decline, and concerns over changes in the culture itself. Russian identity crystallized around "negative solidarities," searches for enemies and scapegoats for social problems.[4] Intolerance looms large in public discourse, as evidenced by the phenomenal popularity of films such as the nationalist revenge scenario *Brother 2*, the best-selling patriotic fiction of Aleksandr Prokhanov, and the presence of black-clad "Russia for Russians" advocates at political demonstrations. The Putin and Medvedev regimes have cleverly exploited such sentiments, as have a range of local leaders in Russia and Russian-dominated regions such as Crimea and southeastern Ukraine.[5]

Religion has also shaped some efforts to define national identity. Svetlana Ryzhova notes the tendency to conflate Russianness and Orthodoxy, which has resulted from the near-doubling of ethnic Russians who identify themselves with this faith. Though Ulitskaya warns that the contemporary Russian Orthodox Church is on a corrupt and "Byzantine path" and is afflicted with an incurable "sickness," she exhibits a more hopeful view of Christianity as "the religion of the impossible."[6] From her viewpoint, this religion is ultimately incompatible with hate. Responding to the ethnic tensions of the past decades, intelligentsia discussions of tolerance have highlighted anti-Semitism and discrimination against people (mainly Muslims) from Central Asia and the Caucasus. Both groups' integration into the USSR showcased fraternity while also supporting the ethnic Russian mandate to enlighten (forcibly or otherwise) "backward" minorities. In the post-Soviet era, Jews and Muslims have been accused of ingratitude to the Russian state that brought them modernity.[7] Ulitskaya sees the written word as one way to counteract such hatred. As her visit to Khanty-Mansiisk demonstrates, there has been a noted rise in children's literature focusing on tolerance, with some cultural commentators devoting special attention to racism and xenophobia among young people. By the beginning of the twenty-first century such texts had become widespread enough to attract the attention of librarians across the country. *Tolerantnost'* is a permanent, if disputed, fixture in public discourse.[8]

Engage and Educate: Tolerance and Ecumenical Dialogue

Tolerance is a value conveyed to readers of all ages, comprising one facet of Ulitskaya's blended literary and public persona. Among the works of children's literature she has authored is *The Story of Antwerp the Sparrow, Mikheev the Cat, Vasia the Aloe Plant, and the Centipede Mar'ia Semenovna and Her Children* (*Istoriia pro vorob'ia Antverpena, kota Mikheeva, stoletnika Vasiu i sorokonozhku Mar'iu Semenovnu s sem'ei*), whose animal (and plant) characters overcome distrust and misunderstanding to make friends and live together. In addition to its emphasis on cooperation, the tale is notable for several reasons. The plot acknowledges the danger of adolescents who harm their environment and other people, treat the weak badly, and hate those who are different.[9] The author as *intelligentka* shows young readers that such behavior should change, in the process asserting that education must promulgate tolerance. This tenet also shapes the series for young readers that Ulitskaya edits. Each book illustrates universal human qualities, begins with a preface by Ulitskaya, and includes a central text composed by another author. One critic, lauding *The Big Green Tent* as a novel embodying *tolerantnost'*, argues that it serves as the final book in the series: Ulitskaya's writings for young and adult readers alike strive to instill respect and curiosity, balancing appreciation for others' traditions with the intelligentsia virtue of personal responsibility.[10]

There is a pressing need for such didacticism in the foreboding atmosphere of contemporary Russia. As a leading voice of the (liberal) thinking class, Ulitskaya proffers political as well as cultural solutions. Discussion of tolerance is meaningless without a concomitant critique of the national shift toward authoritarianism. The most striking example is her correspondence with an unlikely interlocutor: jailed former oligarch Mikhail Khodorkovsky, reined in by Vladimir Putin in 2003 and released from prison in 2013. The tycoon's fate was due to his challenging of Kremlin policies; the state prosecuted an opponent easily associated with the plutocracy and poverty of the 1990s. Ulitskaya developed a special interest in Khodorkovsky because of his social projects and wide-ranging charitable initiatives, particularly his founding of the Podmoskovnyi Lyceum, a school for orphans. Ulitskaya builds the reader's expectations as she introduces Khodorkovsky: "[H]ere was an oligarch who awakened from the mania of personal consumption and learned to receive happiness helping the disadvantaged part of the population. And a few years later I found myself in an astounding school for orphan children, organized by this same oligarch. And now I will say his name: Mikhail Khodorkovsky. Soon this name would thunder throughout the world, and not for the reason that he had become [post-Soviet Russia's] first major philanthropist and benefactor. His international fame is connected with the enormous judicial process that the state undertook against him."[11]

In a rhetorical move designed to sway those readers skeptical of Khodorkovsky's intentions, Ulitskaya first applauds his transformation, then mentions an important result of this shift, and only then states the name of this remarkable man. In her view, the oligarch turned from a life of "personal consumption" (*lichnoe upotreblenie*), the scourge of the consumer era she scorns, to a desire to aid the less fortunate. Khodorkovsky's

Ulitskaya with Boris Akunin (*left*) and Leonid Parfenov (*right*) at the release of the volume *Mikhail Khodorkovsky: Articles, Dialogues, Interviews* in Moscow, January 2011. (RIA Novosti, Grigory Sysoyev)

conversion story, of course, has overtones of hagiography as well as the socialist realist narrative. The business magnate's "awakening" also recalls the mandate of the intelligentsia to help the common people, a duty that the state has shunned. Instead, Putin and Medvedev focused on punishing Khodorkovsky as a political opponent. In Ulitskaya's first letter to him she cites the long tradition of Russian prison literature, a comment that places her—and her correspondent—among such canonical authors as Fyodor Dostoevsky and Anton Chekhov (not to mention Aleksandr Solzhenitsyn). These rationales, however, are secondary to a commonality Ulitskaya implies but never explicitly states: both she and the imprisoned businessman scorn Putin as a throwback to a Soviet past they deeply mistrust.[12]

The correspondence with Khodorkovsky, while unusual for Ulitskaya, recalls the "open letters" that both dissidents and the state used to affect opinion in the last decades of the USSR. In this vein, Ulitskaya's fourth missive to the imprisoned billionaire asserts that his trial will go into the history books, as occurred with Iulii Daniel' and Andrei Siniavskii. Clearly there is scant similarity between these dissident writers and Putin's erstwhile political opponent, yet actual differences are less important than how Khodorkovsky functions as a necessary historical figure for Ulitskaya's image of intelligentsia versus state. As with her advocacy of tolerance, this epistolary discussion signals the integrity of the individual in opposition to the brute power of government. Initially the correspondence places great emphasis on the differences between Ulitskaya and her interlocutor; at least one interviewer was surprised by the harshness with which she addressed Khodorkovsky. Ulitskaya's subsequent statements about the imprisoned oligarch have been less critical, a response to the increasingly aggressive actions of the state.[13]

Within the polarized context of Putin and Medvedev's Russia, Ulitskaya's advocacy of *tolerantnost'* has provoked as much calumny as her support for Khodorkovsky. Conservative critics sometimes identify Ulitskaya with Russophobia or the de facto synonym of non-Russianness; one reviewer questions whether *Daniel Stein, Interpreter* should have received a national award because of the narrative's limited treatment of ethnic Russians and Russian Orthodoxy. Such antagonism underlines the need for the themes of tolerance, empathy, and forgiveness that motivate this novel.[14]

For Ulitskaya, promotion of tolerance comes from the intelligentsia, whose liberal faction deems acceptance of society's variegated nature a virtue to inculcate in the common people. Discussion of *tolerantnost'* is meaningless without those who embody it: the *intelligenty* examined in chapter 3. Scholar Dmitrii Likhachev, writing in the first year of the chaotic post-Soviet period, emphasized the Russian Federation's need for openness and inclusion. This assertion amounted to an intellectual celebrity endorsement. Likhachev, with his integrity, impeccable academic credentials and record of opposing injustice, implied that *tolerantnost'* was an intelligentsia value that had survived the dark Communist years and now must guide society. Since the early 1990s both scholars and the media have highlighted not only the need for tolerance but also its definition. One critic notes that *tolerantnost'* is distinct from *terpimost'* (benevolence): the latter term invokes the condescension the dominant segment (ethnic Russians) displays toward marginal groups.[15] Echoing the rhetoric of the intellectual class, which envisions itself as the guarantor of ethical behavior in society, proponents view tolerance as a moral imperative and thus obligatory for those in the majority. Edith Clowes notes that Ulitskaya endorses this position as a key part of what it means to be Russian. In defining Russianness as embracing tolerance, Ulitskaya follows the precedent of Thaw poet Evgenii Evtushenko, whose poem "Babii Iar" posited that a "real" Russian is one who opposes anti-Semitism. *Tolerantnost'* is the most important of the connections between her narratives grounded in the Soviet period and Ulitskaya's position as a post-1991 author writing about the past.[16]

The author sees the intelligentsia as ethical arbiter and author of history. She likewise posits that the group has an equally important claim to the future through its moral imperative to enlighten the population. This view underlies the children's literature she has penned and the series she has edited to inculcate tolerance, as well as two other areas of her charitable work. The Good Book (*Khoroshaia kniga*) project supplies books to provincial schools and libraries and is funded in part by the liberal Prokhorov Foundation.[17] Ulitskaya's work with hospitals is greatly a tribute to Aleksandr Men' and Georgii Chistiakov: she labels both men the "heart and soul" of an early version of Hospice in Russia, extolling them as priests and scholars. The integrity Ulitskaya upholds calls for individual action guided by the tolerance she posits as a universal value, encoded in the humane approach to the body that runs throughout her writing.[18]

When authors depict *tolerantnost'*, they imply that literature is an extension of reality and a means of directly molding it. Both precepts are central to the intelligentsia. Children and adults alike can be positively guided by writing, as one critic implies when urging Ulitskaya to employ her "sentimental-civic realism" (*sentimental'no-grazhdanstvennyi realizm*) to address (and presumably resolve) social problems.[19] Ulitskaya for her part maintains that young readers are easier to shape. However, the success of these attempts will only be evident when today's readers transmit the cultural inheritance of tolerance to their own children in the next generation. Against the background of Russia's numerous social experiments from New (Soviet) Man to shock therapy, instilling open-mindedness is a project that will, Ulitskaya hopes, shape the future of society.[20]

Ulitskaya's narratives embody the intelligentsia maxim that tolerance must be increased to save Russia from isolation, authoritarianism, and social malaise. This idea recalls the beliefs of Isaiah Berlin, who argues that coexistence is possible despite disagreement. Liberal intellectuals, however, are not the only group advocating tolerance. In her insightful analysis of the Russian Orthodox Church, Irina Papkova demonstrates how its moderates have argued for recognizing the Russian Federation as a multiconfessional society. She observes how the same 1997 law that banned proselytizing also protected Islam, Judaism, and Buddhism as faiths practiced for centuries in the region. This is a welcome gesture, as were the efforts of Men', whom Ulitskaya identifies along with Solzhenitsyn and Sakharov as one of the three defining figures of the post-Thaw era. He influenced Church politics in a positive manner before his mysterious murder in 1990. Himself of Jewish descent, Men' imparted intelligentsia values to the clergy, calling for the ecumenical dialogue that is also central to *Daniel Stein, Interpreter*. Despite Ulitskaya's categorical allegation that Orthodoxy has promoted a lack of culture, its moderate faction was clearly sympathetic to calls for tolerance.[21] This stance was spurred by a centrist group, with liberal and reactionary believers at the fringes. Patriarch Aleksii II, for instance, set the tone when in 1991 he assured New York rabbis that the Church does not pursue a policy of anti-Semitism.[22]

Ulitskaya's own biography is inseparable from the resurgence of the Church and its approach to tolerance; with guidance from Men', she converted to Orthodoxy in the 1960s and later, after meeting Daniel Stein's real-life counterpart, returned to Christianity after a period of disillusionment.[23] As Judith Kornblatt notes, Ulitskaya was one of a small but influential subset of Moscow Jewish intellectuals who converted to Orthodoxy, in the process construing Judaism as the base for Christianity. Ultimately Ulitskaya's characterization of faith is more multifaceted than merely critical: works such as *Seven Saints from Briukho* literally and metaphorically depict the Church as a martyr to Soviet hatred. This viewpoint fits well with Russian Orthodoxy's own narrative of itself as victim of—as opposed to collaborator with—the atheist state.[24]

Faith must instill tolerance. For Ulitskaya, however, the Russian Orthodox Church is moving away from inclusive universalism to isolating nationalism as it grows closer to a government marked by intolerance and corruption. Even if the desire for ecumenical conversation is present, it has been difficult to translate into practice. As Papkova notes, while the Russian Orthodox Church "affirms the right of non-Orthodox Christians who 'acknowledge the Holy Trinity [and] the dual nature of Jesus Christ' to practice their faith in Russia and goes as far as allowing for limited cooperation by the ROC with these groups," the clergy also condemns denominations it sees as "sects." The Church has not officially codified its relationship with any of the non-Christian faiths, in contrast to the thinking of Men', a prominent supporter of ecumenical dialogue. This difference clearly underscores the conflicts between Ulitskaya and the clergy of her chosen religion. In her writing, the Russian Orthodox Church becomes an ambivalent symbol of the people's potential for ignorance, wisdom, hatred, and love. Iurii Maletskii, responding to *Daniel Stein, Interpreter* and its revision of Christianity, asserts that the Church is Russia's most important religious organization—with this, he adds, comes responsibility. In Ulitskaya's novel, the monk Fyodor fails to fulfill this obligation and, in the process, reveals the hypocrisy that undergirds intolerance. Kind priest Father Mikhail worries about Fyodor's morals after the man seduces a girl in Russia. After immigrating to the Holy Land, Fyodor becomes convinced that the Jews have hidden the secrets of their faith, leaving only "scraps" for Christians. This belief, which Ulitskaya decries as horribly deluded, leads him to destroy Daniel's sanctuary in retribution.[25] One critic maintains that the author sees the Church as uneducated, an accusation congruent with her narratorial comments in the novel and unflattering portrayal of zealots such as Fyodor. The *narod*, however, is not to blame for this problem in contemporary Russia. For Ulitskaya, figures such as Men' are the exception to a religious bureaucracy that, unlike the intelligentsia, has no desire to enlighten the common people. She believes that Christianity must articulate tolerance in a way that sways the masses, even if achieving this aim entails sidestepping theological traditions or inventing new ones.[26]

Doctrine must not restrict understanding and acceptance. In this respect Ulitskaya's own adoption of Christianity suggests an alternative: movement from one belief system to another necessitates an exchange of ideas built on mutual respect. This scenario guides the progression of her writing, with intercultural discussion in earlier works preceding the extended ecumenical conversations present in *Daniel Stein*. *The Funeral Party* contains a telling example. In the novel Maika is the daughter of immigrant lawyer Irina and dying artist Alik. She mediates between Irina's immigrant America and Alik's transplanted Russia, functioning as a kind of hybrid character.[27]

In a more overt scenario, the talk between a rabbi and an Orthodox priest later in the narrative is not antagonistic but instead a rare example of Jewish-Christian dialogue. This unusual conversation results from Alik's demand that he will only consider baptism if he can also consult with a rabbi, a stipulation that recalls the common heritage of Judaism and Christianity. It is the first time Reb Menashe has spoken with a priest, an event that Alik and his friends prolong by plying both clerics with drink. Father Victor is the more enthusiastic of the two, happily commenting on his respect for Judaism: "In some ways I'm a Judophile. Every decent Christian must respect the chosen people. You understand how important it is that Jews have poured their precious blood into every culture, every nation. And from this what do we get? It's a worldwide process! The Russians leave their ghetto, and the Chinese. Mark my words, from these young American Chinese we're getting the best musicians, the best mathematicians. I'll go further—mixed marriages! You see what I'm saying? It's the creating of a new people! [. . .] We're living in new times! Neither Jew nor gentile, and in the most direct sense too."[28] Father Victor illuminates several axioms central to Ulitskaya's understanding of faith and tolerance, both of which rely on the body and family as components in "mixed marriages" that are creating "a new people." First, Christianity must respect Judaism as its source. He also notes that Jewish-Christian interaction exists in a global context. The resulting convergence of ethnic and religious identities is positive, stimulating talent as well as mutual understanding in these "new times," which have replaced the isolating "ghetto" of the past.

The Funeral Party establishes a pattern more fully developed by the convert Daniel Stein. This protagonist's dismissal of dogma permits a provocative and compelling interconfessional conversation; for the author, dialogue and orthodoxy are at odds, and faith should never ossify.[29] Ulitskaya asserts that writing *Daniel Stein* taught her that being in a state of "crisis," questioning received assumptions and continually adjusting one's beliefs, is the correct condition for humanity. This theme of the considered life is one to which the author frequently returns. Clearly, religious belief does not imply intellectual independence; the ideology Soviet citizens accepted has been replaced by an analogous acquiescence to religious doctrine. In both cases uncritical adherence to a set of beliefs robs the individual of agency and faith of sincerity. The Russian Orthodox Church constructs edifices such as the imposing Christ the Savior Cathedral, overseen by Iurii Luzhkov, Moscow's former mayor and onetime favorite of Putin. At the same time, Ulitskaya continues, the city's homeless and wounded veterans suffer unnoticed.[30]

Ulitskaya also has little sympathy for ardent believers who fail to acknowledge or understand other viewpoints. Fanatics of any type are antithetical to her postulate of continual reevaluation. *Daniel Stein, Interpreter* portrays both political and religious extremists through personages such as the delusional monk Fyodor and doctrinaire Communist Rita. Single-minded devotion invites disaster, especially when these efforts lay claim to transforming society or the soul. Ulitskaya uses literature's obsession with history to underscore this basic truth: fictional analysis of the past reveals the problem of blind devotion as a constant in Russian culture. In the story "So It Is Written" ("Tak napisano"), Bible-quoting Roza joins autobiographical narrator Zhenia on an excursion to the top of Mount Sinai. The initially skeptical Zhenia experiences an epiphany as the result of her journey, during which she helps an old woman from Novosibirsk reach the summit and is reminded that Christianity is a faith grounded in aiding others. Roza, however, goes mad because of the voices in her head and asks Zhenia to refer her to a psychiatrist who is a religious believer. Abstract belief is dangerous for self and others without the good deeds that give it meaning. Ulitskaya, following the twinned intelligentsia dicta of questioning and compassion, also opposes those whose zealotry closes off dialogue.[31]

Intolerance and the Limits of Understanding

Blind belief in one's rightness leads to prejudice and oppression, whether conveyed by Communism or Orthodoxy. Ulitskaya's works starkly depict the manifold intolerance deforming Russia; it is the shadowy secret of the Great Family, the statist metaphor for relations between ruler and the *narod* that reached its height under Stalin but continues today. The Great Family putatively protects its own, such as the new Pioneers in the story "A Gift Not Made by Hands," who are awed by the prospect of serving Stalin's cause. However, it neglects or brutally punishes both erring members and those whose backgrounds, thoughts, or bodies make them alien. Ulitskaya singles out this coercive kinship, with its false rhetoric of equality, for its persecution of two non-Christian groups discussed earlier in this chapter: Jews and Muslims.[32]

Jews in Ulitskaya's works experience anti-Semitism as a prevalent force in Russian history. They also function as a metaphor for the fate of the intelligentsia—both groups are victims of the state and a *narod* whose attitude to them ranges from disdainful ignorance to spontaneous violence. Expanding on the discussion in chapter 3, we will examine the gravest result of such problems: the Holocaust, which has received limited attention in Russian mainstream literature and national consciousness. *Daniel Stein* is thus remarkable if only for extensively discussing the murder of Jews and their armed resistance in the ghetto of Emsk, a fictional stand-in for the Belarusian city of Mir. The novel depicts how the Nazis exploited prewar hatred and distrust to turn various ethnicities against one another: first Poles and Belarusians helped the occupiers exterminate the Jews, then the Belarusians and Nazis dispatched the Poles.[33]

Ulitskaya's autobiographical narrator asserts that in writing *Daniel Stein* she has poisoned her body with the legacy of hatred stemming from the Jewish question and the Crusades. Written to her editor, this message encapsulates the associations between *telesnost'*, history, and intolerance that run throughout Ulitskaya's works: "I hate the Jewish question! It is the most disgusting question in the history of our civilization. It should be abolished as a fiction, as non-existent. Why do all humanitarian, cultural, and philosophical problems — to say nothing about purely religious problems — constantly dance around the Jews? God has laughed at his chosen people far more than at any of the others. He knew perfectly well that a person cannot love God more than himself."[34]

The narrator pleads for an end to anti-Semitism, which then would mean the world (and Russia in particular) would have no need for the "Jewish Question." Jews' travails, Ulitskaya implies, come from two factors: external oppression and inner doubt, a transcendent lack of faith that also recalls the constant introspection of the intelligentsia. Clearly, it is the first cause that shapes *Daniel Stein*'s illustrations of gentiles' complicity in and indifference to the destruction of Soviet and Polish Jewry. In *My Grandson Veniamin*, Esfir', the last surviving Jew of Bobruisk, notes that today children play on the graves of her relatives and others murdered in what Timothy Snyder terms the "bloodlands." Ulitskaya's depiction of ethnic strife has provoked the ire of nationalist critics, who imply that little room for diversity exists in either Russian literature or its mission to diagnose social ills. *Daniel Stein* chronicles the end result of such thinking: the elimination of imagined enemies, whether Jews or Slavs.[35]

Jews, however, also willingly estrange themselves from other ethnicities. In *The Funeral Party*, Leva Gottlieb, Irina's religiously conservative ex-husband, cuts ties with former acquaintances after becoming more dogmatic in his Judaism. As one critic observes, his distance from others resembles the self-imposed autism that has silenced Irina's daughter Maika, who refuses to talk to adults.[36] For Soviet Jewry and its diaspora, such isolation partially stems from past attacks and present discrimination, yet Ulitskaya demonstrates that separation from others is a limiting solution regardless of circumstances. It is a retreat from tolerance, which involves the presence of the opposing perspectives that philosopher Karl Jaspers identifies as central to communication. Daniel, however, as literal and metaphorical translator, promotes and engages in dialogue as he changes geographical location and religious orientation, converting from Judaism to Catholicism.[37]

The concepts of false kinship we analyze in chapter 2 contribute to a lack of *tolerantnost'*. As Gottlieb demonstrates, Jews may also promote intolerance. *Daniel Stein* elaborates on this idea in depicting Israel, a state formed in response to the horrors of ethnic and religious intolerance. While the first half of the novel focuses on the Holocaust, the work provides ample evidence that the erstwhile victims may also become aggressors. Extremist Jews envision themselves as a family that must repel all who threaten it: Daniel himself, the narrative implies, is cursed by conservative rabbis and consequently dies in a car crash. One critic unwittingly echoes this vein of thought when comparing Ulitskaya to Hitler and the brutal Bohdan Khmelnytsky; all three supposedly glorified the conversion of Jews to Christianity. Such vitriol supports the novel's underlying argument that isolation opens the way to misunderstanding, enmity, and tragedy.[38]

Ulitskaya's texts are also significant for discussing another tragedy unacknowledged within the Great Family: Stalin's 1944 deportation of the Crimean Tatars, a fact elided by recent Russian and Ukrainian struggles over the peninsula. In *The Big Green Tent* dissident Mikha is much more moved by their plight than by that of his fellow Jews who are attempting to emigrate to Israel. As he becomes involved with Tatar activists, the narrator notes: "This alien, Tatar struggle was closer to Mikha's heart than Jewish efforts to be repatriated to Israel. After all, the Jewish exile had lasted two thousand years, far too ancient a history, but the Tatars' exile was still so fresh: their houses and wells in Crimea were not yet destroyed, the Tatars still remembered the Soviet soldiers who had forced them out and the neighbors who had then taken over their homes."[39]

In the Brezhnev era, the narrator explains, the exile of the Tatars was an ongoing injustice. It is not surprising that this less familiar event is introduced by comparing the Tatars to the refuseniks: for Ulitskaya, both peoples are held in literal and metaphorical captivity. By implication, the misunderstandings between Muslims and Jews are secondary to their experience of common oppression. In *The Big Green Tent*, Mikha and his friend Aishe appeal to Sakharov to help free Aishe's father, an imprisoned Tatar activist. This scene recalls Daniel's conversation with Pope John Paul II, in which he persuades the pontiff to begin atoning for centuries of anti-Semitism. In both instances a higher moral authority must right a wrong caused by intolerance; in *The Big Green Tent*, however, Aishe's father dies in prison before he can be helped. *Medea and Her Children* provides a more satisfying resolution: the eponymous protagonist wills her house to Ravil Yusupov, the descendent of exiled Crimean Tatars who had saved her childhood friend during the Civil War. As critic Svetlana Timina perceptively notes, Ravil inheriting Medea's home completes the cyclical movement that dominates the narrative. In a move typical for Ulitskaya's corpus, this novel establishes a theme that a later work—*The Big Green Tent*—explores in more detail. Both narratives maintain that the history of the USSR is founded on division, exclusion, and iniquity.[40]

The intolerance of the Great Family is also reflected in geographical terms. In her engaging discussion of post-Soviet identity, Clowes argues that Ulitskaya's works critique a Russian-dominated, conservative, exclusionary North/center that oppresses a more vibrant, inclusive South/periphery (with its ethnic minorities). In *Medea and Her Children*, Moscow is the focal point of this reactionary zone, while the Black Sea region is its more tolerant antipode. Combining this spatial schema with the kinship metaphor inherited from Stalinism, Ulitskaya's narratives show the controlling center regulating its unruly subalterns in Crimea, a sadly prescient vision of Putin's 2014 seizure of the region.[41]

Most ethnic Russians are uninterested in minorities discussing their plights since, as Lev Gudkov observes, the majority avers that such expressions detract from its own narrative of trauma (e.g., accounts of the Holocaust ignore or deemphasize the massive losses suffered by Russians during the war). The travails of others, according to this logic, dilute Russians' claims to be the "real" victims of history.[42] This exclusionary cult of suffering is crucial to national identity, as Gudkov suggests. Hostility to marginalized voices comes from the myth of the Great Family, which, Ulitskaya alleges, is moving Russia toward authoritarianism. The group most able to counter this dangerous drift is the liberal intelligentsia, the embattled heirs of the late Soviet regime's opponents who support the *tolerantnost'* we discuss in this chapter. However, the fates of several prominent characters question the success of these *intelligenty*.[43]

In Ulitskaya's works scientists receive particular emphasis as thinkers whose preoccupation with seeking truth and understanding the world predisposes them to critique and oppose the state. At the most obvious level, these characters reflect the author's own early career in genetics, when she was taught by survivors of Trofim Lysenko's purges. Doctors form a special subset; to build on our discussion in chapter 1, Ulitskaya makes use of this type's rich pedigree in Russian literature and how it embodies the self-reflexive image of the intelligentsia along with the *intelligent*'s desire to heal what ails society. *The Kukotskii Case* opens with the ominous observation that by the 1920s the doctor's intelligentsia relatives realize that their world has changed for the worse. The state forces them to share their apartment with new neighbors, and after executions and exile "the Bolsheviks had already demonstrated that human life, which these rotten *intelligenty* were used to defending, was not worth a kopeck." Ironically quoting the Soviet regime's scorn for the intellectual class, Ulitskaya's narrator shows that the intelligentsia's old-fashioned ethics are no longer in favor. The novel's ensuing amalgam of Stalinism, kinship, and morality uses the regime's maltreatment of the body to juxtapose the caring intellectual with a bloodthirsty government. Like Daniel Stein, Pavel Alekseevich struggles to improve conditions for humanity and is punished for his efforts. Both men also embody what Boris Engel'gardt in a different context terms the "person-idea" (*chelovek-ideia*), a character whose life is defined by a concept and who exemplifies the intelligentsia value of living one's philosophy.[44] During the anti-cosmopolitan campaign, Pavel Alekseevich begins drinking heavily to avoid meetings at which he would be expected to denounce Jewish colleagues. The ploy is all too effective; he eventually becomes an alcoholic and once even rapes Elena while intoxicated. Kukotskii's addiction is a psychosomatic response to the body politic, whose illness contaminates Pavel Alekseevich along with everyone else connected with it.[45]

Viktor Iul'evich Shengeli is even less fortunate. *The Big Green Tent*'s inspiring teacher never writes his definitive book linking childhood, moral development, and demographic catastrophe. His second manuscript, also unfinished, deals with the problems that arise if fear precipitates an early initiation into adulthood, appropriate given Ulitskaya's statement that the Brezhnev years were ruled by apathy and trepidation. Shengeli falls victim to his own diagnosis of Soviet society, in which the larva-like masses and their state overseers cannot allow genius to illuminate their shortcomings. Visiting his room in a communal apartment, dissident Il'ia is disheartened, regretfully comparing his friends' failures to improve society. This thought crystallizes as he looks with shock at his former teacher: "An unshaven, yellowed, elderly man sleeps. A dark red tablecloth is pulled halfway off the table. On the bare, stained wood, a fat notebook, a pen, a glass of tea dark like iodine. No, it is impossible to write on this velvet tablecloth. [. . .] [I]t's just incomprehensible, what happened with Viktor Iul'evich [. . .] why is he lying here alone, half drunk, among the best of Russia's books?"[46] Viktor Iul'evich's decline is described through the fate of body and intellect, made starker by use of the present tense. His alcoholic slumber occurs in a room that Ulitskaya renders a still life of the failed intelligentsia: writing implements, tablecloth, and Shengeli himself show that nothing here is conducive to bringing thoughts to fruition. The erstwhile teacher has degenerated into a prematurely aged drunk, abandoned by his wife and former student; his decline humanizes history and depicts the fate of the talented individual in the USSR in depressingly physical terms.[47]

The Big Green Tent, despite its intricate plot and numerous characters, is unified by its rehabilitation of those who confront the Soviet state. Ulitskaya summarizes what is abundantly clear in the narrative: the government, not its pro-democracy critics, is to blame for Russia's current poor standard of living. Oppression, the narrative underscores, was the defining attribute of Soviet politics. The doomed poet Mikha, for instance, realizes after the invasion of Czechoslovakia that Marxism only leads to despotism.[48] As with Daniel Stein, the righteous individual is vanquished by unjust authorities; the narrator notes with little subtlety that Mikha is the same age as Jesus and has sacrificed his life for others. One critic observes that Ulitskaya's early novella *Sonechka* is about those whom the USSR wanted to destroy but could not; *The Big Green Tent* is about those whom the government tried to crush and did. Indeed, Ulitskaya's works teem with characters victimized by a brutal state: Gulia in the story of the same name was arrested three times, while the mother of Shurik's lover Alla in *Sincerely Yours, Shurik* was deported to Kazakhstan following Kirov's murder.[49]

Ulitskaya's dissidents provoke the ire of the Great Family and its totalizing ideology. Berlin has stressed that belief in a single truth as a panacea is perilous, as it justifies the horrors of Communism and fascism. Characters such as Mikha and Daniel Stein show that no one should be able to define unity and thus exclude those who fall outside its boundaries. This rejection alarms some conservative critics: Ekaterina Rep'eva argues that the tolerance promoted by characters such as Stein is a source of chaos.[50] Presumably a surfeit of ideas leads to confusion. Ulitskaya's rejection of unitary truth has implications for the intelligentsia, which believes in abstract truth to an exceptional degree. This group forms its identity by assuming that it has the unique right to determine Russia's course (and the moral onus to convince the *narod* to follow it). As Katerina Clark shows, in many respects this messianic mission overlapped with state policies. How then can Ulitskaya reject one proponent of unitary truth while praising another? The difference is that her positive characters—whether successful or doomed in their efforts—embody ideas by modeling them in everyday life. In Ulitskaya's writing, positive characters bring abstract laws of morality down to a human level by living rightly moment to moment and do not impose their values on others through violence. Her works combine ethics and the quotidian, with this confluence tempered by awareness of human fallibility.[51]

In Ulitskaya's corpus there is a strong need to make the ideas of others mutually comprehensible. Given this problem, the high stakes of personal ethics, and the difficulty of negotiating state repression, the translator is a key, polysemous figure for Ulitskaya, and one we examine by building on our discussion in the introduction to this volume. Daniel Stein, not surprisingly, is the most detailed example. He interprets between languages but also between cultures and faiths. Margarita Levantovskaya investigates how the monk likewise operates as a polyglot convert from Judaism to Catholicism.[52] In doing so, Daniel shows that Jewishness is negotiable (as is Christianity) and that the boundary between gentiles and the chosen people can be blurred. As a priest devoted to action over dogma, he experiences translation as embodied experience. For Daniel this is not an abstract discussion but a matter of survival. Growing up in interwar Poland, the Jewish boy quickly absorbs the politics of language: he speaks Polish without a (Yiddish) accent and learns to ride a horse, which keeps him from being recognized as a Jew in occupied Belarus. He is forced to assume a series of identities during the Holocaust but, as critics argue, he maintains his central values: respect for others, intellectual curiosity, and compassion. This preservation of personality denotes the sincerity that underlies intelligentsia identity; Daniel's shifting external roles recall the subtle changes of position that intellectuals such as Pavel Alekseevich needed to survive Stalinism. Both characters also show how the intelligentsia's traits are shaped by its own suffering as well as how it responds to oppression.[53]

While Daniel safeguards his moral constancy, he is still alarmed by wearing a uniform strikingly similar to that of the SS. Indeed, the peril of collaboration is a constant danger for translators. In *The Big Green Tent*, Ol'ga finds temporary work as an interpreter for a Colombian author visiting the Soviet Union. The acquaintance who arranges this job was in part responsible for her earlier expulsion from the university after she supported a dissident professor. Not surprisingly, after accompanying the Latin American writer she is expected to submit a report to the KGB about his activities. Contact with foreigners, who provide a viewpoint independent of the state, must be carefully monitored (as are Soviets' reactions to these encounters).[54]

Translators are not the only group whose depiction complicates the ethics of Ulitskaya's oeuvre. Despite her guiding commitment to *tolerantnost'*, certain groups fall outside of it and receive incomplete or distorted characterization. Our comments do not detract from the fact that, as we have discussed in the preceding chapters, Ulitskaya is the most important author in contemporary Russian literature. Her narratives and *publitsistika* combine a broad readership with key innovations: inclusive approaches to the physical body, reconsidered definitions of kinship, personalization of history, and defense of the embattled liberal intelligentsia. These interconnected factors contribute to her overall message of tolerance, but at times this is a message with disturbing limitations.

These boundaries are strikingly evident in the schematic portrayal of homosexuals. Ulitskaya shows gay characters more as victims than as nuanced individuals. Addressing the controversy surrounding Timenchik's book on families in her tolerance series, Ulitskaya distances herself from the same-sex parents the volume depicts, observing that their portrayal is meant not as an endorsement but as a way to end persecution. The oppression of gays violates intelligentsia values, but she cannot bring herself to advocate fully on this group's behalf. Her well-intentioned attempts at sympathetic depiction are overshadowed by aesthetic or social subtexts that view gays as completely defined by how the state victimizes them. Because they point to ailments of contemporary culture, the narratives restrict these personages' significance to their homosexuality. The result is that queer characters can never transcend otherness, a scenario that recalls perestroika-era depictions of gays as the product and casualty of a cruel society.[55]

Telesnost' and culture connect in Ulitskaya's images of homosexuality. Her approach avoids the shock tactics of authors such as Eduard Limonov and Vladimir Sorokin, whose provocative portrayals, Vitaly Chernetsky argues, merely "reinscribe the society's oppressive and discriminatory attitudes." Ulitskaya's screenplay *The Liberty Sisters* presents her first queer character, polyglot Sergei, who is from the Caucasus and tries to make twins Vera and Liuba into sophisticated models. He seduces the teenage boy Zhenia while listening to Charlie Parker. The boy later dies when Vera grabs him, then throws him and herself out of the window, all while Parker plays in the background. This scene implies that Sergei is responsible for Zhenia's death (if not Vera's); he meets Zhenia while trying to transform the twins from Soviet working-class girls to something more elegant.[56] The link between homosexuality, music, and doom is one that runs throughout Ulitskaya's narratives. In *The Big Green Tent*, musicologist Sania has a blood disease — presumably AIDS — and from adolescence onwards fears female sexuality, even recalling the Sirens who devoured Odysseus's comrades after luring them with beauty and song. As with *The Liberty Sisters*, the ekphrasis of a narrative depicting music becomes embroiled in Russia's cultural anxieties over homosexuality.[57]

"Angel," Ulitskaya's most extensive and important depiction of homosexuals, begins by invoking Vladimir Nabokov's *Lolita*. Like Humbert Humbert, Nikolai Romanovich marries to become close to his new wife's child. He imagines rearing and schooling stepson Slava "lovingly and chastely"; at the same time, it is clear that the teenager is to become his *eromenos*. The classical philosophy professor remains in favor during the Soviet period; the antiquity he specializes in "came to be called Classical Materialism. This fallacy was what the beliefs of Nikolai Romanovich consisted of. He passed them on in full measure to his alumnus [Slava] even as he inserted more personal predilections, cautiously and patiently, with the assistance of his experienced fingers, his sensitive tongue with its discerning tastebuds, and his old withered lance." Sexual corruption is a metaphor for Nikolai Romanovich's distortion of ancient culture as well as his literal seduction of Slava. The professor's relationship with his stepson is not, however, his only transgression. His gravest flaw is venality: the misappropriation of aesthetics for professional and then personal gain, which constitutes an abrogation of sincerity. Nikolai Romanovich thus fails the critical moral test Ulitskaya sets for the intelligentsia, a scenario that implicates queerness as well.[58]

After his stepfather's death, Slava is discomfited and lost. When he meets a new lover at last, he experiences a revelation that is also something entirely new for the Russian reader. The two men meet under the pretext of a chess game, and Slava accompanies him to his apartment: "They did not finish their game of chess. They made love, strong, masculine love, of which Slava had had only an inkling before. The place smelled of vaseline and blood. It was what Slava had been wanting and what Nikolai Romanovich had been unable to give him. It was a night of nuptials, of initiation, and of ecstasy beyond the reach of music. A new life had begun for Slava." This description lacks the light irony that Ulitskaya usually includes with depictions of heterosexual sex. Its emphasis on the physical likewise evokes the images of copulation between men and women that dominate *zhenskaia proza*. Slava's experience with the chess player signals the beginning of another existence, which is, however, not narrated. This elision mars the first scene of consensual gay sex in mainstream Russian literature and Ulitskaya's only detailed portrayal of intercourse between men. It likewise creates a disturbing trend. Ulitskaya's male homosexuals are victims, not fully developed individuals: in the very next scene, Slava's decaying corpse turns up. His history in the intervening decades has included time in the camps, loss of health and Moscow residence permit, and a fictitious marriage: "[o]f his former riches, all that remained was his rare talent for listening to music and his aristocratic hands with their oval nails." Presumably, Slava was murdered by a lover or by anti-gay hoodlums.[59] Ulitskaya's character is a victim of intolerant Soviet society but also, more disturbingly, of his own homosexuality—no positive straight characters meet with such a grisly end. The suicide of poet Mikha in *The Big Green Tent*, for instance, involves him uttering a final, defiant word against the state as he jumps to his death.[60]

The story "Dutch Fruit" ("Frukt gollandskii") clarifies Ulitskaya's personal perspective on queerness via her autobiographical narrator, Zhenia. In the Netherlands, she meets an emaciated and toothless artist who reminds her of a now deceased friend who was imprisoned for being gay. Zhenia admits to a onetime horror of sodomy and her previous view of homosexuality as "a mistake, a misprint, even a crime." As with the protagonist in "Angel," the artist is a personage completely defined by being gay, which has given him the aura of outcast even in relatively tolerant Western Europe. In childhood he was in a concentration camp, a fact clearly unrelated to his homosexuality yet with strong overtones of Slava's imprisonment.[61]

Female homosexuality is less visible in Ulitskaya's works. This limited depiction is not surprising, given the smaller role of lesbians in a gay culture that is itself increasingly marginalized by Russian society; as Chernetsky argues, lesbian scenes in post-Soviet literature often seem manufactured for a (straight) male gaze. Ulitskaya for her part presents not queer female characters, but those who at various moments display "homosexual" behavior. In the story "A Cow's Leg" ("Korov'ia noga") autobiographical narrator Zhenia and her translator arrive at their German hotel and are taken for lesbians because of their appearance. Zhenia's remark that this is an error, but not an offensive one, is a milder version of the simultaneous humanity and alterity ascribed to homosexuals in "Angel" and "Dutch Fruit." The story "Dauntless

Women of the Russian Steppe" ("Zhenshchiny russkikh selenii . . .") depicts lesbian tendencies during a drunken episode that begins with friends in New York conversing about their problems with men. The female bonding of Margot, Emma, and Vera connotes separation from the male world: Vera is widowed, Emma is no longer with her lover, and Margot has never slept with anyone but her former husband. She recalls "the shame and embarrassment of drunken copulation, when you lay there filled with loathing while two hundred pounds of meat jerked up and down on you, braising your dryness, making you feel you were being impaled, and your breasts ended up covered in bruises as if you had been beaten and the brown marks took a year afterward to fade."[62]

This image of marital sex recalls rape, coitus without love, and male drinking—all standard descriptions in women's prose that are atypical for Ulitskaya. It contrasts sharply with Margot's experience when she and Emma, intoxicated, fall into bed together. Emma is nauseated, but Margot enjoys caressing her. When, on the verge of orgasm, Margot detects a suspicious lump in Emma's breast, she sobers up and assumes a practical tone. Ulitskaya's works typically mark unreciprocated sexual encounters as negative, yet Margot's advance results in a potentially life-saving discovery. This dalliance in lesbianism drives Emma back to her rejected lover and implies that Margot is drawn to Emma only after her own dismissal of men (and her ex-husband in particular). The story's title evokes Nikolai Nekrasov's poem "There Are Women in the Russian Steppes . . ." ("Est' zhenshchiny v russkikh selen'iakh . . ."), a paean to stalwart and striking Russian women, but Ulitskaya's version is an exotic adventure localized in an alien land (America) that eclipses any speculation about lesbians in Russia. In "Dauntless Women of the Russian Steppe" an anomalous act of sexuality is merely one event in a larger scenario (the friends' drunken evening, complaints about men, and the discovery of what turns out to be a tumor). The reader senses that homosexuality between women is not a topic Ulitskaya feels compelled to discuss, a situation resulting from the reduced visibility Chernetsky notes. Similarly, her memoir and autobiographical stories acknowledge gay male acquaintances but contain no discussions of lesbians.[63]

Ulitskaya neither substantially engages female homosexuality nor integrates its male counterpart. Her presentation of gay men is revolutionary for its tentative effort to present sympathy and foster tolerance. Nonetheless, she fails to show them leading full and nuanced lives that transcend victimhood. Instead, the physical and emotional trauma of their sexuality dominates them, implying that this liberal author is convinced that queerness is fundamentally alien. This stance stems from Ulitskaya's own upbringing in the deeply homophobic society of late Stalinism; like her narrator Zhenia in "Dutch Fruit," she cannot fully abandon her earlier feelings of fear and repulsion.

Portrayals of sexuality are not the only instance where Ulitskaya's narratives show the limits of tolerance. The author's image of Muslims presents an even more complicated problem. In her novels Crimean Tatars are a civilized, harmonious community, but Chechnya is profoundly troubling. Unlike the exiled Tatars, Chechens are nearly invisible in Ulitskaya's fiction: though two of her novels mention the 1944 deportations in Crimea, she never refers to the similar plight that befell 400,000 Chechens in the same year. Ulitskaya's family history partially explains her focus: one of her grandmothers was from Crimea. However, this choice also reflects Ulitskaya's systemic distinction between a secularized Muslim minority oppressed by the state and a group tainted by the zealotry and aggression that are anathema to the intelligentsia. She supports centuries of discriminatory rhetoric when describing how in the post-Soviet Chechen wars, "Russia is involved with a mountain people, with an ancient and violent way of life. This is a world according to whose laws they nailed the wrist of a vanquished enemy to the gates of one's own home." By implication, the liberal intelligentsia will be unable to engage in dialogue with such people. The ongoing conflict in the Caucasus does not allow Ulitskaya to extend to Chechens the compassion she shows for the less "brutal" Tatars.[64] While such a statement is not new in Russian culture, it is a troubling response from an author who has fearlessly criticized others' xenophobia and intolerance. Equally alarming is her lack of meaningful distinction between Islamic moderates and extremists, a difference she repeatedly underscores in Christianity and Judaism but does not make with Islam.[65]

Her first extensive discussion occurs in an interview following the 2002 theater hostage crisis in Moscow. After decrying the state's failure to defend its citizens against terrorism, Ulitskaya claims that Islamic fundamentalism arises from the untapped sexual energy of Muslim men and a world where males have limited interactions with women. In *Discarded Relics*, she expands on this thesis, linking segregation of the sexes to its extreme manifestation, female suicide bombers: "Muslim women, those same subservient ones in head scarves, inhabitants of the female half of the house, tender beauties with eyes outlined in kohl or matrons with a crowd of children, without taking off their scarves, hang grenades on themselves, put on suicide vests, and blow up living people, neither sparing their own lives nor anyone else's." Loving and nurturing women become suicide bombers. This action, she maintains, is not their choice, but at the demand of Muslim men who "tied [women] to participation in the most horrifying war."[66]

These concerns recall the dichotomies of sexuality/violence and female subservience/male aggression that mark what Edward Said and Susan Layton read as orientalist misconceptions of Muslims. They also reflect Ulitskaya's ongoing belief that relations between men and women are a crucial index of civilization in a given society; relations between bodies determine history. In this context she compares Russia unfavorably with Europe due to the former's "Eastern" habit of marginalizing women in public life. Likewise, her prose and plays have from the beginning validated sexuality as a central component of human existence. To a degree her critique of gender and sexuality in fundamentalist Islam resonates with themes that unite her narratives.[67]

Ulitskaya also posits that this faith's radicalized components negate the values she upholds as an *intelligentka*. In her memoir, after discussing the problem of gender roles in the West, she then turns to Islam, "which, right next to us, lives by other principles. But this world also is alive, developing, and, after having overcome its illnesses, will in the end reach the norms of humanity [*obshchechelovecheskim normam*]: recognizing human life as the highest good, recognizing the equal rights of women, and the right to any choice of religion, if it does not threaten the life of another person."[68] Islam, which she does not qualify in terms of its radical versus progressive or mainstream components, needs to "overcome its illnesses," mature, and "reach the norms of humanity." In a different context her description of this religion's problems could apply to the excesses of Stalinism. These parallels reveal that she sees Islam's shortcomings as threatening values that the intelligentsia also protected from the atheist Soviet establishment: the dignity of the individual, the right of both women and men to freedom, the ability to choose one's faith. Islamists, like the godless totalitarian state, violate these foundational assumptions. In doing so, both ideologies substitute rigid belief for the tolerance and dynamic inquiry that Ulitskaya upholds as central for *intelligenty*. Her worry over this danger precludes the understanding that she extends to other religious traditions. Another factor worries Ulitskaya as well: she notes that the Qu'ran is the sacred text for half the world's population, yet much of this group is illiterate. Thus in the Islamic world, there is not so much reading as "mechanisms, induced by this book: tradition, strict form, Sharia law." She assumes that a high level of illiteracy does not allow for the crucial interaction between word and believer that helped Judaism and much of Christianity to mature. For Ulitskaya as an *intelligentka*, reading is a spiritual as well as hermeneutic act; believers who cannot have direct contact with holy scripture are not full members of the faith.[69]

These intelligentsia fears resemble the very attitudes that are repugnant to its liberal ideal of tolerance. Ulitskaya's warning in *Discarded Relics* that today the "responsible and enlightened" are having fewer children than the less fortunate fits into a broader demographic anxiety: many Russians worry that low birthrates, frequent divorces, immigration, and an impotent or alcoholic male populace will make them a minority in their own nation. This parallel is an uncomfortable one for Ulitskaya, who denounces concerns based on ethnic insecurity as a movement towards fascism. However, both the rhetoric of Russia as dying nation and her own fears of genetic decay signal alarm that the best (whether in terms of *natsional'nost'* or intellect) will be overpowered by the fecund yet inferior. Ulitskaya's conception of history as a pattern of demographic regress limits her endorsement of *tolerantnost'* and Christian love for the poor. In urging the thinking class to save their nation's history from the *narod*, she undermines the mandate for compassion that supposedly motivates the intelligentsia.[70]

Ulitskaya's own intelligentsia background in great part explains her insufficiently critical portrayal of this group. The author's image of the *intelligenty* is selective, deeming only liberals qualified to belong. It thus oversimplifies the worldview of post-Soviet intellectuals, eliding figures such as conservative Prokhanov or mercurial radical Limonov. Another factor is the group's ideals, which focus on critique of the state, not of the intelligentsia's own mythologies. Ulitskaya's oeuvre replaces the "official" fictions of Russian history with an alternative one: the hagiography of the suffering intelligentsia, a group assailed by first the Soviet state and then consumerism. In this sense Mariia Litovskaia errs when she states that Ulitskaya's image of *intelligenty* combats nostalgia. The author's prose certainly militates against the current fondness for the economic stability and mellow coercion of the Brezhnev years. However, while dismantling this misconception, her writing promulgates a more specific fiction: she believes that after 1991 the intelligentsia has continued its mission of making morality comprehensible to the masses. As critics such as Zubok and Dubin show, this supposition has little to do with reality; instead, it proffers a post-Soviet picture of a persevering enlightening class and a common folk eager for instruction. Though compelling, this image is only the latest fabrication of a group that has long claimed the right to interpret (and thus potentially distort) history.[71]

Those who do not share Ulitskaya's liberal intelligentsia worldview are ultimately alien in her works. This stance is clear when she depicts characters who participate in the crimes of the totalitarian state. Their eventual punishment comes in varying forms, but the causal and sometimes crude relationship between transgression and consequence underlies the importance of positive ethics in her oeuvre. In *Daniel Stein*, Belarusian chief of police Ivan Semenovich, an unrepentant and paranoid Nazi collaborator, is a violent drunk. He respects Daniel (who he thinks is Polish)—in Ivan Semenovich's hierarchy, Poles are superior to Belarusians but Jews are inferior. Ulitskaya's novel sentences him to an agonizing death from cancer. Ivan Semenovich's widow recalls how he died as she writes to her sister: "His right leg was amputated a year ago, and that may have been a mistake because afterward that dreadful sarcoma spread like wildfire to his bones and he suffered beyond all measure. He did not want to go into the clinic because till the day he died he was afraid the Jews would kidnap him. [. . .] He had a full file of news clippings about war criminals the Jews had abducted, even from Latin America, and put on trial. Even more than a trial, he feared the children would learn the truth about his past."[72]

Ethics are indivisible from the body—corporeality is the means by which this former collaborator suffers for his sins. Ivan Semenovich is afraid that Jewish doctors will arrest him for crimes against humanity and, worse yet, his children will then discover the horrors of which he knows he is guilty. Nothing can alleviate his pain, which is a literal manifestation of the metastasis of hate during the Holocaust. This agony signals that Ulitskaya's novel knows no other way of dealing with such reprehensible characters. The portrayals of Ivan Semenovich and proponents of Islamic violence recall a key caveat from the philosopher Karl Popper—tolerance must extend to all those who are not themselves intolerant; otherwise, tolerance will permit the tendencies that will eventually destroy it. For Ulitskaya the intelligentsia must determine the content and parameters of *tolerantnost'* and the means by which literature can illustrate them. Breaking with her usual subtle and nuanced characterization, she shows how negative personages unambiguously destroy first the lives of others and then their own.[73]

Depictions of moral compromise are another example of the boundaries of tolerance—Ulitskaya excludes these characters from the dialogue with diversity that she prizes. Her harsh reaction is provoked by their transgression, which is by definition a betrayal of the sincerity that is a central tenet of intellectuals. Likhachev indicates in his discussion of the intelligentsia that its identity stems from a code of behavior founded on *iskrennost'* and integrity. Within this context, in *Sincerely Yours, Shurik* the eponymous protagonist's sexual compromises underscore weakness and a basic amorality at odds with his slavish self-sacrifice. Shurik embraces the consoling dimension of his character, functioning as a caregiver in both sexual and platonic ways. His grandmother Elizaveta Ivanovna, a moral authority in the text, suggests that one of Shurik's gravest flaws is not living his own life (he instead fulfills the desires of others). Guilt and desire for approbation are two key motivators for Shurik, whose drifting existence is subject to chance and the consequences of previous entanglements. The resulting passivity underscores his failure to embody the imperative for action that Ulitskaya ascribes to the intelligentsia.[74]

Compromise can assume other forms. In *The Big Green Tent*, Il'ia believes cooperating with the state to be his only choice. The reward he garners turns out to be worth little; after the KGB permits him to leave the Soviet Union, Il'ia does not survive long in the United States. Mikha's father-in-law Sergei Borisovich, despite his experience as a dissident in the camps and in exile, commits a similar transgression when he holds a press conference where he "repents of all his sins against Soviet power." Characters such as Il'ia and Sergei Borisovich alter their behavior or principles under difficult circumstances, believing they have no other recourse. The same novel provides a powerful counterexample: recalling Gorbanevskaia's participation in the protest on Red Square (and subsequent arrest), the reader realizes that there is always a morally correct response to oppression.[75]

For some, such as Masha's Stalinist parents in "A Writer's Daughter," compromise is a by-product of ambition, as Ulitskaya observes: "Those who want to be winners in this life inevitably lose the contours of their individuality. People on the margins with no ambition to win a better place preserve their selves. That's where my heroes are: the nurse Medea, who doesn't pursue a career and wants to stay in the shadows but doesn't yield anything to the authorities and at a critical moment in her life is not afraid to act according to her conscience. Her husband failed at his career because despite all his revolutionary ideas he was unable to take part in an execution and fainted. 'My [body] couldn't take it!' he says. Those who have nothing to lose—the poor and the invalids—are not afraid of the Soviet regime because they have already lost everything.

Theirs is the special courage of the outcasts. And I don't go looking for them, our life is full of them."[76] Only the humble characters in Ulitskaya's prose and plays avoid the contamination of working with the state. Despite the stigma attached to compromise, this solution was a common element of Stagnation-era culture. In this respect Ulitskaya is influenced by the *shestidesiatniki*; problems of ethical equivocation are central to the works of Solzhenitsyn and Trifonov and to their ambivalent image of the intelligentsia. For Ulitskaya, who identifies closely with this generation, flexible morality as a survival strategy is ethically flawed and doomed to failure.[77]

Ulitskaya maintains that compromise also arises from consumer forces that have replaced Communist ideology, especially in relation to the press. The adulteration of free speech in an effort to continue publishing is a particularly insidious manifestation; though it has not yet spread to prose fiction, Ulitskaya sees this possibility on the horizon. She maintains that today's Russian writers are not compelled by state censorship to modify their aesthetic aims—these barriers are absent largely because Russian authorities do not consider literature important enough to restrict. By contrast, commercial pressures are a greater threat to artistic integrity. This posited link between compromise and consumerism underscores one of the contradictions of Ulitskaya's writing, which strives to maintain its prized sincerity despite profitability. Likewise, while her body of writing has developed by modeling and defending tolerance, such *tolerantnost'* has its limits, and at times they undermine Ulitskaya's calls for inclusion and acceptance.[78]

From Orthodoxy to Orthopraxis: Living Rightly and Gathering Difference

Morality and compromise exist alongside another crucial opposition: dogma and practice. Daniel Stein, the protagonist whose views are closest to Ulitskaya's own, asserts that Rome is not the mother of the Church but merely a sister; it is no better than the numerous other branches of Christianity. This is congruent with the monk's suspicion of religious bureaucracy, which opposes the simplicity and ecumenical egalitarianism at the heart of his faith. Rome as mother is problematic in a more specific way. In the novel the papal hierarchy, which ultimately bans the monk from mass, stands in for a system closer to home: the Russian Orthodox Church. Although Ulitskaya herself is a convert, for her Orthodoxy exemplifies the dangers of caesaropapism, drawing ever closer to the state. It is no coincidence that she became a Christian in the 1960s, a time when this faith was persecuted. Her memoir describes attending services in a house that evoked the humble secret sanctuaries of the first years of Christianity: "My experience began in a church that could be called a catacomb. It was a church in the home of Father Andrei Sergeenko, where around two dozen people gathered, and the service itself occurred in a room in his home on the outskirts of the city of Aleksandrov, where [the priest] lived until his death. It was a community whose spirit suggested that of early Christianity."[79] Father Andrei Sergeenko provided Ulitskaya with a church that was both simple and far removed from the current machinations between high-ranking Orthodox clergy and Putin's state. In both the Soviet and Roman contexts, the true faithful were marginalized and victimized by unjust rulers. For Ulitskaya, Christianity—like the intelligentsia—must speak the truth, defend the weak, and oppose the powerful.

Medea models the positive aspects of Orthodoxy. Visiting Elena in Tashkent, she recalls that the religious instruction imparted by her mother has allowed her to lead a Christian life. In doing so, she need not trouble herself with "philosophical questions which it is by no means essential for each individual to try to resolve." Instead, she continues, one must live according to the knowledge that nothing can turn evil into good and that many people have strayed from righteousness. This statement is the closest Medea ever comes to formalizing the ethical system reflected in her everyday life, where it is the individual who is ultimately responsible.[80] Impoverished Zina in "The Chosen People" proposes a similarly quiet yet crucial concept. After begging outside a church, she argues with her friend and protector Katia the Redhead. When challenged to explain the Mother of God, she defines the *Bogoroditsa* as the "Mother of her daughter." To build on our discussion in chapter 1, Katia's scoffing reaction misses the underlying wisdom of the remark: Christianity is a family of believers. Choosing to belong to it is an inalienable part of human existence—as when Medea shuns arcane theology, Zina identifies belief and support as the true bulwarks of Orthodoxy. It is all the more telling that the bearer of this message is also someone who desperately needs it; for Ulitskaya, Christianity exists for the dispossessed and meek, not the powerful and proud.[81]

Faith should not be complicated by abstract theory. Daniel Stein takes particular issue with manifestations of theology that lack redeeming action. In an anomalous instance of anger, he drives from his church a

Balkan woman selling cloth that, she claims, brings protection by the Virgin Mary. He later explains his actions to Hilda in a manner that elaborates on Zina's statement: "Personally I cannot accept the dogma of the Virgin Mary's Immaculate Conception as it is currently presented by the Church. I greatly admire Miriam, quite irrespective of how she conceived. She was a holy woman, and a suffering woman, but we really do not have to turn her into the progenitor of the world." Daniel objects heatedly not to the sale of the cloth itself but to the contention that Mary is important as a holy "progenitor" rather than a suffering mother. What makes this distortion even more galling is its creation of an artificial rupture where none exists: Daniel does not accept the division of soul and *telesnost'*.[82] This lack of separation is crucial to Ulitskaya's revision of theology and literalizes her claim that Stein bridges the gap between Judaism and Christianity with his body. The gulf between flesh and spirit, by analogy, is as false as the partitioning of the faithful into Jews and gentiles. Conservative Jewish and Russian Orthodox critics were outraged at these statements, marking a shift toward more ideological attacks on Ulitskaya. Ironically, both contingents make the same argument: *Daniel Stein* advocates the merger of Christianity and Judaism. The presumed compatibility (and potential merging) of the two religions recalls the belief of some Russian Orthodox converts that Jewish holy tradition can be reduced to the Hebrew Bible. From the standpoint of *Daniel Stein*'s conservative critics the rift between the two religions is a natural and necessary demarcation: overcoming it would destroy one faith to the benefit of the other.[83]

Ulitskaya's refashioned theology operates in everyday life, that overlooked realm of banal wonders and understated wisdom. Ivan Isaevich, a modest man from an Old Believer family who marries Medea's sister Alexandra, develops a holistic view of family, *byt*, and *bytie*: "He was touched by [Alexandra's] prayerful sigh, but only much later, when he was already her husband, did he realize that the crucial point was the amazingly simple way she had solved the problem which had tormented him all his life. For him the worship of a righteous God simply could not be reconciled with the living of an unrighteous life, but [Alexandra] brought everything together in a splendidly straightforward way: she painted her lips and dressed to kill, and could throw herself into having fun with total abandon, but when the time came, she would sigh and weep and pray, and suddenly give generous help to someone in need." Alexandra is full of contradictions and is far from sinless, as her last husband senses and the narrative reveals. However, Ivan Isaevich values the broader implications of her living in harmony with *byt*, namely being at peace with self and God in daily life. With this focus Ulitskaya follows a long tradition of Russian novelists who depict what Gary Saul Morson terms the "philosophy of the ordinary." The most celebrated is Leo Tolstoy who, as Berlin evinces in his seminal essay, shows readers how to live righteously not through dogma but by following "rules of thumb." For Ulitskaya these practical guidelines mandate that the sincerity and tolerance of the intelligentsia should shape everyday existence.[84]

Life is more important than ideas; ideas without life take on a terrible abstraction, leading to the horrors of the twentieth century that Ulitskaya documents. Daniel Stein concludes that Jesus teaches us to endorse existence over theology; for this reason the monk sees the present as more important than the eventual Last Judgment. In doing so, Ulitskaya's protagonist rescues faith from the teleological justifications that created religious brutality (the Crusades) and its rationalist counterparts (Stalinism).[85]

The principle of upholding deeds over dogma unites Ulitskaya's oeuvre. She articulates this assertion in an interview, stating, "I am no longer interested at all in dogmatic theology . . . All that interests me is behavior—how people treat their neighbors. It doesn't even matter to me very much what they think." As a number of critics have noted, the protagonist of *Daniel Stein, Interpreter* stresses "orthopraxis" over "orthodoxy," endorsing a practical philosophy steeped in Judeo-Christian tradition. This opposition accompanies a refusal to privilege any one religion over another. During the discussions with German schoolchildren about the Holocaust that form the backbone of the novel, he answers the question a Muslim girl poses about his attitude towards non-believers: "Dear Fatima, I have to admit that I have never in my life come across an unbeliever. Well, almost never. The majority of people, apart from those who completely and unconditionally accept the faith they have chosen or inherited from their parents, have their own ideas about a Supreme Power, a Mover of the world which we believers call the Creator."[86] The schoolchildren, like the reader, are another flock to whom the priest ministers. This audience makes it even more important that Daniel explain how dogma and denomination do not connote belief. Instead, actions are key. As one critic melodramatically but perceptively proclaims, faith is dead without deeds. One source for this idea is clear: Men', Ulitskaya's mentor, reminds believers that Christianity is neither an ideology nor a frozen system of rituals.[87]

Ulitskaya's emphasis on actions over theology increases personal accountability instead of eliding it through a claim to save souls or, in a different vein, to build Communism. One fractious critic scoffs that *Daniel Stein, Interpreter* promotes a permissive god who pats sinners on the head and is a comfortable deity for the consumer era. In truth Ulitskaya's stance could not be more different. With all the righteousness of the marginalized intelligentsia, she denounces abstract ideology, moral laxity, and the culture of gratification that has come with the era of capitalism; her cry for responsibility echoes a central concern of women's prose. The author argues for a practical faith that relies on productive acts in place of empty phrases and promotes unity instead of division.[88]

Difference can lead to strife or, as Stuart Hall has argued, to a new, liberating sense of self. Hybrid characters who combine disparate ethnic, ideational, and religious heritages embody Ulitskaya's philosophy that unity triumphs over conflict. The first major example of this type is Gulia from the early story of the same title, who observes holidays celebrated by her German, Polish, and Russian ancestors. As we note, Ulitskaya's oeuvre develops: it shifts from simply depicting such characters to elaborating on the discourse of tolerance that underlies their depiction. Gulia's mixed origins, for instance, anticipate the diverse backgrounds and beliefs of characters such as Maika and Alik in *The Funeral Party.* Shengeli in *The Big Green Tent*, with his Russian, Georgian, and Jewish roots, incarnates the same principle. Daniel Stein is the apotheosis of hybridity, exemplifying and commenting on the harmonious combination of linguistic, ethnic, and religious difference.[89] Ulitskaya also highlights Daniel's literalized connection of *byt* and *bytie*; what Levantovskaya labels his "gestures of translation" likewise show the bond between physical, quotidian existence and convictions. Ulitskaya herself is a hybrid figure, as her position between secular Jewish and Orthodox Christian identity indicates. In reflecting on her background, she asserts that she need not choose between its varied elements. As "My Favorite Arab" ("Moi liubimyi arab") recounts, the author is reluctant to represent Russians or Russianness. She feels comfortable only speaking for herself, an atypical figure who is "Russian by culture, Jewish by blood, and Christian by faith."[90]

Hybridity recurs across Ulitskaya's oeuvre and reinforces a central part of her philosophy: homogenous groups and monolithic thinking are untenable in an inclusive society. One critic compares this presumption to polyphony: a mixture of viewpoints and distinct character voices shapes Ulitskaya's story cycles. E. F. Shafranskaia theorizes in a parallel way that writing about other ethnicities generates "alien texts" (*inoteksty*) in *Daniel Stein*, which in turn create points of contact between self and other. She sees the existence of the novel—and the coexistence of faiths—as a hopeful sign, despite Daniel's death and failure to transform his principles fully into practice.[91]

Diversity and community are organizing devices in Ulitskaya's work. Mikhail Bakhtin famously charts how Dostoevsky's prose moves from one scandal scene to another. Our analysis examines how Ulitskaya relies on an opposite structure: nearly all of her longer works contain a central moment when relatives, friends, or survivors of a tragedy gather to celebrate or remember. One critic observes that, for a healthy family, celebration is tautological; the quotidian is itself a coming together that provides support through kinship. Nevertheless, to build on our discussion in chapter 2, Ulitskaya's emphasis on the family of affinity—particularly its multicultural dimension—is reinforced when relatives convene, often creating a focal point for plot and theme as well.[92]

The early work *Sonechka* establishes this pattern when a motley assortment of friends, fellow artists, and admirers meet for a posthumous exhibit of Robert Viktorovich's paintings. *Medea and Her Children* transforms the principle of gathering into a rationale for the novel's existence, as its final paragraph makes clear when extolling Medea's clan.[93] This utopian vision of kinship overcoming loss, a favorite for citation by critics, helps explain Ulitskaya's enormous popularity with both intellectuals and ordinary readers eager for a believable but optimistic image of human behavior in difficult times. Earlier in the novel, Masha's suicide and the ensuing funeral have drawn Medea to Alexandra, the one person whom she has not been able to forgive throughout the plot. The service and wake, while following Greek Orthodox tradition, encompass a multitude of faiths and ethnicities.

This scenario has already occurred in the novel with the unusual combination of guests that commemorated Samuel's death decades ago: "Alexandra came with Sergei, Fyodor with Georgii and Natasha, brother Dimitry with his son Gvidas from Lithuania, and all the men of the family from Tbilisi. [. . .] Medea did not allow any baking of pies or a big funeral party. There was traditional kutiya with rice, raisins and honey, there was bread, cheese, a bowl of Central Asian greens, and hard-boiled eggs. When Natasha asked Medea why she had arranged it this way, she replied: 'He was a Jew, Natasha, and Jews don't have funeral parties at all. [. . .] I don't like our parties where people always eat and drink too much. Let it be this way.'" Food portrays unity and the combination of different traditions, ranging from the *kutiya* of Russian Orthodoxy to Central Asian greens. Despite being a strictly observant Christian, Medea melds the wake with Jewish belief, reminding readers that these sometimes antagonistic faiths are also related. The third element present is a natural reluctance to promote the overindulgence alien to her own upbringing and values.[94] The multiethnic wake is a momentous occasion for the author, as *The Funeral Party* also demonstrates. The scene that gives the novel its name gathers a colorful set of guests in the melting pot of New York's Russophone diaspora. It is significant that this coming together occurs outside the USSR: having moved abroad, friends and relatives can now replace the counterfeit unity of the Great Family with the family of affinity. These events reflect a main theme underlying Ulitskaya's oeuvre, namely, that supportive kinship comes from harmony based on personal ethics and tolerance solidified during times of crisis.[95]

Daniel Stein, Interpreter more explicitly reveals the ideals behind this conception of family. In 1992 Daniel travels to Emsk to take part in the fiftieth anniversary of the escape he organized from the ghetto. The event, which involves Jewish survivors from around the world, begins with Kaddish. When the priest who had planned a mass cannot attend, Daniel is the logical choice to replace him, and he conducts services in the church where he took refuge after fleeing from the Gestapo. This circular construction emphasizes that Daniel's life has overcome the enmity between Jew and gentile that helped cause the Holocaust, thus binding plot development to the protagonist enacting a core idea (e.g., faith as a call for reconciliation). In doing so, the novel gives readers the crucial impression that humanity is, indeed, one extended family.[96]

This kinship does not end with people. After Daniel's death and the ransacking of his sanctuary by the crazed Fyodor, Hilda finds an icon that has escaped destruction: "It was a marvelous depiction of 'Praise the Lord the Highest Heavens.' On the icon the sprightly hand of Mother Ioanna had represented Adam with a beard and moustache and Eve with a long pigtail, hares, squirrels, birds, and serpents, and all of creation which had formed a long queue to embark on Noah's Ark and was now leaping and rejoicing and praising the Lord. The flowers and the leaves gleamed, palms and willows waved their branches. A child's train crawled along the earth and childish smoke spiraled joyfully from the funnel. A plane flew in the sky, leaving a slender white vapor trail behind it. The old lady had been a genius. She had envisaged all creation praising the Lord: rocks, plants, animals, and even the iron creations of man."[97] The image that has survived is one of hope that comes from unity under the gaze of a kind deity. Hilda admires the icon that Mother Ioanna has adapted, acknowledging both the original image and the creativity of the artist, a woman of solid faith and good deeds throughout the novel. The *obraz* displays all of the Lord's creation waiting to board the ark: from the first son and daughter to the smallest animal, all will be saved from the impending flood. Even humanity's "iron creations" will be spared, suggesting a need for the descendants of Adam and Eve to recognize their imprint on the world.

Given *Daniel Stein, Interpreter*'s revision of theology, it is appropriate that Mother Ioanna has diverged from the rules of icon painting, which privilege immediate recognition and reverence instead of revisionism and playfulness. The scene she crafts is emblematic of the monk's church. For Daniel all things are connected; there is no division between God's creatures, just as the Lord sees all the faithful as a single flock regardless of religion. The narrative within the icon also resonates with the novel's ideational trajectory: Daniel has perished because he was cursed, and Fyodor has wrecked his sanctuary. In a similar manner, the horrors of the Holocaust and Soviet rule have warped the lives of many whom the Carmelite priest served. However, as the symbol of Noah's ark implies, ultimately all will be saved by a deity who sides with the sufferers and not the persecutors. As in the closing paragraph of *Medea and Her Children*, the reader infers that all people have the chance to belong to the Christian family of affinity if they act with responsibility and tolerance.

The icon in this passage is a multilayered work that addresses the faithful. The legend of Noah and the flood is narrated in scripture, which in turn inspired the creation of the original icon Praise the Lord the Highest Heavens. Then Mother Ioanna reworks this image, which is depicted in the final pages of Ulitskaya's novel. In *The Funeral Party* Alik's version of the Last Supper fulfills a similar function: "Opposite [. . .] hung a large painting of Alik's, depicting the Chamber of the Last Supper, with a triple window and a table covered in a white cloth. There were no people seated at the table, just twelve large pomegranates, drawn in meticulous detail in delicate shades of lilac, crimson and pink, rough and full of seeds, their jagged, hypertrophied crowns and vivid dents evoking their internal partitioned structure. Beyond the triple window lay the Holy Land, seen as it is now rather than in the imagination of Leonardo da Vinci." Ekphrasis combines with veneration. Alik, like Mother Ioanna, has reworked a classic representation of a scene (painted by Leonardo da Vinci) based on a written source (the New Testament). Both the icon and the painting rely on their viewer's conviction that these layers of representation are built on a real event but are also tied to a contemporary context. In *The Funeral Party*, the rabbi who has come to convert Alik recalls that some believed the pomegranate (not the apple) was the source of temptation; likewise, the cleric remembers how the Last Supper supposedly took place on top of the tomb of David. As throughout Ulitskaya's corpus, here Judaism and Christianity are inextricably linked by ties that are corporeal and familial as well as theological and historical.[98]

Like Mother Ioanna's icon, Alik's painting implies the need to recognize all of God's creations, not just the human. Taken together, the images link the Old and New Testaments to the present day, advocating for a living and flexible faith (orthopraxis) instead of ossified dogma. Both works of art convey images of community via an oddly successful mixture of the reverent and the ludic that suits Daniel and Alik. The two men, born Jewish, are depicted as forces of reconciliation, whether through religion or art. It is no coincidence that even in death they cause diverse groups to come together in their honor. These and Ulitskaya's other images of gathering the likeminded contrast vividly with the *narod*'s unthinking stampede at Stalin's funeral.

The icon and painting metaphorically depict the family of affinity, an image of kinship and inclusiveness that acquires added importance when viewed within the context of the intelligentsia. In promoting tolerance as part of an ethical, reflective life, Ulitskaya embodies this group's principles. The author reiterates intellectuals' mandate to educate and enlighten the rest of the population but does so through a new definition of belonging. This shift replaces post-Soviet exclusionary "negative solidarities" and their "patriotism of despair" with the more accepting model of *tolerantnost'*. Literature is the medium for both depicting togetherness and making it a reality. Just as Viktor Iul'evich in *The Big Green Tent* notes that books aid the moral development needed to ensure human survival, Ulitskaya's tolerance project uses writing to create a more inclusive society. Both efforts rely on the power of the text, a supposition with Judeo-Christian overtones of a people united by faith, love, and the word. This utopian scenario resonates with the messianic role Russian literature has long professed.[99]

Christianity for its part can provide a basis for rethinking community. Ulitskaya's attempts to apply it to heal interethnic rifts, clashes between religions, and relations between individual and society reveal a fundamentally optimistic viewpoint about the potential for change and unity. Her literary works (for children and adults) and *publitsistika* play an essential role, educating readers and engendering the awareness that is the precursor to action. Ultimately Ulitskaya's works illustrate not only the intelligentsia's claim to the writing of history but an even loftier goal: the resolution of deep-seated conflicts in past and present.[100]

CONCLUSION

ULITSKAYA, INTELLIGENTSIA, AND THE ETHICS OF THE ORDINARY

Ludmila Ulitskaya completed the novel *Daniel Stein, Interpreter* in the summer of 2006. After acknowledging her debt to dissidents, scholars, and longtime friends, she closes the book with a curious mixture of regret and audacity: "I beg forgiveness of all those I will disappoint, those who will be irritated by my outspokenness, or who will totally reject me. I hope my work will lead nobody astray but serve only to encourage personal responsibility in matters of life and faith. My excuse is my sincere wish to tell the truth as I understand it, and the craziness of that ambition."[1] These final sentences, stark in their combination of contradictory appeals, succinctly summarize the author's worldview. Ulitskaya's novel of reconciliation between Jews and gentiles ends on a personal note that encapsulates the quotidian philosophy of her oeuvre. Conveying the truth—a privilege and duty of the intelligentsia—is its own justification, regardless of who listens. The desire to voice one's morality is "sincere," recalling the strict ethics Ulitskaya ascribes to *intelligenty*, whose values center on honesty and personal responsibility in everyday life. Positive morality, her novel concludes, is meaningless without a corresponding embodiment in *byt*.

This statement is a natural one for Ulitskaya, whose works erase the boundaries between society and writing, self and other, flesh and soul. Her integrative approach is evident in prose that reveals the suffering and sincerity of the body, showing how the physical form also reflects the call for tolerance that structures her oeuvre. *Telesnost'* is more than a subservient shell waiting to be filled with meaning, whether by the state or by the ideas that obsess Russian literature. Early works such as

"Bronka" and *Sonechka* use corporeality to evince the same ethics and actions that more explicitly mold later novels as her corpus develops. Just as Daniel Stein brooks no division between body and spirit, Ulitskaya casts the physical and ideational as an indivisible expression of intelligentsia mores. In this respect she sidesteps the grim physicality that came to dominate the Yeltsin era; the *chernukha* body, as Eliot Borenstein outlines, demarcated the nation's bifurcation into predator and prey, foreign and familiar, enemy and friend. Ulitskaya's texts instead stress how corporeality literally and metaphorically joins characters in daily life. Such connections do not subsume individual identities. Critiquing the Great Family apotheosized by Stalin and revived by Putin, she shows that community need not entail subordination of body and mind to invidious ideology.[2]

Togetherness must instead come from willingly shared values; kinship and belonging result from the intelligentsia virtues of tolerance, responsibility, and *iskrennost'*. The consequent family of affinity, which dominates *Medea and Her Children*, provides a model for the groups of relatives that populate Ulitskaya's prose and plays. Borrowing heavily from two centuries of previous Russian writing, she envisions family as protection against the hostile forces of history. It does not, however, form an impervious barrier: estranged children, broken marriages, and sundry betrayals demonstrate how external forces such as the state strain relations between relatives. This susceptibility explains why shared values, not common genes, are the best guarantor of stable kinship. By supporting the family of affinity, Ulitskaya avoids the false choice that has deformed literature since perestroika: characters must belong either to the coercive Great Family (whether as builders of socialism or Putin's restorers of national pride) or its centrifugal counterpart (*chernukha* families, where only misery and misanthropy link relatives).

The intelligentsia, a mythologized group in Ulitskaya's writing, is itself a family of affinity, in terms of both creativity (as her use of intertexts suggests) and morality. Only intellectuals can correctly interpret Russia's troubled history; literature is more reliable than official records and textbooks subject to government whims. Scientists find similar favor—for Ulitskaya, the nation's decline is evident through genetic degradation as well as the wars and repression causing it. The intelligentsia is not, however, merely a physical presence. Dissidents in *The Big Green Tent* demonstrate that while individual *intelligenty* may fail, their collective ideas do not. Intellectuals are distinct from both the *narod* and the state, and these separations contribute to the independent thought that scholar Dmitrii Likhachev lauds as critical to the group's identity.³ Self-definition must lead to action, or at least the attempt to act. *Daniel Stein, Interpreter* makes this conviction clear with its revision of Christianity, which the novel depicts as the family of Judaism with the addition of Jesus as favorite son. This utopian scenario has little to do with traditional theology. Instead, it reveals that faith is kinship based on belonging, not exclusion. For Ulitskaya religion is empty without the intelligentsia trinity—*tolerantnost'*, responsibility, and sincerity—that inspires her. Despite her prose's limited understanding of groups such as gays and Chechens, Ulitskaya is an author guided by tolerance. Faith, literature, and charitable projects all contribute to an optimism at odds with the despair of the 1990s that preceded the increasingly pompous glory of Putin's Russia. At times gender also plays a role, as Rosalind Marsh notes when discussing how this author has expanded the images provided by women's prose. In one interview Ulitskaya speculates that the course of history suggests that "male" priorities—capturing space and consolidating power—will give way to "female" goals: continuing the species and thus preserving and nurturing offspring.⁴

History and current events have tempered Ulitskaya's belief in basic human goodness. After the punk protest group Pussy Riot's April 2012 trial for hooliganism and inciting religious hatred, she sharply criticized a regime that, along with the Russian Orthodox Church, has become more brazen and less tolerant. Though Nadezhda Tolokonnikova and Mariia Alekhina were released from prison in December 2013, just before the Winter Olympic Games in Sochi, Pussy Riot's continued persecution by police illustrates the regime's proclivity for providing visible reminders of its power.⁵ Ulitskaya has opposed the Russian seizure of Crimea; given her hopes for interethnic tolerance as a means of overcoming past trauma, she is also understandably worried by Putin's actions concerning eastern Ukraine. Ulitskaya likewise bemoans the limited success of her social programs, claiming, for instance, that the children's literature project on tolerance is her "most foolish," in part because of the continued promotional efforts it requires.⁶ However, the cultural rhetoric of such endeavors evokes a much larger problem that informs her worldview: Russia after 1991 has been infantilized by capitalism and its greed, excess, and self-gratification, problems that began in the postwar era. "Physics, chemistry, and biology got involved, medicine expanded, with all its wonderful accomplishments in dentistry, cosmetology, and surgery. Psychology raced ahead with convincing arguments. Many ways were thought up for a person to express love for himself. Plants and factories started up, traveling salesmen worked intensively. It turned out to be a gold mine!"[7]

This criticism is clearly directed at the West as much as the USSR, whose consumer industry was still in its infancy after the Great Patriotic War. Today, however, Ulitskaya worries that the developed nations' love for self, abetted by an avaricious society, has eclipsed care for others or the environment. In Putin's Russia these disturbing traits exist in tandem with an unyielding state that increasingly distances itself from Europe and the tenets of civil society. Between the (corrupting) pleasures of the market and the heavy hand of government, scant room remains for individuals to improve society on their own terms.[8]

Ulitskaya's interviews reflect this foreboding scenario, along with a lament over limited authorial ability that devolves into the trope of exhaustion. She has long maintained that each novel will be her last: the process is too tiring and, as *Daniel Stein*'s autobiographical narrator complains, can literally poison the writer. A professed reluctance to create longer narratives (which subsequently garner profit and critical acclaim) is a part of the Ulitskaya phenomenon. Her high print runs, public visibility, and recognition among all types of readers exemplify how Ulitskaya can sell books, ideas, and even the concept that writing remains relevant in the changed circumstances of post-Soviet Russia.[9]

Her most recent book is *Poet: A Book of Memories: Natal'ia Gorbanevskaia*, a collection of Ulitskaya's and others' essays and reminiscences about the famous dissident. She also recently published *Childhood 45–53: There Will Be Happiness Tomorrow*. Ulitskaya, the volume's compiler, introduces chapters comprised of others' letters about daily life during late Stalinism, the era that dominated her childhood. This encyclopedia of *byt* combines nostalgia for a way of life now vanished and scorn for a state that subjected its citizens to fear and privation. Her *Discarded Relics*, a collection of interviews and essays, signaled a turn away from fiction toward a genre one critic likens to Dostoevsky's *Diary of a Writer*.[10] While in the future she may produce other novels, the seeds of her shift toward documentary prose were present even in Ulitskaya's first stories and novellas, set against the autobiographical backdrop of postwar Moscow. A staple of contemporary literature, memoirs suggest a balance between reliability and personal expression. For Ulitskaya, this translates into verisimilitude, a value inherited from the *shestidesiatniki*, which in turn reliably conveys the sincerity that motivates the intelligentsia. Documentary genres effectively emphasize *iskrennost'* and an (unacknowledged) authorial narcissism as they highlight intellectuals' favorite subject: themselves. Such writing promotes the debate about the past that shapes Ulitskaya's narratives and *publitsistika*, in the process testifying to the survival and importance of intellectuals. In recent decades, Beth Holmgren observes, structural disjuncture has marked aestheticized memoirs. This characterization is true of both *Daniel Stein* and *The Big Green Tent*, despite their generic affinities with fiction. With elaborate plots and appeals to conscience, the novels are memoirs of ideas that privilege dialogue, independent thought, and the need to resist authoritarianism. These rambling narratives likewise underscore the impossibility of imposing unitary meaning on the richly chaotic realms of *byt* and personal experience.[11]

Memoirs document the trauma Mark Lipovetsky and Alexander Etkind identify as the central preoccupation of post-1991 literature. Ulitskaya, however, endorses intelligentsia virtues that, having survived the Soviet period, can now save Russia from repeating past errors. Ideas can overcome individual destinies: ecumenically enlightened Daniel dies after conservative rabbis curse him, and the iconoclasts in *The Big Green Tent* capitulate, emigrate, or commit suicide after confronting the state. Yet while characters perish, their causes persist. Formerly imprisoned oligarch Mikhail Khodorkovsky offers another example of enduring ideals. Ulitskaya's correspondence with him transforms his shift from rapacious capitalist to concerned philanthropist into a plea to resist the twin evils of state and greed. Such scenarios reiterate the intelligentsia's belief in the ascendancy of the spiritual over the material, a tenet central to Ulitskaya's optimism.[12]

Ulitskaya's identity is inseparable from the thinking class whose background and ethics she shares. For several decades the intelligentsia has been in crisis: the collusive state support it previously enjoyed has vanished, replaced by freedoms rendered meaningless by poverty, chaos, and the threat of irrelevance. Katerina Clark argues that the group cannot survive without the regime it opposed; in this sense, the recent authoritarian turn may be an ironically hopeful development for intellectuals. Increasing censorship, broadened state powers, and Putin's posturing inspired demonstrations that—at least in Moscow and Saint Petersburg—roused the nation's dissipated and dispirited thinking class. Ulitskaya's support for Pussy Riot and Khodorkovsky indicates a prominently politicized role both for her and the *intelligenty* she represents. Russia's recent moves to crush dissent may rekindle opposition fueled by national and world attention as well as the deleterious effects of Western sanctions.[13]

The much-maligned market economy is another source of hope. The intelligentsia lost much of its credibility by supporting Yeltsin's disastrous economic "reforms" and the nefarious Western values they connoted. Ulitskaya, while scorning capitalism and its excesses, undoubtedly has benefited from the rise of giant post-Soviet publishers such as Eksmo and Astrel'. She now reaches a population that never would have seen her works outside the narrow circles of *samizdat* (or the miniscule print runs of early 1990s high literature). Though Ulitskaya worries about the lack of serious readers, she is unique in delivering intelligentsia values to a mass market that eagerly awaits her next volume.[14]

Ulitskaya's status as author, *intelligentka*, and enemy of Putin permits her to introduce both a serious critique of the past and the need for tolerance in the present. She models a new role for intellectuals by bringing a message of everyday compassion to millions of readers. From the beginning her works have favored honest simplicity over suspect abstraction. The most erudite characters fail, while their humble counterparts spread kindness by making ethical choices in ordinary life. This second group, Ulitskaya's true heroes, lives the modest morality that unites flesh, family, idea, and faith.

APPENDIX: MAJOR WORKS BY ULITSKAYA, 1988–2013

The Big Green Tent, novel
(*Zelenyi shater*, 2010)

The Big Green Tent is a series of stories that, taken together, form a loosely structured novel. Outsiders Il'ia, Sania, and Mikha meet at school and form a strong bond with Viktor Iul'evich Shengeli, who teaches them about literature and life and is researching Russian childhood. Later all three former students develop into fully fledged members of the dissident intelligentsia as, respectively, photographer, musicologist, and poet, and each experiences his own tragedy alongside the key historical events of the Thaw and Stagnation years. Though Anna Aleksandrovna, Sania's grandmother, is a positive adult influence from the older generation, Il'ia, Sania, and Mikha—like so many of their contemporaries—ultimately remain in a larval state of moral and personal development and cannot avoid ethical compromise or disaster. Even Ol'ga, Il'ia's wife and a dissident herself, does not completely transform. Russian poetry, *samizdat*, and *tamizdat* literature, especially Pasternak's *Doctor Zhivago*, are all important intertexts in the novel.

Childhood 45–53: There Will Be Happiness Tomorrow, edited volume of memoirs
(*Detstvo 45–53: A zavtra budet schast'e*, 2013)

Ulitskaya introduces each section of this compilation of others' letters and memoirs from 1945 to 1953, the years of her childhood. Together these texts comprise an encyclopedia of *byt* in late Stalinism, with Ulitskaya's tone ranging from outrage and horror to nostalgia as she presents the material (selected from the more than six hundred letters she received). The first section concerns the commemoration of May 9 (Victory Day) and how this holiday now signals a return to militarism. The next two parts deal with drinking and eating (and the 1946-1947 famine). Clothing, bathing, playing, and the courtyard (*dvor*) comprise the following sections. Ulitskaya then recalls the communal apartment where she lived until she was twenty-three. The next portions describe others' memories of animals, school, and orphanages; later parts depict life in the city and village, as well as the handicapped, and prisoners of war and the Gulag. Ulitskaya discusses fear as a factor shaping late Stalinism and follows this with a section on the death of the Father of the Peoples. The volume concludes with a series of letters too long to include in the previous sections but too fascinating to omit.

Daniel Stein, Interpreter, novel
(*Daniel' Shtain, perevodchik,* 2006)

Through a series of letters, newspaper clippings, interviews, and other materials, this loosely structured novel depicts the life of Daniel Stein, a fictionalized version of Oswald Rufeisen, who was born a Polish Jew, converted to Catholicism after World War II, and eventually became a priest and resided in Israel. The narratives of several characters help to form a composite picture of Daniel, who attempts to reconcile Christianity, Judaism, and Islam. Ewa, the daughter of a Holocaust survivor, seeks to understand her family's history and her complicated relationship with her mother as she struggles with an unfaithful husband and a gay son. German Hilda comes to Israel to assist Daniel and atone for the sins of the Holocaust. Examples of religious faith and extremism illustrate that, in Daniel's words, all people are believers in some way—but the consequences of rigid belief can be devastating.

Discarded Relics, memoir
(*Sviashchennyi musor,* 2012)

One commentator likens this memoir to Dostoyevsky's *Diary of a Writer*. Ulitskaya notes that the title comes from her inability to part with the things whose material presence shaped her life. The volume is comprised of previously unpublished nonfiction as well as interviews and *publitsistika*, in some cases revised since their original publication. In the introductory section Ulitskaya bemoans the decreased role books play in modern life. The first portion of the volume focuses on Ulitskaya's relatives, friends, and coworkers, with particular attention to her grandparents. She also discusses her early writing career and critiques feminism. In the following section she addresses topics such as politics, post-Soviet poverty, and her reevaluation of Mikhail Khodorkovsky. The next part of the memoir describes her fraught relationship with Christianity, including her experiences while writing *Daniel Stein, Interpreter* and *The Big Green Tent*. This section also details her problems with breast cancer and concludes with Ulitskaya's observation that Christianity is the religion of the poor, not the powerful.

The Funeral Party, novel
(*Veselye pokhorony,* 1997)

In this novel of emigration, artist Alik's death in New York becomes a celebration of life. His visitors and the atmosphere surrounding him present a hybrid array of cultures and religions (thus prefiguring *Daniel Stein, Interpreter*). Shared ideals define family and friendship, a crucial theme throughout Ulitskaya's corpus. It is primarily women who gather around Alik, and their physical depiction emphasizes sexuality and acceptance of the body; the novel also contains one of Ulitskaya's first sympathetic portrayals of a gay character. As they watch the 1991 coup on television, those in the novel observe from afar as history is made.

The Kukotskii Case, novel
(*Kazus Kukotskogo*, 2001)

Prominent gynecologist Pavel Alekseevich Kukotskii meets Elena during wartime evacuation, later marrying her and adopting Tanya, her daughter. A second adopted daughter, Toma, joins the family when her mother dies as the result of an illegal abortion. Eventually the Kukotskii family fractures after the spouses have a fateful argument about the legal and moral aspects of terminating pregnancy. Elena, whose interior life is depicted through an extended dream narrative in the novel, slowly loses her mind. Kukotskii's friend Il'ia Gol'dberg is an inveterate truth-teller who has spent time in the camps and later develops a theory of cultural decline based on his research on the Soviet gene pool. (This decline plays a more prominent role in *The Big Green Tent*.) Despite the sad fates of Kukotskii, Elena, and Tanya, Tanya's daughter Zhenia offers hope for the future, and at the end of the novel Elena experiences a vision that affirms life and human community.

Medea and Her Children, novel
(*Medeia i ee deti*, 1996)

Adopting the structure of the family chronicle, *Medea and Her Children* depicts the history of its protagonist through her reminiscences and the annual visits of relatives to her Crimean home in the 1970s. History and memory intertwine for Medea, and events tend to recur across generations, as when the fateful affair that divides Medea and her sister Alexandra finds an echo in the love triangle of Nike, Masha, and former gymnast Butonov. Ulitskaya's humanized treatment of the body and female sexuality, which are significant elements in her later work, figure prominently in this novel. Childless Medea defines family as inclusive and expanding, and she eventually leaves her home to Crimean Tatar Ravil Yusupov.

My Grandson Veniamin, play
(*Moi vnuk Veniamin*, 1988)

Esfir' tells her cousin Elizaveta how Esfir' left Bobruisk in Belarus just before the Nazis attacked. All her relatives were killed, and today children play on their gravestones. She wants her son Leva to marry Sonia, a Jew from Bobruisk who will visit Esfir' in Moscow. Leva and Sonia marry, but Leva soon leaves her. Adopted by a Jewish woman, Sonia defined herself as Jewish in solidarity with her adoptive mother. Vitia, a childhood (gentile) friend visits Sonia and they have sex. Esfir' wants Sonia to have a Jewish grandson who will be named Veniamin. Upon learning that Sonia is not ethnically Jewish, Esfir' declares that in fact Sonia is the most Jewish of all, since she is an orphan. When Vitia makes anti-Semitic comments, Sonia orders him to leave, despite Esfir' now wanting her to marry him. This early play's discussion of the Holocaust foreshadows more extensive discussion in *Daniel Stein, Interpreter*.

Russian Jam, play
(*Russkoe varen'e*, 2008)

In a decaying dacha in the post-Soviet era an intelligentsia family unwittingly reenacts Chekhov's *Cherry Orchard*. The father of Natal'ia Ivanovna and Andrei Ivanovich received the dacha for supporting Stalin and creating a new type of gooseberry (another evident reference to Chekhov). The various family members each suggest a social problem in 1990s Russia, whether it be Varvara the Slavophile or Liza, who makes phone-sex calls to foreigners. Rostislav, Natal'ia Ivanovna's son, is a developer who wants to buy the dacha. As the play progresses the dacha falls apart, and the greedy handyman Semyon is little help in making repairs. Andrei Ivanovich is moving to Barcelona and has sold the dacha at a ridiculously low price to Semyon, who in turn sells it to Rostislav. The play ends with Rostislav destroying the dacha to make way for the expansion of the Moscow metro.

Seven Saints from Briukho, play
(*Semero sviatykh iz derevni Briukho*, 2008)

During the Russian Civil War Dusia and Mania Gorelia are holy women. Dusia's fiancé abandoned her before their wedding. Father Vasilii and the villagers in Briukho are worried that the Red Army, headed by the violent Rogov, will destroy the village's miraculous icon. Mania, Dusia's former fiancé, is Ulitskaya's only transgendered character. Timosha, who has deserted from the Reds, is commanded by Rogov to shoot Dusia, her helpers, and Father Vasilii. After the execution Timosha sees seven crowns floating into the sky. He becomes a holy fool, and the village is later renamed Rogovsk.

Sincerely Yours, Shurik, novel
(*Iskrenne Vash Shurik*, 2003)

Shurik, whose prototype appears in the short story "Gulia," is raised by his mother Vera and grandmother Elizaveta Ivanovna. His feminized upbringing sets the stage for Shurik's later passivity and sexual involvement with many women, and upbringing itself becomes a central theme of the novel. Through Shurik's lovers and partners, Ulitskaya introduces themes that recur in her texts, such as emigration, the irregular body, redefined family relationships, and the fate of the intelligentsia from the Thaw to the 1990s.

Sonechka, novella
(1992)

In 1941 naïve reader Sonechka is evacuated to Sverdlovsk, where she works in a library and catches the attention of artist Robert Viktorovich, who is in exile. The two marry and have a daughter, Tanya, finally returning to Moscow during the Thaw. When Tanya becomes a teenager she experiments with sex and also meets Jasia, a Polish orphan. Jasia lives with the family, and she and Robert Viktorovich begin an affair that lasts for many years—Robert Viktorovich dies in Jasia's arms. Sonechka, who has long known about them but pities Jasia, continues to support Jasia. At the end of her life Sonechka is alone with the books that she loves. The novella's focus on sexuality, family, creativity, and Stalinist repression establishes these topics as important themes that will appear throughout Ulitskaya's works.

NOTES

Foreword

1. A Russian writer of Georgian origin, Boris Akunin (b. 1956), the pseudonym of Grigorii Chkhartishvili, is the author of an unprecedentedly successful series of detective novels, set at the end of nineteenth-century Russia and featuring Erast Fandorin as the intrepid sleuth, which attempted to "elevate" the genre to middlebrow status. Dar'ia Dontsova achieved enormous popularity in the first decade of the twenty-first century with what she calls her "ironic" crime novels with female protagonists, in which crime takes a back seat to romance and consumerism.

2. From Italy, the Penne Prize in 1997 and again in 2006 for *The Kukotskii Case* (*Kazus Kukotskogo*), as well as the Giuseppe Acerbi Award in 1998 for *Sonechka*; from France, the Medici Prize in 1998, the Chevalier of the Ordre des Palmes académiques in 2003 and the Chevalier of the Ordre des Arts et des Lettres the following year, plus the Simone de Beauvoir Prize in 2011; from China, the National Literature Prize for *Sincerely Yours, Shurik* (*Iskrenne vash Shurik*) in 2005; from Germany and Russia, the Father Alexander Men Award (2008); from South Korea, the Park Kyong-ni Prize (2012); and in 2014 the Austrian State Prize for European Literature. Despite Russian audiences' unflagging enthusiasm for her fiction, official recognition on home terrain lagged behind Europe's. Nonetheless, in 2001 Ulitskaia became the first woman to win the Russian Booker Prize (for *The Kukotskii Case*), and three years later her *Sincerely Yours, Shurik* in Italy received the Grinzane Cavour Literary Award (2008) and in Russia was named Novel of the Year, while she was hailed as Best Writer of the Year—an honor that carries the frivolously labeled Ivanushka Prize. And 2007 brought her the National Olympia Prize of the Russian Academy of Business [*sic*] and the Big Book National Literary Prize for *Daniel Stein, Interpreter* (*Daniel' Shtain, perevodchik*)—the novel that reportedly sold a million copies in Russia.

3. Private conversation in Moscow in 1993.

4. "Ia kak by vremennyi pisatel', vot napishu vse i poidu delat' chto-to drugoe." See http://www.ulickaya.ru/content/view/1271/.

5. I posed the question informally to a range of women in Helsinki, Uppsala, and Łódź during residency fellowships at the Aleksanteri Institute and the Centre for

Russian and Eurasian Studies, as well as during an invited talk at Łódź University in early 2014.

6. See Mikhail Zolotonosov, "Sentimentalizm s pristavkoi 'neo,'" *Moskovskie novosti* 7 February 1992, 26; Mark Lipovetsky, "Literature on the Margins: Russian Fiction in the Nineties," *Studies in 20th Century Literature* 24, no. 1 (Winter 2000): 139-68. Zolotonosov subsequently characterized *Sincerely Yours, Shurik* as ridiculing her own earlier sentimentalism, "rooted in the nineteenth century."

7. See the long dialogue between Mark Lipovetsky and Alexander Etkind, "The Salamander's Return: The Soviet Catastrophe and the Post-Soviet Novel," *Russian Studies in Literature*, no. 4 (2010): 6-48.

8. "Pochemu vmesto togo, chtob rasskazyvat' pro glavnoe, Vy topite Bol'shuiu Istoriiu v chastnoi, seroi, povsednevnoi, obvolakivaete Bol'shie Sobytiia obiliem chastnostei?" "Strogo govoria, imenno sud'ba chastnogo cheloveka menia interesuet. A sud'by gosudarstv—udel istorikov, politologov." Interview of February 2011, reprinted in Ulitskaia's pointedly titled *Sviashchennyi musor [Discarded Relics]* (Moscow: Astrel', 2012), 442-51; specifically 444, 448. Danilkin constantly calls her a guru, ignoring her disclaimers.

9. "Moia zadacha—voprosy stavit', a ne reshat'." Interview available on Ulitskaia's website at http://www.ulickaya.ru/content/view/1284.

10. Perhaps the difference between Ulitskaia's focus and that of many of her male contemporaries may be compared fruitfully to that between two novelists of the early nineteenth century, Walter Scott (1771-1832) and Jane Austen (1775-1817): his historical novels addressed national conflicts and the fate of kingdoms, while hers examined daily life and social mores—what in a letter she famously called "the little bit (two inches wide) of ivory" that constituted her literary purview.

11. In subsequent editions, the title was amended to "Vtorogo marta togo zhe goda." See, for example, Liudmila Ulitskaia, *Veselye pokhorony* (Moscow: Vagrius, 2000).

12. The textual juxtaposition of the two events recalls the synchrony in *Anna Karenina* of Nikolai Levin's death and Kitty's discovery of new life—her pregnancy.

13. Liudmila Ulitskaia, *Bednye rodstvenniki* (Moscow: Slovo, 1994), 178. This, of course, describes Ulitskaia's own authorial manner.

14. "Menia v te moi molodye gody Pasternak ubedil, chto mir spleten iz tonchaishikh nitei [. . .] ona sama vedet tebia v glubinu uzora, cherez napriazhenie strastei, boli, stradaniia, liubvi. [. . .] Eto kusok moei zhizni, skrestivshiisia s mnogochislennymi nitiami drugikh zhiznei, myslei i kartin." The manuscript of her talk, "Sviazi," sent to me by Ulitskaia in March 2003 (I functioned as her interpreter).

15. Liudmila Ulitskaia, *Medea and Her Children*, trans. Arch Tait (New York: Schocken Books, 2002), 4.

16. Ibid., 312.

17. Stishova contends that, unlike in Andrei Tarkovsky's cinema, post-Soviet cinema no longer tropes the yearning for a normal life as the paternal Home/House ("Toska po normal'noi zhizni ne oboznachaetsia bol'she obrazom otchego Doma, kak u Tarkovskogo"). Elena Stishova, "Kto vy, mastera kul'tury?," *Iskusstvo kino*, no. 6 (1993): 66.

18. Robert Viktorovich, her husband, is a splendid painter, her daughter Tanya's extraordinary facility in languages lands her in the United Nations, Tanya's admirer

Vladimir becomes a renowned musician (based on Vladimir Ashkenazy), and the beauty of Jasia ("her other daughter") renders her an ambulatory work of art.

19. "Schastlivye," in Ulitskaia, *Bednye rodstvenniki*, 7. The English translation, made from Ulitskaia's manuscript, appeared as "Lucky," trans. Helena Goscilo, in *From the Soviets*, special issue of *Nimrod* 2, no. 2 (Spring/Summer 1990): 66–70; specifically 68.

20. "Nevazhno, chto my dumaem o vere, o problemakh religioznoi zhizni. Vazhno to, chto my delaem." See the interview titled "Stala pisatelem, kogda menia vygnali s raboty," available at http://ulickaya.ru/content/view/1281/.

21. Ibid.

22. See Brian James Baer, *Other Russias: Homosexuality and the Crisis of Post-Soviet Identity* (New York: Palgrave Macmillan, 2009), 116–18. The only available English translation of the story bears the title "Angel." See Liudmila Ulitskaia, *Sonechka: A Novella and Stories*, trans. Arch Tait (New York: Schocken Books, 2005), 173–94.

23. "[G]omoseksual'nymi ubiistvami militsiia ne osobenno interesovalas'." Ulitskaia, *Veselye pokhorony*, 451. Though homosexuality was decriminalized in 1993, the government and large segments of the population remain virulently homophobic. The law Putin signed in June 2013 banning homosexual "propaganda," obviously intended to eliminate all LGBT activities, tacitly encourages the violence against gays that erupts on a steady basis and has led to the closure of such gay clubs as Moscow's Central Station. See Sunnivie Brydum, "Moscow's Largest Gay Club Shuts Its Doors," *The Advocate* (18 March 2014), available at http://www.advocate.com/world/2014/03/18/moscows-largest-gay-club-shuts-its-doors, and Patricia Herlihy, "Russia's 'Family Values' Experiment: Laws Restricting Abortion, Divorce and Gay Rights Mask Russia's Real Problems," *Los Angeles Times* (19 June 2013), available at http://articles.latimes.com/2013/jun/19/opinion/la-oe-herlihy-russia-anti-gay-20130619.

24. Ulitskaia, *Veselye pokhorony*, 451.

25. *Sviashchennyi musor*, 445.

26. Nikolai Romanovich, in fact, follows the Greek model of homosexual conduct, whereby an older man introduces a young male (*puer delicatus*) to same-sex activity. Called the "Greek vice" by the Romans, ephebic love gradually entered Roman life. See Craig Arthur Williams, *Roman Homosexuality: Ideologies of Masculinity in Classical Antiquity* (Oxford: Oxford University Press, 1999).

27. It is instructive to compare Ulitskaia's treatment of homosexual activity with that portrayed in Sorokin's prose, where it functions as a trope, thoroughly politicized, repellent, and completely devoid of intimacy (see *Blue Lard* [*Goluboe salo*, 1999]). A related presentation of homosexual anal intercourse as rape occurs in Aleksei German's *Khrustalev, My Car!* (*Khrustalev, mashinu!*, 1998).

28. I normally render *chernukha*, derived from the word for black (*chernyi*), as "crime and slime." *Chernukha* designates a radical naturalism comprising an overwhelmingly grim, atavistic world of violence, poverty, drunkenness, random and brutal sexual activity, addiction of all sorts, a seedy environment, and a reduction of most behavior to physiological impulses. It envisions neither respite nor escape from desperately destructive circumstances.

29. A genetic abnormality that duplicates chromosome 21, Down syndrome retards mental, physical, and social development, affecting thought processes, appearance, and

social interaction. Tat'iana Tolstaia's story "Night" ("Noch'," 1987) also depicts a male with Down syndrome, likewise cared for by a loving mother.

30. For an analysis of this story in the context of post-Soviet physiology in women's prose, see Helena Goscilo, *Dehexing Sex: Russian Womanhood during and after Glasnost* (Ann Arbor: University of Michigan Press, 1996), 98–99.

31. Siniavskii critiqued the intelligentsia for endorsing Yeltsin's 1993 shelling of the White House, for having lost touch with popular interests, and for abandoning conscience so as to reap the rewards of alliance with the authorities. See Andrei Sinyavsky, *The Russian Intelligentsia* (New York: Columbia University Press, 1997).

32. Ferran Mateo, "On Being Chosen: The Great Writer Ludmila Ulitskaya Speaks Up," *Russia Beyond the Headlines*, 30 June 2013, available at http://rbth.ru/2013/06/30/on_being_chosen_the_great_writer_ludmila_ulitskaya_speaks_up_27549.html.

33. For the full text of her speech and those of the Austrian officials presiding over the event in Mozarts Geburtshaus in Salzburg, see http://www.penrussia.org/new/2014/1818. An appreciably different view of the 1960s, though with an analogous emphasis on discourse, emerges in the smart and opinionated monograph by Petr Vail' and Aleksandr Genis, *60-e: Mir sovetskogo cheloveka* (Moscow: Novoe literaturnoe obozrenie, 1996).

34. Miscellaneous Russian commentators in thrall to Richard Florida's highly assailable concept of the "creative class" have ascribed the various anti-Putin demonstrations to Russia's creative class, but no one has defined the nature of that putative class in Russia. See Richard Florida, *The Rise of the Creative Class* (New York: Basic Books, 2002). For cogent criticism of Florida's theory, see, among numerous others, Eugene McCann, "Inequality and Politics in the Creative-City Region: Questions of Livability and State Strategy," *International Journal of Urban and Regional Research* 31, no. 1 (2007): 188–96; J. Peck, "Struggling with the Creative Class," *International Journal of Urban and Regional Affairs* 29, no. 4 (2005): 749–70; and D. Ponzini and U. Rossi, "Becoming a Creative City: The Entrepreneurial Mayor, Network Politics and the Promise of Urban Renaissance," *Urban Studies* 47, no. 5 (2010): 1037–57.

35. Elizabeth Day, "Ludmila Ulitskaya: Why I'm Not Afraid of Vladimir Putin," *The Observer*, 16 April 2011. Available at http://www.theguardian.com/world/2011/apr/17/lyudmila-ulitskaya-dissident-putin-interview.

36. Mateo, "On Being Chosen," translation adjusted, HG.

37. For a laudatory review of the volume, see Richard Sakwa, "Mikhail Khodorkovsky: Putin's Prisoner, Russia's Hero," *Times Literary Supplement*, 28 September 2011. Available at http://www.the-tls.co.uk/tls/public/article785939.ece.

38. On this volume, Akunin's participation in it, and in an exchange with Khodorkovsky printed in *Esquire*, see Anna Stroganova, "Boris Akunin: 'Dlia menia perepiska s Khodorkovskim znachila ochen' mnogoe," *RFI Russkii: Literaturnyi perekrestok* (6 April 2011). Available at http://www.russian.rfi.fr/prava-cheloveka/20110416-boris-akunin-dlya-menya-perepiska-s-khodorkovskim-znachila-ochen-mnogoe.

39. Day, "Ludmila Ulitskaya."

40. See note 28.

41. Ulitskaia, "Lucky," 69.

42. "Gor'ko i besslovesno plakala plot' do utra." In Liudmila Ulitskaia, *Skvoznaia liniia* (Moscow: Eksmo, 2004), 164–82; specifically 181. The published English version, by Arch Tait, is in *Sonechka: A Novella and Stories*, 195–219; specifically 218: "Wordlessly

the flesh lamented until morning." Apart from omitting an equivalent for "gor'ko," however, the translation fails to use a verb that communicates the notion of fluids, secreted during sexual activity—a euphemistic displacement important for the scene.

43. "[Seans zakonchilsia] kratkim vvedeniem—v priamom i perenosnom smysle— v novyi predmet." *Sonechka*, in *Bednye rodstvenniki*, 231-87; specifically 257.

44. "Vse budet pravil'no, na etom mir postroen." Mikhail Bulgakov, *Sobranie sochinenii* (Ann Arbor: Ardis, 1988), 8:378.

45. In subsequent editions, this collection of stories carried the shortened title of *Devochki*. Whereas *Bednye rodstvenniki* had a print run of three thousand copies, once she became popular, the print runs of her publications increased accordingly.

46. "The Student," trans. Michael Henry Heim, *Anton Chekhov's Selected Stories*, ed. Cathy Popkin (New York: W. W. Norton, 2014), 290-93, specifically 293.

47. Cathy Popkin, introduction to *Anton Chekhov's Selected Stories*, xviii.

Introduction

1. Ulitskaia canceled her reading at the last minute due to illness, yet the gathering that expected her reflects an obvious but crucial truth: writers' identities stem in part from their audience. On Limonov, see Andrew Wachtel, *Remaining Relevant after Communism: The Role of the Writer in Eastern Europe* (Chicago: University of Chicago Press, 2006), 94.

2. For stylistic reasons our analysis uses necessarily imprecise synonyms ("thinking caste," "intellectuals," etc.) to designate the varied social groups that together form the intelligentsia. The seminal discussion of *intelligenty* in English is Isaiah Berlin, "Introduction," in *Russian Intellectual History: An Anthology*, ed. Marc Raeff (New York: Harcourt, Brace, and World, 1966), 3-11.

3. Vladimir Pomerantsev, "Ob iskrennosti v literature," *Novyi mir*, no. 12 (1953): 218-45. Svetlana Boym discusses sincerity in *Common Places: Mythologies of Everyday Life in Russia* (Cambridge: Harvard University Press, 1994), 95-97. On the importance of the individual over the state, see Liudmila Ulitskaia, "Ulitskaia: Podlinnyi sopernik Khodorkovskogo—Putin," interview with Mikhail Shevelev, *Radio Svoboda*, 11 September 2009, http://www.svobodanews.ru/articleprintview/1820056.html.

4. On "new sincerity," see Ellen Rutten, *Sincerity after Communism: A Cultural History*, unpublished manuscript. For a discussion of the periphery in post-Soviet Russia, see Edith Clowes, *Russia on the Edge: Imagined Geographies and Post-Soviet Identity* (Ithaca, NY: Cornell University Press, 2011). Masha Gessen is one of the latest critics to notice Ulitskaia's optimism. See "The Weight of Words: One of Russia's Most Famous Writers Confronts the State," *New Yorker*, 6 October 2014, 34, http://www.newyorker.com/magazine/2014/10/06/weight-words.

5. The first Anglophone article on Ulitskaia was a study of the novella *Sonechka*. See Deuk-Jae Lee, "The Terrible Journey to Self-Identification," *Rusistika*, no. 17 (1998): 31-34; Clowes, *Russia on the Edge*; Benjamin Sutcliffe, *The Prose of Life: Russian Women Writers from Khrushchev to Putin* (Madison: University of Wisconsin Press, 2009).

6. Edit Gilbert, ed., *Embertan és irodalom: Elbeszélésbe oltott gének Ljudmila Ulickaja regényeiben* (Pécs: Muvészetek Háza, 2005); Margarita Levantovskaya, "The Russian-Speaking Jewish Diaspora: Liudmila Ulitskaia's *Daniel Stein, Translator*," *Slavic Review*,

no. 1 (2012): 91-107; see also Rimgaila Salys, "Ljudmila Ulickaja's Sonečka: Gender and the Construction of Identity," *Russian, Croatian and Serbian, Czech and Slovak, Polish Literature*, no. 3 (2011): 443-66. Among the dissertations are: Jenne Powers, "Novel Histories: Repudiation of Soviet Historiography in the Works of Iurii Trifonov, Vladimir Makanin, and Liudmila Ulitskaia" (PhD diss., University of North Carolina at Chapel Hill, 2009); Natal'ia Egorova, "Proza L. Ulitskoi 1980-2000-kh godov: Problematika i poetika" (Kand. diss., Astrakhanskii gosudarstvennyi universitet, 2007); and Peri Israfil gyzy Mamedova, "Khudozhestvennoe prostranstvo i vremia v sovremennoi russkoi proze (na material tvorchestva L. Ulitskoi)" (Kand. diss., Bakinskii slavianskii universitet, 2011).

7. On the problem of global culture and consumerism, see Liudmila Ulitskaia, interview with Elizabeth Skomp, 5 May 2012. For connections between poverty and consumer culture, see Ulitskaia, interview with Elizabeth Skomp and Benjamin Sutcliffe by e-mail, 17 June 2011. In this message she qualifies her disdain for those ensnared by the market, admitting that price determines what consumers can afford. Nikolai Aleksandrov, "V Moskve vruchena premiia 'Bol'shaia kniga,'" *Novoe vremia*, no. 42 (2007): 51.

8. Helena Goscilo and Vlad Strukov, "Introduction," in *Celebrity and Glamour in Contemporary Russia: Shocking Chic*, ed. Helena Goscilo and Vlad Strukov (London: Routledge, 2011), 6. For a discussion of the Ulitskaia phenomenon and popularity, see Aleksandrov, "V Moskve vruchena premiia," 51.

9. A substantial body of scholarship explores the dark fate of the book market in the 1990s. See Helena Goscilo, "Big-Buck Books: Pulp Fiction in Post-Soviet Russia," *The Harriman Review*, nos. 2-3 (1999/2000), 8. On the post-Soviet decline of the publishing industry within the broader context of developing consumer culture, one example is Nancy Condee and Vladimir Padunov, "The ABCs of Russian Consumer Culture: Readings, Ratings, and Real Estate," in *Soviet Hieroglyphics: Visual Culture in Late Twentieth-Century Russia*, ed. Nancy Condee (Bloomington: Indiana University Press; London: British Film Institute, 1995).

10. Liudmila Ulitskaia, "'Krizis—pravil'noe sostoianie,'" in *Vazhnee, chem politika: Pochemu my tak zhivem i kak mogli by zhit'?*, ed. Aleksandr Arkhangel'skii (Moscow: AST, 2011), 24, 36.

11. The education official is quoted in Pavel Basinskii, "Novosti: Rossiia vo Frankfurte," *Rossiiskaia gazeta*, 19 October 2005, 1. For a discussion of Ulitskaia's popularity abroad, see, for example, Klarisa Pul'son's interview with Slavist Hélène Melat, "Ideal'noe chtenie," *Profil'*, 9 April 2012, http://www.profile.ru/article/idealnoe-chtenie-70028. On worries about literature, commercialization, and commodities, see Boym, *Common Places*, 61.

12. For an excellent though dated overview of Ulitskaia's biography, see Maria Litovskaia, "Lyudmila Ulitskaya," trans. Seth Graham, *Russian Writers since 1980*, ed. Marina Balina and Mark Lipovetsky, Dictionary of Literary Biography 285 (Detroit: Gale, 2004), 330. On the author's grandfathers, see Liudmila Ulitskaia, "Tri avtora: Khristianstvo bez miloserdiia?," *Moskovskie novosti*, 2 December 2003, 5; and Ulitskaia, "Mladshaia shestidesiatnitsa," interview with Mariia Sedykh, *Obshchaia gazeta*, no. 20 (2002): 8.

13. Ulitskaia discusses her grandmother in *Sviashchennyi musor* (Moscow: Astrel', 2012), 237; and Ulitskaia, comp., *Detstvo 45-53: A zavtra budet schast'e* (Moscow: AST, 2013), 103.

14. Litovskaia, "Lyudmila Ulitskaya," 330; Ulitskaia, "Ulitskaia—Khodorkovskii: Bez protokola," *Novaia gazeta*, 11 September 2009, http://www.novayagazeta.ru/society/43627.html. Ulitskaia discusses her experience with *samizdat* in Liudmila Ulitskaia, "Ravnenie na Medeiu," interview with O. Nikolaeva and A. Nikolaev, *Novye Izvestiia*, 24 February 2000, 7; and "Vstrechi: Liudmila Ulitskaia: Ne mogli by vyzhit', esli b," interview with Vladimir Prikhod'ko, *Moskovskaia pravda*, 27 January 2001, 6. On her mother's death, see Ulitskaia, "Liudmila Ulitskaia otvetila na nashi voprosy," *Snob*, http://www.snob.ru/selected/entry/28919.

15. For mention of her marriages and divorces, see, for example, "Korzina, kartina, kartonka i malen'kaia sobachonka," interview with Iana Zhiliaeva, *Moskovskii komsomolets*, 30 January 1999, 3.

16. Litovskaia, "Lyudmila Ulitskaya," 329. On the author's early reception, see also Mariia Litovskaia, "Smena sotsial'nykh stereotipov i fenomen populiarnosti pisatelia: Sluchai Liudmily Ulitskoi," in *Noveishaia russkaia literatura rubezha XX-XXI vekov: Itogi i perspektivy*, comp. and ed. M. A. Cherniak and A. M. Novozhilova (St. Petersburg: LEMA, 2007). Ulitskaia has authored two books for children: *Skuchnaia shuba* (Moscow: Malysh, 1982) and *Sto pugovits* (Moscow: Detskaia literatura, 1983). Her first play, which would be reissued decades later by Eksmo, is *Moi vnuk Veniamin* (Moscow: VAAP-inform, 1988). Liudmila Ulitskaia, "Bron'ka," *Ogonek*, no. 52 (1989): 2-23; Ulitskaia, *Sonechka*, *Novyi mir*, no. 7 (1992): 61-89; Ulitskaia, *Medeia i ee deti*, *Novyi mir*, nos. 3-4 (1996): 3-46, 7-79. For a partial list of Ulitskaia's journal publications (beginning in 1994), see *Zhurnal'nyi zal*, http://magazines.russ.ru/authors/u/ulitskaya/. Ulitskaia has moved from publisher to publisher: first Vagrius, then Eksmo, and most recently Astrel'.

17. Liudmila Ulitskaia, *Kazus Kukotskogo* (Moscow: Eksmo, 2001); Iurii Grymov, director, *Kazus Kukotskogo* (Moscow: NTV, 2005); Ulitskaia, *Daniel' Shtain, perevodchik* (Moscow: Eksmo, 2006). For a list of Ulitskaia's awards, see the website of her agent, Elena Kostiukovich, http://www.elkost.com/authors/ulitskaya. Ulitskaia's novel *The Big Green Tent* (*Zelenyi shater*, 2010) had an initial print run of 200,000 and has been reissued multiple times. The first printing of *Discarded Relics* (*Sviashchennyi musor*, 2012) is also notable: 100,000 copies were published. Astrel' is now republishing all of her works from the 1990s and beyond.

18. On Ulitskaia's characteristic style, see Tat'iana Frolova, "Shater s tablichkoi 'vykhod,'" *Neva*, no. 8 (2011): 200. For a discussion of morality, profit, and consumers as eternal adolescents, see Galina Iuzefovich, "Gospozha nabliudatel'," *Itogi*, no. 8 (2011), http://www.itogi.ru/iskus/2011/8/162194.html. Concerning Ulitskaia's universal appeal, see I. V. Nekrasova, "O raznykh sposobakh povestvovaniia v proze Liudmily Ulitskoi," in *Izmeniaiushchaiasia Rossiia—izmeniaiushchaiasia literatura: Khudozhestvennyi opyt XX-nachala XXI vekov, sbornik nauchnykh trudov*, comp. A. I. Vaniukov (Saratov: Nauka, 2008), 2:303. In 2011 Benjamin Sutcliffe observed a bookstore in central Moscow using Ulitskaia's name to market volumes in which she was the author of the introduction.

19. Liudmila Ulitskaia, "A Conversation with Ludmila Ulitskaya," reading and talk at Cooper Union, New York, 4 May 2012; Vladislav Zubok, *Zhivago's Children: The Last Russian Intelligentsia* (Cambridge, MA: Belknap, 2009), 353, 355. On the symbiosis between intelligentsia and state, see the provocative study by Katerina Clark, "The King Is Dead, Long Live the King: Intelligentsia Ideology in Transition," paper presented at the conference "Russia at the End of the Twentieth Century: Culture and Its Horizons

in Politics and Society," Stanford University, October 1998, http://www.stanford.edu/group/Russia20/volumepdf/clark_fin99.pdf.

20. Zubok, *Zhivago's Children*, 351. For a survey of intelligentsia narratives of defeat, see Dmitrii Shalin, "Intellectual Culture," in *Russian Culture at the Crossroads: Paradoxes of Postcommunist Consciousness*, ed. Dmitrii Shalin (Boulder, CO: Westview Press, 1996), 41.

21. Boris Dubin, "Rossiiskaia intelligentsiia mezhdu klassikoi i massovoi kul'turoi," in *Slovo-pis'mo-literatura: Ocherki po sotsiologii sovremennoi kul'tury* (Moscow: Novoe literaturnoe obozrenie, 2001), 341.

22. Evgeniia Shcheglova, "Nesbyvshaiasia mechta: O proze Liudmily Ulitskoi," *Zvezda*, no. 3 (2012): 229. On the USSR's effects on history, see Irina Paperno, "Personal Accounts of the Soviet Experience," *Kritika*, no. 4 (2002): 597; Lev Gudkov, *Negativnaia identichnost': Stat'i 1997–2002 godov* (Moscow: Novoe literaturnoe obozrenie, 2004), 14. Ulitskaia voices her fears over books' disappearance in her memoirs: *Sviashchennyi musor*, 13. On literature and culture tying humanity to its world, see ibid., 55.

23. Wolfgang Iser, "Foreword: Intertextuality; The Epitome of Culture," in *Memory and Literature: Intertextuality in Russian Modernism*, by Renate Lachmann, trans. Roy Sellars and Anthony Wall (Minneapolis: University of Minnesota Press, 1997), xi.

24. Liudmila Ulitskaia, *Zelenyi shater* (Moscow: Eksmo, 2011), 5; Guy de Mallac, *Boris Pasternak: His Life and Art* (Norman: University of Oklahoma Press, 1981), 293. On the epigraph to *The Big Green Tent* and Ulitskaia's works as a whole, see Frolova, "Shater s tablichkoi 'vykhod,'" 207.

25. Ulitskaia, *Sviashchennyi musor*, 203; Liudmila Ulitskaia, *Zhenshchina dlia vsekh*, unpublished screenplay, 13; M. E. Poriadina, "Aktualizatsiia 'tolerantnykh' motivov v detskoi knige na sovremennom rossiiskom rynke," *Bibliografiia*, no. 1 (2009): 63.

26. Our definition of intertextuality is borrowed from Andrew Wachtel, *Plays of Expectations: Intertextual Relations in Twentieth-Century Russian Drama* (Seattle: University of Washington Press, 2006), 3–4; Ulitskaia, *Zelenyi shater*, 459, 460. On Pasternak's pre-1917 worldview, see de Mallac, *Boris Pasternak*, 297.

27. Wachtel, *Plays of Expectations*, 6. On intertextuality and cultural memory, see Iser, "Foreword," xiii.

28. Harold Bloom, *The Anxiety of Influence: A Theory of Poetry* (New York: Oxford University Press, 1973), 5–6; Sandra Gilbert and Susan Gubar, *The Madwoman in the Attic: The Woman Writer and the Nineteenth-Century Literary Imagination* (New Haven and London: Yale University Press, 1979), 48. On the stage adaptation of *Sonechka*, see Liudmila Ulitskaia, "Novyi roman 'Daniel' Shtain, perevodchik,'" interview with Kseniia Larina, *Ekho Moskvy*, 19 November 2006, http://www.echo.msk.ru/programs/kazino/47588.

29. Liudmila Ulitskaia, *Liudi nashego tsaria* (Moscow: Eksmo, 2005), 5, 7; Ulitskaia, *Sviashchennyi musor*, 468.

30. Dubin, "Rossiiskaia intelligentsiia," in *Slovo-pis'mo-literatura*," 332; Ulitskaia, *Zelenyi shater*, 52–53.

31. On Ulitskaia as representative of a moribund intelligentsia, see Evgenii Belzhelarskii, "My nikogda ne stanem starshe," *Itogi*, no. 52 (2010), http://www.itogi.ru/arts-kniga/2010/52/160445.html. For an evaluation of Ulitskaia as a writer for the common reader, see Elena Plakhova, "Proza: Velikolepnyi ochevidets," *Moskovskaia pravda*, 17 August 2005, 4.

32. On Ulitskaia and Chekhov, see N. A. Baksaraeva, "'Dushevnost' bez dukhovnosti'? (Chekhovskaia traditsiia v povesti L. Ulitskoi 'Sonechka')," in *Tvorchestvo A. P. Chekhova: Mezhvuzovskii sbornik nauchnykh trudov*, ed. G. I. Tamarli (Taganrog: Taganrogskii gosudarstvennyi pedagogicheskii institut, 2004), 108; Ulitskaia, *Zelenyi shater*, 540-41.

33. Mikhail Zolotonosov, "Chitatel': Muzhchiny ee mechty," *Moskovskie novosti*, 13 February 2004, 25. For other views linking Ulitskaia and the classic Russian novel, see Daniel Rondeau, "La grande Ludmila," *L'Express*, no. 2802 (2005): 61; and B. Tesmer, "Proza Liudmily Ulitskoi na rubezhe XX-XXI veka (spetsifika tvorcheskoi manery)," in *Traditsii russkoi klassiki XX veka i sovremennost': Materialy mezhdunarodnoi nauchnoi konferentsii*, comp. and ed. S. M. Kormilov (Moscow: Izdatel'stvo Moskovskogo universiteta, 2002), 281.

34. On the nineteenth-century novel's interest in the quotidian, see Gary Saul Morson, "Philosophy in the Nineteenth-Century Novel," in *The Cambridge Companion to the Classic Russian Novel*, ed. Malcolm Jones and Robin Feuer Miller (Cambridge: Cambridge University Press, 1998), 150, 166.

35. For a discussion of the author's favorite writers, see Ulitskaia, *Sviashchennyi musor*, 205. Ulitskaia, *Medeia i ee deti* (Moscow: Eksmo, 2002), 162. On Medea and betrayal, see M. A. Bologova, "Rozhdenie liriki iz dukha parodii: L. Ulitskaia; 'Veselye pokhorony' vs 'Medeia i ee deti,' 'Sonechka' & 'Kazus Kukotskogo,'" in *Parodiia v russkoi literature XX v.: Sbornik statei*, ed. A. I. Kuliapin et al. (Barnaul: Izdatel'stvo Altaiskogo gosudarstvennogo universiteta, 2002), 147.

36. Tat'iana Grigor'eva, "Liudmila Ulitskaia: Zelenyi shater," *OpenSpace.ru arkhiv*, 24 January 2011, http://os.colta.ru/literature/events/details/20064/. On Ulitskaia, *Anna Karenina*, and Chechnya, see Tat'iana Samoilycheva, "Absoliutnyi zvon," *Literaturnaia gazeta*, no. 44 (2012): 7.

37. Ulitskaia, *Zelenyi shater*, 173. Ulitskaia discusses Pushkin in *Sviashchennyi musor*, 37; Ulitskaia, *Zelenyi shater*, 43.

38. Zolotonosov, "Chitatel'," 25. Other critics comment on neosentimentalism as a pattern in Ulitskaia criticism: Litovskaia, "Lyudmila Ulitskaya," 331; Sun' Chao, "Tvorchestvo L. Ulitskoi v kontekste russkoi literatury kontsa XX v. Novatorstvo i traditsiia," in *Aktual'nye problemy sotsiogumanitarnogo znaniia: Sbornik nauchnykh trudov kafedry filosofii MPGU. Vypusk 27* (Moscow: Prometei, 2004), 184.

39. For an overview of the problematics of male and female writing in the nineteenth century, see Barbara Heldt's foundational work: *Terrible Perfection: Women and Russian Literature* (Bloomington: Indiana University Press, 1987). On the link between sincerity and sentimentalism, see Rutten, *Sincerity after Communism*.

40. For an exploration of family and literature, see Robert Stephens, *The Family Saga in the South: Generations and Destinies* (Baton Rouge: Louisiana State University Press, 1995), 3-6. Jenne Powers called our attention to this reference. Irina Savkina, "Rod/dom: Semeinaia khronika Liudmily Ulitskoi i Vasiliia Aksenova," in *Semeinye uzy: Modeli dlia sborki*, comp. and ed. Sergei Ushakin (Moscow: Novoe literaturnoe obozrenie, 2004), 1:173, 157; Leonid Bakhnov, "Genio loci," *Druzhba narodov*, no. 8 (1996): 179.

41. Analysis of Ulitskaia and the family chronicle is adapted from Benjamin Sutcliffe, "Everyday Life and the Ties That Bind in Liudmila Ulitskaia's *Medea and Her Children*," in *Everyday Life in Russia: Subjectivities, Perspectives, and Lived Experience*,

ed. David Ransel, Mary Cavender, Karen Petrone, and Choi Chatterjee (Bloomington: Indiana University Press, forthcoming).

42. Concerning Mandel'shtam, see Ulitskaia, interview with Skomp; Ulitskaia, "Liudmila Ulitskaia: I Accept Everything That Is Given," interview with Anastasiia Gosteva, *Russian Studies in Literature*, no. 2 (2001): 92; on Ulitskaia and Nabokov, see E. V. Larieva, "'Est' igry, v kotorye ia ne igraiu'. Ili 'igraiu'? Nabokovskii intertekst v povesti L. Ulitskoi 'Sonechka,'" in *Siuzhet, motiv, istoriia: Sbornik nauchnykh statei*, vypusk 8, ed. E. V. Kapinos (Novosibirsk: Nauka, 2009), 223.

43. Ulitskaia, *Sviashchennyi musor*, 34, 41. On Nabokov and Pasternak, see Liudmila Ulitskaia, reading and talk at Columbia University, New York, 3 May 2012. Ulitskaia, *Sviashchennyi musor*, 37.

44. For Ulitskaia's comments on *Doctor Zhivago*, see "Ravnenie na Medeiu," 7. For comparisons between Ulitskaia and Pasternak, see, for example, Dominique Fernandez, "Tolstoï et les bébés," *Le Nouvel Observateur*, no. 2038 (2003): 59; Mikhail Edel'shtein, "Za vsiu sredu," *Ekspert*, no. 12 (2011): 72.

45. Tat'iana Skokova, "Proza Liudmily Ulitskoi v kontekste russkogo postmodernizma: Avtoreferat" (Kand. diss., Moskovskii gosudarstvennyi gumanitarnyi universitet, 2010), 4-5; Jasmina Vojvodić, "Ljudmila Ulickaja i ruski postmodernizam," *Književna republika*, nos. 5-7 (2008): 245. On Russian postmodernism, see the informative study by Mark Lipovetsky, *Russian Postmodernist Fiction: Dialogue with Chaos*, trans. Eliot Borenstein (Armonk, NY: M. E. Sharpe, 1999).

46. Ulitskaia, reasonably enough, denies she is a postmodernist: Liudmila Ulitskaia, "Schitaite menia retrogradom," interview with I. Evseev, *Sankt-Peterburgskii universitet*, nos. 28-29 (1998): 4, quoted in Larieva, "'Est' igry,'" 222. On preserving versus destroying, see "Liudmila Ulitskaia: Dumala, ne dozhivu do finala svoego poslednego romana," interview with Maksim Chizhikov, *Komsomol'skaia pravda*, 21 February 2008, http://www.kp.ru/daily/24053/104935/.

47. Ulitskaia, "Mladshaia shestidesiatnitsa," 8. For a sustained comparison of Ulitskaia and Trifonov, see Jenne Powers, "Novel Histories." On Ulitskaia's perception of Solzhenitsyn, see Liudmila Ulitskaia, "Bez bol'shikh illiuzii, no . . . ," *Zhurnal Indeks/Dos'e na tsenzuru*, no. 16 (2001), http://www.index.org.ru/journal/16/ulizkaya.html.

48. Ulitskaia, *Zelenyi shater*, 240. On the intelligentsia's right to interpret history, see Irina Paperno, *Stories of the Soviet Experience: Memoirs, Diaries, Dreams* (Ithaca, NY: Cornell University Press, 2009), xii; Ulitskaia, Russian Literary Series, Brooklyn Public Library, Brooklyn, NY, 5 May 2012.

49. Concerning Pomerantsev, see Rutten, *Sincerity after Communism*. Lipovetsky and Etkind, "The Salamander's Return," 9-11. On Ulitskaia's novels and ethics, see Evgeniia Shcheglova, "Nesbyvshaiasia mechta: O proze Liudmily Ulitskoi," *Zvezda*, no. 3 (2012): 218.

50. On connections between everyday life and women's prose, see Sutcliffe, *The Prose of Life*, 3-23. For a strong survey of women's prose and the body, see Goscilo, *Dehexing Sex*, 87-116. On Ulitskaia and women's prose, see Goscilo, "Perestroika and Post-Soviet Prose: From Dazzle to Dispersal," in *A History of Women's Writing in Russia*, ed. Adele Barker and Jehanne Gheith (Cambridge: Cambridge University Press, 2002), 303, 309-310.

51. Tat'iana Kazarina, "Bednye rodstvenniki," *Preobrazhenie*, no. 4 (1996): 169. See also I. A. Mart'ianova, "Metapoetika zhivopisi i kino v proze L. Ulitskoi, L. Petrushevskoi

i D. Rubinoi," in *Metapoetika: Sbornik statei nauchno-metodicheskogo seminara "Textus,"* ed. V. P. Khodus (Stavropol: Stavropol'skii gosudarstevnnyi universitet, 2008), 1:336.

52. On Ulitskaia, Petrushevskaia, and Chekhov, see L. G. Tiutelova, "Chekhovskaia traditsiia v otechestvennoi drame XX veka i p'esa L. Ulitskoi 'Russkoe varen'e, ili Afterchekhov,'" in *Sovremennaia russkaia drama: Sbornik statei i materialov mezhdunarodnoi nauchnoi konferentsii (27-29 sentiabria 2007 g.)*, ed. I. Bidermann, E. N. Shevchenko, and T. S. Shakhmatova (Kazan: RITs shkola, 2008), 164. Ulitskaia comments on Petrushevskaia's prose as brutal but correct in "Plokhoi chitatel'," *Voprosy literatury*, no. 1 (1996): 34; on Petrushevskaia's talent, see Liudmila Ulitskaia, "Priznanie Liudmily Ulitskoi: 'V sleduiushchei knige ia vynuzhdena budu sebia ubit,'" interview with Alla Bossart, *Vecherniaia Moskva*, 18 June 2001, 3. Ulitskaia praises Petrushevskaia's *Number One* in *Sviashchennyi musor*, 215. Petrushevskaia's bizarre novel, which depicts cannibalism and transmigration of souls, has little affinity with Ulitskaia's work, aside from the dream state Elena experiences in *The Kukotskii Case*. Liudmila Petrushevskaia, *Nomer Odin, ili V sadakh drugikh vozmozhnostei* (Moscow: Eksmo, 2006). Ulitskaia and Petrushevskaia both identify their literature teachers as formative influences (Ulitskaia, *Sviashchennyi musor*, 19; Liudmila Petrushevskaia, *Deviatyi tom* [Moscow: Eksmo, 2003], 126).

53. In Petrushevskaia's oeuvre unsavory men run the gamut from would-be rapist intellectual Zhora in *Our Crowd* (*Svoi krug*) to recidivist son Andrei in *The Time: Night* (*Vremia noch'*) who locks himself in his mother's room with two women. Liudmila Petrushevskaia, *Svoi krug*, in *Dom devushek* (Moscow: Vagrius, 1998), 329; Petrushevskaia, *Vremia noch'*, in *Dom devushek*, 368, 396.

54. Nina Sadur, "Worm-Eaten Sonny," trans. Wendi Fornoff, in *Lives in Transit: Recent Russian Women's Writing*, ed. Helena Goscilo (Dana Point, CA: Ardis, 1995), 203-4. For a discussion of Sadur and gendered violence, see Elizabeth Skomp, "Violence, Madness, and the Female Grotesque in Nina Sadur's *The South* and Svetlana Vasilenko's *Little Fool*," in *Times of Trouble: Violence in Russian Literature and Culture*, ed. Marcus Levitt and Tatyana Novikov (Madison: University of Wisconsin Press, 2007), 287-95. On the supposed relationship between the state and emasculation, see Mar'a-Leena Raunio, "Kak ia ne stala pisatel'nitsei," in *Mariia: Literaturnyi al'manakh*, comp. Galina Skvortsova (Petrozavodsk: Kareliia, 1990), 1:272.

55. Ulitskaia, *Kazus Kukotskogo*, 67, 422.

56. Helena Goscilo, "Women's Wards and Wardens: The Hospital in Contemporary Russian Women's Fiction," *Canadian Women's Studies/Les Cahiers de la femme*, no. 4 (1989): 83-84.

57. On Petrushevskaia's dark depictions of gay men, see Sutcliffe, *The Prose of Life*, 89.

58. Liudmila Ulitskaia, *Sestrichki "Liberti,"* unpublished screenplay. For one instance of how Tolstaia connects beauty and artificiality, see her story "Krug," in *Reka Okkervil'* (Moscow: Podkova, 2004), 62.

59. Ulitskaia, reading and talk at Columbia University. She critiques women's prose and feminism in Ulitskaia, *Sviashchennyi musor*, 225, 222. On reactions to feminism and women's prose, see Goscilo, *Dehexing Sex*, 12-13.

60. On Ulitskaia not belonging among the authors of women's prose, see, for example, T. M. Koliadich, "L. E. Ulitskaia," in *Russkaia proza kontsa XX veka*, ed. T. M. Koliadich (Moscow: Academia, 2005), 372; and Elena Elina and Svetlana Ishekova, "Obrazy Rossii v tsikle rasskazov L. Ulitskoi 'Devochki,'" in *Mir Rossii v zerkale*

noveishei khudozhestvennoi literatury: Sbornik nauchnykh trudov, ed. A. I. Vaniukov (Saratov: Izdatel'stvo Saratovskogo universiteta, 2004), 187.

61. On Ulitskaia, women's prose, and nineteenth-century literature, see Sergei Malashenok, "Kak napisat' roman Ulitskoi," *Topos: Literaturno-filosofskii zhurnal*, 1 July 2005, http://topos.ru/article/3762. Concerning physiology and characters ruled by their vaginas, see Lev Kuklin, "Kazus Ulitskoi," *Neva*, no. 7 (2003): 179. Other critics ascribe to Ulitskaia the putative pleasantness of *zhenskaia proza*, e.g., Andrei Nemzer, "Pervaia ledi: Laureatom premii Smirnoff-Buker stala Liudmila Ulitskaia," *Vremia novostei*, 7 December 2001, http://www.vremya.ru/2001/226/10/17407.html.

62. On women's prose and the intelligentsia, see Sutcliffe, *The Prose of Life*, 72–73.

63. On the Red Pinkerton, see Catharine Nepomnyashchy, "Markets, Mirrors, and Mayhem: Aleksandra Marinina and the Rise of the New Russian *Detektiv*," in *Consuming Russia: Popular Culture, Sex, and Society since Gorbachev*, ed. Adele Barker (Durham, NC: Duke University Press, 1999), 162–63, 165.

64. For a sense of the cataclysmic Yeltsin era, see Vladimir Korobov, "So Many Books, Yet So Few, or the New Publishing Crisis," trans. Marian Schwartz, ed. Deming Brown, *Russian Social Science Review*, no. 1 (1997): 82–89. On the absence of censorship in literature, see Ulitskaia, "A Conversation with Ludmila Ulitskaya."

65. Ulitskaia, reading and talk at Columbia University; Ulitskaia, *Sviashchennyi musor*, 60.

66. For comments on an ecology of reading, see Ulitskaia, "'Krizis—pravil'noe sostoianie,'" 46. Iuzefovich discusses Ulitskaia as social commentator in "Gospozha nabliudatel'."

67. See the bizarre comment inserted by the editor following I. A. Ostrenko's article: "Subkul'tura detstva v tsikle L. Ulitskoi 'Devochki,'" in *Mirovaia slovesnost' dlia detei i o detiakh*, ed. I. G. Mineralova (Moscow: Moskovskii gosudarstvennyi pedagogicheskii universitet, 2004), 9:1:62. On Ulitskaia and the *telenovela*, see "Liudmila Ulitskaia: Obshchestvo podrostkov menia pugaet," interview with Lev Danilkin, *Afisha*, 16 February 2011, http://www.afisha.ru/article/8621/.

68. On Ulitskaia's difference from mass literature, see E. V. Chumakevich, "Postrealizm v sovremennoi russkoi proze: Romany D. Rubinoi i L. Ulitskoi," *Vestnik Brestskaga universiteta. Seriia filologichnykh nauk*, no. 2 (2009): 33. Ulitskaia's revival of the *roman* is implicit in discussions about her using the chronotope of the nineteenth-century novel, e.g., I. V. Nekrasova, "Siuzhetoobrazuiushchaia funktsiia khronotopa v romane L. Ulitskoi 'Kazus Kukotskogo,'" in *Prostranstvo i vremia v khudozhestvennom proizvedenii: Sbornik nauchnykh trudov*, comp. and ed. A. G. Prokof'eva, V. Iu. Prokof'eva, and S. M. Skibin (Orenburg: Orenburgskii gosudarstvennyi pedagogicheskii universitet, 2002), 86. On literary criticism and reading, see Ulitskaia, reading and talk at Columbia University.

69. Ulitskaia discusses reading Akunin in: Liudmila Ulitskaia, "Iskrenne vasha, Liudmila Ulitskaia," interview with Ivana Ignat'eva, *Versiia*, no. 15 (2004): 25. On Akunin and history, see Elena Baraban, "A Country Resembling Russia: The Use of History in Boris Akunin's Detective Novels," *Slavic and East European Journal*, no. 3 (2004): 396–420.

70. Ulitskaia has authored an introduction to Limonov's book on Russian prisons; see Eduard Limonov, *Mes prisons* (Arles: Actes Sud, 2008); Wachtel, *Remaining Relevant after Communism*, 92.

71. On the "stroll with authors" protest, see Artem Efimov, "Samaia chitaiushchaia strana," *Lenta.ru*, 13 May 2012, http://lenta.ru/articles/2012/05/13/reading/; Dmitrii Bykov, *Opravdanie* (Moscow: ProzaiK, 2010).

72. Dina Rubina, *Na solnechnoi storone ulitsy* (Moscow: Eksmo, 2011). For a comparison of Rubina and Ulitskaia, see Ol'ga Os'mukhina, "V poiskakh utrachennoi tolerantnosti: Liudmila Ulitskaia," *Voprosy literatury*, no. 1 (2011): 146. Chumakevich discusses the image of Tashkent in "Postrealizm v sovremennoi russkoi proze," 30, 32.

73. "Liudmila Ulitskaia: U nas kak-to dazhe modno — byt' neschastnoi," interview with Irina Slavinskaia, *Ukrains'ka pravda*, 24 November 2011, http://life.pravda.com.ua/person/2011/11/24/90088/. On Ulitskaia's readership, see Ulitskaia, interview with Skomp.

74. For discussion of how books form personality, see Ulitskaia, *Sviashchennyi musor*, 29, 31.

75. On Ulitskaia's son, see *Sviashchennyi musor*, 310. Ulitskaia, *Zelenyi shater*, 140. See Clowes, *Russia on the Edge*, 2. Another critic makes the contentious argument that those from a mixed cultural background avoid the dichotomized trap of "backwards" Russian thinking and its misguided Western neo-liberal counterpart: Madina Tlostanova, "The Imagined Freedom: Post-Soviet Intellectuals between the Hegemony of the State and the Hegemony of the Market," *South Atlantic Quarterly*, no. 3 (2006): 655.

76. Liudmila Ulitskaia, *Daniel Stein, Interpreter: A Novel in Documents*, trans. Arch Tait (New York: Overlook, 2011), 19. On moving between many languages and a single one, see N. V. Logunova, "Transformatsiia zhanrovogo kanona epistoliarnogo romana v knige L. Ulitskoi 'Daniel' Shtain, perevodchik,'" in *Russkaia literatura v formirovanii sovremennoi iazykovoi lichnosti: Sankt-Peterburg 24–27 oktiabria 2007 g.*, vol. 1, *Literatura v formirovanii iazykovoi lichnosti: Etapy i varianty*, ed. P. E. Bukharkin, N. O. Rogozhina, and E. E. Iurkov (St. Petersburg: Mirs, 2007), 171. On Stein as translator between heaven and earth, see Elena D'iakova, "Bol'shoi knigoi nazvano zhitie," *Novaia gazeta*, 26 November 2007, 19; Kapitolina Koksheneva, "Dyra novogo ateizma: O romane Liudmily Ulitskoi 'Daniel' Shtain, perevodchik,'" *Moskva*, no. 4 (2008): 209. On the image of the translator, see Anja Tippner, "Konversion(en): Translation und Identität in Ljudmila Ulickajas Roman *Daniel' Štajn — perevodčik* // Daniel Stein — Ubersetzer," in *Trans-lation — Trans-nation — Trans-formation: Übersetzen und jüdische Kulturen*, ed. Petra Ernst et al. (Innsbruck: StudienVerlag, 2012), 217–33.

77. Yuri Slezkine, *The Jewish Century* (Princeton, NJ: Princeton University Press, 2004), 1.

78. Andrew Wachtel, "Translation, Imperialism, and National Self-Definition in Russia," *Public Culture*, no. 1 (1999): 69, 55. For the most famous discussion of Russian culture as universal, see Fyodor Dostoevsky, "Pushkin (A Sketch)," in *A Writer's Diary*, trans. Kenneth Lantz, ed. Gary Saul Morson (Evanston, IL: Northwestern University Press, 1993), 2:1281–95.

79. On Ulitskaia and multiethnic cultural exchange, see Olaf Terpits, "'Zdes' i tam': Aspekt 'kul'turnogo transfera' v literaturnom diskurse 1990-kh godov," trans. A. I. Godina, in *Evreiskaia emigratsiia iz Rossii, 1881–2005*, ed. O. V. Budnitskii (Moscow: ROSSPEN, 2008), 357, 358; Jasmina Vojvodić, "Transfery Danielia Shtaina," *Russian Literature*, no. 1 (2011): 141–55; Levantovskaya, "The Russian-Speaking Jewish Diaspora." Liudmila Ulitskaia, *Veselye pokhorony* (Moscow: Eksmo, 2006), 161.

80. The mention of New York evokes Sergei Dovlatov's prose about Soviet exiles; on Ulitskaia and Dovlatov, see Nina Malygina, "Zdes' i seichas: Poetika ischeznoveniia," *Oktiabr'*, no. 9 (2000): 156; Adrian Wanner, *Out of Russia: Fictions of a New Translingual Diaspora* (Evanston, IL: Northwestern University Press, 2011), 10.

81. On Ulitskaia as traitorous emigrant, see, for example, Ol'ga Nadezhdina, "Naviazannaia subkul'tura," *Literaturnaia gazeta*, no. 19 (2008): 10. Shcheglova, "Nesbyvshaiasia mechta," 219-20, 218.

82. Liberals are only a subset of the heterogeneous post-1991 intelligentsia: see Masha Gessen, *Dead Again: The Russian Intelligentsia after Communism* (London: Verso, 1997), 18. The comments on the similarities between readers in different countries come from Ulitskaia, reading and talk at Columbia University; Ulitskaia, interview with Skomp.

83. Ulitskaia distinguishes honesty from falsehood in *Sviashchennyi musor*, 166. On Men', Solzhenitsyn, and Sakharov, see Liudmila Ulitskaia, "'Krizis—pravil'noe sostoianie,'" 34, 35, 44. On Iulii Daniel', see Ulitskaia, "My v zerkale iskusstva: Vash Iu," *Obshchaia gazeta*, no. 47 (2000): 10; on Men', Sakharov, and Solzhenitsyn, see Ulitskaia, "Tri avtora," 5.

84. The *narod* is as much a cultural construct as the intelligentsia. In late Soviet culture this became evident when both of these groups shaped village prose, whose sometimes retrograde values Ulitskaia eschews. For an overview of these authors, see Kathleen Parthé, *Russian Village Prose: The Radiant Past* (Princeton, NJ: Princeton University Press, 1992).

85. Liudmila Ulitskaia, "Ia ne khochu golosovat' za men'shee zlo," *Russkii kur'er*, 10 March 2004, 1; on the intelligentsia's presumptions about the *narod*, see Masha Gessen, *Dead Again*, 7. For a discussion of the intelligentsia's perception of values and survival, see Paperno, "Personal Accounts," 610. On the shared emphasis on writing, common dislike of free trade, and other similarities between *intelligenty* and the state, see Clark, "The King Is Dead."

86. Ulitskaia, "'Krizis—pravil'noe sostoianie,'" 20.

87. For a recent (if slanted) discussion of Stalinism and public debate, see David Satter, *It Was a Long Time Ago, and It Never Happened Anyway: Russia and the Communist Past* (New Haven, CT: Yale University Press, 2012).

88. "Liudmila Ulitskaia: Obshchestvo podrostkov." On commercializing the Soviet past, see Ulitskaia, "Predislovie: Trudnyi podrostok protiv Velikogo mifa," in *Khochu zhit'! Dnevnik sovetskoi shkol'nitsy*, by Nina Lugovskaia (Moscow: RIPOL-klassik, 2010), 3.

89. Ulitskaia frequently expresses concern about the common people and the future of the nation. For a fuller discussion of the "society of adolescents," see Ulitskaia, "Lichinki, deti lichinok," interview with Anastasiia Gosteva, *Gazeta.ru*, http://www.gazeta.ru/culture/2010/12/21/a_3472805.shtml.

90. For an overview of xenophobic fears over birthrates and the gene pool, see Serguei Oushakine, *The Patriotism of Despair: Nation, War, and Loss in Russia* (Ithaca, NY: Cornell University Press, 2009), 100-105.

91. On her disavowal of literature as instruction, see Ulitskaia, "Liudmila Ulitskaia: Kak dlia vzroslykh, tol'ko luchshe," interview with A. Onoprienko, *Trud*, 14 September 2004, 6.

92. Concerning Ulitskaia's work with hospitals, see her foreword to *Chelovek popal v bol'nitsu*, comp. Liudmila Ulitskaia (Moscow: Eksmo, 2009). For one of Ulitskaia's

first commentaries on the tolerance series, see "Pisatel' Liudmila Ulitskaia: 'Nashi knigi o cheloveke, kotoryi ne takov, kak vy,'" *Izvestiia*, 19 June 2006, 12.

93. Oushakine, *The Patriotism of Despair*.

94. For an image of Ulitskaia's novels as a unified text, see Radostina Veleva, "Romanite na Liudmila Ulitskaia—mezhdu traditsiiata i novata slovesnost," *Bol'garskaia rusistika*, nos. 1–2 (2010): 155. On Ulitskaia's own description of her works as continuations of their predecessors, see the article discussing the author's visit to Vologda, "Liudmila Ulitskaia: Pishu to, o chem znaiu," http://www.cultinfo.ru/home/0975/15.htm.

Chapter 1. Redeeming the Body

1. Ulitskaia, *Daniel Stein, Interpreter*, 294–95.
2. Ulitskaia, *Sviashchennyi musor*, 210.
3. Judith Butler, *Bodies That Matter: On the Discursive Limits of "Sex"* (London: Routledge, 1993), 2; Elizabeth Grosz, *Volatile Bodies: Toward a Corporeal Feminism*, Theories of Representation and Difference (Bloomington: Indiana University Press, 1994), 19.
4. On sentiment and sentimentalism, see Rutten, *Sincerity after Communism*; Mikhail Zolotonosov, "Chitatel'," 25.
5. Helena Goscilo and Andrea Lanoux, "Introduction: Lost in the Myths," in *Gender and National Identity in Twentieth-Century Russian Culture*, ed. Helena Goscilo and Andrea Lanoux (DeKalb: Northern Illinois University Press, 2006), 20. On the mind/body binary, see Rolf Hellebust, *Flesh to Metal: Soviet Literature and the Alchemy of Revolution* (Ithaca, NY: Cornell University Press, 2003), 149.
6. One key example of Stalinist physique appears in the film *Circus* (*Tsirk*), which depicts an American circus star who finds refuge in the USSR with her mixed-race son; Grigorii Aleksandrov, director (Moscow: Mosfil'm, 1936). Lilya Kaganovsky depicts its opposite: the male body sacrificed for the glory of the state. See Kaganovsky, *How the Soviet Man Was Unmade: Cultural Fantasy and Male Subjectivity under Stalin* (Pittsburgh, PA: University of Pittsburgh Press, 2008).
7. Yury Trifonov, *The Exchange and Other Stories*, trans. Ellendea Proffer et al. (Evanston, IL: Northwestern University Press, 2002). For an even more influential view of middle age, see *Moscow Does Not Believe in Tears* (*Moskva slezam ne verit*); Vladimir Men'shov, director (Moscow: Mosfil'm, 1979).
8. Vasilii Pichul, director, *Malen'kaia Vera* (Moscow: Kinostudiia im. M. Gor'kogo, 1988). For the classic discussion of the Great Family, see Katerina Clark, *The Soviet Novel: History as Ritual* (Chicago: University of Chicago Press, 1981), 114, 115. This translation of *chernukha* comes from Helena Goscilo. On perestroika and bodily trauma, see Goscilo, "Perestroika and Post-Soviet Prose," 309.
9. Aleksandr Rogozhkin, director, *Osobennosti natsional'noi okhoty* (St. Petersburg: Lenfil'm, 1995). For an overview of 1990s fears of population decline, see Michele Rivkin-Fish, "From 'Demographic Crisis' to 'Dying Nation': The Politics of Language and Reproduction in Russia," in Goscilo and Lanoux, *Gender and National Identity*, 151–73. On the sexualized female body, see Eliot Borenstein, *Overkill: Sex and Violence in Contemporary Russian Popular Culture* (Ithaca, NY: Cornell University Press, 2008).
10. For an overview of homosexuality after 1991, a discussion of selective tolerance, and a nuanced reading of Ulitskaia's "Golubchik," see Brian James Baer, *Other Russias:*

Homosexuality and the Crisis of Post-Soviet Identity (New York: Palgrave Macmillan, 2009). Baer discusses the relationship between Yeltsin-era homophobia and literature in "Engendering Suspicion: Homosexual Panic in the Post-Soviet *Detektiv*," *Slavic Review* 64, no. 1 (2005): 24-42.

11. Aleksei Balabanov, director, *Brat 2* (Moscow: STV, 2000). On Putin as physical image and ideological brand, see Helena Goscilo, "Russia's Ultimate Celebrity: VVP as VIP *Objet d'art*," in *Putin as Celebrity and Cultural Icon*, ed. Helena Goscilo (London: Routledge, 2012), 6-36.

12. For a discussion of Dontsova and Robski, see Olga Mesropova, "Crime, Byt, and Fairy-Tales: Daria Dontsova and Post-Soviet Ironical Detective Fiction," *Slavic and East European Journal*, no. 1 (2008): 113-28; Mesropova, "The Discreet Charm of the Russian Bourgeoisie," *Russian Review*, no. 1 (2009): 89-101; Borenstein, *Overkill*, 18.

13. Ulitskaia, *Kazus Kukotskogo*, 19; Grymov, *Kazus Kukotskogo*.

14. Ulitskaia, *Kazus Kukotskogo*, 18.

15. Marianne Hirsch, *The Mother/Daughter Plot: Narrative, Psychoanalysis, Feminism* (Bloomington: Indiana University Press, 1989), 12.

16. Ulitskaia, *Kazus Kukotskogo*, 11-12, 14.

17. Ibid., 31; Goscilo and Lanoux, "Introduction," 13.

18. Ulitskaia, *Kazus Kukotskogo*, 73.

19. Ibid., 76.

20. Ibid., 238.

21. Ibid., 306.

22. Ibid., 347, 344; Lev Pirogov, "Kipiatok ne dlia chainikov: Ulitskaia, Tolstaia i natsional'nyi vopros," *Nezavisimaia gazeta, Ex Libris*, 12 January 2006, 5.

23. Ulitskaia, "Pevchaia Masha," in *Liudi nashego tsaria*, 126, 130, 131, 132, 135.

24. Liudmila Ulitskaia, "Doch' Bukhary," in *Bednye, zlye, liubimye* (Moscow: Eksmo, 2002), 50, 57.

25. Liudmila Ulitskaia, "Lialin dom," in *Bednye, zlye, liubimye*, 71. The description of Kazia exemplifies the female gaze Yelena Furman discusses. See Furman, "Writing the Body in New Women's Prose: Sexuality and Textuality in Contemporary Russian Fiction" (PhD diss., University of California-Los Angeles, 2004).

26. Ulitskaia, "Doch' Bukhary," in *Bednye, zlye, liubimye*, 53-54; Ulitskaia, "Lialin dom," in *Bednye, zlye, liubimye*, 73, 75, 71.

27. Ulitskaia, *Veselye pokhorony*, 55, 63-64, 234.

28. Simi Linton, *Claiming Disability: Knowledge and Identity* (New York: New York University Press, 1998), 11. Keith Livers, *Constructing the Stalinist Body: Fictional Representations of Corporeality in the Stalinist 1930s* (Lanham, MD: Lexington Books, 2004).

29. On the damaged male body, see Kaganovsky, *How the Soviet Man Was Unmade*, 11; Kuklin, "Kazus Ulitskoi," 179.

30. Ulitskaia, "Podkidysh," in *Bednye, zlye, liubimye*, 155, 161-62, 152.

31. Liudmila Ulitskaia, *Iskrenne Vash Shurik* (Moscow: Eksmo, 2005), 208, 178. On disability and marginalization, see Linton, *Claiming Disability*, 12.

32. Liudmila Ulitskaia, "The Chosen People," trans. Isabel Heaman, in *Lives in Transit: A Collection of Recent Russian Women's Writing*, ed. Helena Goscilo (Dana Point, CA: Ardis, 1995), 90, 92.

33. Ibid., 91. On the importance of contemplation, see Ulitskaia and Khodorkovskii, "Dialogi: Liudmila Ulitskaia—Mikhail Khodorkovskii," in *Stat'i, dialogi, interv'iu*, by Mikhail Khodorkovskii (Moscow: Eksmo, 2010), 132.

34. Ulitskaia, "Doch' Bukhary," in *Bednye, zlye, liubimye*, 56, 58, 59, 50, 52, 55. Tat'iana Kazarina observes Ulitskaia's women employing seemingly superhuman strength. Ailing Alya, for example, manages to prolong her life so that her daughter will be old enough to marry before Alya dies. See Kazarina, "Bednye rodstvenniki," 170.

35. Andrei Sinyavsky, *Ivan the Fool: Russian Folk Belief; A Cultural History*, trans. Joanne Turnbull and Nikolai Formozov (Moscow: Glas, 2007), 260. The *iurodivaia* (female holy fool) in Ulitskaia's works manifests humility more than other behaviors typical of the holy fool.

36. Svetlana Vasilenko's *Little Fool* (*Durochka*) contains the best-developed example of the *iurodivaia*, who travels through time to mitigate suffering. On Vasilenko, see Svitlana Kobets, "From Fool to Mother to Savior: The Poetics of Orthodox Christianity and Folklore in Svetlana Vasilenko's Novel-Vita *Little Fool* (Durochka)," *Slavic and East European Journal*, no. 1 (2007): 87-110.

37. Liudmila Ulitskaia, "Dar nerukotvornyi," in *Bednye, zlye, liubimye*, 114, 124-25, 120, 121.

38. Liudmila Ulitskaia, *Semero sviatykh iz derevni Briukho*, in *Russkoe varen'e i drugoe* (Moscow: Eksmo, 2008), 9, 36, 69, 66, 68, 7, 71.

39. On the literary pedigree of the holy fool, see Ulitskaia, "Iskrenne vasha," 25. Vasilenko's novella *Shamara* offers another positive image of a transgendered character: the mercurial but ultimately kind hermaphrodite Lera. See Sutcliffe, *The Prose of Life*, 89.

40. For a scandalous critique of women's prose and the body, see Pavel Basinskii, "Pozabyvshie dobro? Zametki na poliakh 'novoi zhenskoi prozy,'" *Literaturnaia gazeta*, no. 7 (1991): 10.

41. See, for example, the acerbic comments by Vladimir Rudinskii, "Liudmila Ulitskaia. 'Liudi nashego tsaria,'" *Nasha strana* (Buenos Aires), 24 September 2005, 3. On the link between biology and the physiological, see Kuklin, "Kazus Ulitskoi," 177-83.

42. Ulitskaia, *Sviashchennyi musor*, 427.

43. Ibid., 462.

44. Liudmila Ulitskaia, *Medea and Her Children*, trans. Arch Tait (New York: Schocken Books, 2002), 65, 69, 187.

45. Ulitskaia, *Medeia i ee deti*, 154, 153.

46. Ulitskaia, *Kazus Kukotskogo*, 95, 169, 269.

47. Aleksandr Solzhenitsyn, *Cancer Ward*, trans. Rebecca Frank (New York: Dial, 1968). Petrushevskaia likewise links totalitarianism and illness in her grim novella *Little Terrible* (*Malen'kaia Groznaia*): Liudmila Petrushevskaia, *Malen'kaia Groznaia*, in *Dom devushek*. On the relationship between Stalinism and illness in this novella, see Tat'iana Rovenskaia, "Opyt novogo zhenskogo mifotvorchestva: 'Medeia i ee deti' L. Ulitskoi i 'Malen'kaia Groznaia' L. Petrushevskoi," *Adam i Eva: Al'manakh gendernoi istorii*, ed. L. P. Repina (Moscow: Institut vseobshchei istorii RAN, 2001), 156-57.

48. On men and the *sharashka*, see Aleksandr Solzhenitsyn, *The First Circle*, trans. Thomas P. Whitney (New York: Harper and Row, 1968). Ulitskaia, *Kazus Kukotskogo*, 35, 54. Predecessors focused less on assault of the body and more on domesticity; the first major work to do so—Lidiia Chukovskaia's terrifying *Sof'ia Petrovna*—was penned

during the Stalin period itself. Given Anglophone Slavists' fascination with this era, it is all the more unfortunate that *The Kukotskii Case* has not yet been translated into English.

49. Ulitskaia, *Medea and Her Children*, 67.

50. For the connections between biology and medicine, see Ulitskaia, "Liudmila Ulitskaia: I Accept Everything," 74. On Pavel Alekseevich and Spasokukotskii, see Ulitskaia, "Ia ne khochu," 1; Ulitskaia, *Kazus Kukotskogo*, 32.

51. Ulitskaia, *Kazus Kukotskogo*, 165, 140, 73–75, 77–78, 211, 31.

52. See I. Grekova, Perelom, in *Na ispytaniiakh* (Moscow: Sovetskii pisatel', 1990); Marina Palei, "The Bloody Women's Ward," trans. Arch Tait, in *Women's View*, ed. Natasha Perova and Andrew Bromfield (Moscow: Glas, 1992). One critic notes that uncaring doctors contributed to women's persistent feeling of shame connected with the body, yet another instance of ideology manifested through corporeality: Tat'iana Rovenskaia, "Vinovata li ia . . . ? Ili fenomen gendernoi viny (na materiale zhenskoi prozy 80-kh-nachalo 90-kh godov)," *Gendernye issledovaniia*, no. 3 (1999): 218.

53. On *The Death of Ivan Ilyich*, see Mariia Remizova, "Grandes dames proshedshego sezona: Zametki o literaturnykh premiiakh," *Kontinent*, no. 112 (2002): 396–405.

54. Liudmila Ulitskaia, *The Funeral Party*, trans. Cathy Porter (New York: Schocken Books, 1999), 145.

55. Ulitskaia, *Veselye pokhorony*, 283.

56. Ol'ga Slavnikova posits that female nakedness in the novel denotes community and lack of competition among the women rather than eroticism. See Slavnikova, "Nedolet ukazyvaet na tsel'," *Ural*, no. 2 (1999): 184. The film adaptation of this work is striking and supports Slavnikova's argument: Vladimir Fokin, director, *Niotkuda s liubov'iu ili Veselye pokhorony* (Moscow: Fora-fil'm, 2007). On the significance of the body, see Grosz, *Volatile Bodies*, vii.

57. Aleksei Balabanov, director, *Brat* (Moscow: STV, 1997). For a discussion of the economic and social crises facing the elderly in the 1990s, see, for example, Victoria Velkoff and Kevin Kinsella, "Russia's Aging Population," in *Russia's Torn Safety Nets: Health and Social Welfare during the Transition*, ed. Mark Field and Judy Twigg (New York: St. Martin's, 2000), 231–50.

58. Liudmila Ulitskaia, "Pisatel' Liudmila Ulitskaia: 'Vsekh interesuet tol'ko—kakoe imenno bel'e nosila Knipper-Chekhova," interview with Natal'ia Kochetkova, *Izvestiia*, 27 July 2005, 12. On the author's admiration of the older generation, see Ulitskaia, *Sviashchennyi musor*, 67.

59. Aleksandr Solzhenitsyn, "Matryona's House," *Stories and Prose Poems*, trans. Michael Glenny (New York: Farrar, Straus and Giroux, 1971), 3–52; Liudmila Ulitskaia, "March 1953," trans. Arch Tait, in *Present Imperfect: Stories by Russian Women*, ed. Ayesha Kagal and Natasha Perova (Boulder, CO: Westview Press, 1996), 12.

60. Ulitskaia, *Moi vnuk Veniamin*, in *Russkoe varen'e i drugoe*.

61. For analysis of this discourse, see Rivkin-Fish, "From 'Demographic Crisis' to 'Dying Nation.'" Ulitskaia, *Kazus Kukotskogo*, 444; Ulitskaia, "Vtorogo marta togo zhe goda," in *Bednye, zlye, liubimye*, 176. See Ulitskaia's comments about Russians accepting death while Americans are unwilling to discuss the subject: "Liudmila Ulitskaia: I Accept Everything," 81–82.

62. Ulitskaia, *Kazus Kukotskogo*, 21–22, 395.

63. For the description of Vasilisa in the bathhouse, see ibid., 410. On the need for feminists to reconsider corporeality, see Grosz, *Volatile Bodies*, xi, xiii.

64. Ulitskaia, *Kazus Kukotskogo*, 442. The discussion of bathing in *The Kukotskii Case* is based on Benjamin Sutcliffe, "Mother, Daughter, History: Embodying the Past in Liudmila Ulitskaia's *Sonechka* and *The Case of Kukotskii*," *Slavic and East European Journal*, no. 4 (2009): 606–22.

65. Ulitskaia, *Zelenyi shater*, 335, 340.

66. On the role of the widow, see Helena Goscilo, "Widowhood as Genre and Profession à la Russe: Nation, Shadow, Curator, and Publicity Agent," in Goscilo and Lanoux, *Gender and National Identity*, 55–74; Ulitskaia, *Medea and Her Children*, 149.

67. Ulitskaia, "Gulia," in *Bednye, zlye, liubimye*, 93, 86, 91. On Ulitskaia versus Baranskaia, see Helena Goscilo, "Introduction: Squaring the Circle," in *Lives in Transit*, xv.

68. Ulitskaia notes that Shurik was the prototype for the protagonist in *Sincerely Yours, Shurik*; perhaps compassion as well as attraction motivates Gulia's latest admirer (Ulitskaia et al., "Roman li to, chto ia pishu? Otchet o Bukerovskoi konferentsii," *Voprosy literatury*, no. 2 [2005]: 28). On Russia as a weak nation, see Oushakine, *The Patriotism of Despair*, 5.

69. Liudmila Ulitskaia, "Logika erosa," interview with Natal'ia Dardykina, *Moskovskii komsomolets*, 24 December 2001, 6. On women's prose and the visibly traumatized female body, see Goscilo, "Perestroika and Post-Soviet Prose," and Goscilo, *Dehexing Sex*, 87–116.

70. Julia Kristeva, *Black Sun: Depression and Melancholia*, trans. Leon Roudiez (New York: Columbia University Press, 1989), 48.

71. Liudmila Ulitskaia, "Chuzhie deti," in *Bednye, zlye, liubimye*, 132, 137; Kazarina, "Bednye rodstvenniki," 171.

72. Ulitskaia, "Lialin dom," in *Bednye, zlye, liubimye*, 78, 80.

73. Hirsch, *The Mother/Daughter Plot*, 16, emphasis in original; Ulitskaia, *Kazus Kukotskogo*, 13–14, 445. On the function of dreams in *The Kukotskii Case*, see Iuliia Semikina, "Khudozhestvennaia fenomenologiia izobrazheniia bytiia i inobytiia v romane L. Ulitskoi 'Kazus Kukotskogo,'" *Studia Universitatis Babeș-Bolyai, Philologia*, no. 1 (2008): 123–30.

74. Ulitskaia's screenplay for *The Liberty Sisters* is her work most shaped by *chernukha*. For a critique of how Ulitskaia depicts sexuality, see Ol'ga Ryzhova, "Kumirnia: Koitus Kukotskogo, ili Samaia intelligentnaia domokhoziaika," *Literaturnaia gazeta*, no. 37 (2004): 11.

75. Ostrenko, "Subkul'tura detstva," 60; Ulitskaia, "March 1953," 11, 12, 20.

76. Liudmila Ulitskaia, "Vetrianaia ospa," in *Sonechka* (Moscow: Eksmo, 2008), 369, 391. Kazarina views the sexualized elements in "Chicken Pox" as a principally nonerotic rite of passage rooted in biology. See Kazarina, "Bednye rodstvenniki," 172.

77. Liudmila Ulitskaia, "Liudmila Ulitskaia: Rugat' intelligentsiiu—uzhasnaia poshlost'," interview with Ol'ga Mozgovaia, *Vecherniaia Moskva*, 29 May 2005, 5; Liudmila Ulitskaia, "Bronka," in *Sonechka and Other Stories*, trans. Arch Tait (Moscow: Glas, 1998), 125, 126, 127.

78. On the male gaze and the pleasures of looking, see Laura Mulvey, "Visual Pleasure and Narrative Cinema," in *Feminist Film Theory: A Reader*, ed. Susan Thornham (New York: New York University Press, 1999), 58–69. See Palei, *Kabiriia s Obvodnogo kanala*, in *Long Distance, ili Slavianskii aktsent* (Moscow: Vagrius, 2000).

79. Evgeniia Shcheglova discusses the novel's supposed emphasis on sexuality in

"O spokoinom dostoinstve—i ne tol'ko o nem: Liudmila Ulitskaia i ee mir," *Neva*, no. 7 (2003): 184.

80. Ulitskaia, *Kazus Kukotskogo*, 286, 291, 328, 334, 337-38.

81. On reading as romance, see Ulitskaia, *Sviashchennyi musor*, 33-34. Liudmila Ulitskaia, *Sonechka*, in *Sonechka: A Novella and Other Stories*, trans. Arch Tait (New York: Schocken Books, 2005), 7, 11, emphasis in original.

82. Ulitskaia, *Sonechka*, 9.

83. Ibid., 33-34, 43-44, 39, 52.

84. Nina Voronel', "Sekret Don Zhuana," *Novoe vremia*, no. 40 (2006): 35; Ulitskaia, *Iskrenne Vash Shurik*, 168.

85. Ulitskaia ascribes the sensation of weightlessness, suspension, or flight to several other characters, usually during sex, including Valentina in *The Funeral Party*, Masha in *Medea and Her Children*, and Kazia in "Lialia's Home." Ulitskaia, *Veselye pokhorony*, 283; Ulitskaia, *Medeia i ee deti*, 238-39; Ulitskaia, "Lialin dom," in *Bednye, zlye, liubimye*, 262; Susan Rubin Suleiman, "(Re)Writing the Body: The Politics and Poetics of Female Eroticism," in *The Female Body in Western Culture*, ed. Susan Rubin Suleiman (Cambridge, MA: Harvard University Press, 1986), 10.

86. Ulitskaia, *Iskrenne Vash Shurik*, 337.

87. Ulitskaia, "Bednaia, schastlivaia Kolyvanova," in *Bednye, zlye, liubimye*, 213-14; Ulitskaia, "Telo krasavitsy" and "Pristavnaia lestnitsa," in *Liudi nashego tsaria*, 79-89 and 26-31.

88. Ulitskaia, "Strashnaia dorozhnaia istoriia," in *Liudi nashego tsaria*, 261, 265.

89. Liudmila Ulitskaia, *Sonechka*, in *Bednye, zlye, liubimye*, 256-57, 267. On the need for understanding instead of dogma, see Ulitskaia, "Rezul'tat uvidim ne srazu," interview with Maiia Kucherskaia, *Vedomosti piatnitsa*, 11 July 2008, http://friday.vedomosti.ru/article.shtml?2008/07/11/13071.

Chapter 2. Ideas That Bind

1. Liudmila Ulitskaia, "Subbotnee inter'viu: Liudmila Ulitskaia," interview with Arslan Saidov, *Radio Svoboda*, 3 May 2003, http://www.svobodanews.ru/content/article/24188014.html.

2. Ulitskaia, *Sviashchennyi musor*, 210. For a sense of Russia's claims to Crimea, see, for example, Viktor Martynok, "Rossiia ne imeet prava predat' russkikh v Krymu," *Komsomol'skaia pravda*, 27 February 2014, http://www.km.ru/world/2014/02/27/protivo stoyanie-na-ukraine-2013-14/733415-rossiya-ne-imeet-prava-predat-russkikh-v-.

3. On family as a structuring metaphor in Ulitskaia's work, see, among others, Andrei Arkhangel'skii, "Zhizn' ulitskaia," *Ogonek*, no. 9 (2008), http://ogoniok.com/5036/27/. Several interviews discuss the centrality of the family in her work: see, for example, Ulitskaia, "Liudmila Ulitskaia: I Accept Everything," and Ulitskaia, "Zapretnykh tem net," interview with Andrei Zaitsev, *Nezavisimaia gazeta, Religii*, 17 December 2003, 8.

4. On *Daniel Stein*, Aksenov, and history, see Larisa Romanovskaia, "Apokrif ot dobrogo diadi," *Kul'tura*, no. 44 (2006): 2.

5. Concerning the shift from public to private, see, among others, Josephine Woll, *Real Images: Soviet Cinema and the Thaw* (London: I. B. Tauris, 2000), xiii; Sergei Ushakin, "Mesto-imeni-ia: Sem'ia kak sposob organizatsii zhizni," in *Semeinye uzy:*

Modeli dlia sborki, comp. and ed. Sergei Ushakin (Moscow: Novoe literaturnoe obozrenie, 2004), 1:10.

6. Irina Savkina, "Rod/dom: Semeinaia khronika Liudmily Ulitskoi i Vasiliia Aksenova," in Ushakin, *Semeinye uzy*, 1:157; on the Great Family, see Clark, *The Soviet Novel*, 114, 115.

7. Mikhail Chiaureli, director, *Padenie Berlina* (Moscow: Mosfil'm, 1949). For an important discussion of state, kinship, and intimacy, see Michael Herzfeld, *Cultural Intimacy: Social Poetics in the Nation-State* (New York: Routledge, 1997), 2.

8. I. Grekova, "Letom v gorode," in *Na ispytaniiakh*, 486-87, 492; for a discussion of "Summer in the City," see Sutcliffe, *The Prose of Life*, 44. On the relationship between ideology and national shifts in intimacy, see Herzfeld, *Cultural Intimacy*, 30.

9. Helena Goscilo and Yana Hashamova, "Cinepaternity: The Psyche and Its Heritage," in *Cinepaternity: Fathers and Sons in Soviet and Post-Soviet Film*, ed. Helena Goscilo and Yana Hashamova (Bloomington: Indiana University Press, 2010), 10; Georgii Daneliia, director, *Osennii marafon* (Moscow: Mosfil'm, 1979); Vladimir Men'shov, director, *Moskva slezam ne verit* (Moscow: Mosfil'm, 1979).

10. Petrushevskaia, *Svoi krug*, in *Dom devushek*, 347-48; Seth Graham, "Models of Male Kinship in Perestroika Cinema," in Goscilo and Hashamova, *Cinepaternity*, 73-75. On the breakdown of the Great Family, see Goscilo and Hashamova, "Cinepaternity," 14.

11. On the symbolism of prostitution, see Eliot Borenstein, "Selling Russia: Prostitution, Masculinity, and Metaphors of Nationalism after Perestroika," in Goscilo and Lanoux, *Gender and National Identity*, 186. On the family's shifting image, see Alexander Prokhorov, "From Family Reintegration to Carnivalistic Degradation: Dismantling Soviet Communal Myths in Russian Cinema of the Mid-1990s," *Slavic and East European Journal*, no. 2 (2007): 272; Balabanov, *Brat* and *Brat 2*.

12. Andrei Zviagintsev, director, *Vozvrashchenie* (Moscow: REN TV, 2003). On Putin as father figure, see Goscilo and Hashamova, "Cinepaternity," 10; Ushakin, "Mesto-imeni-ia," 10.

13. One perceptive critic argues in an early article that Ulitskaia's strong focus on kinship explains her emphasis on Jewish and Eastern ethnicities. Kazarina, "Bednye rodstvenniki," 169; for a similar discussion that focuses on Russian Orthodoxy, see E. V. Larieva, "Sviatye i greshnye: Dva rasskaza L. Ulitskoi o sem'e ('Oni zhili dolgo,' '. . . i umerli v odin den')," *Filologiia i chelovek* (Barnaul), no. 3 (2008): 190.

14. On Solzhenitsyn and Ulitskaia, see Powers, "Novel Histories," 154.

15. Ulitskaia, *Medea and Her Children*, 18.

16. Ibid.

17. The comparison of Medea with the elderly women of *derevenskaia proza* comes from Shcheglova, "O spokoinom dostoinstve," 187. For a sense of conservative mores in village prose, see Valentin Rasputin, "Cherchez la femme," *Nash sovremennik*, no. 3 (1990): 168-72.

18. Ulitskaia, "Ustanovlenie ottsovtsva," in *Liudi nashego tsaria*, 111, 115, 119.

19. Ulitskaia discusses scientific study of the family in "Korzina, kartina," 3.

20. Ulitskaia, *Kazus Kukotskogo*, 92, 96. In her Lacanian reading of *The Kukotskii Case*, Irina Zherbkina underscores that Pavel Alekseevich is a stepfather and not a father per se (Zherbkina, *Gendernye 90-e, ili Fallosa ne sushchestvuet* [St. Petersburg: Aleteiia, 2003], 183-84). Ulitskaia, *Kazus Kukotskogo*, 169; Savkina, "Rod/dom," 179-80;

Ulitskaia, *Kazus Kukotskogo*, 153. Ulitskaia comments on the novel and death in "Ravnenie na Medeiu," 7.

21. Ulitskaia, *Kazus Kukotskogo*, 389. Vladimir Iarantsev identifies revision of family relationships as an important feature of Ulitskaia's work. See Iarantsev, "Vzgliad iz Sibiri," *Literaturnaia Rossiia*, no. 41 (2006): 12-13; Anna Starobinets, "Te zhe i volshebnik," *Ekspert*, no. 33 (2002), http://expert.ru/expert/2002/33/33ex-books_36445/.

22. On preserving family, see Ulitskaia, "Pisatel' Liudmila Ulitskaia: 'Vsekh interesuet tol'ko," 12.

23. Ulitskaia, *Sonechka*, in *Bednye, zlye, liubimye*, 266, 267, 271, 274. Mariia Remizova acknowledges Pavel Alekseevich's dual emphases when she claims that "love and blood" are the novel's two main themes. See Remizova, "Grandes dames proshedshego sezona." On Ulitskaia and Turgenev, see Nadezhdina, "Naviazannaia subkul'tura," 10.

24. Ulitskaia, *Medeia i ee deti*, 83; Ulitskaia, *Sonechka*, 23.

25. For an analysis of representation in *Sonechka*, see Christina Parnell, "Hiding and Using Sexuality: The Artist's Controversial Subject in Modern Russian Women's Literature," in *Gender and Sexuality in Russian Civilization*, ed. Peter Barta (London: Routledge, 2001), 311–24.

26. Baksaraeva, "'Dushevnost' bez dukhovnosti'?," 106; Ulitskaia, *Sonechka*, 71.

27. Ulitskaia, *Sonechka*, 3.

28. Herzfeld, *Cultural Intimacy*, 4; Ulitskaia, "Dar nerukotvornyi," in *Bednye, zlye, liubimye*, 113, 115; Elina and Ishekova, "Obrazy Rossii," 182.

29. Ulitskaia, "Vtorogo marta togo zhe goda ... ," in *Bednye, zlye, liubimye*, 170.

30. Ulitskaia, *Daniel' Shtain, perevodchik*, 317, 18, 66.

31. Ibid., 479, 489–90.

32. Ulitskaia, *The Funeral Party*, 59–60.

33. On the link between Noah's ark and the novel, see Maiia Karapetian, "Aristokraty dukha, brazhniki i bludnitsy: 'Legkoe dykhanie' geroev Liudmily Ulitskoi," *Kul'tura*, no. 27 (1998): 10; Ulitskaia, *Veselye pokhorony*, 232.

34. For discussion of Ulitskaia and values uniting humanity, see V. Ia. Skvortsov and A. I. Skvortsova, "Samobytie cheloveka v povesti Liudmily Ulitskoi 'Veselye pokhorony,'" *Vestnik Volgogradskogo gosudarstvennogo universiteta. Seriia 2: Filologiia, zhurnalistika*, no. 5 (2000): 110. Discussion of Alik's wake is adapted from Benjamin Sutcliffe, "Liudmila Ulitskaia's Literature of Tolerance," *Russian Review*, no. 68 (2009): 495–509.

35. Ulitskaia, *Medea and Her Children*, 312; Svetlana Timina, "Ritmy vechnosti: Roman Liudmily Ulitskoi *Medeia i ee deti*," in *Perom i prelest'iu: Zhenshchiny v panteone russkoi literatury; sbornik statei*, ed. Wanda Laszczak and Daria Ambroziak (Opole: Wydawca Dariusz Karbowiak, 1999), 147. On non-interference and Medea's family, see Ol'ga Berezkina, "Issledovanie istorii rasshirennoi sem'i na materiale romana L. Ulitskoi 'Medei i ee deti,'" *Zhurnal prakticheskoi psikhologii i psikhoanaliza*, no. 4 (2005), http://psyjournal.ru/psyjournal/articles/detail.php?ID=2679. A. Baranova gives a similar view in "Semeinaia problematika v sovremennom psikhologicheskom romane (L. Ulitskaia, Medeia i ee deti)," *Caucasus philologia*, no. 1 (2006): 70–71, reprinted in *Epicheskii tekst: Perspektivy izucheniia*, http://mith.ru/epic/litoi.htm.

36. Powers discusses the inclusion of the reader in "Novel Histories," 190. On kindness and home, see Tat'iana Rovenskaia, "Arkhetip doma v novoi zhenskoi proze, ili Kommunal'noe zhitie i kommunal'nye tela," *Inoi vzgliad*, no. 3 (2001): 25. For ideas

about human nature and Medea's family, see the overview of Ulitskaia's writing in Litovskaia, "Lyudmila Ulitskaya," 332. Discussion of the end of the novel comes from Sutcliffe, "Everyday Life."

37. Goscilo and Lanoux, "Introduction," 4. On maternal categories, see Elizabeth Podnieks and Andrea O'Reilly, "Introduction: Maternal Literatures in Text and Tradition: Daughter-Centric, Matrilineal, and Matrifocal Perspectives," in *Textual Mothers/ Maternal Texts: Motherhood in Contemporary Women's Literatures*, ed. Elizabeth Podnieks and Andrea O'Reilly (Waterloo, ON: Wilfred Laurier University Press, 2010), 12-24.

38. Ulitskaia, "Rugat' intelligentsiiu," 5.

39. On women's prose and mothers, see Helena Goscilo, "Coming a Long Way, Baby: A Quarter-Century of Russian Women's Fiction," *The Harriman Institute Forum*, no. 1 (1992): 1-17; Ulitskaia, *Sviashchennyi musor*, 223.

40. Ulitskaia, *Kazus Kukotskogo*, 93.

41. Ibid., 347, 376. On Petrushevskaia and repetition, see Sutcliffe, *The Prose of Life*, 82-83.

42. Ulitskaia, *Kazus Kukotskogo*, 443, 445.

43. Rovenskaia, "Opyt novogo zhenskogo mifotvorchestva," 139; Anja Grothe, "Medusa, Cassandra, Medea: Re-Inscribing Myth in Contemporary German and Russian Women's Writing" (PhD diss., City University of New York, 2000), 267. See also Mary Childs's discussion of Medea and her classical referent in "Classical Allusions and Imperial Desire: Problems of Identity in Georgian and Russian Literature" (PhD diss., University of Washington, Seattle, 2012), http://hdl.handle.net/1773/21796.

44. Ulitskaia, *Medea and Her Children*, 7. Rovenskaia sees in Medea an alternative to the trajectory of traditional womanhood. See Rovenskaia, "Opyt novogo zhenskogo mifotvorchestva," 145.

45. Ulitskaia, *Medea and Her Children*, 100-101, 212.

46. Ulitskaia, *Daniel Stein, Interpreter*, 26, 70, 320, 252.

47. Ibid., 160. For a discussion of family as geobiographical document, see Ushakin, "Mesto-imeni-ia," 40.

48. Ulitskaia, "Diana," in *Skvoznaia liniia*, 14, 30-31; Aleksandr Solzhenitsyn, "The Smatterers," in *From under the Rubble*, trans. A. M. Brock et al. (Boston: Little, Brown, and Company, 1975), 275.

49. Malashenok, "Kak napisat' roman Ulitskoi"; Ulitskaia, "Zapretnykh tem net," 8; Liudmila Ulitskaia, *Women's Lies*, trans. Arch Tait, ed. Natasha Perova, Arch Tait, and Joanne Turnbull, *Glas: New Russian Writing*, no. 30 (2003): 239-40.

50. Helene Deutsch, *The Psychology of Women: A Psychoanalytic Interpretation* (New York: Bantam, 1973), 479.

51. Ulitskaia, *Skvoznaia liniia*, 29-30, 32.

52. For a discussion of how the fictional father devolves in perestroika-era women's prose, see Sutcliffe, *The Prose of Life*, 77-78.

53. Ulitskaia, "Telo krasavitsy," in *Liudi nashego tsaria*, 89.

54. Ulitskaia, *Kazus Kukotskogo*, 127, 419, 422, 95. For a discussion of ethics and the intelligentsia, see Ulitskaia, "Rugat' intelligentsiiu," 5.

55. Ulitskaia, *Iskrenne Vash Shurik*, 59, 374. Gena in the story "Paper Victory" ("Bumazhnaia pobeda") is also fatherless, but not because of a wartime loss as one might expect. Liudmila Ulitskaia, "Bumazhnaia pobeda," in *Istorii pro zverei i liudei* (Moscow: Eksmo, 2006), 189. See the problematic analysis of this story in: Oksana Lushchevska,

"Ulitskaia's Writing for Children: Transcending Limitations of the Graphic Novel Genre," *Bookbird*, no. 2 (2013): 23-31.

56. Ulitskaia, *Medea and Her Children*, 104-5.

57. Ulitskaia, *Medeia i ee deti*, 85, 88, 96.

58. Ulitskaia, "Pisatel'skaia doch'," in *Liudi nashego tsaria*, 214, 239. On fathers and sons in Stalinism, see Clark, *The Soviet Novel*, 126.

59. Ulitskaia, "Velikii uchitel'," in *Liudi nashego tsaria*, 46, 53.

60. Ulitskaia, *Daniel' Shtain, perevodchik*, 87, 153, 362, 364.

61. One critic decries Hilda's affair with a married Arab, rhetorically wondering what would have happened if the heroine of Aleksandr Pushkin's *Eugene Onegin* had behaved in such a promiscuous manner. This comment is an irrelevant but fascinating reminder of how Ulitskaia's reception is inseparable from the cult of classical Russian literature. Ekaterina Rep'eva, "Roman kak oruzhie globalizma," *Literaturnaia Rossiia*, nos. 2-3 (2007), http://www.litrossia.ru/2007/02-03/01111.html; Ulitskaia, *Daniel' Shtain, perevodchik*, 165.

62. *Vospitanie* is a capacious term denoting upbringing, child-rearing, parenting, education, nurturing, training, or the instilling of morality. See R. Bamm et al., *Semeinoe vospitanie: Slovar' dlia roditelei* (Moscow: Prosveshchenie, 1967), 39, 40. On Ulitskaia's ideas about *vospitanie*, see "Liudmila Ulitskaia: I Accept Everything," 78-79; Ulitskaia, *Iskrenne Vash Shurik*, 313-14.

63. Ulitskaia, *Iskrenne Vash Shurik*, 362.

64. On the intersection of ideology and *vospitanie*, see Rebecca Knight, "Representations of Soviet Childhood in Post-Soviet Texts by Liudmila Ulitskaia and Nina Gabrielian," *Modern Language Review*, no. 3 (July 2009): 805.

65. Ulitskaia, *Medeia i ee deti*, 127, 132-33; Clowes, *Russia on the Edge*, 126-27; Ulitskaia, *Medea and Her Children*, 162.

66. For an influential discussion of childhood in Russian literature, see Andrew Wachtel, *The Battle for Childhood: Creation of a Russian Myth* (Stanford, CA: Stanford University Press, 1990). On gynocentric plots and women's prose, see Tat'iana Rovenskaia, "Zhenskaia proza serediny 1980-kh-nachala 1990-kh godov. (Problematika, mental'nost', identifikatsiia)" (Kand. diss., Moskovskii gosudarstvennyi universitet, 2000), 50.

67. See Ulitskaia, "Zapretnykh tem net," 8. As we explain in chapter 4, Ulitskaia's approach to Islam is both more complex and far less charitable.

68. Ulitskaia, "Chuzhie deti," in *Bednye, zlye, liubimye*, 126; Ulitskaia, "Podkidysh," in *Bednye, zlye, liubimye*, 140. On the significance of twins, see O. V. Pobivailo, "Bliznechnyi mif v rasskaze L. E. Ulitskoi 'Vtoroe litso,'" *Filologiia i chelovek* (Barnaul), no. 2 (2008): 115-19.

69. Liudmila Ulitskaia, "The Foundling," trans. Alla Zbinovsky, in *Childhood: Zip and Other Stories* (Moscow: Glas, 1998), 48. On family as initial social interaction, see the discussion in Ulitskaia, "Pisatel' Liudmila Ulitskaia: Vsekh interesuet tol'ko," 12. On contemplation, see Ulitskaia and Khodorkovskii, "Dialogi," 132.

70. Ulitskaia, "The Foundling," 40.

71. Ulitskaia, "Podkidysh," in *Bednye, zlye, liubimye*, 141-42; Liudmila Ulitskaia "Tvorets znal, chto delal!," interview with Inessa Tsiporkina, *Knizhnoe obozrenie*, no. 33 (2000): 5.

72. Ulitskaia, *Medea and Her Children*, 164.

73. Ibid., 286. On women writers and responsibility, see Goscilo, "Coming a Long Way, Baby," 5.
74. Ulitskaia, *Medea and Her Children*, 258.
75. Ulitskaia, *Medeia i ee deti*, 26, 43. Though Medea eventually discovers a brother who has become a monk on Mount Athos, he plays no meaningful role in the plot. Ibid., 259.
76. Liudmila Ulitskaia, *Russkoe varen'e*, in *Russkoe varen'e i drugoe*, 132, 187, 149.

Chapter 3. An Obsession with History

1. For an eyewitness account of the "stroll" on 13 May 2012, see Efimov, "Samaia chitaiushchaia strana."
2. Andrew Wachtel, *An Obsession with History: Russian Writers Confront the Past* (Stanford, CA: Stanford University Press, 1994), 1. For a discussion of Karamzin, see ibid., 46-65. The idea of inherited discourse comes from, among others, Aleksandr Prokhorov, *Unasledovannyi diskurs: Paradigmy stalinskoi kul'tury v literature i kinematografe "ottepeli"* (St. Petersburg: Akademicheskii proekt/Izdatel'stvo DNK, 2007).
3. For a discussion of objective truth, see Berlin, "Introduction," 6. On the dying intelligentsia, see R. V. Ryvkina, "The Expiration of the Intelligentsia's Social Role in Post-Soviet Russia," *Russian Education and Society*, no. 7 (2007): 17. Oushakine outlines the idea of past as trauma in *The Patriotism of Despair*, 5.
4. Concerning authors creating their own version of history, see Wachtel, *An Obsession with History*, 11; Margaret Ziolkowski, *Literary Exorcisms of Stalinism: Russian Writers and the Soviet Past* (Columbia, SC: Camden House, 1997), 6-7. For an excellent analysis of post-Soviet authors "processing" the trauma of the Soviet experience, see Lipovetsky and Etkind, "The Salamander's Return."
5. On the intelligentsia's varied views of history, see Rosalind Marsh, *Literature, History and Identity in Post-Soviet Russia, 1991-2006* (New York: Peter Lang, 2007), 18-19; Ulitskaia, "Rugat' intelligentsiiu," 5. On *The Big Green Tent* as documenting the sufferings of liberal dissidents, see Zoia Svetova, "Ne bylo pobeditelei u vremeni," *Novoe vremia*, no. 43 (2010): 46. For a critical view of Daniel, see Valentina Erofeeva, "Bol'shaia natsional'naia?!," *Den' literatury*, no. 136 (2007), http://coollib.com/b/121010/read.
6. Leona Toker, writing about the Gulag, makes an analogous argument: critiquing fictional representations of the prison system does not detract from the real and evident trauma suffered by its victims: Toker, *Return from the Archipelago: Narratives of Gulag Survivors* (Bloomington: Indiana University Press, 2000), 2.
7. Dmitrii Likhachev, "O russkoi intelligentsii," in *Vospominaniia, razdum'ia, raboty raznykh let*, ed. O. V. Panchenko et al. (St. Petersburg: ARS, 2006), 2:382, 389.
8. For two classic discussions of the positive hero and his sources, see Rufus Mathewson, *The Positive Hero in Russian Literature* (New York: Columbia University Press, 1958); and Clark, *The Soviet Novel*.
9. Ulitskaia, "Rugat' intelligentsiiu," 5; Paperno, *Stories of the Soviet Experience*, 60. For a survey of (self-ascribed) intelligentsia traits, see Andrei Sinyavsky, *Soviet Civilization: A Cultural History*, trans. Joanne Turnbull with Nikolai Formozov (New York: Arcade, 1990), 134-35.
10. Solzhenitsyn, "The Smatterers," 240-42; Ulitskaia, "'Pisatel'skaia doch,'" in *Liudi nashego tsaria*, 213.

11. Ulitskaia, *Sviashchennyi musor*, 71, 77.

12. Ulitskaia, *Iskrenne Vash Shurik*, 11. For one example of the author's polemical praise of the intelligentsia, consider the full title and content of the interview "Rugat' intelligentsiiu": "To curse the intelligentsia is incredibly crass."

13. A number of critics discuss the diminished (or simply defunct) role of the intelligentsia, e.g., Gessen, *Dead Again*, 4; Paperno, *Stories of the Soviet Experience*, 47; and Ryvkina, "The Expiration of the Intelligentsia's Social Role." For commentary on print culture, see Clark, "The King Is Dead."

14. On fear of consumer culture, see for example, Liudmila Ulitskaia, "Vse konchilos': My v"ekhali v novuiu zhizn'," *Ogonek*, no. 50 (2008): 13. Zubok discusses the end of the intelligentsia in *Zhivago's Children*, 353; Ryvkina, "The Expiration of the Intelligentsia's Social Role," 9, 11. Ulitskaia laments the structure of today's culture in "A Conversation with Ludmila Ulitskaya." Concerning consciousness, see Ulitskaia, "Portret iavleniia: Kul't mass," *Novaia gazeta*, 15 November 2004, 23.

15. On trauma, see Lipovetsky and Etkind, "The Salamander's Return," 9, 30. On Crimea and Russian national identity, see Orlando Figes, *The Crimean War: A History* (New York: Metropolitan Books, 2010), 484-93. For a discussion of the debates over history textbooks, see, for example, A. S. Kan, "Istoriografiia, istochnikovedenie, metody istoricheskogo issledovaniia: Postsovetskoe issledovanie o politicheskikh repressiiakh v Rossii i SSSR," *Otechestvennaia istoriia*, no. 1 (2003): 120-33, and Iu. N. Smirnov, "Istorik v meniaiushchemsia prostranstve rossiiskoi kul'tury," *Rossiiskaia istoriia*, no. 6 (2007): 201-7.

16. Denis Kozlov, "Writing about the Thaw in Post-Soviet Russia," *Russian Studies in History*, no. 4 (2011): 4, 5-6. On critiques of the *shestidesiatniki* and the ties between intelligentsia and state, see Clark, "The King Is Dead."

17. Clark, *The Soviet Novel*, 189. For the link between youth and Thaw intelligentsia, see Dubin, "Rossiiskaia intelligentsiia," in *Slovo-pis'mo-literatura*, 341.

18. On culpability and the *shestidesiatniki*, see Galina Artemenko, "Liudmila Ulitskaia: 'Ia napisala obo vsem, o chem khotela,'" *Sankt-Peterburgskie vedomosti*, 7 November 2011, http://www.spbvedomosti.ru/article.htm?id=10282070@SV_Articles; Edel'shtein, "Za vsiu sredu," 72. Ulitskaia notes that Russian literature today is "written for a small audience": Ulitskaia, reading and talk at Columbia University.

19. Ulitskaia, "Bez bol'shikh illiuzii, no . . ."; Ulitskaia, *Zelenyi shater*, 260.

20. Marsh, *Literature, History and Identity in Post-Soviet Russia*, 308; Ulitskaia, "Mladshaia shestidesiatnitsa," 8; Ulitskaia, *Zelenyi shater*, 74-75.

21. Shengeli's surname recalls poet and critic Georgii Shengeli. As Guy de Mallac notes, Pasternak was also interested in the links between Moscow's streets and the city's cultural status; this commonality is one of a number of links between Shengeli and the author of *Doctor Zhivago* (de Mallac, *Boris Pasternak*, 291). For a sense of the intelligentsia's mythos of place, see Paperno, "Personal Accounts," 598. Interestingly, Ulitskaia discusses Trifonov neither in her literary works nor in interviews. It is inconceivable that she did not read his works while living in Moscow in the 1960s and 1970s.

22. On documentary literature in a broader context, see Irina Kaspe, "Certificate of What? Document and Documentation in Contemporary Russian Literature," trans. Birgit Beumers, *Russian Review*, no. 4 (2010): 563-84. Dubin discusses the moral qualities of the intelligentsia in "Intelligentsiia i professionalizatsiia," in *Slovo-pis'mo-literatura*, 189. For a survey of documentary genres and their impact on Thaw and Stagnation

literature, see Sutcliffe, *The Prose of Life*, 19–22. Clark indicates that *iskrennost'* was shared by both state and alienated intellectuals during the Thaw years: "The King Is Dead."

23. On the common plots of Ulitskaia's works, see Liudmila Ulitskaia, "Liudmila Ulitskaia: Pishu o tom, chto znaiu," *Cultinfo.ru: Kul'tura v Vologodskoi oblasti*, http://www.cultinfo.ru/home/0975/15.htm. The idea of the master plot comes from Clark, *The Soviet Novel*, 5.

24. Alexei Yurchak, *Everything Was Forever, Until It Was No More: The Last Soviet Generation* (Princeton, NJ: Princeton University Press, 2006).

25. Paperno, *Stories of the Soviet Experience*, 41, 240; Ulitskaia, *Zelenyi shater*, 130.

26. Boris Dubin, "Kniga i dom (k sotsiologii knigosobiratel'stva)," in *Slovo-pis'mo-literatura*, 49; Ulitskaia, *Sviashchennyi musor*, 30; Ulitskaia, *Zelenyi shater*, 125, 445.

27. Ulitskaia, *Kazus Kukotskogo*, 287; Ulitskaia, *Medea and Her Children*, 53.

28. Concerning the relationship between knowing the world and one's own body, see the discussion by Ostrenko, "Subkul'tura detstva," 60; Paperno, "Personal Accounts," 609.

29. Paperno, *Stories of the Soviet Experience*, 9, 15. For a thoughtful survey of the memoir in late Soviet and post-Soviet culture, see Beth Holmgren, "Introduction," in *The Russian Memoir: History and Literature*, ed. Beth Holmgren (Evanston, IL: Northwestern University Press, 2003), ix–xxxix. Ulitskaia, *Zelenyi shater*, 291.

30. Ulitskaia, *Daniel Stein, Interpreter*, 61.

31. Mikhail Gorelik, "Proshchanie s ortodoksiei," *Novyi mir*, no. 5 (2007): 168; Ulitskaia, *Zelenyi shater*, 432. On Ulitskaia as a future emigrant, see Nadezhdina, "Naviazannaia subkul'tura," 10.

32. On Jews and the intelligentsia as victims of the *narod*, see I. Grekova's overlooked masterpiece dealing with Tsarist and Stalinist anti-Semitism: *Svezho predanie* (Moscow: Eksmo, 2002).

33. Ulitskaia, *Daniel Stein, Interpreter*, 247–48.

34. For strong opinions about acceptable behavior for the intelligentsia, see Ulitskaia, "Rugat' intelligentsiiu," 5; Ulitskaia, *Daniel' Shtain, perevodchik*, 21. On the beneficence of crisis, see Ulitskaia, "'Krizis—pravil'noe sostoianie,'" 20.

35. Ulitskaia, *Zelenyi shater*, 229, 52.

36. Ulitskaia, *Skvoznaia liniia*, 65.

37. Ulitskaia, *Russkoe varen'e*, 95, 132; Arkhangel'skii, "Zhizn' ulitskaia." For an interesting discussion of how *Russian Jam* critiques the intelligentsia, see E. N. Petukhova, "Dialog s Chekhovym: 'Russkoe varen'e' L. Ulitskoi," in *Dialog s Chekhovym: Sbornik nauchnykh trudov v chest' 70-letiia V. B. Kataeva*, ed. P. N. Dolzhenkov (Moscow: Moskovskii gosudarstvennyi universitet, 2009), 371.

38. Ulitskaia, *Russkoe varen'e*, 172, 104; Anton Chekhov, "Gooseberries," in *Eleven Stories*, trans. Ronald Hingley (London: Oxford University Press, 1975).

39. Ulitskaia, *Russkoe varen'e*, 121, 166, 127; Ulitskaia, "Novyi roman."

40. Belzhelarskii, "My nikogda ne stanem starshe."

41. On the intellectual's choice between commercialization and righteous poverty, see Ulitskaia, "Rugat' intelligentsiiu," 5. For a discussion of *intelligenty* who have survived by working with business or the state, see Ryvkina, "The Expiration of the Intelligentsia's Social Role," 15. In the 1990s, presumably to earn needed money, Ulitskaia herself wrote the screenplay for a simplistic psychological thriller involving sex, photography, and vengeance (Aleksandr Khvan, director, *Umirat' legko* [Moscow: NTV-Profit, 1999]).

42. Iuzefovich, "Gospozha nabliudatel'," 61.

43. For a scholarly assessment mentioning popular hostility to the intelligentsia, see Edel'shtein, "Za vsiu sredu," 72. A less academic critique of *intelligenty* is evident on commentary linked to sites such as Sinton: http://forum.syntone.ru/index.php?showtopic=14258&st=15. Ulitskaia, *Zelenyi shater*, 289, 295.

44. Concerning the failed 1991 coup as a moment of redemption for the intelligentsia, see Zubok, *Zhivago's Children*, 351; Ulitskaia, *Veselye pokhorony*, 167, 171; Ulitskaia, *The Funeral Party*, 88.

45. For a positive portrayal, see the plumber and part-time KGB agent Gena, who makes a good husband for Galina in *The Big Green Tent* (Ulitskaia, *Zelenyi shater*, 254, 258). On thieving, anti-Semite neighbors, see Ulitskaia, "Gulia," in *Bednye, zlye, liubimye*, 88; Ulitskaia, *Zelenyi shater*, 417; Ulitskaia, *Russkoe varen'e*, 98. On the communal apartment and intelligentsia, see Boym, *Common Places*, 121–67, and the multifaceted study by Il'ia Utekhin, *Ocherki kommunal'nogo byta* (Moscow: OGI, 2001).

46. T. N. Doronina, "'Prinimaiu vse, chto daetsia': Liudmila Ulitskaia i sel'skii chitatel'," *Panorama bibliotechnoi zhizhni oblasti: Opyt, novye idei, tendentsii razvitiia* (Nizhnii Novgorod), no. 3 (2006): 35. For extensive commentary on center and periphery, see Clowes, *Russia on the Edge*.

47. Ulitskaia, "Moskva-Podrezkovo, 1992," in *Liudi nashego tsaria*, 281.

48. Ibid., 283, 285. On Ulitskaia's love of *The Captain's Daughter*, see Ulitskaia, "'Krizis—pravil'noe sostoianie,'" 45; Venedikt Erofeev, *Moskva-Petushki* (Paris: YMCA-Press, 1977).

49. Ulitskaia, *Zelenyi shater*, 517; Ludmila Alexeyeva, *Soviet Dissent: Contemporary Movements for National, Religious, and Human Rights*, trans. Carol Pearce and John Glad (Middletown, CT: Wesleyan University Press, 1985), 5. For a seminal account of tension between the intelligentsia and the *narod* in the Gulag, see Eugenia Ginzburg, *Journey into the Whirlwind*, trans. Paul Stevenson and Max Hayward (New York: Harcourt, Brace and World, 1967).

50. Ulitskaia, *Daniel' Shtain, perevodchik*, 498; Ulitskaia, *Zelenyi shater*, 388, 390.

51. On Ulitskaia's respect for Siniavskii, see *Sviashchennyi musor*, 440, 446. Sinyavsky, *Ivan the Fool*, 14. Ulitskaia, "Finist Iasnyi Sokol," in *Liudi nashego tsaria*, 90–93.

52. Anatolii Mateshko, director, *Zhenshchina dlia vsekh* (Kiev: Kinostudiia im. A. Dovzhenko and Piramida-Menatep, 1991). Ulitskaia wrote the screenplay for this film. Ulitskaia, "Oni zhili dolgo," in *Liudi nashego tsaria*; Ulitskaia, "... i umerli v odin den'," in *Liudi nashego tsaria*, 179, 180.

53. Ulitskaia, *Kazus Kukotskogo*, 437, 438. Savkina astutely observes that Toma exhibits the mediocrity Ulitskaia sees dominating the gene pool after decades of death and emigration (Savkina, "Rod/dom," 180).

54. Ulitskaia, *Kazus Kukotskogo*, 138; Ulitskaia, *Zelenyi shater*, 67, 69, 73.

55. Ulitskaia, *Zelenyi shater*, 467; Ulitskaia, "Karpaty, Uzhgorod," in *Liudi nashego tsaria*, 255; Ulitskaia, "A Conversation with Ludmila Ulitskaya." Ulitskaia's eulogy for Gorbanevskaia appeared on the *Novaia gazeta* blog: see "Liudmila Ulitskaia pro Natal'iu Gorbanevskuiu," reproduced at http://masha-tim.livejournal.com/. On the author's admiration for Gorbanevskaia, see Ulitskaia, "Persona: Ulitskaia na sklone," interview with Iunna Chuprinina, *Itogi*, no. 10 (2005): 98. We discuss her volume on Gorbanevskaia in the conclusion.

56. Ulitskaia, *Kazus Kukotskogo*, 299–300.

57. Ulitskaia, *Zelenyi shater*, 78-81; Ulitskaia, *Sviashchennyi musor*, 27.

58. Boris Pasternak, "The Childhood of Zhenya Luvers," in *Collected Short Prose*, trans. Christopher Barnes (New York: Praeger, 1977); Ulitskaia, *Sviashchennyi musor*, 19-20; Ulitskaia, *Zelenyi shater*, 95-96, 79.

59. Ulitskaia, *Zelenyi shater*, 306.

60. Ibid., 541.

61. Quoted in Gessen, *Dead Again*, 11. On the relationship between the Thaw, poetry, and sincerity, see Holmgren, "Introduction," xxix.

62. Ulitskaia, *Zelenyi shater*, 90; *Zapiski dekabristov* (London: Vol'naia russkaia tipografiia, 1862-1863); Zubok, *Zhivago's Children*, 246.

63. Sinyavsky, *Soviet Civilization*, 233; Ulitskaia, *Zelenyi shater*, 501.

64. Ulitskaia, *Zelenyi shater*, 76, 107.

65. Ibid., 99. Alexander Gerschenkron, "Notes on Doctor Zhivago," *Modern Philology*, no. 3 (1961): 200, quoted in de Mallac, *Boris Pasternak*, 317. Ulitskaia notes that Pasternak himself faced the problem of moral compromise and attempted to compensate for it by helping other writers: Ulitskaia, interview with Skomp. On the publication of *Doctor Zhivago*, see Ulitskaia, *Sviashchennyi musor*, 452.

66. Shengeli identifies Pasternak's work as a continuation of the nineteenth-century novelistic tradition he values so highly (Ulitskaia, *Zelenyi shater*, 99). Some critics have located other echoes of *Zhivago*'s plot within *The Big Green Tent*: Edel'shtein, for instance, views Vinberg's unremarkable and unrecognized death on board a plane as akin to Zhivago's demise. See Edel'shtein, "Za vsiu sredu," 72. On coincidences in Pasternak's novel, see Angela Livingstone, *Boris Pasternak: Doctor Zhivago* (Cambridge: Cambridge University Press, 1989), 84-86.

67. Christopher Barnes references Pasternak on the connections between everyday life and moral truth: Boris Pasternak, *Sobranie sochinenii v piati tomakh* (Moscow: Khudozhestvennaia literatura, 1989-1992), 3:575, quoted in Christopher Barnes, *Boris Pasternak: A Literary Biography*, vol. 2, *1928-1960* (Cambridge: Cambridge University Press, 1998), 244. Boris Pasternak, *Doctor Zhivago*, trans. Max Hayward and Manya Harari (New York: Bantam, 1985), 10. For mention of Pasternak sharing Nikolai Nikolaevich's values, see de Mallac, *Boris Pasternak*, 309.

68. Pasternak, *Doctor Zhivago*, 42. On the link between art and freedom, see Ulitskaia, *Sviashchennyi musor*, 449. Pasternak, *Doctor Zhivago*, 437. Concerning the "primacy and autonomy of language" for Pasternak, see de Mallac, *Boris Pasternak*, 352; on art and history, see 287. Ulitskaia, *Zelenyi shater*, 236.

69. Ulitskaia, *Zelenyi shater*, 559. As an author, Ulitskaia privileges the verbal (prose, drama, memoir) over the nonverbal in ekphrasis. In doing so she continues a practice long linked to literature's subordination of the other arts (Michael Squire, *Image and Text in Graeco-Roman Antiquity* [New York: Cambridge University Press, 2009], 121). The authors thank Emily Rush for suggesting this source.

70. de Mallac, *Boris Pasternak*, 307; Pasternak, *Doctor Zhivago*, 453, 285, 147.

71. Ulitskaia, "My v zerkale iskusstva," 10; Alla Latynina, "Vsekh sovetskaia vlast' ubila," *Novyi mir*, no. 6 (2011): 172.

72. Ulitskaia, *Zelenyi shater*, 162-63. For Ulitskaia's own explanation of this image, see Anna Chupriian, "Ulitskaia raskinula shater," *Tribuna*, no. 6 (2011): 14.

73. Ulitskaia, *Zelenyi shater*, 584; Aleksandr Sokurov, *Russkii kovcheg* (St. Petersburg: Hermitage Bridge Studio, 2002).

74. On the intelligentsia's shared guilt in state crimes, see O. Altaev, "The Dual Consciousness of the Intelligentsia and Pseudo-Culture," in *The Political, Social and Religious Thought of Russian "Samizdat": An Anthology*, trans. Nickolas Lupinin, ed. Michael Meerson-Aksenov and Boris Shragin (Belmont, MA: Nordland, 1977), 131. Solzhenitsyn, "The Smatterers," 251.

Chapter 4. Writing Tolerance

1. Ulitskaia received a much warmer response from the university where the discussion occurred. For Ulitskaia's reflections on the tolerance series, see Liudmila Ulitskaia, "'Detskii proekt', ili Nemnogo o kul'turnoi antropologii," *Biblioteka v shkole*, no. 12 (2008), http://lib.1september.ru/view_article.php?ID=200801203; Liudmila Ulitskaia, "Odna khoroshaia kniga sposobna proizvesti deistvie, kotoroe ne mozhet vagon plokhikh," interview with Ol'ga Drobot, *Inostrannaia literatura*, no. 7 (2009), http://magazines.russ.ru/inostran/2009/7/h019.html.

2. For the text of the parents' letter, see http://arhiv.oodvrs.ru/article/index.php?id_page=71& id+article=972. Parents in this region are not the only Russians skeptical of initiatives promoting tolerance; for objections by the bishop of Perm (and Ulitskaia's response, including commentary on the events in Khanty-Mansiisk), see Mikhail Pozdniaev, "Russiia—ne dom terpimosti'," *Novye Izvestiia*, 19 February 2009, http://www.newizv.ru/society/2009-02-12/105581-rossija-ne-dom-terpimosti.html.

3. For an overview of these problems, see Gudkov, *Negativnaia identichnost'*.

4. Oushakine, *The Patriotism of Despair*, 5. On 1990s threats to national pride and negative solidarities, see Svetlana Ryzhova, "Tolerance and Extremism: Russian Ethnicity in the Orthodox Discourse of the 1990s," in *Religion and Identity in Modern Russia: The Revival of Orthodoxy and Islam*, ed. Juliet Johnson, Marietta Stepanianits, and Benjamin Forest (Aldershot, UK: Ashgate, 2005), 66.

5. Liberal intellectual Oleg Panfilov blames state control of mass media for heightened intolerance. See Panfilov, "Rebirth of Russian Nationalism," trans. Arch Tait, *Index on Censorship*, no. 1 (2006): 142–48. For a discussion of anti-Semitism in comparison with other forms of xenophobia and racism, see Lev Gudkov, "Attitudes toward Jews in Post-Soviet Russia and the Problem of Anti-Semitism," in *Revolution, Repression, and Revival: The Soviet Jewish Experience*, ed. Zvi Gitelman and Yaacov Ro'i (Lanham, MD: Rowman and Littlefield, 2007). On Prokhanov, see, for instance, "Aleksandr Prokhanov: Rossiia stanet imperiei ili ischeznet," *Nevskoe vremia*, 21 April 2010, http://www.nvspb.ru/tops/aleksandr-prohanov-rossiya-stanet-imperiey-ili-ischeznet-42272.

6. Fifty-eight percent of ethnic Russians self-identified as Orthodox in 2002, as compared to 30 percent in 1989: Ryzhova, "Tolerance and Extremism," 68; Ulitskaia, "Bez bol'shikh illiuzii, no . . ."; "Liudmila Ulitskaia otvetila na nashi voprosy."

7. Concerning the relationship between enforced modernity and Russian/Soviet rule, see Douglas Northrop, *Veiled Empire: Gender and Power in Stalinist Central Asia* (Ithaca, NY: Cornell University Press, 2004); Anna Shternshis, *Soviet and Kosher: Jewish Popular Culture in the Soviet Union, 1923–1939* (Bloomington: Indiana University Press, 2006).

8. On tolerance initiatives, see Iuliia Zelenina, "Tolerantnost' po-russki," *Vecherniaia Moskva*, 16 November 2005, http://www.vmdaily.ru/showarticle.php?id=263308. On librarians and tolerance, see Poriadina, "Aktualizatsiia 'tolerantnykh' motivov."

9. Ulitskaia, *Istoriia pro vorob'ia Antverpena, kota Mikheeva, stoletnika Vasiu i sorokonozhku Mar'iu Semenovnu s sem'ei* (Moscow: Eksmo, 2005), 68.

10. Edel'shtein, "Za vsiu sredu," 72. Another critic notes the correspondences between the characters in Ulitskaia's writing for adults and her children's books: Ol'ga Bugoslavskaia, "Vzroslye i deti," *Znamia*, no. 10 (2005): 219.

11. Ulitskaia, *Sviashchennyi musor*, 350.

12. Ulitskaia's correspondence with Khodorkovsky appeared in the liberal newspaper *New Paper* (*Novaia gazeta*), the literary journal *Banner* (*Znamia*), and on the pro-Western Radio Liberty (*Radio Svoboda*) website. Ulitskaia and Khodorkovskii, "Dialogi," 112.

13. See, for example, Ulitskaia, "A Conversation with Ludmila Ulitskaya."

14. For a conservative opinion, see Erofeeva, "Bol'shaia natsional'naia?!" By contrast, another critic defines a Russian writer in a simple yet inclusive way: any author who writes in Russian. E. F. Shafranskaia, "Russkaia literatura o nerusskoi zhizni i nerusskikh geroiakh," *Russkaia slovesnost'*, no. 7 (2007): 41.

15. Likhachev, "O russkoi intelligentsii," 392. For a discussion of *tolerantnost'* versus *terpimost'*, see Dar'ia Krasnoperova, "Zachem nam novoe slovo? Ili Zametki o tolerantnosti," *Sankt-Peterburgskie vedomosti*, 4 March 2003, 5. "Tolerast," a pejorative term for those who support tolerance, has recently appeared, as online definitions show: see, for example, "Slovar' molodezhnogo slenga," http://teenslang.su/id/15659.

16. On the vicissitudes of *terpimost'*, see Zelenina, "Tolerantnost' po-russki"; Clowes, *Russia on the Edge*, xiv.

17. Ulitskaia gives an overview of the "Good Book" project in "Ia protivnitsa togo, chtoby gosudarstvo rukovodilo kul'turoi," interview with Aleksandr Shatalov, *Novoe vremia*, no. 32 (2009): 50-51.

18. On her work with hospitals, see Ulitskaia, comp., *Chelovek popal v bol'nitsu*. Ulitskaia, "Kakoe vremia zhizni nam dostalos'," interview with Iuliia Shigareva, *Argumenty i fakty*, 19 May 2004, 21.

19. On sentimental-civic realism, see Belzhelarskii, "My nikogda ne stanem starshe."

20. For a discussion of tolerance, see Ulitskaia, "My i drugie," interview with Adilia Zaripova, *Rossiiskaia gazeta*, 13 April 2010, 1. Zelenina discusses tolerance and ensuing generations in "Tolerantnost' po-russki." Ulitskaia, "Rezul'tat uvidim ne srazu." On transmitting values through reading, see Maiia Kucherskaia, "Vot oni tak i zhili," *Vedomosti*, 29 December 2010, 6.

21. Isaiah Berlin, "The Pursuit of the Ideal," in *Moral Disagreements: Classical and Contemporary Readings*, ed. Christopher Gowans (London: Routledge, 2000), 199-200; Irina Papkova, *The Orthodox Church and Russian Politics* (New York: Oxford University Press, 2011), 33, 35, 53-54; Ulitskaia, "Tri avtora," 5; Ulitskaia, *Daniel' Shtain, perevodchik*, 498-99.

22. Papkova, *The Orthodox Church*, 11. Ryzhova analyzes the patriarch's comments in "Tolerance and Extremism," 77. Aleksii II, "Vashi proroki—nashi proroki," *Moskovskie novosti*, 26 January 1992, 24.

23. On her conversion, see Ulitskaia, "Portret iavleniia," 23. A number of interviews and essays discuss Men', e.g. Ulitskaia, "Bez bol'shikh illiuzii, no . . ." The author mentions Oswald Rufeisen (Daniel's historical model) and her return to faith in *Daniel' Shtain, perevodchik*, 497-98.

24. On late Soviet converts, see Judith Kornblatt, *Doubly Chosen: Jewish Identity, the Soviet Intelligentsia, and the Russian Orthodox Church* (Madison: University of

Wisconsin Press, 2004), 9, 124, 136. Ulitskaia, *Semero sviatykh*, in *Russkoe varen'e*, 36, 38.

25. Ulitskaia, "Portret iavleniia," 23; Iurii Maletskii, "Roman Ulitskoi kak zerkalo russkoi intelligentsii," *Novyi mir*, no. 5 (2007), http://www.portal-slovo.ru/philology/37290.php. The idea that Christianity is a remnant of the rich repast of Judaism earlier appears in Ulitskaia, *Veselye pokhorony*, 113; Ulitskaia, *Daniel' Shtain, perevodchik*, 331, 509, 511–12.

26. On Ulitskaia and the ignorance of the Orthodox Church, see Koksheneva, "Dyra novogo ateizma," 217. Concerning Ulitskaia's assessment of the clergy as bureaucratic, see "Politik ili pastyr'?," *Nezavisimaia gazeta, Religii*, 4 February 2009, 4.

27. For an attempt to find common ground amid differing beliefs, see Liudmila Ulitskaia, "Trudnye knigi Ulitskoi," interview with Iuliia Rakhaeva, *Novoe vremia*, no. 46 (2007): 73–76. On Maika, see Terpits, "'Zdes' i tam,'" 355.

28. Mikhail Krutikov examines the meeting of the rabbi and priest in "Opyt rossiiskoi evreiskoi emigratsii i ego otrazhenie v proze 90-kh godov," *Diaspora*, no. 3 (2000): 220. Ulitskaia, *The Funeral Party*, 67.

29. Ulitskaia, "'Krizis—pravil'noe sostoianie,'" 20. Ulitskaia also discusses the importance of the considered life in Ulitskaia and Khodorkovskii, "Dialogi," 132. On *Daniel Stein* rejecting dogma in favor of positive actions, see Koksheneva, "Dyra novogo ateizma," 211.

30. Concerning the switch from ideology to religion and free will, see Ulitskaia, "Liudmila Ulitskaia: 'Proshu ne gadit' v pod"ezde!,'" interview with Valentina Oberemko, *Argumenty i fakty*, 12 December 2007, 70. Ulitskaia also acknowledges that an individual's beliefs are impermanent and will necessarily evolve: "Liudmila Ulitskaia napishet o sviashchennom musore," *Izvestiia*, 1 May 2012, http://www.izvestia.ru/news/523290. On the Christ the Savior Cathedral, see Ulitskaia, *Sviashchennyi musor*, 99.

31. Ulitskaia, "Tak napisano," in *Liudi nashego tsaria*, 313, 319.

32. Ulitskaia's survey of the calamitous Soviet experience also touches on the tragedy of other ethnicities, such as Lithuanians deported under Stalin (Ulitskaia, *Medeia i ee deti*, 43, 194). On "A Gift Not Made by Hands," see Elina and Ishekova, "Obrazy Rossii," 184.

33. Two authors—Anatolii Rybakov and Vasilii Grossman—have depicted the Holocaust at great length in their prose. Brief but harrowing images of this period also appear in Aleksandr Askol'dov's film *Commissar* (*Kommisar*) (Moscow: Kinostudiia M. Gor'kogo, 1967). The discussion of intolerance between Jews and gentiles comes from Sutcliffe, "Liudmila Ulitskaia's Literature of Tolerance."

34. Ulitskaia, *Daniel Stein, Interpreter*, 295.

35. Ulitskaia, *Moi vnuk Veniamin*, 194, 196, 211; Timothy Snyder, *Bloodlands: Europe between Hitler and Stalin* (New York: Basic Books, 2010). For one conservative reaction, see Erofeeva, "Bol'shaia natsional'naia?!"

36. On Gottlieb and Maika, see Krutikov, "Opyt rossiiskoi evreiskoi emigratsii," 221.

37. Karl Jaspers, "Communication: The Loving Struggle," in *Karl Jaspers: Basic Philosophical Writings* (Athens: Ohio University Press, 1986), 77-78. For an analysis of Daniel's shifts, see Vojvodić, "Transfery Danielia Shtaina," 149, 150. See also the discussion by Brian Baer: "Interpreting *Daniel Stein*: Or What Happens When Fictional Translators Get Translated," in *Transfiction: Research into the Realities of Translation*

Fiction, ed. Klaus Kaindl and Karlheinz Spitzl (Philadelphia: John Benjamins, 2014), 160-68.

38. Ulitskaia, *Daniel' Shtain, perevodchik*, 473, 495, 507. On Ulitskaia and the Christianization of Jews, see Gennadii Razumov, "Knizhnye vykresty L. Ulitskoi," *Narod moi*, no. 17 (2007), http://ami-moy.narod.ru/A405/A405-051.html.

39. Ulitskaia, *Zelenyi shater*, 465-66.

40. Ulitskaia, *Zelenyi shater*, 470-71, 528; Ulitskaia, *Daniel' Shtain, perevodchik*, 365-66; Ulitskaia, *Medeia i ee deti*, 10-12, 252; Timina, "Ritmy vechnosti," 152.

41. Clowes, *Russia on the Edge*, 126, 127.

42. One critic, for instance, complains that *Daniel Stein* focuses on anti-Semitism too much for a literary work—see Koksheneva, "Dyra novogo ateizma," 210.

43. Lev Gudkov, "Antisemitizm i ksenofobiia v postsovetskoi Rossii," in *Negativnaia identichnost'*, 249. On Putin and authoritarianism, see Ulitskaia, "Ulitskaia: 'Podlinnyi sopernik Khodorkovskogo.'" Ulitskaia suggests the ameliorative role of the intelligentsia in "Nevezhestvo poddaetsia lecheniiu," *Izvestiia*, 31 January 2006, 6.

44. On the author's experience with geneticists, see Ulitskaia, "Mladshaia shesti-desiatnitsa," 8. Ulitskaia, *Kazus Kukotskogo*, 13; Boris Engel'gardt, "Ideologicheskii roman Dostoevskogo," in *Dostoevskii: Stat'i i materialy*, ed. A. S. Dolinin (Leningrad: Mysl', 1925), 2:89.

45. Ulitskaia, *Kazus Kukotskogo*, 126, 127, 94. On Pavel Alekseevich's drinking, see Céline Bricaire, "Les recits de soiffards du nouveau millénaire: Figures de l'alcoolisme chez A. Guelassimov (La soif), V. Popov (Le troisième souffle), A. Matveieva (Le vin italien), L. Oulitskaïa (Le cas du Dr Koukotski)," in *Le premier quinquennat de la prose russe du XXIe siècle*, ed. Hélène Mélat (Paris: Institut d'études slaves, 2006), 292, 294.

46. Ulitskaia, *Zelenyi shater*, 103-5, 305-6.

47. Ulitskaia's narrator discusses the Brezhnev era in the story "A Son of Noble Parents" ("Syn blagorodnykh roditelei," in *Liudi nashego tsaria*, 152). On Shengeli as history with a human face, see Frolova, "Shater s tablichkoi 'vykhod,'" 202.

48. Ulitskaia, *Zelenyi shater*, 467. In *The Big Green Tent* Vinberg, a Jew who fled the Nazis only to be imprisoned in the Gulag, is reminded of Hitler's Berlin when discussing Petr Nichiporuk's arrest for stating that the USSR has betrayed Lenin's principles. As Oushakine notes in a different context, Nichiporuk's real-life prototype also aided the exiled Crimean Tartars; this link reveals Ulitskaia's complex reworking of historical material in the novel. Ulitskaia, *Zelenyi shater*, 396; Serguei Oushakine, "The Terrifying Mimicry of Samizdat," *Public Culture*, no. 2 (2001): 200. For a validation of the dissident movement, see Ulitskaia, "Lichinki, deti lichinok."

49. Ulitskaia, *Zelenyi shater*, 532, 541; on *Sonechka*, see the first response to Ulitskaia's work by a critic: Inna Prusakova, "Liudmila Ulitskaia. Sonechka. Povest'. 'Novyi mir' 1992, No. 7," *Neva*, no. 1 (1993): 236; Ulitskaia, "Gulia," in *Bednye, zlye, liubimye*, 89; Ulitskaia, *Iskrenne Vash Shurik*, 67.

50. Berlin, "The Pursuit of the Ideal," 201. On Daniel Stein and the problem of defining unity, see the interesting discussion in Kaspe, "Certificate of What?," 574; Rep'eva, "Roman kak oruzhie globalizma."

51. Berlin discusses unitary truth and the thinking class in "Introduction," 6. On state and intelligentsia messianism, see Clark, "The King Is Dead."

52. On Daniel's revision of Jewish identity, see Levantovskaya, "The Russian-Speaking Jewish Diaspora," 94, 107.

53. Ulitskaia, *Daniel' Shtain, perevodchik*, 39, 40-41, 174. For a discussion of Daniel's unchanging values, see Levantovskaya, "The Russian-Speaking Jewish Diaspora," 100, and Vojvodić, "Transfery Danielia Shtaina," 146.

54. Ulitskaia, *Daniel' Shtain, perevodchik*, 102; Ulitskaia, *Zelenyi shater*, 359-60, 370-71.

55. Ulitskaia, *Sviashchennyi musor*, 319-20.

56. Vitaly Chernetsky, *Mapping Postcommunist Cultures: Russia and Ukraine in the Context of Globalization* (Montreal: McGill-Queen's University Press, 2007), 149; Ulitskaia, *Sestrichki Liberti*.

57. Ulitskaia, *Zelenyi shater*, 579, 224, 218-19. In *The Big Green Tent*, Sania's disgust with the corporeality of heterosexual sex and other factors hint that he is gay, but the novel never clarifies this presumably important part of his identity (ibid., 125; Ulitskaia, interview with Skomp and Sutcliffe by e-mail).

58. Liudmila Ulitskaia, "Angel," in *Sonechka*, 175, 180, 178-79, 188.

59. On the "trope of the tragic homosexual" in Russian literature, see Baer, *Other Russias*, 97. Ulitskaia, "Angel," in *Sonechka*, 184, 186, 190, 191.

60. Some critics have misapprehended Ulitskaia's treatment of homosexuality; for instance, Andrei Arkhangel'skii claims that the professor in "Angel" adopts a young boy only to corrupt him after ten years. See Arkhangel'skii, "Zhizn' ulitskaia."

61. Ulitskaia, "Frukt gollandskii," in *Liudi nashego tsaria*, 293, 294, 297.

62. Chernetsky, *Mapping Postcommunist Cultures*, 149-50; Ulitskaia, "Korov'ia noga," in *Liudi nashego tsaria*, 274; Liudmila Ulitskaia, "Dauntless Women of the Russian Steppe," in *Sonechka*, 224, 234, 235.

63. Ulitskaia, "Zhenshchiny russkikh selenii . . . ," in *Skvoznaia liniia*, 131-32.

64. For a discussion of the Chechen deportation, see Margaret Ziolkowski, *Alien Visions: The Chechens and the Navajos in Russian and American Literature* (Newark: University of Delaware Press, 2005), 270. On Ulitskaia's familiarity with Crimean Tatars, see Baranova, "Semeinaia problematika v sovremennom psikhologicheskom romane (L. Ulitskaia, Medeia i ee deti)," *Caucasus philologia*, no. 1 (2006): 70-71; Ulitskaia, *Sviashchennyi musor*, 372.

65. The overly broad characterization of Islam appears in Liudmila Ulitskaia, "Mirom praviat troechniki," *Moskovskie novosti*, 5 September 2004, 6, and Liudmila Ulitskaia: "'Vse delo—v otsutstvii normal'nogo seksa': Pisatel' polagaet, chto 'Makdonalds' sposoben primirit' molodezh' vsekh natsional'nostei," interview with Mark Smirnov, *Nezavisimaia gazeta*, 1 November 2002, 7. For examples of differentiation between various types of Christianity and Judaism, see Ulitskaia, *Sviashchennyi musor*, 465, 468; Ulitskaia, *Veselye pokhorony*, 121-22.

66. Ulitskaia, "'Vse delo,'" 7; Ulitskaia, *Sviashchennyi musor*, 313.

67. On links between "Eastern"/Muslim sexuality and Western stereotypes, see the foundational work: Edward Said, *Orientalism* (New York: Pantheon, 1978). Susan Layton provided the first extensive discussion of orientalism in Russian literature: *Russian Literature and Empire: Conquest of the Caucasus from Pushkin to Tolstoy* (Cambridge: Cambridge University Press, 1994). Ulitskaia, *Sviashchennyi musor*, 213.

68. Ulitskaia, *Sviashchennyi musor*, 234.

69. Ulitskaia, "'Krizis—pravil'noe sostoianie,'" 20; Ulitskaia, *Sviashchennyi musor*, 60. The early story "The Daughter of Bokhara" hints at a more nuanced image of Muslim believers: protagonist Alya's father wrote about the Prophet Mohammed's

night journey, a religious topic that prejudiced atheist Uzbek Communists against him (Ulitskaia, "Doch' Bukhary," 54.) For a broader discussion of Ulitskaia's ideas about Islams and Muslims (including the Arab-Israeli conflict), see Benjamin Sutcliffe, "Secular Victims, Religious Aggressors: Liudmila Ulitskaia's Muslims, Radical Islam, and the Russian Intelligentsia," *Russian Review*, forthcoming.

70. On reproduction, see Ulitskaia, *Sviashchennyi musor*, 253. Oushakine observes that population worries create the sense of a "Russian cross" (*russkii krest*) borne by the nation: Oushakine, *The Patriotism of Despair*, 100-105. For a discussion of the link between ethnic tension and impending fascism, see Ulitskaia, "Liudmila Ulitskaia otvetila na nashi voprosy."

71. See Litovskaia's otherwise quite insightful article: Litovskaia, "Smena sotsial'nykh stereotipov," 26.

72. Ulitskaia, *Daniel' Shtain, perevodchik*, 172; Ulitskaia, *Daniel Stein, Interpreter*, 151.

73. Karl Popper, *The Open Society and Its Enemies* (Princeton, NJ: Princeton University Press, 1966), 1:235n6, 265n4.

74. Likhachev, "O russkoi intelligentsii," 382; Ulitskaia, *Iskrenne Vash Shurik*, 313-14.

75. Ulitskaia, *Zelenyi shater*, 515.

76. Liudmila Ulitskaia, "Ludmila Ulitskaya," in *Contemporary Russian Fiction: A Short List; Russian Authors Interviewed by Kristina Rotkirch*, trans. Charles Rougle, ed. Anna Ljunggren and Kristina Rotkirch (Moscow: Glas, 2008), 182-83.

77. As we discuss in chapter 3, Trifonov is an obvious yet unacknowledged influence on Ulitskaia's treatment of history, morality, and the intelligentsia. His early, pro-Stalinist novel *Students* (*Studenty*, 1950), which was implicated in postwar persecution of Jewish intellectuals, may be one reason why she does not mention him. Iurii Trifonov, *Studenty*, in *Sobranie sochinenii v chetyrekh tomakh*, ed. S. A. Baruzdin et al. (Moscow: Khudozhestvennaia literatura, 1985), 1:21-406.

78. Liudmila Ulitskaia, "Nel'zia zhit' vo vremeni, pol'nost'iu ego ignoriruia," *Moskovskie novosti*, 1 April 2011, 11; Ulitskaia, reading and talk at Columbia University.

79. Ulitskaia, *Daniel' Shtain, perevodchik*, 365. Ulitskaia discusses church and state in "Bez bol'shikh illiuzii, no . . ."; Ulitskaia, *Sviashchennyi musor*, 470.

80. Ulitskaia, *Medea and Her Children*, 224. In "The Great Teacher," working-class Gena does the opposite: he rejects his grandmother's humble Orthodoxy in favor of the refined theories of anthroposophy (Ulitskaia, "Velikii uchitel'," in *Liudi nashego tsaria*, 46, 52). On "The Great Teacher," see Liu Na, "Povestvovatel'naia strategiia L. Ulitskoi v knige 'Liudi nashego tsaria,'" *Vestnik Tambovskogo universiteta. Seriia: gumanitarnye nauki*, no. 11 (2009): 243. Discussion of orthopraxis is partially taken from Sutcliffe, "Liudmila Ulitskaia's Literature of Tolerance."

81. Ulitskaia, "The Chosen People," 84-85, 90. On Christianity as antithetical to wealth, see Ulitskaia, "Tak napisano," in *Liudi nashego tsaria*, 311.

82. Ulitskaia, *Daniel' Shtain, perevodchik*, 280-81; Ulitskaia, *Daniel Stein, Interpreter*, 228; Ulitskaia, *Daniel' Shtain, perevodchik*, 120. See Rufeisen's views on labeling and dogma: Kornblatt, *Doubly Chosen*, 117.

83. On Daniel Stein's body, see Ulitskaia, "Novyi roman." On the subordination of Christianity to Judaism, see, for example, Andrei Vorontsov, "Oshibka patera Shtaina," *Literaturnaia gazeta*, no. 5 (2007): 7. For a view from a conservative Jewish critic, see Razumov, "Knizhnye vykresty L. Ulitskoi."

84. For a good outline of the differences between *byt* and *bytie*, see Stephen Hutchings, *Russian Modernism: The Transfiguration of the Everyday* (Cambridge: Cambridge University Press, 1997), 38; Ulitskaia, *Medea and Her Children*, 139; Morson, "Philosophy in the Nineteenth-Century Novel," 166; Isaiah Berlin, *The Hedgehog and the Fox: An Essay on Tolstoy's View of History* (London: Weidenfeld and Nicolson, 1967), 69.

85. Ulitskaia, *Daniel' Shtain, perevodchik*, 171. On *Daniel Stein*, ethics, and the everyday, see I. V. Kuznetsov, "'Daniel' Shtain' L. Ulitskoi v russkoi literaturnoi traditsii," *Russkaia slovesnost'*, no. 6 (2008): 40.

86. Ulitskaia, "Ludmila Ulitskaya," in *Contemporary Russian Fiction*, 186-87. On Ulitskaia's views of orthodoxy and orthopraxis, see "Mladshaia shestidesiatnitsa," 8. For critics' discussions of these two terms, see the following: Gorelik, "Proshchanie s ortodoksiei," 172; Svetlana Shishkova-Shipunova, "Kod Danielia Shtaina, ili Dobryi chelovek iz Khaify," *Znamia*, no. 9 (2007): 194; Evgenii Ermolin, "Ubitoe vremia: Zhivye litsa," *Kontinent*, no. 134 (2007), http://magazines.russ.ru/continent/2007/134/ee19.html; Ulitskaia, *Daniel Stein, Interpreter*, 366.

87. On faith and deeds, see Chumakevich, "Postrealizm v sovremennoi russkoi proze," 34; Aleksandr Men', "Osnovnye zhiznennye printsipy khristianstva," in *O sebe... Vospominaniia, interv'iu, besedy, pis'ma*, comp. Natal'ia Grigorenko and Pavel Men' (Moscow: Izdatel'stvo Zhizn' s Bogom, 2007), 285.

88. Ermolin, "Ubitoe vremia."

89. Stuart Hall, "Cultural Identity and Diaspora," in *Identity: Community, Culture, Difference*, ed. Jonathan Rutherford (London: Lawrence and Wishart, 1990), 223, 235. On Gulia's ancestry, see Iasmina Voivodich [Jasmina Vojvodić], "Chto otmechaet Gulia? O prazdnikakh v proizvedeniiakh Liudmily Ulitskoi," *Russian Literature*, no. 1 (2007): 116.

90. Levantovskaya, "The Russian-Speaking Jewish Diaspora," 100; Ulitskaia, "Ludmila Ulitskaya," in *Contemporary Russian Fiction*, 186. On atypicality, see Ulitskaia, "Moi liubimyi arab," in *Liudi nashego tsaria*, 269.

91. Ulitskaia, "Ludmila Ulitskaya," in *Contemporary Russian Fiction*, 186; V. S. Abramova, "'Kaleidoskop' kak khudozhestvennyi printsip v knige 'Liudi nashego tsaria,'" in *Natsional'no-kul'turnaia spetsifika teksta: Mezhvuzovskii sbornik nauchnykh trudov*, ed. G. S. Dvinianinova et al. (Perm: Permskii gosudarstvennyi universitet, 2007), 273; Shafranskaia, "Russkaia literatura," 41.

92. Mikhail Bakhtin, *Problems of Dostoevsky's Poetics*, trans. and ed. Caryl Emerson (Minneapolis: University of Minnesota Press, 1999), 146; Voivodich, "Chto otmechaet Gulia?," 116. On family as metaphor, see Clowes, *Russia on the Edge*, 138.

93. Ulitskaia, *Sonechka*, 272. Powers contends that this passage also includes the reader in Medea's family: "Novel Histories," 189.

94. Ulitskaia, *Medea and Her Children*, 305-7, 196-97. Portions of this discussion are adapted from Sutcliffe, "Everyday Life."

95. Ulitskaia, *Veselye pokhorony*, 264-83. On crisis as strengthening family, see Timina, "Ritmy vechnosti," 147. One critic argues that Alik's reinterpreted painting of the Last Supper is a symbol of the novel as a whole: Natal'ia Egorova, "Zhizn' ili 'Veselye pokhorony?' L. Ulitskaia o russkoi literature v sovremennom zapadnom mire," in *Vostok-zapad: Prostranstvo russkoi literatury; materialy Mezhdunarodnoi nauchnoi konferentsii. (Zaochnoi). Volgograd 25 noiabria 2004 g. Volgogradskii gosudarstvennyi*

pedagogicheskii universitet, ed. N. E. Tropkina et al. (Volgograd: Volgogradskoe nauchnoe izdatel'stvo, 2005), 114.

96. Ulitskaia, *Daniel' Shtain, perevodchik*, 431-32; Elena Stepanian, "'Eto my, Gospodi': O diletantakh, professionalakh i o mirovom kholode," *Znamia*, no. 2 (2010): 195. On the connection between Daniel's faith and the human family, see Ulitskaia, "'Krizis—pravil'noe sostoianie,'" 31-32.

97. Ulitskaia, *Daniel Stein, Interpreter*, 402.

98. Ulitskaia, *The Funeral Party*, 60.

99. Ulitskaia, *Zelenyi shater*, 76.

100. Ulitskaia, "Portret iavleniia," 23.

Conclusion

1. Ulitskaia, *Daniel Stein, Interpreter*, 408.

2. Ulitskaia, *Daniel' Shtain, perevodchik*, 120. On predator and prey, see Borenstein, *Overkill*.

3. For a representative (liberal) view of the intelligentsia's fate in *The Big Green Tent*, see Latynina, "Vsekh sovetskaia vlast' ubila"; Likhachev, "O russkoi intelligentsii," 382.

4. A number of critics discuss action versus thought in *Daniel Stein*; for example Gorelik, "Proshchanie s ortodoksiei," 172. Rosalind Marsh, "New Mothers for a New Era? Images of Mothers and Daughters in Post-Soviet Prose in Historical and Cultural Perspective," *Modern Language Review*, no. 4 (2012): 1214. For comments on male and female priorities, see Ulitskaia, *Sviashchennyi musor*, 231.

5. On the formation and fate of Pussy Riot, see Masha Gessen, *Words Will Break Cement: The Passion of Pussy Riot* (New York: Riverhead, 2014).

6. See Ulitskaia's comments on a liberal radio program: "Svoimi glazami," *Ekho Moskvy*, 7 August 2012, http://echo.msk.ru/programs/svoi-glaza/916652-echo/. For Ulitskaia's remarks on Crimea, see "Izvestnoi pisatel'nitse 'otvratitel'no' nasilie Rossii," *15 minut*, 11 March 2014, http://15minut.org/article/izvestnoj-pisatelnice-otvratitelno-nasilie-rossii-ona-hochet-chtoby-tatarskij-k. She discusses Russia and Ukraine in "Liudmila Ulitskaia: Otnosheniia Rossii s Ukrainoi isporcheny na neskol'ko pokolenii vpered," interview with Iurii Volodarskii, *Forbes Ukraina*, 2 May 2014, http://forbes.ua/lifestyle/1370187-lyudmila-ulickaya-otnosheniya-rossii-s-ukrainoj-isporcheny-na-neskolko-pokolenij-vpered. On the tolerance project, see Ulitskaia, "A Conversation with Ludmila Ulitskaya."

7. For putative links between consumerism and immaturity, see Ulitskaia, "Vse konchilos'," 12-13. On the rise of consumerism after the Great Patriotic War, see Ulitskaia, *Sviashchennyi musor*, 266.

8. On Putin and Europe, see Liudmila Ulitskaia, "Liudmila Ulitskaia: Evropa, proshchai!" interview with Andrei Sharyi, *Radio Svoboda*, 20 August 2014, http://www.svoboda.org/content/article/26541088.html.

9. Ulitskaia first prognosticated the end of her career as novelist following the publication of *Sincerely Yours, Shurik*: Liudmila Ulitskaia, "Liudmila Ulitskaia napisala, vozmozhno, svoi poslednii roman," *Newsru.com*, 8 April 2004, http://www.newsru.com/cinema/08apr2004/uli.html. On the author poisoned by her material, see Ulitskaia, *Daniel' Shtain, perevodchik*, 372. Ulitskaia maintains that finishing *Daniel Stein* almost killed her: "Liudmila Ulitskaia: Dumala, ne dozhivu do finala."

10. Liudmila Ulitskaia, *Poetka: Kniga o pamiati: Natal'ia Gorbanevskaia* (Moscow: AST, 2014). For a nostalgic look at the postwar courtyard, for example, see Ulitskaia, *Detstvo 45–53*, 161. On Ulitskaia and Dostoevsky, see Tat'iana Filippova, "Intelligent obyknovennyi," *Profil'*, 5 November 2012, 65.

11. For an interview that discusses *Discarded Relics*, see "Liudmila Ulitskaia napishet"; Holmgren, "Introduction," x. On memoirs as testament to survival, see Paperno, *Stories of the Soviet Experience*, 1; Holmgren, "Introduction," xxx. For a discussion of *Daniel Stein*, documents, and meaning, see Kaspe, "Certificate of What?," 574.

12. Lipovetsky and Etkind, "The Salamander's Return," 9–12; Ulitskaia, *Daniel' Shtain, perevodchik*, 495, 507. Concerning Khodorkovsky's transformation, see Ulitskaia, *Sviashchennyi musor*, 350.

13. Clark, "The King Is Dead." Berlin discusses the intelligentsia's obligation to speak the truth: Berlin, "Introduction," 7. For Ulitskaia's discussion of the Pussy Riot incident and trial, see "Liudmila Ulitskaia: 'Nekotorye nadezhdy na osvobozhdenie Pussy Riot u menia poiavilis,'" *Kommersant.ru*, 3 August 2012, http://www.kommersant.ru/doc/1995459.

14. Zubok, *Zhivago's Children*, 353. On the dearth of good readers, see Ulitskaia, reading and talk at Columbia University.

WORKS CITED

Works by, Coauthored by, and Compiled by Liudmila Ulitskaia

Biriukov, Ivan, Liudmila Ulitskaia, and Grigorii Riazhskii. *Umirat' legko*. Unpublished screenplay.
Ulitskaia, Liudmila. *Bednye rodstvenniki*. Moscow: Slovo, 1994.
———. *Bednye, zlye, liubimye*. Moscow: Eksmo, 2002.
———. "Bron'ka." *Ogonek*, no. 52 (1989): 2-23.
———. "The Chosen People." Translated by Isabel Heaman. In *Lives in Transit: A Collection of Recent Russian Women's Writing*, edited by Helena Goscilo, 84-92. Dana Point, CA: Ardis, 1995.
———. *Daniel' Shtain, perevodchik*. Moscow: Eksmo, 2006.
———. *Daniel Stein, Interpreter: A Novel in Documents*. Translated by Arch Tait. New York: Overlook, 2011.
———. "The Foundling." Translated by Alla Zbinovsky. In *Childhood: Zip and Other Stories*, edited by Natasha Perova, 35-64. Moscow: Glas, 1998.
———. *The Funeral Party*. Translated by Cathy Porter. New York: Schocken, 1999.
———. *Iskrenne Vash Shurik*. Moscow: Eksmo, 2005.
———. *Istoriia pro vorob'ia Antverpena, kota Mikheeva, stoletnika Vasiu i sorokonozhku Mar'iu Semenovnu s sem'ei*. Moscow: Eksmo, 2005.
———. *Istorii pro zverei i liudei*. Moscow: Eksmo, 2006.
———. *Kazus Kukotskogo*. Moscow: Eksmo, 2001.
———. *Liudi nashego tsaria*. Moscow: Eksmo, 2005.
———. "Lucky." Translated by Helena Goscilo. In *From the Soviets*. Special issue of *Nimrod* 2, no. 2 (Spring/Summer 1990): 66-70.
———. "March 1953." Translated by Arch Tait. In *Present Imperfect: Stories by Russian Women*, edited by Ayesha Kagal and Natasha Perova, 11-24. Boulder, CO: Westview Press, 1996.
———. *Medea and Her Children*. Translated by Arch Tait. New York: Schocken Books, 2002.
———. *Medeia i ee deti*. *Novyi mir*, nos. 3-4 (1996): 3-46, 7-79.
———. *Medeia i ee deti*. Moscow: Eksmo, 2002.
———. *Russkoe varen'e i drugoe*. Moscow: Eksmo, 2008.

———. *Sestrichki Liberti.* Unpublished screenplay.
———. *Skuchnaia shuba.* Moscow: Malysh, 1982.
———. *Skvoznaia liniia.* Moscow: Eksmo, 2004.
———. *Sonechka. Novyi mir*, no. 7 (1992): 61–89.
———. *Sonechka.* Moscow: Eksmo, 2008.
———. *Sonechka and Other Stories.* Translated by Arch Tait. Moscow: Glas, 1998.
———. *Sto pugovits.* Moscow: Detskaia literatura, 1983.
———. *Sviashchennyi musor.* Moscow: Astrel', 2012.
———. *Tsiu-iurikh'.* Moscow: Eksmo, 2002.
———. *Veselye pokhorony.* Moscow: Vagrius, 2000.
———. *Veselye pokhorony.* Moscow: Eksmo, 2006.
———. *Women's Lies.* Translated by Arch Tait. Edited by Natasha Perova, Arch Tait, and Joanne Turnbull. *Glas: New Russian Writing*, no. 30 (2003): 237–81.
———. *Zelenyi shater.* Moscow: Eksmo, 2011.
———. *Zhenshchina dlia vsekh.* Unpublished screenplay.
Ulitskaia, Liudmila, comp. *Chelovek popal v bol'nitsu.* Moscow: Eksmo, 2009.
———. *Detstvo 45–53: A zavtra budet schast'e.* Moscow: AST, 2013.
———. *Poetka: Kniga o pamiati: Natal'ia Gorbanevskaia.* Moscow: AST, 2014.

Interviews with, Opinion Pieces by, and Lectures by Liudmila Ulitskaia

Ulitskaia, Liudmila. "Bez bol'shikh illiuzii, no . . ." *Zhurnal Indeks/Dos'e na tsenzuru*, no. 16 (2001). http://www.index.org.ru/journal/16/ulizkaya.html.
———. "A Conversation with Ludmila Ulitskaya." Reading and talk at Cooper Union, New York, 4 May 2012.
———. "'Detskii proekt', ili Nemnogo o kul'turnoi antropologii." *Biblioteka v shkole*, no. 12 (2008). http://lib.1september.ru/view_article.php?ID=200801203.
———. "Ia ne khochu golosovat' za men'shee zlo." *Russkii kur'er*, 10 March 2004, 1.
———. "Ia protivnitsa togo, chtoby gosudarstvo rukovodilo kul'turoi." Interview with Aleksandr Shatalov. *Novoe vremia*, no. 32 (2009): 50–51.
———. Interview with Elizabeth Skomp. 5 May 2012.
———. Interview with Elizabeth Skomp and Benjamin Sutcliffe by e-mail. 17 June 2011.
———. "Iskrenne vasha, Liudmila Ulitskaia." Interview with Ivana Ignat'eva. *Versiia*, no. 15 (2004): 25.
———. "Izvestnoi pisatel'nitse 'otvratitel'no' nasilie Rossii." *15 minut*, 11 March 2014. http://15minut.org/article/izvestnoj-pisatelnice-otvratitelno-nasilie-rossii-ona-hochetchtoby-tatarskij-k.
———. "Kakoe vremia zhizni nam dostalos'." Interview with Iuliia Shigareva. *Argumenty i fakty*, 19 May 2004, 21.
———. "Korzina, kartinka, kartonka i malen'kaia sobachonka." Interview with Iana Zhiliaeva. *Moskovskii komsomolets*, 30 January 1999, 3.
———. "'Krizis—pravil'noe sostoianie.'" In *Vazhnee, chem politika: Pochemu my tak zhivem i kak mogli by zhit'?* Edited by Aleksandr Arkhangel'skii, 18–53. Moscow: AST, 2011.
———. "Lichinki, deti lichinok." Interview with Anastasiia Gosteva. *Gazeta.ru*. http://www.gazeta.ru/culture/2010/12/21/a_3472805.shtml.
———. "Liudmila Ulitskaia: Dumala, ne dozhivu do finala svoego poslednego romana." Interview with Maksim Chizhikov. *Komsomol'skaia pravda*, 21 February 2008. http://www.kp.ru/daily/24053/104935/.

———. "Liudmila Ulitskaia: Evropa, proshchai!" Interview with Andrei Sharyi. *Radio Svoboda*, 20 August 2014. http://www.svoboda.org/content/article/26541088.html.

———. "Liudmila Ulitskaia: I Accept Everything That Is Given." Interview with Anastasiia Gosteva. *Russian Studies in Literature*, no. 2 (2001): 72-93.

———. "Liudmila Ulitskaia: Kak dlia vzroslykh, tol'ko luchshe." Interview with A. Onoprienko. *Trud*, 14 September 2004, 6.

———. "Liudmila Ulitskaia napisala, vozmozhno, svoi poslednii roman." *Newsru.com*, 8 April 2004. http://www.newsru.com/cinema/08apr2004/uli.html.

———. "Liudmila Ulitskaia napishet o sviashchennom musore." *Izvestiia*, 1 May 2012. http://www.izvestia.ru/news/523290.

———. "Liudmila Ulitskaia: 'Nekotorye nadezhdy na osvobozhdenie Pussy Riot u menia poiavilis.'" *Kommersant.ru*, 3 August 2012. http://www.kommersant.ru/doc/1995459.

———. "Liudmila Ulitskaia: Obshchestvo podrostkov menia pugaet." Interview with Lev Danilkin. *Afisha*, 16 February 2011. http://www.afisha.ru/article/8621/.

———. "Liudmila Ulitskaia: Otnosheniia Rossii s Ukrainoi isporcheny na neskol'ko pokolenii vpered." Interview with Iurii Volodarskii. *Forbes Ukraina*, 2 May 2014. http://forbes.ua/lifestyle/1370187-lyudmila-ulickaya-otnosheniya-rossii-s-ukrainoj-isporcheny-na-neskolko-pokolenij-vpered.

———. "Liudmila Ulitskaia otvetila na nashi voprosy." *Snob*. http://www.snob.ru/selected/entry/28919.

———. "Liudmila Ulitskaia: Pishu o tom, chto znaiu." *Cultinfo.ru: Kul'tura v Vologodskoi oblasti*. http://www.cultinfo.ru/home/0975/15.htm.

———. "Liudmila Ulitskaia pro Natal'iu Gorbanevskuiu." *Blog Novoi gazety*, 30 November 2013. http://masha-tim.livejournal.com/.

———. "Liudmila Ulitskaia: 'Proshu ne gadit' v pod"ezde!'" Interview with Valentina Oberemko. *Argumenty i fakty*, 12 December 2007, 70.

———. "Liudmila Ulitskaia: Rugat' intelligentsiiu—uzhasnaia poshlost'." Interview with Ol'ga Mozgovaia. *Vecherniaia Moskva*, 29 May 2005, 5.

———. "Liudmila Ulitskaia: Tvorets znal, chto delal!" Interview with Inessa Tsiporkina. *Knizhnoe obozrenie*, no. 33 (2000): 5.

———. "Liudmila Ulitskaia: U nas kak-to dazhe modno—byt' neschastnoi." Interview with Irina Slavinskaia. *Ukrains'ka pravda*, 24 November 2011. http://life.pravda.com.ua/person/2011/11/24/90088/.

———. "Liudmila Ulitskaia: 'Vse delo—v otsutstvii normal'nogo seksa': pisatel' polagaet, chto 'Makdonalds' sposoben primirit' molodezh' vsekh natsional'nostei." Interview with Mark Smirnov. *Nezavisimaia gazeta*, 1 November 2002, 7.

———. "Logika erosa." Interview with Natal'ia Dardykina. *Moskovskii komsomolets*, 24 December 2001, 6.

———. "Ludmila Ulitskaya." In *Contemporary Russian Fiction: A Short List; Russian Authors Interviewed by Kristina Rotkirch*, translated by Charles Rougle, edited by Anna Ljunggren and Kristina Rotkirch, 174-92. Moscow: Glas, 2008.

———. "Mirom praviat troechniki." *Moskovskie novosti*, 5 September 2004, 6.

———. "Mladshaia shestidesiatnitsa." Interview with Mariia Sedykh. *Obshchaia gazeta*, no. 20 (2002): 8.

———. "My i drugie." Interview with Adilia Zaripova. *Rossiiskaia gazeta*, 13 April 2010, 1.

———. "My v zerkale iskusstva: Vash Iu." *Obshchaia gazeta*, no. 47 (2000): 10.

———. "Nel'zia zhit' vo vremeni, pol'nost'iu ego ignoriruia." *Moskovskie novosti*, 1 April 2011, 11.
———. "Nevezhestvo poddaetsia lecheniiu." *Izvestiia*, 31 January 2006, 6.
———. "Novyi roman 'Daniel' Shtain, perevodchik.'" Interview with Kseniia Larina. *Ekho Moskvy*, 19 November 2006. http://www.echo.msk.ru/programs/kazino/47588.phtml.
———. "Odna khoroshaia kniga sposobna proizvesti deistvie, kotoroe ne mozhet vagon plokhikh." Interview with Ol'ga Drobot. *Inostrannaia literatura*, no. 7 (2009): 245-50.
———. "Persona: Ulitskaia na sklone." Interview with Iunna Chuprinina. *Itogi*, no. 10 (2005): 94-98.
———. "Pisatel' Liudmila Ulitskaia: 'Nashi knigi o cheloveke, kotoryi ne takov, kak vy.'" Interview with Nikolai Aleksandrov. *Izvestiia*, 19 June 2006, 12.
———. "Pisatel' Liudmila Ulitskaia: 'Vsekh interesuet tol'ko — kakoe imenno bel'e nosila Knipper-Chekhova.'" Interview with Natal'ia Kochetkova. *Izvestiia*, 27 July 2005, 12.
———. "Plokhoi brak ili chestnyi razvod?" Interview with O. Nesterova. *Trud*, 10 March 2005, 29.
———. "Plokhoi chitatel'." *Voprosy literatury*, no. 1 (1996): 33-36.
———. "Portret iavleniia: Kul't mass." *Novaia gazeta*, 15 November 2004, 23.
———. "Predislovie: Trudnyi podrostok protiv Velikogo mifa." In *Khochu zhit'! Dnevnik sovetskoi shkol'nitsy*, by Nina Lugovskaia, 3-10. Moscow: RIPOL-klassik, 2010.
———. "Priznanie Liudmily Ulitskoi: 'V sleduiushchei knige ia vynuzhdena budu sebia ubit'.'" Interview with Alla Bossart. *Vecherniaia Moskva*, 18 June 2001, 3.
———. "Ravnenie na Medeiu." Interview with Ol'ga Nikolaeva and Aleksandr Nikolaev. *Novye Izvestiia*, 24 February 2000, 7.
———. Reading and talk at Columbia University, New York. 3 May 2012.
———. "Rezul'tat uvidim ne srazu." Interview with Maiia Kucherskaia. *Vedomosti piatnitsa*, 11 July 2008. http://friday.vedomosti.ru/article.shtml?2008/07/11/13071.
———. Russian Literary Series. Brooklyn Public Library, Brooklyn, NY. 5 May 2012.
———. "Schitaite menia retrogradom." Interview with I. Evseev. *Sankt-Peterburgskii universitet*, nos. 28-29 (1998): 4.
———. "Subbotnee inter'viu: Liudmila Ulitskaia." Interview with Arslan Saidov. *Radio Svoboda*, 3 May 2003. http://www.svobodanews.ru/content/article/24188014.html.
———. "Svoimi glazami." *Ekho Moskvy*, 7 August 2012. http://echo.msk.ru/programs/svoi-glaza/916652-echo/.
———. "Tri avtora: Khristianstvo bez miloserdiia?" *Moskovskie novosti*, 2 December 2003, 5.
———. "Trudnye knigi Ulitskoi." Interview with Iuliia Rakhaeva. *Novoe vremia*, no. 46 (2007): 73-76.
———. "Ulitskaia — Khodorkovskii: Bez protokola." *Novaia gazeta*, 11 September 2009. http://www.novayagazeta.ru/society/43627.html.
———. "Ulitskaia: Podlinnyi sopernik Khodorkovskogo — Putin." Interview with Mikhail Shevelev. *Radio Svoboda*, 11 September 2009. http://www.svobodanews.ru/articleprintview/1820056.html.
———. "Vse konchilos': My v"ekhali v novuiu zhizn'." *Ogonek*, no. 50 (2008): 13.
———. "Vstrechi: Liudmila Ulitskaia; ne mogli by vyzhit', esli b . . ." Interview with Vladimir Prikhod'ko. *Moskovskaia pravda*, 27 January 2001, 6.

———. "Zapretnykh tem net." Interview with Andrei Zaitsev. *Nezavisimaia gazeta, Religii,* 17 December 2003, 8.
Ulitskaia, Liudmila, and Mikhail Khodorkovskii. "Dialogi: Liudmila Ulitskaia—Mikhail Khodorkovskii." In *Stat'i, dialogi, interv'iu,* by Mikhail Khodorkovskii, 110-41. Moscow: Eksmo, 2010.
Ulitskaia, Liudmila, et al. "Roman li to, chto ia pishu? Otchet o Bukerovskoi konferentsii." *Voprosy literatury,* no. 2 (2005): 3-40.

Secondary Literature and Other Sources

Abdullaev, E. "Detskii proekt Liudmily Ulitskoi." *Voprosy literatury,* no. 6 (2007): 352-55.
Abramova, V. S. "'Kaleidoskop' kak khudozhestvennyi printsip v knige 'Liudi nashego tsaria.'" In *Natsional'no-kul'turnaia spetsifika teksta: Mezhvuzovskii sbornik nauchnykh trudov,* edited by G. S. Dvinianinova et al., 270-78. Perm: Permskii gosudarstvennyi universitet, 2007.
Aleksandrov, Grigorii, director. *Tsirk.* Moscow: Mosfil'm, 1936.
Aleksandrov, Nikolai. "V Moskve vruchena premiia 'Bol'shaia kniga.'" *Novoe vremia,* no. 42 (2007): 50-51.
Aleksii II. "Vashi proroki—nashi proroki." *Moskovskie novosti,* 26 January 1992, 24.
Alexeyeva, Ludmila. *Soviet Dissent: Contemporary Movements for National, Religious, and Human Rights.* Translated by Carol Pearce and John Glad. Middletown, CT: Wesleyan University Press, 1985.
Altaev, O. "The Dual Consciousness of the Intelligentsia and Pseudo-Culture." In *The Political, Social and Religious Thought of Russian "Samizdat": An Anthology.* Translated by Nickolas Lupinin, edited by Michael Meerson-Aksenov and Boris Shragin, 116-47. Belmont, MA: Nordland, 1977.
Arkhangel'skii, Andrei. "Zhizn' ulitskaia." *Ogonek,* no. 9 (2008). http://ogoniok.com/5036/27/.
Artemenko, Galina. "Liudmila Ulitskaia: 'Ia napisala obo vsem, o chem khotela.'" *Sankt Peterburgskie vedomosti,* 7 November 2011. http://www.spbvedomosti.ru/article.htm?id=10282070@SV_Articles.
Askol'dov, Aleksandr, director. *Kommisar.* Moscow: Kinostudiia M. Gor'kogo, 1967.
Baer, Brian James. "Engendering Suspicion: Homosexual Panic in the Post-Soviet *Detektiv.*" *Slavic Review* 64, no. 1 (2005): 24-42.
———. "Interpreting *Daniel Stein*: Or What Happens When Fictional Translators Get Translated." In *Transfiction: Research into the Realities of Translation Fiction,* edited by Klaus Kaindl and Karlheinz Spitzl, 157-75. Philadelphia: John Benjamins, 2014.
———. *Other Russias: Homosexuality and the Crisis of Post-Soviet Identity.* New York: Palgrave Macmillan, 2009.
Bakhnov, Leonid. "Genio loci." *Druzhba narodov,* no. 8 (1996): 178-80.
Bakhtin, Mikhail. *Problems of Dostoevsky's Poetics.* Translated and edited by Caryl Emerson. Theory and History of Literature 8. Minneapolis: University of Minnesota Press, 1999.
Baksaraeva, N. A. "'Dushevnost' bez dukhovnosti'? (Chekhovskaia traditsiia v povesti L. Ulitskoi 'Sonechka')." In *Tvorchestvo A. P. Chekhova: Mezhvuzovskii sbornik nauchnykh trudov,* edited by G. I. Tamarli, 105-10. Taganrog: Taganrogskii gosudarstvennyi pedagogicheskii institut, 2004.

Balabanov, Aleksei, director. *Brat*. Moscow: STV, 1997.
———. *Brat 2*. STV, 2000.
Bamm, R., et al. *Semeinoe vospitanie: Slovar' dlia roditelei*. Moscow: Prosveshchenie, 1967.
Baraban, Elena. "A Country Resembling Russia: The Use of History in Boris Akunin's Detective Novels." *Slavic and East European Journal*, no. 3 (2004): 396-420.
Baranova, A. "Semeinaia problematika v sovremennom psikhologicheskom romane (L. Ulitskaia, Medeia i ee deti)." *Caucasus philologia*, no. 1 (2006): 70-71. Reprinted in *Epicheskii tekst: Perspektivy izucheniia*. http://mith.ru/epic/lit01.htm.
Barnes, Christopher. *Boris Pasternak: A Literary Biography*. Vol. 2, *1928-1960*. Cambridge: Cambridge University Press, 1998.
Basinskii, Pavel. "Novosti: Rossiia vo Frankfurte." *Rossiiskaia gazeta*, 19 October 2005, 1.
———. "Pozabyvshie dobro? Zametki na poliakh 'novoi zhenskoi prozy.'" *Literaturnaia gazeta*, no. 7 (1991): 10.
Belzhelarskii, Evgenii. "My nikogda ne stanem starshe." *Itogi*, no. 52 (2010). http://www.itogi.ru/arts-kniga/2010/52/160445.html.
Berezkina, Ol'ga. "Issledovanie istorii rasshirennoi sem'i na materiale romana L. Ulitskoi 'Medeia i ee deti.'" *Zhurnal prakticheskoi psikhologii i psikhoanaliza*, no. 4 (2005). http://psyjournal.ru/psyjournal/articles/detail.php?ID=2679.
Berlin, Isaiah. *The Hedgehog and the Fox: An Essay on Tolstoy's View of History*. London: Weidenfeld and Nicolson, 1967.
———. "Introduction." In *Russian Intellectual History: An Anthology*, edited by Marc Raeff, 3-11. New York: Harcourt, Brace, and World, 1966.
———. "The Pursuit of the Ideal." In *Moral Disagreements: Classical and Contemporary Readings*, edited by Christopher Gowans, 193-203. London: Routledge, 2000.
Bloom, Harold. *The Anxiety of Influence: A Theory of Poetry*. New York: Oxford University Press, 1973.
Bologova, M. A. "Rozhdenie liriki iz dukha parodii: L. Ulitskaia. 'Veselye pokhorony' vs 'Medeia i ee deti,' 'Sonechka' & 'Kazus Kukotskogo.'" In *Parodiia v russkoi literature XX v.: Sbornik statei*, edited by A. I. Kuliapin et al., 135-56. Barnaul: Izdatel'stvo Altaiskogo gosudarstvennogo universiteta, 2002.
Borenstein, Eliot. *Overkill: Sex and Violence in Contemporary Russian Popular Culture*. Ithaca, NY: Cornell University Press, 2008.
———. "Selling Russia: Prostitution, Masculinity, and Metaphors of Nationalism after Perestroika." In *Gender and National Identity in Twentieth-Century Russian Culture*, edited by Helena Goscilo and Andrea Lanoux, 174-95. DeKalb: Northern Illinois University Press, 2006.
Boym, Svetlana. *Common Places: Mythologies of Everyday Life in Russia*. Cambridge: Harvard University Press, 1994.
Bricaire, Céline. "Les recits de soiffards du nouveau millénaire: Figures de l'alcoolisme chez A. Guelassimov (La soif), V. Popov (Le troisième souffle), A. Matveieva (Le vin italien), L. Oulitskaïa (Le cas du Dr Koukotski)." In *Le premier quinquennat de la prose russe du XXIe siècle*, ed. Hélène Mélat, 285-98. Paris: Institut d'études slaves, 2006.
Bugoslavskaia, Ol'ga. "Vzroslye i deti." *Znamia*, no. 10 (2005): 217-20.
Bulgakov, Mikhail. *Sobranie sochinenii*. Vol. 8. Ann Arbor, MI: Ardis, 1988.

Butler, Judith. *Bodies That Matter: On the Discursive Limits of "Sex."* London: Routledge, 1993.
Bykov, Dmitrii. *Opravdanie.* Moscow: ProzaiK, 2010.
Chao, Sun'. "Tvorchestvo L. Ulitskoi v kontekste russkoi literatury kontsa XX v. Novatorstvo i traditsiia." In *Aktual'nye problemy sotsiogumanitarnogo znaniia: Sbornik nauchnykh trudov kafedry filosofii MPGU.* Vypusk 27, 182–87. Moscow: Prometei, 2004.
Chekhov, Anton. *Eleven Stories.* Translated by Ronald Hingley. London: Oxford University Press, 1975.
———. "The Student." In *Anton Chekhov's Selected Stories,* edited by Cathy Popkin, 290–93. New York: W. W. Norton, 2014.
Chernetsky, Vitaly. *Mapping Postcommunist Cultures: Russia and Ukraine in the Context of Globalization.* Montreal: McGill-Queen's University Press, 2007.
Chiaureli, Mikhail, director. *Padenie Berlina.* Moscow: Mosfil'm, 1949.
Childs, Mary. "Classical Allusions and Imperial Desire: Problems of Identity in Georgian and Russian Literature." PhD diss., University of Washington, Seattle, 2012. http://hdl.handle.net/1773/21796.
Chumakevich, E. V. "Postrealizm v sovremennoi russkoi proze: Romany D. Rubinoi i L. Ulitskoi." *Vestnik Brestskaga universiteta. Seriia filologichnykh nauk,* no. 2 (2009): 29–34.
Chupriian, Anna. "Ulitskaia raskinula shater." *Tribuna,* no. 6 (2011): 14.
Clark, Katerina. "The King Is Dead, Long Live the King: Intelligentsia Ideology in Transition." Paper presented at the conference "Russia at the End of the Twentieth Century: Culture and Its Horizons in Politics and Society." Stanford University, October 1998. http://www.stanford.edu/group/Russia20/volumepdf/clark_fin99.pdf.
———. *The Soviet Novel: History as Ritual.* Chicago: University of Chicago Press, 1981.
Clowes, Edith. *Russia on the Edge: Imagined Geographies and Post-Soviet Identity.* Ithaca, NY: Cornell University Press, 2011.
Condee, Nancy, and Vladimir Padunov. "The ABCs of Russian Consumer Culture: Readings, Ratings, and Real Estate." In *Soviet Hieroglyphics: Visual Culture in Late Twentieth-Century Russia,* edited by Nancy Condee, 130–72. Bloomington: Indiana University Press; London: British Film Institute, 1995.
Daneliia, Georgii, director. *Osennii marafon.* Moscow: Mosfil'm, 1979.
Day, Elizabeth. "Ludmila Ulitskaya: Why I'm Not Afraid of Vladimir Putin." *The Observer,* 16 April 2011. http://www.theguardian.com/world/2011/apr/17/lyudmila-ulitskaya-dissident-putin-interview.
de Mallac, Guy. *Boris Pasternak: His Life and Art.* Norman: University of Oklahoma Press, 1981.
Deutsch, Helene. *The Psychology of Women: A Psychoanalytic Interpretation.* New York: Bantam, 1973.
D'iakova, Elena. "Bol'shoi knigoi nazvano zhitie." *Novaia gazeta,* 26 November 2007, 19.
Doronina, T. N. "'Prinimaiu vse, chto daetsia': Liudmila Ulitskaia i sel'skii chitatel'." *Panorama bibliotechnoi zhizhni oblasti: Opyt, novye idei, tendentsii razvitiia* (Nizhnii Novgorod), no. 3 (2006): 33–35.
Dostoevsky, Fyodor. *A Writer's Diary.* Translated by Kenneth Lantz. Edited by Gary Saul Morson. 2 vols. Evanston, IL: Northwestern University Press, 1993.

Dubin, Boris. *Slovo-pis'mo-literatura: Ocherki po sotsiologii sovremennoi kul'tury*. Moscow: Novoe literaturnoe obozrenie, 2001.
Edel'shtein, Mikhail. "Za vsiu sredu." *Ekspert*, no. 12 (2011): 72.
Efimov, Artem. "Samaia chitaiushchaia strana." *Lenta.ru*, 13 May 2012. http://lenta.ru/articles/2012/05/13/reading/.
Egorova, Natal'ia. "Proza L. Ulitskoi 1980-2000-kh godov: Problematika i poetika." Kand. diss., Astrakhanskii gosudarstvennyi universitet, 2007.
———. "Zhizn' ili 'Veselye pokhorony?' L. Ulitskaia o russkoi literature v sovremennom zapadnom mire." In *Vostok-zapad: Prostranstvo russkoi literatury; materialy Mezhdunarodnoi nauchnoi konferentsii. (Zaochnoi). Volgograd 25 noiabria 2004 g. Volgogradskii gosudarstvennyi pedagogicheskii universitet*, edited by N. E. Tropkina et al., 109-16. Volgograd: Volgogradskoe nauchnoe izdatel'stvo, 2005.
Egoshina, Ol'ga. "Dukhovnost' i 'dukhovka.'" *Novye izvestiia*, 11 January 2010, 4.
Elina, Elena, and Svetlana Ishekova. "Obrazy Rossii v tsikle rasskazov L. Ulitskoi 'Devochki.'" In *Mir Rossii v zerkale noveishei khudozhestvennoi literatury: Sbornik nauchnykh trudov*, edited by A. I. Vaniukov, 181-87. Saratov: Izdatel'stvo Saratovskogo universiteta, 2004.
Engel'gardt, Boris. "Ideologicheskii roman Dostoevskogo." In *Dostoevskii: Stat'i i materialy*, edited by A. S. Dolinin, 2:79-109. Leningrad: Mysl', 1925.
Ermolin, Evgenii. "Ubitoe vremia: Zhivye litsa." *Kontinent*, no. 134 (2007). http://magazines.russ.ru/continent/2007/134/ee19.html.
Erofeev, Venedikt. *Moskva-Petushki*. Paris: YMCA-Press, 1977.
Erofeeva, Valentina. "Bol'shaia natsional'naia?!" *Den' literatury*, no. 136 (2007). http://coollib.com/b/121010/read.
Evtushenko, Evgenii. "Babii Iar." *Literaturnaia gazeta*, no. 112 (1961): 4.
Fernandez, Dominique. "Tolstoï et les bébés." *Le Nouvel Observateur*, no. 2038 (2003): 59.
Figes, Orlando. *The Crimean War: A History*. New York: Metropolitan Books, 2010.
Filippova, Tat'iana. "Intelligent obyknovennyi." *Profil'*, 5 November 2012, 64-66.
Florida, Richard. *The Rise of the Creative Class*. New York: Basic Books, 2002.
Fokin, Vladimir, director. *Niotkuda s liubov'iu ili Veselye pokhorony*. Moscow: Fora-fil'm, 2007.
Frolova, Tat'iana. "Shater s tablichkoi 'vykhod.'" *Neva*, no. 8 (2011): 198-208.
Furman, Yelena. "Writing the Body in New Women's Prose: Sexuality and Textuality in Contemporary Russian Fiction." PhD diss., University of California-Los Angeles, 2004.
Gerschenkron, Alexander. "Notes on Doctor Zhivago." *Modern Philology*, no. 3 (1961): 194-200.
Gessen, Masha. *Dead Again: The Russian Intelligentsia after Communism*. London: Verso, 1997.
———. "The Weight of Words: One of Russia's Most Famous Writers Confronts the State." *New Yorker*, 6 October 2014, 34. http://www.newyorker.com/magazine/2014/10/06/weight-words.
———. *Words Will Break Cement: The Passion of Pussy Riot*. New York: Riverhead, 2014.
Gilbert, Edit, ed. *Embertan és irodalom: Elbeszélésbe oltott gének Ljudmila Ulickaja regényeiben*. Pécs: Muvészetek Háza, 2005.

Gilbert, Sandra, and Susan Gubar. *The Madwoman in the Attic: The Woman Writer and the Nineteenth-Century Literary Imagination*. New Haven and London: Yale University Press, 1979.

Ginzburg, Eugenia. *Journey into the Whirlwind*. Translated by Paul Stevenson and Max Hayward. New York: Harcourt, Brace and World, 1967.

Gorelik, Mikhail. "Proshchanie s ortodoksiei'." *Novyi mir*, no. 5 (2007): 168–72.

Goscilo, Helena. "Big-Buck Books: Pulp Fiction in Post-Soviet Russia." *The Harriman Review*, nos. 2–3 (1999/2000): 6–24.

———. "Coming a Long Way, Baby: A Quarter-Century of Russian Women's Fiction." *The Harriman Institute Forum*, no. 1 (1992): 1–17.

———. *Dehexing Sex: Russian Womanhood during and after Glasnost*. Ann Arbor: University of Michigan Press, 1996.

———. "Introduction: Squaring the Circle." In *Lives in Transit: Recent Russian Women's Writing*, edited by Helena Goscilo, xi–xx. Dana Point, CA: Ardis, 1995.

———. "Perestroika and Post-Soviet Prose: From Dazzle to Dispersal." In *A History of Women's Writing in Russia*, edited by Adele Barker and Jehanne Gheith, 297–312. Cambridge: Cambridge University Press, 2002.

———. "Russia's Ultimate Celebrity: VVP as VIP *Objet d'art*." In *Putin as Celebrity and Cultural Icon*, edited by Helena Goscilo, 6–36. London: Routledge, 2012.

———. "Widowhood as Genre and Profession à la Russe: Nation, Shadow, Curator, and Publicity Agent." In *Gender and National Identity in Twentieth-Century Russian Culture*, edited by Helena Goscilo and Andrea Lanoux, 55–74. DeKalb: Northern Illinois University Press, 2006.

———. "Women's Wards and Wardens: The Hospital in Contemporary Russian Women's Fiction." *Canadian Women's Studies/Les Cahiers de la femme*, no. 4 (1989): 83–86.

Goscilo, Helena, and Yana Hashamova. "Cinepaternity: The Psyche and Its Heritage." In *Cinepaternity: Fathers and Sons in Soviet and Post-Soviet Film*, edited by Helena Goscilo and Yana Hashamova, 1–25. Bloomington: Indiana University Press, 2010.

Goscilo, Helena, and Andrea Lanoux. "Introduction: Lost in the Myths." In *Gender and National Identity in Twentieth-Century Russian Culture*, edited by Helena Goscilo and Andrea Lanoux, 3–29. DeKalb: Northern Illinois University Press, 2006.

Goscilo, Helena, and Vlad Strukov. "Introduction." In *Celebrity and Glamour in Contemporary Russia: Shocking Chic*, edited by Helena Goscilo and Vlad Strukov, 1–26. London: Routledge, 2011.

Graham, Seth. "Models of Male Kinship in Perestroika Cinema." In *Cinepaternity: Fathers and Sons in Soviet and Post-Soviet Film*, edited by Helena Goscilo and Yana Hashamova, 70–86. Bloomington: Indiana University Press, 2010.

Grammatikov, Vladimir, director. *Sestrichki Liberti*. Moscow: Kinostudiia im. M. Gor'kogo, 1990.

Grekova, I. *Na ispytaniiakh*. Moscow: Sovetskii pisatel', 1990.

———. *Svezho predanie*. Moscow: Eksmo, 2002.

Grigor'eva, Tat'iana. "Liudmila Ulitskaia: Zelenyi shater." *OpenSpace.ru arkhiv*, 24 January 2011. http://os.colta.ru/literature/events/details/20064/.

Grosz, Elizabeth. *Volatile Bodies: Toward a Corporeal Feminism*. Bloomington: Indiana University Press, 1994.

Grothe, Anja. "Medusa, Cassandra, Medea: Re-Inscribing Myth in Contemporary German and Russian Women's Writing." PhD diss., City University of New York, 2000.
Grymov, Iurii, director. *Kazus Kukotskogo*. Moscow: NTV, 2005.
Gudkov, Lev. "Attitudes toward Jews in Post-Soviet Russia and the Problem of Anti-Semitism." In *Revolution, Repression, and Revival: The Soviet Jewish Experience*, edited by Zvi Gitelman and Yaacov Ro'i, 193–217. Lanham, MD: Rowman and Littlefield, 2007.
———. *Negativnaia identichnost': Stat'i 1997–2002 godov*. Moscow: Novoe literaturnoe obozrenie, 2004.
Hall, Stuart. "Cultural Identity and Diaspora." In *Identity: Community, Culture, Difference*, edited by Jonathan Rutherford, 222–37. London: Lawrence and Wishart, 1990.
Heldt, Barbara. *Terrible Perfection: Women and Russian Literature*. Bloomington: Indiana University Press, 1987.
Hellebust, Rolf. *Flesh to Metal: Soviet Literature and the Alchemy of Revolution*. Ithaca, NY: Cornell University Press, 2003.
Herzfeld, Michael. *Cultural Intimacy: Social Poetics in the Nation-State*. New York: Routledge, 1997.
Hirsch, Marianne. *The Mother/Daughter Plot: Narrative, Psychoanalysis, Feminism*. Bloomington: Indiana University Press, 1989.
Holmgren, Beth. "Introduction." In *The Russian Memoir: History and Literature*, edited by Beth Holmgren, ix–xxxix. Evanston, IL: Northwestern University Press, 2003.
Hutchings, Stephen. *Russian Modernism: The Transfiguration of the Everyday*. Cambridge: Cambridge University Press, 1997.
Iarantsev, Vladimir. "Vzgliad iz Sibiri." *Literaturnaia Rossiia*, no. 41 (2006): 12–13.
Iser, Wolfgang. "Foreword: Intertextuality; The Epitome of Culture." In *Memory and Literature: Intertextuality in Russian Modernism* by Renate Lachmann, translated by Roy Sellars and Anthony Wall, vii–xviii. Minneapolis: University of Minnesota Press, 1997.
Iuzefovich, Galina. "Gospozha nabliudatel'." *Itogi*, no. 8 (2011). http://www.itogi.ru/iskus/2011/8/162194.html.
Jaspers, Karl. *Karl Jaspers: Basic Philosophical Writings*. Athens: Ohio University Press, 1986.
Kaganovsky, Lilya. *How the Soviet Man Was Unmade: Cultural Fantasy and Male Subjectivity under Stalin*. Pittsburgh, PA: University of Pittsburgh Press, 2008.
Kan, A. S. "Istoriografiia, istochnikovedenie, metody istoricheskogo issledovaniia: Postsovetskoe issledovanie o politicheskikh repressiiakh v Rossii i SSSR." *Otechestvennaia istoriia*, no. 1 (2003): 120–33.
Karapetian, M. "Aristokraty dukha, brazhniki i bludnitsy: 'Legkoe dykhanie' geroev Liudmily Ulitskoi." *Kul'tura*, no. 27 (1998): 10.
Kaspe, Irina. "Certificate of What? Document and Documentation in Contemporary Russian Literature." Translated by Birgit Beumers. *Russian Review*, no. 4 (2010): 563–84.
Kazarina, Tat'iana. "Bednye rodstvenniki." *Preobrazhenie*, no. 4 (1996): 169–72.
Khvan, Aleksandr, director. *Umirat' legko*. Moscow: NTV-Profit, 1999.
Knight, Rebecca. "Representations of Soviet Childhood in Post-Soviet Texts by Liudmila Ulitskaia and Nina Gabrielian." *Modern Language Review*, no. 3 (2009): 790–808.

Kobets, Svitlana. "From Fool to Mother to Savior: The Poetics of Orthodox Christianity and Folklore in Svetlana Vasilenko's Novel-Vita *Little Fool* (Durochka)." *Slavic and East European Journal*, no. 1 (2007): 87–110.
Koksheneva, Kapitolina. "Dyra novogo ateizma: O romane Liudmily Ulitskoi 'Daniel' Shtain, perevodchik.'" *Moskva*, no. 4 (2008): 209–17.
Koliadich, T. M. "L. E. Ulitskaia." In *Russkaia proza kontsa XX veka*, edited by T. M. Koliadich, 369–91. Moscow: Academia, 2005.
Kornblatt, Judith. *Doubly Chosen: Jewish Identity, the Soviet Intelligentsia, and the Russian Orthodox Church*. Madison: University of Wisconsin Press, 2004.
Korobov, Vladimir. "So Many Books, Yet So Few, or the New Publishing Crisis." Translated by Marian Schwartz. Edited by Deming Brown. *Russian Social Science Review*, no. 1 (1997): 82–89.
Kozlov, Denis. "Writing about the Thaw in Post-Soviet Russia." *Russian Studies in History*, no. 4 (2011): 3–17.
Krasnoperova, Dar'ia. "Zachem nam novoe slovo? Ili Zametki o tolerantnosti." *Sankt-Peterburgskie vedomosti*, 4 March 2003, 5.
Kristeva, Julia. *Black Sun: Depression and Melancholia*. Translated by Leon Roudiez. New York: Columbia University Press, 1989.
Krutikov, Mikhail. "Opyt rossiiskoi evreiskoi emigratsii i ego otrazhenie v proze 90-kh godov." *Diaspora*, no. 3 (2000): 212–34.
Kucherskaia, Maiia. "Vot oni tak i zhili." *Vedomosti*, 29 December 2010, 6.
Kuklin, Lev. "Kazus Ulitskoi." *Neva*, no. 7 (2003): 177–89.
Kuznetsov, I. V. "'Daniel' Shtain' L. Ulitskoi v russkoi literaturnoi traditsii." *Russkaia slovesnost'*, no. 6 (2008): 38–42.
Larieva, E. V. "'Est' igry, v kotorye ia ne igraiu'. Ili 'igraiu'? Nabokovskii intertekst v povesti L. Ulitskoi 'Sonechka.'" In *Siuzhet, motiv, istoriia: Sbornik nauchnykh statei*, vypusk 8, edited by E. V. Kapinos, 222–35. Novosibirsk: Nauka, 2009.
———. "Sviatye i greshnye: Dva rasskaza L. Ulitskoi o sem'e ('Oni zhili dolgo,' '. . . i umerli v odin den')." *Filologiia i chelovek* (Barnaul), no. 3 (2008): 186–92.
Latynina, Alla. "Vsekh sovetskaia vlast' ubila." *Novyi mir*, no. 6 (2011): 169–77.
Layton, Susan. *Russian Literature and Empire: Conquest of the Caucasus from Pushkin to Tolstoy*. Cambridge: Cambridge University Press, 1994.
Lee, Deuk-Jae. "The Terrible Journey to Self-Identification." *Rusistika*, no. 17 (1998): 31–34.
Levantovskaya, Margarita. "The Russian-Speaking Jewish Diaspora in Translation: Liudmila Ulitskaia's *Daniel Stein, Translator*." *Slavic Review*, no. 1 (2012): 91–107.
Likhachev, Dmitrii. *Vospominaniia, razdum'ia, raboty raznykh let*. 3 vols. Edited by O. V. Panchenko et al. St. Petersburg: ARS, 2006.
Limonov, Eduard. *Mes prisons*. Arles: Actes Sud, 2008.
Linton, Simi. *Claiming Disability: Knowledge and Identity*. New York: New York University Press, 1998.
Lipovetsky, Mark. "Literature on the Margins: Russian Fiction in the Nineties." *Studies in 20th Century Literature* 24, no. 1 (Winter 2000): 139–68.
———. *Russian Postmodernist Fiction: Dialogue with Chaos*. Translated by Eliot Borenstein. Armonk, NY: M. E. Sharpe, 1999.
Lipovetsky, Mark, and Alexander Etkind. "The Salamander's Return: The Soviet Catastrophe and the Post-Soviet Novel." *Russian Studies in Literature*, no. 4 (2010): 6–48.

Litovskaia, Maria. "Lyudmila Ulitskaya." Translated by Seth Graham. In *Russian Writers since 1980*, edited by Marina Balina and Mark Lipovetsky, 329-35. Dictionary of Literary Biography 285. Detroit: Gale, 2004.

———. "Smena sotsial'nykh stereotipov i fenomen populiarnosti pisatelia: Sluchai Liudmily Ulitskoi." In *Noveishaia russkaia literatura rubezha XX-XXI vekov: Itogi i perspektivy*, compiled and edited by M. A. Cherniak and A. M. Novozhilova, 23-28. St. Petersburg: LEMA, 2007.

Livers, Keith. *Constructing the Stalinist Body: Fictional Representations of Corporeality in the Stalinist 1930s*. Lanham, MD: Lexington Books, 2004.

Livingstone, Angela. *Boris Pasternak: Doctor Zhivago*. Cambridge: Cambridge University Press, 1989.

Logunova, N. V. "Transformatsiia zhanrovogo kanona epistoliarnogo romana v knige L. Ulitskoi 'Daniel' Shtain, perevodchik.'" In *Russkaia literatura v formirovanii sovremennoi iazykovoi lichnosti: Sankt-Peterburg 24-27 oktiabria 2007 g.* Vol. 1, *Literatura v formirovanii iazykovoi lichnosti: Etapy i varianty*, edited by P. E. Bukharkin, N. O. Rogozhina, E. E. Iurkov, 164-74. St. Petersburg: Mirs, 2007.

"Ludmila Ulitskaya." *Elkost International Literary Agency*. http://www.elkost.com/authors/ulitskaya.

Lushchevska, Oksana. "Ulitskaia's Writing for Children: Transcending Limitations of the Graphic Novel Genre." *Bookbird*, no. 2 (2013): 23-31.

Malashenok, Sergei. "Kak napisat' roman Ulitskoi." *Topos: Literaturno-filosofskii zhurnal* (1 July 2005). http://topos.ru/article/3762.

Maletskii, Iurii. "Roman Ulitskoi kak zerkalo russkoi intelligentsii." *Novyi mir*, no. 5 (2007). http://www.portal-slovo.ru/philology/37290.php.

Malygina, Nina. "Zdes' i seichas: Poetika ischeznoveniia." *Oktiabr'*, no. 9 (2000): 152-59.

Mamedova, Peri Israfil gyzy. "Khudozhestvennoe prostranstvo i vremia v sovremennoi russkoi proze (na material tvorchestva L. Ulitskoi)." Kand. diss., Bakinskii slavianskii universitet, 2011.

Marsh, Rosalind. *Literature, History and Identity in Post-Soviet Russia, 1991-2006*. New York: Peter Lang, 2007.

———. "New Mothers for a New Era? Images of Mothers and Daughters in Post-Soviet Prose in Historical and Cultural Perspective." *Modern Language Review*, no. 4 (2012): 1191-219.

Mart'ianova, I. A. "Metapoetika zhivopisi i kino v proze L. Ulitskoi, L. Petrushevskoi i D. Rubinoi." In *Metapoetika: Sbornik statei nauchno-metodicheskogo seminara "Textus,"* edited by V. P. Khodus, 1:336-40. Stavropol: Izdatel'stvo Stavropol'skogo gosudarstvennogo universiteta, 2008.

Martynok, Viktor. "Rossiia ne imeet prava predat' russkikh v Krymu." *Komsomol'skaia pravda*, 27 February 2014. http://www.km.ru/world/2014/02/27/protivostoyanie-na-ukraine-2013-14/733415-rossiya-ne-imeet-prava-predat-russkikh-v-.

Mateo, Ferran. "On Being Chosen: The Great Writer Ludmila Ulitskaya Speaks Up." *Russia Beyond the Headlines*, 30 June 2013. http://rbth.ru/2013/06/30/on_being_chosen_the_great_writer_ludmila_ulitskaya_speaks_up_27549.html.

Mateshko, Anatolii, director. *Zhenshchina dlia vsekh*. Kiev: Kinostudiia im. A. Dovzhenko and Piramida-Menatep, 1991.

Mathewson, Rufus. *The Positive Hero in Russian Literature*. New York: Columbia University Press, 1958.

McCann, Eugene. "Inequality and Politics in the Creative-City Region: Questions of Livability and State Strategy." *International Journal of Urban and Regional Research* 31, no. 1 (2007): 188-96.
Men', Aleksandr. *O sebe... Vospominaniia, interv'iu, besedy, pis'ma*, compiled by Natal'ia Grigorenko and Pavel Men'. Moscow: Izdatel'stvo Zhizn' s Bogom, 2007.
Men'shov, Vladimir, director. *Moskva slezam ne verit*. Moscow: Mosfil'm, 1979.
Mesropova, Olga. "Crime, Byt, and Fairy-Tales: Daria Dontsova and Post-Soviet Ironical Detective Fiction." *Slavic and East European Journal*, no. 1 (2008): 113-28.
———. "The Discreet Charm of the Russian Bourgeoisie." *Russian Review*, no. 1 (2009): 89-101.
Morson, Gary Saul. "Philosophy in the Nineteenth-Century Novel." In *The Cambridge Companion to the Classic Russian Novel*, edited by Malcolm Jones and Robin Feuer Miller, 150-68. Cambridge: Cambridge University Press, 1998.
Mulvey, Laura. "Visual Pleasure and Narrative Cinema." In *Feminist Film Theory: A Reader*, edited by Susan Thornham, 58-69. New York: New York University Press, 1999.
Na, Liu. "Povestvovatel'naia strategiia L. Ulitskoi v knige 'Liudi nashego tsaria.'" *Vestnik Tambovskogo universiteta. Seriia gumanitarnye nauki*, no. 11 (2009): 241-43.
Nadezhdina, Ol'ga. "Naviazannaia subkul'tura." *Literaturnaia gazeta*, no. 19 (2008): 10.
Nekrasova, I. V. "O raznykh sposobakh povestvovaniia v proze Liudmily Ulitskoi." In *Izmeniaiushchaiasia Rossiia — izmeniaiushchaiasia literatura: Khudozhestvennyi opyt XX-nachala XXI vekov; sbornik nauchnykh trudov*, compiled by A. I. Vaniukov, 2:303-7. Saratov: Nauka, 2008.
———. "Siuzhetoobrazuiushchaia funktsiia khronotopa v romane L. Ulitskoi 'Kazus Kukotskogo.'" In *Prostranstvo i vremia v khudozhestvennom proizvedenii: Sbornik nauchnykh trudov*, compiled and edited by A. G. Prokof'eva, V. Iu. Prokof'eva, and S. M. Skibin, 86-90. Orenburg: Orenburgskii gosudarstvennyi pedagogicheskii universitet, 2002.
Nemzer, Andrei. "Pervaia ledi: Laureatom premii Smirnoff-Buker stala Liudmila Ulitskaia." *Vremia novostei*, 7 December 2001. http://www.vremya.ru/2001/226/10/17407.html.
Nepomnyashchy, Catharine. "Markets, Mirrors, and Mayhem: Aleksandra Marinina and the Rise of the New Russian *Detektiv*." In *Consuming Russia: Popular Culture, Sex, and Society since Gorbachev*, edited by Adele Barker, 161-91. Durham, NC: Duke University Press, 1999.
Northrop, Douglas. *Veiled Empire: Gender and Power in Stalinist Central Asia*. Ithaca, NY: Cornell University Press, 2004.
Os'mukhina, Ol'ga. "V poiskakh utrachennoi tolerantnosti: Liudmila Ulitskaia." *Voprosy literatury*, no. 1 (2011): 144-58.
Ostrenko, I. A. "Subkul'tura detstva v tsikle L. Ulitskoi 'Devochki.'" In *Mirovaia slovesnost' dlia detei i o detiakh*, edited by I. G. Mineralova, 1:9:55-62. Moscow: Moskovskii pedagogicheskii gosudarstvennyi universitet, 2004.
Oushakine, Serguei. "Mesto-imeni-ia: Sem'ia kak sposob organizatsii zhizni." In *Semeinye uzy: Modeli dlia sborki*, compiled and edited by Sergei Ushakin, 1:7-52. Moscow: Novoe literaturnoe obozrenie, 2004.
———. *The Patriotism of Despair: Nation, War, and Loss in Russia*. Ithaca, NY: Cornell University Press, 2009.
———. "The Terrifying Mimicry of Samizdat." *Public Culture*, no. 2 (2001): 191-214.

Palei, Marina. "The Bloody Women's Ward." Translated by Arch Tait. In *Women's View*, edited by Natasha Perova and Andrew Bromfield, 74-91. Moscow: Glas, 1992.
———. *Long Distance, ili Slavianskii aktsent*. Moscow: Vagrius, 2000.
Panfilov, Oleg. "Rebirth of Russian Nationalism." Translated by Arch Tait. *Index on Censorship*, no. 1 (2006): 142-48.
Paperno, Irina. "Personal Accounts of the Soviet Experience." *Kritika*, no. 4 (2002): 577-610.
———. *Stories of the Soviet Experience: Memoirs, Diaries, Dreams*. Ithaca, NY: Cornell University Press, 2009.
Papkova, Irina. *The Orthodox Church and Russian Politics*. New York: Oxford University Press, 2011.
Parnell, Christina. "Hiding and Using Sexuality: The Artist's Controversial Subject in Modern Russian Women's Literature." In *Gender and Sexuality in Russian Civilization*, edited by Peter Barta, 311-24. London and New York: Routledge, 2001.
Parthé, Kathleen. *Russian Village Prose: The Radiant Past*. Princeton, NJ: Princeton University Press, 1992.
Pasternak, Boris. *Collected Short Prose*. Translated by Christopher Barnes. New York: Praeger, 1977.
———. *Doctor Zhivago*. Translated by Max Hayward and Manya Harari. New York: Bantam, 1985.
———. *Sobranie sochinenii v piati tomakh*. 5 vols. Moscow: Khudozhestvennaia literatura, 1989-1992.
Peck, J. "Struggling with the Creative Class." *International Journal of Urban and Regional Affairs* 28, no. 4 (2005): 749-70.
Petrushevskaia, Liudmila. *Deviatyi tom*. Moscow: Eksmo, 2003.
———. *Dom devushek*. Moscow: Vagrius, 1998.
———. *Nomer Odin, ili V sadakh drugikh vozmozhnostei*. Moscow: Eksmo, 2006.
Petukhova, E. N. "Dialog s Chekhovym: 'Russkoe varen'e' L. Ulitskoi." In *Dialog s Chekhovym: Sbornik nauchnykh trudov v chest' 70-letiia V. B. Kataeva*, edited by P. N. Dolzhenkov, 363-72. Moscow: Moskovskii gosudarstvennyi universitet, 2009.
Pichul, Vasilii, director. *Malen'kaia Vera*. Moscow: Kinostudiia im. M. Gor'kogo, 1988.
Pirogov, Lev. "Kipiatok ne dlia chainikov: Ulitskaia, Tolstaia i natsional'nyi' vopros." *Nezavisimaia gazeta, Ex Libris*, 12 January 2006, 5.
Plakhova, E. "Proza: Velikolepnyi ochevidets." *Moskovskaia pravda*, 17 August 2005, 4.
Pobivailo, O. V. "Bliznechnyi mif v rasskaze L. E. Ulitskoi 'Vtoroe litso.'" *Filologiia i chelovek* (Barnaul), no. 2 (2008): 115-19.
Podnieks, Elizabeth, and Andrea O'Reilly, eds. *Textual Mothers/Maternal Texts: Motherhood in Contemporary Women's Literatures*. Waterloo, ON: Wilfred Laurier University Press, 2010.
"Politik ili pastyr'?" *Nezavisimaia gazeta, Religii*, 4 February 2009, 4.
Pomerantsev, Vladimir. "Ob iskrennosti v literature." *Novyi mir*, no. 12 (1953): 218-45.
Ponzini, D., and U. Rossi. "Becoming a Creative City: The Entrepreneurial Mayor, Network Politics, and the Promise of Urban Renaissance." *Urban Studies* 47, no. 5 (2010): 1037-57.
Popper, Karl. *The Open Society and Its Enemies*. 2 vols. Princeton, NJ: Princeton University Press, 1966.

Poriadina, M. E. "Aktualizatsiia 'tolerantnykh' motivov v detskoi knige na sovremennom rossiiskom rynke." *Bibliografiia*, no. 1 (2009): 58–63.
Powers, Jenne. "Novel Histories: Repudiation of Soviet Historiography in the Works of Iurii Trifonov, Vladimir Makanin, and Liudmila Ulitskaia." PhD diss., University of North Carolina at Chapel Hill, 2009.
Pozdniaev, Mikhail. "Russiia — ne dom terpimosti'." *Novye Izvestiia*, 19 February 2009. http://www.newizv.ru/society/2009-02-12/105581-rossija-ne-dom-terpimosti.html.
Prokhanov, Aleksandr. "Aleksandr Prokhanov: Rossiia stanet imperiei ili ischeznet." *Nevskoe vremia*, 21 April 2010. http://www.nvspb.ru/tops/aleksandr-prohanov-rossiya-stanet-imperiey-ili-ischeznet-42272.
Prokhorov, Alexander. "From Family Reintegration to Carnivalistic Degradation: Dismantling Soviet Communal Myths in Russian Cinema of the Mid-1990s." *Slavic and East European Journal*, no. 2 (2007): 272–94.
———. *Unasledovannyi diskurs: Paradigmy stalinskoi kul'tury v literature i kinematografe "ottepeli."* St. Petersburg: Akademicheskii proekt/Izdatel'stvo DNK, 2007.
Prusakova, Inna. "Liudmila Ulitskaia. Sonechka. Povest'. 'Novyi mir' 1992, No. 7." *Neva*, no. 1 (1993): 236.
Pul'son, Klarisa. "Ideal'noe chtenie." *Profil'*, 9 April 2012. http://www.profile.ru/article/idealnoe-chtenie-70028.
Rasputin, Valentin. "Cherchez la femme." *Nash sovremennik*, no. 3 (1990): 168–72.
Raunio, Mar'a-Leena. "Kak ia ne stala pisatel'nitsei." In *Mariia: Literaturnyi al'manakh*, compiled by Galina Skvortsova, 1:268–75. Petrozavodsk: Kareliia, 1990.
Razumov, Gennadii. "Knizhnye vykresty L. Ulitskoi." *Narod moi*, no. 17 (2007). http://ami-moy.narod.ru/A405/A405-051.html.
Remizova, Mariia. "Grandes dames proshedshego sezona: Zametki o literaturnykh premiiakh." *Kontinent*, no. 112 (2002): 396–405.
Rep'eva, Ekaterina. "Roman kak oruzhie globalizma." *Literaturnaia Rossiia*, nos. 2–3 (2007). http://www.litrossia.ru/2007/02-03/01111.html.
Rivkin-Fish, Michele. "From 'Demographic Crisis' to 'Dying Nation': The Politics of Language and Reproduction in Russia." In *Gender and National Identity in Twentieth-Century Russian Culture*, edited by Helena Goscilo and Andrea Lanoux, 151–73. DeKalb: Northern Illinois University Press, 2006.
Rogozhkin, Aleksandr, director. *Osobennosti natsional'noi okhoty*. St. Petersburg: Lenfil'm, 1995.
Romanovskaia, Larisa. "Apokrif ot dobrogo diadi." *Kul'tura*, no. 44 (2006): 2.
Rondeau, Daniel. "La grande Ludmila." *L'Express*, no. 2802 (2005): 61.
Rovenskaia, Tat'iana. "Arkhetip doma v novoi zhenskoi proze, ili Kommunal'noe zhitie i kommunal'nye tela." *Inoi vzgliad*, no. 3 (2001): 24–26.
———. "Opyt novogo zhenskogo mifotvorchestva: 'Medeia i ee deti' L. Ulitskoi i 'Malen'kaia Groznaia' L. Petrushevskoi." In *Adam i Eva: Al'manakh gendernoi istorii*, edited by L. P. Repina, 137–62. Moscow: Institut vseobshchei istorii RAN, 2001.
———. "Vinovata li ia . . . ? Ili fenomen gendernoi viny (na materiale zhenskoi prozy 80-kh-nachalo 90-kh godov)." *Gendernye issledovaniia*, no. 3 (1999): 214–24.
———. "Zhenskaia proza serediny 1980-kh-nachala 1990-kh godov. (Problematika, mental'nost', identifikatsiia)." Kand. diss., Moskovskii gosudarstvennyi universitet, 2000.
Rubina, Dina. *Na solnechnoi storone ulitsy*. Moscow: Eksmo, 2011.

Rudinskii, Vladimir. "Liudmila Ulitskaia. 'Liudi nashego tsaria.'" *Nasha strana* (Buenos Aires), 24 September 2005, 3.
"Rukovoditeliu sluzhby po kontroliu i nadzoru v sfere obrazovaniia KhMAO-Iugry Strebkovoi N.V." http://arhiv.oodvrs.ru/article/index.php?id_page=71& id+ article=972.
Rutten, Ellen. *Sincerity after Communism: A Cultural History*. Unpublished manuscript.
Ryvkina, R. V. "The Expiration of the Intelligentsia's Social Role in Post-Soviet Russia." *Russian Education and Society*, no. 7 (2007): 5-20.
Ryzhova, Ol'ga. "Kumirnia: Koitus Kukotskogo, ili Samaia intelligentnaia domokhoziaika." *Literaturnaia gazeta*, no. 37 (2004): 11.
Ryzhova, Svetlana. "Tolerance and Extremism: Russian Ethnicity in the Orthodox Discourse of the 1990s." In *Religion and Identity in Modern Russia: The Revival of Orthodoxy and Islam*, ed. Juliet Johnson, Marietta Stepaniants, and Benjamin Forest, 65-90. Aldershot, UK: Ashgate, 2005.
Sadur, Nina. "Worm-Eaten Sonny." Translated by Wendi Formoff. In *Lives in Transit: Recent Russian Women's Writing*, edited by Helena Goscilo, 203-4. Dana Point, CA: Ardis, 1995.
Said, Edward. *Orientalism*. New York: Pantheon, 1978.
Sait Sintona. http://forum.syntone.ru/index.php?showtopic=14258&st=15.
Sakwa, Richard. "Mikhail Khodorkovsky: Putin's Prisoner, Russia's Hero." *Times Literary Supplement*, 28 September 2011. http://www.the-tls.co.uk/tls/public/article 785939.ece.
Salys, Rimgaila. "Ljudmila Ulickaja's Sonečka: Gender and the Construction of Identity." *Russian, Croatian and Serbian, Czech and Slovak, Polish Literature*, no. 3 (2011): 443-66.
Samoilycheva, Tat'iana. "Absoliutnyi zvon." *Literaturnaia gazeta*, no. 44 (2012): 7.
Satter, David. *It Was a Long Time Ago, and It Never Happened Anyway: Russia and the Communist Past*. New Haven, CT: Yale University Press, 2012.
Savkina, Irina. "Rod/dom: Semeinaia khronika Liudmily Ulitskoi i Vasiliia Aksenova." In *Semeinye uzy: Modeli dlia sborki*, compiled and edited by Sergei Ushakin, 1:156-82. Moscow: Novoe literaturnoe obozrenie, 2004.
Semikina, Iuliia. "Khudozhestvennaia fenomenologiia izobrazheniia bytiia i inobytiia v romane L. Ulitskoi 'Kazus Kukotskogo.'" *Studia Universitatis Babeş-Bolyai, Philologia*, no. 1 (2008): 123-30.
Shafranskaia, E. F. "Russkaia literatura o nerusskoi zhizni i nerusskikh geroiakh." *Russkaia slovesnost'*, no. 7 (2007): 41-45.
Shalin, Dmitrii. "Intellectual Culture." In *Russian Culture at the Crossroads: Paradoxes of Postcommunist Consciousness*, edited by Dmitrii Shalin, 41-98. Boulder, CO: Westview Press, 1996.
Shcheglova, Evgeniia. "Nesbyvshaiasia mechta: O proze Liudmily Ulitskoi." *Zvezda*, no. 3 (2012): 216-29.
———. "O spokoinom dostoinstve—i ne tol'ko o nem: Liudmila Ulitskaia i ee mir." *Neva*, no. 7 (2003): 183-89.
Shishkova-Shipunova, Svetlana. "Kod Danielia Shtaina, ili Dobryi chelovek iz Khaify." *Znamia*, no. 9 (2007): 193-97.
Shternshis, Anna. *Soviet and Kosher: Jewish Popular Culture in the Soviet Union, 1923-1939*. Bloomington: Indiana University Press, 2006.

Sinyavsky, Andrei. *Ivan the Fool: Russian Folk Belief; A Cultural History*. Translated by Joanne Turnbull and Nikolai Formozov. Moscow: Glas, 2007.

———. *The Russian Intelligentsia*. New York: Columbia University Press, 1997.

———. *Soviet Civilization: A Cultural History*. Translated by Joanne Turnbull with Nikolai Formozov. New York: Arcade, 1990.

Skokova, Tat'iana. "Proza Liudmily Ulitskoi v kontekste russkogo postmodernizma: Avtoreferat." Kand. diss., Moskovskii gosudarstvennyi gumanitarnyi universitet, 2010.

Skomp, Elizabeth. "Violence, Madness, and the Female Grotesque in Nina Sadur's *The South* and Svetlana Vasilenko's *Little Fool*." In *Times of Trouble: Violence in Russian Literature and Culture*, edited by Marcus Levitt and Tatyana Novikov, 287–95. Madison: University of Wisconsin Press, 2007.

Skvortsov, V. Ia., and A. I. Skvortsova. "Samobytie cheloveka v povesti Liudmily Ulitskoi 'Veselye pokhorony.'" *Vestnik Volgogradskogo gosudarstvennogo universiteta. Seriia 2: Filologiia, zhurnalistika*, no. 5 (2000): 105–12.

Slavnikova, Ol'ga. "Nedolet ukazyvaet na tsel'." *Ural*, no. 2 (1999): 183–86.

Slezkine, Yuri. *The Jewish Century*. Princeton, NJ: Princeton University Press, 2004.

Smirnov, Iu. N. "Istorik v meniaiushchemsia prostranstve rossiiskoi kul'tury." *Rossiiskaia istoriia*, no. 6 (2007): 201–7.

Snyder, Timothy. *Bloodlands: Europe between Hitler and Stalin*. New York: Basic Books, 2010.

Sokurov, Aleksandr, director. *Russkii kovcheg*. St. Petersburg: Hermitage Bridge Studio, 2002.

Solzhenitsyn, Aleksandr. *Cancer Ward*. Translated by Rebecca Frank. New York: Dial, 1968.

———. *The First Circle*. Translated by Thomas P. Whitney. New York: Harper and Row, 1968.

———. "The Smatterers." In *From under the Rubble*. Translated by A. M. Brock et al., 229–78. Boston: Little, Brown, and Company, 1975.

———. *Stories and Prose Poems*. Translated by Michael Glenny. New York: Farrar, Straus and Giroux, 1971.

Squire, Michael. *Image and Text in Graeco-Roman Antiquity*. New York: Cambridge University Press, 2009.

Starobinets, Anna. "Te zhe i volshebnik." *Ekspert*, no. 33 (2002). http://expert.ru/expert/2002/33/33ex-books_36445/.

Stepanian, Elena. "'Eto my, Gospodi': O diletantakh, professionalakh i o mirovom kholode." *Znamia*, no. 2 (2010): 191–99.

Stephens, Robert. *The Family Saga in the South: Generations and Destinies*. Baton Rouge: Louisiana State University Press, 1995.

Stishova, Elena. "Kto vy, mastera kul'tury?" *Iskusstvo kino*, no. 6 (1993): 57–68.

Stroganova, Anna. "Boris Akunin: 'Dlia menia perepiska s Khodorkovskim znachila ochen' mnogoe." *RFI Russkii: Literaturnyi perekrestok*, 6 April 2011. http://www.russian.rfi.fr/prava-cheloveka/20110416-boris-akunin-dlya-menya-perepiska-s-khodorkovskim-znachila-ochen-mnogoe.

Suleiman, Susan Rubin. "(Re)Writing the Body: The Politics and Poetics of Female Eroticism." In *The Female Body in Western Culture*, edited by Susan Rubin Suleiman, 7–29. Cambridge, MA: Harvard University Press, 1986.

Sutcliffe, Benjamin. "Everyday Life and the Ties That Bind in Liudmila Ulitskaia's *Medea and Her Children*." In *Everyday Life in Russia: Subjectivities, Perspectives, and Lived Experience*, edited by David Ransel, Mary Cavender, Karen Petrone, and Choi Chatterjee. Bloomington: Indiana University Press, forthcoming.

———. "Liudmila Ulitskaia's Literature of Tolerance." *Russian Review*, no. 68 (2009): 495–509.

———. "Mother, Daughter, History: Embodying the Past in Liudmila Ulitskaia's *Sonechka* and *The Case of Kukotskii*." *Slavic and East European Journal*, no. 4 (2009): 606–22.

———. *The Prose of Life: Russian Women Writers from Khrushchev to Putin*. Madison: University of Wisconsin Press, 2009.

———. "Secular Victims, Religious Aggressors: Liudmila Ulitskaia's Muslims, Radical Islam, and the Russian Intelligentsia." *Russian Review*. Forthcoming.

Svetova, Zoia. "Ne bylo pobeditelei u vremeni." *Novoe vremia*, no. 43 (2010): 44–47.

Terpits, Olaf. "'Zdes' i tam': Aspekt 'kul'turnogo transfera' v literaturnom diskurse 1990-kh godov." Translated by A. I. Godina. In *Evreiskaia emigratsiia iz Rossii, 1881–2005*, edited by O. V. Budnitskii, 347–62. Moscow: ROSSPEN, 2008.

Tesmer, B. "Proza Liudmily Ulitskoi na rubezhe XX–XXI veka (spetsifika tvorcheskoi manery)." In *Traditsii russkoi klassiki XX veka i sovremennost': Materialy mezhdunarodnoi nauchnoi konferentsii*, compiled and edited by S. M. Kormilov, 280–83. Moscow: Izdatel'stvo Moskovskogo universiteta, 2002.

Timina, Svetlana. "Ritmy vechnosti: Roman Liudmily Ulitskoi *Medeia i ee deti*." In *Perom i prelest'iu: Zhenshchiny v panteone russkoi literatury; sbornik statei*, edited by Wanda Laszczak and Daria Ambroziak, 146–60. Opole: Wydawca Dariusz Karbowiak, 1999.

Tippner, Anja. "Konversion(en): Translation und Identität in Ljudmila Ulickajas Roman *Daniel' Štajn—perevodčik // Daniel Stein—Übersetzer*." In *Trans-lation—Trans-nation—Trans-formation: Übersetzen und jüdische Kulturen*, edited by Petra Ernst et al., 217–33. Innsbruck: StudienVerlag, 2012.

Tiutelova, L. G. "Chekhovskaia traditsiia v otechestvennoi drame XX veka i p'esa L. Ulitskoi 'Russkoe varen'e, ili Afterchekhov.'" In *Sovremennaia russkaia drama: Sbornik statei i materialov mezhdunarodnoi nauchnoi konferentsii (27–29 sentiabria 2007 g.)*, edited by I. Bidermann, E. N. Shevchenko, and T. S. Shakhmatova, 160–66. Kazan: RITs shkola, 2008.

Tlostanova, Madina. "The Imagined Freedom: Post-Soviet Intellectuals between the Hegemony of the State and the Hegemony of the Market." *South Atlantic Quarterly*, no. 3 (2006): 637–59.

Toker, Leona. *Return from the Archipelago: Narratives of Gulag Survivors*. Bloomington: Indiana University Press, 2000.

Tolstaia, Tat'iana. *Reka Okkervil'*. Moscow: Podkova, 2004.

Trifonov, Iurii. *The Exchange and Other Stories*. Translated by Ellendea Proffer et al. Evanston, IL: Northwestern University Press, 2002.

———. *Studenty*. In *Sobranie sochinenii v chetyrekh tomakh*, edited by S. A. Baruzdin et al., 1:21–406. Moscow: Khudozhestvennaia literatura, 1985.

Utekhin, Il'ia. *Ocherki kommunal'nogo byta*. Moscow: OGI, 2001.

Vail', Petr, and Aleksandr Genis. *60-e: Mir sovetskogo cheloveka*. Moscow: Novoe literaturnoe obozrenie, 1996.

Veleva, Radostina. "Romanite na Liudmila Ulitskaia—mezhdu traditsiiata i novata slovesnost." *Bol'garskaia rusistika*, nos. 1–2 (2010): 154–60.

Velkoff, Victoria, and Kevin Kinsella. "Russia's Aging Population." In *Russia's Torn Safety Nets: Health and Social Welfare during the Transition*, edited by Mark Field and Judith Twigg, 231-50. New York: St. Martin's, 2000.
Vojvodić, Jasmina [Iasmina Voivodich]. "Chto otmechaet Gulia? O prazdnikakh v proizvedeniiakh Liudmily Ulitskoi." *Russian Literature*, no. 1 (2007): 113-20.
———. "Ljudmila Ulickaja i ruski postmodernizam." *Književna republika*, nos. 5-7 (2008): 238-45.
———. "Transfery Danielia Shtaina." *Russian Literature*, no. 1 (2011): 141-55.
Voronel', Nina. "Sekret Don Zhuana." *Novoe vremia*, no. 40 (2006): 34-35.
Vorontsov, Andrei. "Oshibka patera Shtaina." *Literaturnaia gazeta*, no. 5 (2007): 7.
Wachtel, Andrew. *The Battle for Childhood: Creation of a Russian Myth*. Stanford, CA: Stanford University Press, 1990.
———. *An Obsession with History: Russian Writers Confront the Past*. Stanford, CA: Stanford University Press, 1994.
———. *Plays of Expectations: Intertextual Relations in Russian Twentieth-Century Drama*. Seattle: University of Washington Press, 2006.
———. *Remaining Relevant after Communism: The Role of the Writer in Eastern Europe*. Chicago: University of Chicago Press, 2006.
———. "Translation, Imperialism, and National Self-Definition in Russia." *Public Culture*, no. 1 (1999): 49-73.
Wanner, Adrian. *Out of Russia: Fictions of a New Translingual Diaspora*. Evanston, IL: Northwestern University Press, 2011.
Williams, Craig Arthur. *Roman Homosexuality: Ideologies of Masculinity in Classical Antiquity*. Oxford: Oxford University Press, 1999.
Woll, Josephine. *Real Images: Soviet Cinema and the Thaw*. London: I. B. Tauris, 2000.
Yurchak, Alexei. *Everything Was Forever, Until It Was No More: The Last Soviet Generation*. Princeton, NJ: Princeton University Press, 2006.
Zapiski dekabristov. London: Vol'naia russkaia tipografiia, 1862-1863.
Zelenina, Iuliia. "Tolerantnost' po-russki." *Vecherniaia Moskva*, 16 November 2005. http://www.vmdaily.ru./showarticle.php?id=263308.
Zherebkina, Irina. *Gendernye 90-e, ili Fallosa ne sushchestvuet*. St. Petersburg: Aleteiia, 2003.
Ziolkowski, Margaret. *Alien Visions: The Chechens and the Navajos in Russian and American Literature*. Newark: University of Delaware Press, 2005.
———. *Literary Exorcisms of Stalinism: Russian Writers and the Soviet Past*. Columbia, SC: Camden House, 1997.
Zolotonosov, Mikhail. "Chitatel': Muzhchina ee mechty." *Moskovskie novosti*, 13 February 2004, 25.
———. "Sentimentalizm s pristavkoi 'neo.'" *Moskovskie novosti*, 7 February 1993, 26.
Zubok, Vladislav. *Zhivago's Children: The Last Russian Intelligentsia*. Cambridge, MA: Belknap, 2009.
Zviagintsev, Andrei, director. *Vozvrashchenie*. Moscow: REN TV, 2003.

INDEX

Page numbers in italic indicate photographs

abortion, 19–20, 38, 50–52, 70, 81
adolescence, 29, 60–61, 61–62
adoption, 38, 39, 70, 74, 75, 88, 175
aging, 10, 53–57, 60, 77, 93
ailing body, 29, 30–31, 48–50, 53–57
Aksenov, Vasilii, 69
Akunin, Boris (Grigorii Chkhartishvili), xi, xviii, xix, 23, 100, *134*, 179n1
alcoholism, 34, 74, 88, 144, 145, 150, 153
Alekhina, Mariia, 168
Aleksandrov, Grigorii, 193n6
Aleksandrov, Nikolai, 5, 6
Aleksii II, Patriarch, 137, 209n22
Alexeyeva, Ludmila, 118, 123–24
Aliger, Margarita, 104
Altaev, O. (Vladimir Kormer), 128, 208n74
"Angel" ("Golubchik"), xvi, 148–49, 181n26
Anna Karenina (Tolstoy), 14, 86, 180n12
anthroposophy, 213n80
anti-Semitism, 32, 112–13, 117, 132, 137, 140–41, 205n32, 208n5
Arabs, 77, 160, 202n61, 213n69
art: the body in, 56–57; domestic scenes in, 75–76; in history, 127–28; "Last Supper" (painting), 78, 163–64, 214n95; music, xv, xvi, 17, 53, 104, 107, 126, 127, 148; redemptive nature of, 124–27. *See also* ekphrasis; intertexts and intertextuality
Austen, Jane, 180n10

Autumn Marathon (*Osennii marafon*) (Danieliia), 70

"Babii Iar" (Evtushenko), 135–36
Bach, Johann Sebastian, 127, 128
Baer, Brian, xvi
Bakhnov, Leonid, 16
Bakhtin, Mikhail, 140, 160, 161
Baksaraeva, N. A., 76
Balabanov, Aleksei, 30, 70–71
Baranskaia, Natal'ia, 21, 57, 87
Barnes, Christopher, 126, 127, 207n67
benevolence (*terpimost'*), 135
Berlin, Isaiah, 31, 101, 108, 136, 145, 159, 216n13
Beslan (terrorist attack), 131
Biblical narratives, 54, 94, 95, 96, 97
The Big Green Tent (*Zelenyi shater*): art in, 126, 127, 128; books as aid to moral development, 164; denunciation in, 112; *Doctor Zhivago* (Pasternak) as intertext for, xi, xiv, 17, 109, 122, 124–27, 175, 207n66; emigration from Soviet Union, 142, 155; genetics and demographic degradation discussed in, 122; immaturity of younger generation, 28–29, 145, 173; intelligentsia in, xviii, 10, 12–13, 102–3, 106–7, 109, 113, 119, 121–22, 124, 145, 167, 170; Jewish identity depicted, 112, 142; KGB interrogation, 107, 111, 115–6; kinship in, 11, 12–13, 17, 109; literature

237

The Big Green Tent (continued)
  discussed in, 10, 12–13, 15, 107, 110, 124–25, 127; Moscow literary excursions, 107, 124; poets and poetry in, 13, 15, 102–3, 110, 112, 118, 120, 123–24, 127; political activism, 118, 120–21, 142; readership of, 22; sexuality in, 122, 148, 212n57; Soviet dystopia, 13, 110, 118, 145; Soviet history in, 28–29, 119, 120, 127–28, 142, 145, 211n48; Stalin's funeral described in, 120; suicide of, 13, 123, 127, 149; translators in, 24–25, 146

biological family, 3, 77, 81, 83–85, 87–89, 90–91, 109

Bloom, Harold, 11–12, 14

Bobruisk, Nazi massacre at, 54–55, 175

the body: abortion, 19–20, 38, 50–52, 70, 81; acrobatic body, 42–43, 193n6; aging body, 10, 53–57, 60, 77, 93; ailing body, 29, 30–31, 48–50, 53–57; catatonic states, 50, 52, 57, 58, 59, 64, 74; childbirth, 8, 29, 34, 36, 38–40, 58–59, 80, 83–84, 153, 175; corporeality and sincerity, xv, 29–33, 50, 52, 57–59, 64, 66, 74, 76–77, 80, 89; creativity, 85, 86; deformed female bodies, 18, 30, 46–48, 49, 122, 176, 195n39; the elderly, xiii, 6–7, 29, 53–57, 60, 73, 77, 93, 103, 124–25, 196n56, 199n17; eroticism, 53, 57, 59, 61–62, 63, 64–65, 196n56, 198n85; fetishized damaged male body, 30, 43, 51; the handicapped (irregular) body, 29–30, 43, 44–48, 60, 76–77, 87, 176, 195n39; heterosexuality, xvi–xvii, 35, 62–63, 65–66; humility, 45, 48, 61; illness, xvii, 19–20, 29–32, 45–46, 48–50, 52–57, 181n29, 195n47; male physique, xxii, 33–34, 35, 42, 98, 114, 136, 193n6; nakedness and, 55–57, 58, 196n56; the New Man, 33–34; problematic beauty, xvii, 20–21, 30, 40–43; sexual discovery, xiii, 60–61, 62, 64, 122; state co-option of, 43–45, 50–51, 89, 122. *See also* corporeality; death; disability; homosexuality; kinship; masculinity; mothers and motherhood; sexuality; tolerance

"The Body of a Beauty" ("Telo krasavitsy"), 65, 87, 88

Bolsheviks and Bolshevism: body's oppression by, 48, 51; Civil War, 51, 73, 98, 143; false kinship of ideology under, 84, 93; on the intelligentsia, 144; Marxism, 28, 104, 145

Borenstein, Eliot, 35, 67, 167

Boris Godunov (Pushkin), 15

Brezhnev era: exile of Tatars, 142; family in, 70, 109, 110; literature during, 18, 34; nostalgia for, 153; physicality in, 34; as Stagnation, 10, 13, 70, 123–24, 156, 204n22

Brodsky, Joseph, 14, 26, 124

"Bronka" ("Bron'ka"), xiii, xvi, xvii, 8, 61–62, 66, 85, 122, 167

Brother (*Brat*) (Balabanov), 54, 71

Brother 2 (*Brat 2*) (Balabanov), 35, 71, 131

Bulgakov, Mikhail, xxi

Bunin, Ivan, 12, 14

Butler, Judith, 33

Bykov, Dmitrii, xii, 23–24, 105

byt: in Chekhov's works, 13; connections to history, 18, 126–27; corporeality used to interpret the past in, 110; as feature of Ulitskaya's works, 21, 29, 69, 78, 101, 107–9, 145–46, 170; as locus of religious values and ethics, 158–59, 160, 166; nostalgia for, 169, 174; and the realm of ideas, 110, 170; in *zhenskaia proza*, 18–19

bytie (meaningful existence), 21, 128, 158, 160

"Cabiria from the Bypass" ("Kabiriia s Obvodnogo kanala") (Palei), 61–62

Cancer Ward (*Rakovyi korpus*) (Solzhenitsyn), 50

capitalism, 5, 9, 98, 160, 168–69, 171

The Captain's Daughter (*Kapitanskaia dochka*) (Pushkin), 117

"The Carpathians, Uzhgorod" ("Karpaty, Uzhgorod"), 120

catatonia, 50, 52, 57, 58, 59, 64, 74

cemeteries. *See* graveyards

censorship, xx, 22, 156, 170

Chechens and Chechnya, 14, 71, 151, 168, 212n64

Chekhov, Anton: *Cherry Orchard*, xxii, 98, 114, 115, 176; everyday life in works of, 13; "Gooseberries" ("Kryzhovnik"), 114, 176; as intertext for Ulitskaya's works, 76, 98, 114, 115; prison literature of, 134

Chernetsky, Vitaly, 147, 149, 150

chernukha, xvii, xx, 8, 34, 50, 59, 66, 167, 181n28, 197n74

Chernyshevsky, Nikolai, 16, 97
Cherry Orchard (*Vishnevyi sad*) (Chekhov), xxii, 98, 114, 115, 176
Chiaureli, Mikhail, 70
"Chicken Pox" ("Vetrianaia ospa"), 60–61, 197n76
childbirth, 8, 29, 34, 36, 38–40, 58–59, 80, 83–84, 153, 175
Childhood 45–53: There Will Be Happiness Tomorrow (*Detstvo 45–53: A zavtra budet schast'e*), 169, 173
Childhood of Luvers (*Detstvo Liuvers*) (Pasternak), 122
childlessness, 3, 55–56, 58, 83, 84, 175
children: abandonment of, 42, 45; adolescence, 29, 60–61, 61–62; adoption, 38, 39, 70, 74, 75, 88, 175; in alternative biography, 85, 86; culture transmitted to, 29, 54–55, 136; Down syndrome, xvii, 45, 181n29; playacting, 60–61, 62, 64, 95–96; sexual discovery, 60–61, 62, 64
children's literature, 4, 8, 101, 130–33, 208nn1–2
Chkhartishvili, Grigorii. *See* Akunin, Boris
"Chosen People" ("Narod izbrannyi"), xvii, 45, 157, 158
Christianity. *See* "Chosen People"; *Daniel Stein, Interpreter*; Orthodoxy
Chukovskaia, Lidiia, 195n48
Circus (*Tsirk*) (Aleksandrov), 193n6
Civil War, 51, 73, 98, 143
Clark, Katerina: generational political maturity, 90; the Great Family and, 34, 70; on the intelligentsia, 9, 27–28, 105, 170; messianic mission of the intelligentsia, 145; sincerity, 205n22
Clowes, Edith, 5, 25, 93, 135, 143
collaborators and collaboration as problem, 46–47, 60, 73, 76–77, 89–90, 92, 104, 140, 146
collectivization, 56, 70, 121
common people. *See narod*
communal apartments, 66, 90, 117, 120, 144, 173, 206n45
Communism, 18, 90–91, 105, 145, 160
consumerism: capitalism, 5–6, 9, 98, 160, 168–69, 171; gratification in post-1991 Russia, 133–34, 160, 168–69; sincerity, 5–6, 9, 18, 27, 105, 156, 160, 168–69, 184n9, 204n14; as threat to intelligentsia, 9, 105, 205n41. *See also* Yeltsin, Boris
corporeality (*telesnost'*): aging body, 53–57; beauty, xvii, 20–21, 30, 40–43; body and spirit, 158, 167; brutality, 49, 51, 56, 108–9, 118, 127, 145, 195n48; catatonic states, 50, 52, 57, 58, 59, 64, 74; *chernukha*, xvii, xx, 34, 50, 181n28; of the elderly, 53–57, 196n56; eroticism, 53, 57, 59, 61–62, 63, 64–65, 196n56, 198n85; the handicapped (irregular) body, 29–30, 43, 44–48, 60, 76–77, 87, 176, 195n39; in history, 18, 33–34, 110–11; illness, xvii, 19–20, 29–32, 45–46, 48–50, 52–57, 181n29, 195n47; kinship, 74, 82, 85–86; motherhood, 35–37, 80; physical perfection, 45–46; procreation, 36–37; sexuality, xvi–xvii, 35–37, 56, 57–58, 62–63, 65–66, 147, 148, 212n57; sincerity, xv, 29, 33, 50, 52, 55, 57–59, 64, 74, 76–77, 80, 89; as state property, 42–43, 44; stylized images, 36, 41, 46; suffering, 34, 54–55, 146, 154; in *zhenskaia proza*, 50. *See also* disability
"A Cow's Leg" ("Korov'ia noga"), 149
Crimea, 5, 25, 68, 72–73, 85, 142–43, 151, 168, 212n64
culture and cultural values: decline of, 5, 29; of gratification, 133–34, 160, 168–69; problem of consumerism and, 5–6, 9, 18, 27, 29, 105, 156, 160, 168–69, 184n9, 204n14; translator and, xiv, 24–25, 146, 160; transmission of, 29, 54–55, 136
Czechoslovakia, invasion of, 120, 145

Daniel', Iulii, 27, 29, 112, 127–28, 134
Daniel Stein, Interpreter (*Daniel' Shtain, perevodchik*): *byt* and *bytie* connected by, 160; collaboration with totalitarian state, 154; commemoration of ghetto escape, 162; critics' response to, 69, 135, 138, 159, 160, 179n2, 202n61, 211n42; on dogma and practice, 128, 145, 146, 156–59; false kinship of ideology in, 77, 84, 99; family in, 79, 84–85, 90, 91, 113; as force of reconciliation, 164; ghetto escapes, 77, 140, 162; history and fiction conjoined in, 108, 170; Holocaust in, xv, 25, 77, 140, 142, 154, 159, 162–63, 174;

Daniel Stein, Interpreter (continued)
hostility towards, 142, 170; icon of Mother Ioanna, 163, 164; intelligentsia in, 102, 103, 137, 170; Jewish-gentile relations, 138–39, 140–41, 146, 158–59, 162–64, 167; Jews portrayed in, 61, 141, 142; life of, 102, 138, 142, 146, 158, 160, 162; nondenominational spirituality, xv–xvi, 25, 32, 138–39, 158–59, 162, 164–65, 167, 174; orthopraxis in, 156–58, 164; papacy in, 90, 142, 156–57; person-idea, 144; on religious bureaucracy, 156–57; religious conversion in, 77, 84, 141; responsibility for educating others, 111–12; tolerance in, 25, 26, 91, 135, 138, 141, 142; translation, xiv, 25, 146, 160; Ulitskaya on the writing of, 141, 166, 215n9. *See also* Arabs; Jews; Judaism; Muslims

Danilkin, Lev, xii–xiii, 23, 28–29, 180n8
"Darling." *See* "Angel"
"Daughter of Bokhara" ("Doch' Bukhary"), xiii, xvii, 41, 42, 45–46, 212n69
"Dauntless Women of the Russian Steppe" ("Zhenshchiny russkikh selenii"), 149–50
death: acceptance of, 54, 60, 173; aging, 10, 53–57, 60, 77, 93; as celebration of memory, 52–53; cemetery visits and, 72–73, 76; gatherings connected to, 52–53, 78, 162, 174; kinship motivated by, 78; rituals of folklore, 119; wakes and, 52–53, 55, 78, 161–62. *See also The Funeral Party*
Death of Ivan Ilyich (Smert' Ivana Il'icha) (Tolstoy), 52
Decembrists, 115–16, 124–25
defection, 42–43
de Mallac, Guy, 10, 126, 127, 204n21, 207n65
dementia, 39, 40, 52, 58
demographic crises: collectivization, 56, 70, 121; decimation of male population, 38, 97–98; falling birthrates, 8, 34; genetic decay, 29, 121–22, 153, 167; Stalin's pronatalist policies, 36, 38, 50–52, 70, 81–82; xenophobia, 131, 153. *See also* narod
deportations, 72, 142–43, 145, 151, 212n64
derevenskaia proza. See village prose
Deutsch, Helene, 86
Diary of a Writer (Dnevnik pisatelia) (Dostoevsky), 169

disability: "Chosen People," xvii, 45, 157, 158; connection to sexuality, 64; Down syndrome, xvii, 45, 46, 181n29; feeling of inadequacy, 44; the handicapped (irregular) body, 29–30, 43, 44–48, 60, 76–77, 87, 176, 195n39; illness, xvii, 19–20, 29–32, 45–46, 48–50, 52–57, 181n29, 195n47; medicalization of, 43; parents' responses to, 45–46; personal gain and, 46–47, 60, 76–77; and Soviet misuses of corporeality, 45. *See also* corporeality

Discarded Relics (Sviashchennyi musor): cancer treatments, 49, 53; demographic anxiety in, 153; *Diary of a Writer* (Dostoevsky) compared with, 169; importance of books in, 110, 174; on intelligentsia and its failures, 103–4; Islamic fundamentalism critiqued in, 151–52; on maternal happiness, 80; on reading Nabokov's *The Gift*, 16; Ulitskaya's religious conversion, 157; on "The Writer's Daughter," 104

dissidents, 115, 118, 119, 120–23, 134–35, 145, 211n48. *See also The Big Green Tent*; Sakharov, Andrei; Siniavskii, Andrei; Solzhenitsyn, Aleksandr

The Divine Comedy (Dante), xiv
doctors, 36–38, 41, 50–52, 196n52
Doctor Zhivago (Doktor Zhivago) (Pasternak), xi, xiv, 17, 109, 125–27, 173, 207n66, 207n67
documentary genres, 108, 169–70
Dontsova, Dar'ia, xi, 35, 179n1
Dostoevsky, Fyodor, xxii, 4, 12, 25, 47, 116, 134, 161, 169
Down syndrome, xvii, 45, 46, 181n29
Dubin, Boris, 10, 12–13, 106, 108, 110, 153
"Dutch Fruit" ("Frukt gollandskii"), 149

education, 18, 102, 109, 111–12, 153, 164
ekphrasis, 19, 20, 56, 75–76, 127, 148, 163, 165, 207n69
the elderly, xiii, 6–7, 29, 53–57, 60, 73, 77, 91, 93, 103, 124–25, 196n56, 199n17
elektrichka, 117
emigration, 26, 28, 78, 89, 124–25, 142, 155
"Ende Gut—Alles Gut" (Bach), 127, 128
Engel'gardt, Boris, 144
Erofeev, Venedikt, 118

eroticism, 53, 57, 59, 61–62, 63, 64–65, 196n56, 198n85
Etkind, Alexander, xii, 18, 30, 105, 127, 170
Eugene Onegin (*Evgenii Onegin*) (Pushkin), 63, 116, 202n61
everyday life (*byt*). *See byt*
Evtushenko, Evengii, 135–36

The Fall of Berlin (*Padenie Berlina*) (Chiaureli), 70
false family, 46–47, 60, 76–77, 84, 99, 142
false intelligentsia, 103–4, 148
family: adoption, 38, 39, 70, 74, 75, 88, 175; biological family, 3, 77, 81, 83–85, 87–89, 90–91, 109; consanguinity, 69, 71, 85, 99, 109, 111; in *Daniel Stein, Interpreter*, 79, 84–85, 91; false images of, 75–76; false kinship of ideology, 46–47, 60, 76–77, 84, 90–91, 99, 148; gatherings of, 42, 52–54, 78–79, 161–62, 164, 174; male authority, 35–39, 41, 50, 52, 74, 87, 88; *mysl' semeinaia* (family idea) (Tolstoy), 69; siblings, 43–44, 57–59, 62, 72, 75, 83, 93–98, 203n75; support networks in, 73; vulnerability of, 167. *See also* family of affinity; fatherhood; kinship; *The Kukotskii Case*; *Medea and Her Children*; mothers and motherhood
family of affinity: biological connections less important than, 77–78; creation of, 53, 78–80, 93, 107; false kinship of ideology as opposed to, 46–47, 60, 76–77, 84, 90–91, 99, 148; gatherings of, 42, 52–54, 78–79, 161–62, 164, 174; genetics less important than, 77–78; motherhood in, 86–87; in Russophone diaspora, 42, 52–53, 78, 138, 141, 162; same-sex partnerships, 35, 130, 147; shared values of, 167; tolerance in, 79. *See also* intelligentsia; kinship
fascism, 44, 54–55, 70, 98, 112, 145, 153
fatherhood: adoption, 35, 39, 70, 74, 75, 88; disappearance of, 70, 97; fatherlessness, causes of, 70, 87, 88, 201n55; men's experience of, 80; positive role models of, 87, 90; and state corruption, 89–90; surrogacy, 87, 88–89, 90, 91–92, 113
feelings. *See* neosentimentalism
feminism, xii, 21, 174

film, Soviet, xiv–xv, 11, 34–35, 54, 70–71, 119, 131, 180, 193n6
"Finist the Bright Falcon" ("Finist Iasnyi Sokol"), 119
flight (sensation of during sex), 65, 198n85
Florida, Richard, 182n34
folklore and folktales, 11, 46, 48, 95, 119, 195n35, 206n51
"The Foundling" ("Podkidysh"), 43–44, 58, 94, 95, 96
The Funeral Party (*Veselye pokhorony*): acrobatic body, 42–43; coup, 115, 116, 174; death in, xvii, 52–53, 57, 78, 82; *Death of Ivan Ilyich* (Tolstoy) compared with, 52; eroticism in, 53, 196n56; *Eugene Onegin* (Pushkin) and, 116; everydayness of life, 78; family of affinity in, 42, 52–54, 78–79, 162, 174; flight (sensation of during sex), 198n85; Jewish-Christian dialogue in, 138–39; "Last Supper" painting, 78, 163–64, 214n95; reconciliation in, 164; tolerance in, 26, 141–42; women in, 42, 138, 141
Furman, Yelena, 194n25

gatherings, images of, 42, 52–54, 78–79, 161–62, 164, 174
gays. *See* homosexuality
genetics: family of affinity and, 77–78; genetic decay, 29, 121–22, 167; Ulitskaya's training in, 48, 68, 80, 143. *See also* narod
geography, xiv, 26, 107, 117, 141, 143
Georgians, 65–66
Gessen, Masha, 115
The Gift (*Dar*) (Nabokov), 16
"A Gift Not Made by Hands" ("Dar nerukotvornyi"), 46–47, 60, 76–77, 140
Gilbert, Edit, 5
Gilbert, Sandra, and Susan Gubar, 12
girls: playacting, 60–61, 62, 64, 95–96; sexual discovery, 60–61, 62, 64
Girls cycle (*Devochki*), xx, 43–44, 95
Gogol, Nikolai, 65
Goldstein, Baruch, 77
Good Book (*Khoroshaia kniga*) initiative, 29, 136
"Gooseberries" ("Kryzhovnik") (Chekhov), 114, 176

Gorbachev era, 21, 30, 116, 131
Gorbanevskaia, Natal'ia, 120–21, 124, 155, 169, 206n55, 215n10
Gorelik, Mikhail, 112
Goscilo, Helena: on abortion, 38; the body in Russian culture, 33–34; disappearance of fathers, 70, 97; on gender and gender roles, 21, 31, 65, 80; critiques Putin-era culture, 5; on Ulitskaya's depiction of the body, 19
Graham, Seth, 70
grandparents, xiii, 54–55, 57, 60, 77, 91, 93, 124–25, 141, 175
gratification in post-1991 Russia, 133–34, 160, 168–69
graveyards, 72–73, 76
the Great Family: appropriation of the body by, 43, 50–51, 89; characters identified with, 167; corporeal suffering and, 34; deportation of Chechens and Tatars, 72, 142–43, 151; the disabled in, 46–47, 60, 76–77; dissidents as victims, 145; the elderly in, 53–54, 92–93, 106; false kinship of ideology, 46–47, 60, 76–77, 84–85, 99; families of affinity and, 31, 79–80; intolerance of, 140, 143; myth of, 70, 143. *See also* kinship; Stalinism
Great Patriotic War, 36, 81, 98, 121, 169, 173
"The Great Teacher" ("Velikii uchitel'"), 90, 213n80
Grekova, I. (Elena Venttsel'), 8, 21, 52, 70, 85, 205n32
Grossman, Vasilii, 210n33
Grosz, Eliabeth, 33
Grothe, Anja, 83
Grymov, Iurii, 36
Gudkov, Lev, 10, 143
Gulag, 10, 44, 118, 119, 173, 195n48, 203n6, 211n48
Gulag Archipelago (*Arkhipelag GULag*) (Solzhenitsyn), 18, 107
"Gulia," xvi–xvii, 57, 145, 160, 176, 197n68

Hall, Stuart, 160
handicapped (irregular) bodies, 29–30, 43, 44–48, 60, 76–77, 87, 176, 195n39
"A Happy Incident" ("Schastlivyi sluchai"), 114
Hashamova, Yana, 31, 70, 97
Hellebust, Rolf, 43

Herzen, Aleksandr, 111
Herzfeld, Michael, 70, 76
heterosexuality, xvi–xvii, 35, 62–63, 65–66
Hirsch, Marianne, 37, 59
history: Chechens and Chechnya, 14, 71, 151, 168, 212n64; Civil War, 51, 73, 98, 143; Communism, 18, 90–91, 105, 145, 160; corporeality in, 18, 33–34, 111; Crimea, 5, 25, 68, 72–73, 85, 142–43, 151, 168, 212n64; Decembrists, 115–16, 124–25; deportations, 72, 142–43, 145, 151, 212n64; gender in, 152, 168; Great Patriotic War, 36, 81, 98, 169, 173; intelligentsia on, 18, 27, 29, 100, 102–3, 111–12, 122, 125, 167; literature's relation to, 15, 18, 28, 31, 69–70, 108–9, 117–18, 125, 139–40, 167, 170; Marxism, 28, 104, 145; myths in, 28, 44–45, 70, 143; *narod* and deformation of, 121–23; nostalgia, 29, 108, 153, 169; personalization of, xiii, 54–55, 59–60, 92–93, 211n48; political protests, xix, 23, 100, 101, 120, 168, 170; reassessment of, 105–6; recording of, 111–12; *samizdat* literature, 107, 110, 112, 124, 128, 171, 175; Soviet state narratives concerning, xii, xiii, 21, 28–29, 106, 168. *See also* Brezhnev era; Holocaust; Leninism; Putin, Vladimir; Solzhenitsyn, Aleksandr; Stalin, Joseph; Stalinism; Yeltsin, Boris
Holocaust: anti-Semitism, 32, 112–13, 117, 132, 137, 140–41, 205n32, 208n5; "Babii Iar" (Evtushenko), 135–36; commemoration of, xv, 162; *in Daniel Stein, Interpreter*, xv, 25, 77, 140, 142, 146, 159, 163, 174; Nazi massacre at Bobruisk, 54–55, 175; Russian disinterest concerning, 140, 143, 210n33; survival during, 77, 140, 146, 162; as trauma, 154, 163
holy fool (*iurodivaia*), 30, 46–48, 176, 195nn35–36, 195n39
home as sanctuary, xiv–xv
homosexuality: ephebic love, 181n26, 212n60; first depiction as consensual sex, 148–49; homophobia, xvi, 20, 35, 147–49, 181n23; lesbians, 149–50, 168, 170; *The Liberty Sisters*, 20, 147–48, 197n74; music and doom linked with, 148; Nabokov's *Lolita* and, 148; queerness, 20, 34, 35, 148, 149, 151; same-sex partnerships, 35, 130, 147; self-identification

as, 149, 212n57; in Sorokin's prose, 181n27; Ulitskaya on, xvi, 35, 130, 147, 168, 181n27, 197n74, 211n60

House on the Embankment (Dom na naberezhnoi) (Trifonov), 50, 107

humility, 45, 48, 50, 61, 119

hybridity, xvi-xvii, 57, 145, 158-59, 160-62

icons, 36, 41, 48, 162-63, 164, 176

intelligentsia (*intelligenty*): art, redemptive nature of, 124-25; collusion with the state, 88, 104, 114, 128, 205n41, 208n74; consumerism as threat to, 9, 105, 205n41; Decembrists, 115-16, 124-25; decline of, 101-2, 104, 106-7, 114-15, 121-23, 144-45, 155; denunciation of colleagues, 88, 112, 114, 115-16, 144; dissidents, 115, 118, 119, 120-23, 134-35, 145, 211n48; doctors as subset of, 143-44; as educators, 102, 109, 111-12, 117, 135, 153, 164; false intelligentsia, 103-4, 148; on history, 18, 27, 100, 103, 111-12, 125, 167; intertextual portrayals, 98, 114, 115; Jews as, 103, 112-13, 137, 140; on literature and reading, 10-13, 22, 24, 85-86, 105, 110, 123, 125, 153; moral compromises of, xviii, 88, 115-16, 122, 124, 126, 128, 129, 155-56, 182n31, 205n41, 207n65, 208n74; mythos of place, 3, 18, 19, 107-8, 204n21; *narod* and, 27-28, 61, 105, 112, 116-20, 123, 139, 145, 153, 167, 192nn84-85, 206n43; prejudices of, 120, 132, 147, 151-52; religious belief, 139-41, 168, 210n30; responsibility as virtue of, 111-12, 120-21, 128, 131, 133-34, 144-46, 166; *shestidesiatniki*, xviii-xix, 17-18, 23, 78, 106, 108, 114, 116, 156, 169; sincerity, 4, 18, 43, 66, 85, 102, 106, 111-12, 126, 146, 159, 167; smatterers, 103-4; Stalinism, xviii, 36, 106, 107, 114, 124; suffering of, 102-3, 118, 127-28, 146; survival of, 28, 103, 105, 125; tolerance defined by, 45, 135, 136, 154, 159, 167; *zhenskaia proza* on, 18-19. See also *The Big Green Tent*; *Daniel Stein, Interpreter*; *The Funeral Party*; Men', Aleksandr; Sakharov, Andrei; Solzhenitsyn, Aleksandr; tolerance; Trifonov, Iurii

intertexts and intertextuality: *Anna Karenina* (Tolstoy) as, 14-15, 86; art, 56-57, 78, 123, 124-25, 127, 128, 163-64, 214n95; for *The Big Green Tent*, xi, xiv, 15, 17, 109, 122, 124-27, 175, 207n66; Chekhov's works as intertext for *Russian Jam*, 98, 114, 115; from classical literature, 14-15, 85-86; and critics' responses, 14-15; cultural memory, 11-12, 15; of diaspora authors, 26; *Eugene Onegin* (Pushkin) as intertext in *Funeral Party*, 116; *The Gift* (Nabokov), 16; Gogol's "The Overcoat" as intertext for *Sincerely Yours, Shurik*, 65; *narod* depicted in, 117-18; poets and poetry, 13, 15-16, 102-3, 110, 112, 118, 120, 123-24, 127; Pushkin, 15, 47, 63

intolerance: anti-Semitism, 32, 112-13, 117, 132, 137, 140-41, 205n32, 208n5; atonement for, 142-43, 174, 175; Chechens, 151, 168; Crimean Tatars, 72, 118, 142-43, 211n48; geography of, 143; religious extremism, 77, 138, 139-40, 141-42, 151-53. See also Arabs; Holocaust

irregular (handicapped) bodies, 29-30, 43, 44-48, 60, 76-77, 87, 176, 195n39

Iser, Wolfgang, 10, 11, 12

iskrennost' (sincerity). See sincerity

Islam, 132, 140, 142-43, 151-52, 159, 160, 212n69

Israel, 24, 77, 91, 142, 174. See also *Daniel Stein, Interpreter*

iurodivaia. See holy fool

Jaspers, Karl, 141

Jews: anti-Semitism, 32, 112-13, 117, 132, 137, 140-41, 205n32, 208n5; and Arabs, 77, 160, 202n61, 213n69; continuity of Jewish culture, 54; elders of, xiii, 54-55, 60, 77, 93; Israel, 24, 91, 142, 174; as members of intelligentsia, 103, 112-13, 140, 213n77; Muslim relations with, 142; and Russian Orthodoxy, 31, 50, 77, 84, 137-38, 141, 142, 164; under Stalin, 213n77. See also *Daniel Stein, Interpreter*; Holocaust

Judaism: Biblical narratives, 54, 94, 95, 96, 97; conversion to Christianity, 31, 50, 77, 84, 137-38, 141, 142, 164; in *Daniel Stein, Interpreter*, 158; identification with, 162, 168, 175; Jewish extremists, 77, 142; Jewish-gentile relations, 78-139, 140-41, 146, 158-59, 162-64, 167; principles of, 112-13

Kaganovsky, Lilya, 30, 43, 47, 48, 193n6
Karamzin, Nikolai, 33, 100
Kaspe, Irina, 31
Kazarina, Tat'iana, 18, 58, 197n76
KGB, 111, 115–16, 117, 122, 146, 155, 206n45
Khanty-Mansiisk, 130–31, 132, 208nn1–2
Khodorkovsky, Mikhail, xviii, xix, 133–35, 170, 174
Khoroshaia kniga initiative. *See* Good Book initiative
kinship: adoption, 38, 39, 70, 74, 75, 88, 175; of aged survivors, 54–55; biological family, 3, 77, 81, 83–85, 87–89, 90–91, 109; cemeteries as symbols of, 72; Christianity, 157; disintegration of, 19–20, 35, 38–40, 50–51, 74–75, 80, 88, 144, 175, 200n21; false kinship of ideology, 46–47, 60, 76–77, 84, 99, 148; family, 69, 198n3; Jewish-gentile relations, 95, 138–39, 146, 158, 162, 164, 167; linked to history, 69–70, 108–9; and reading, 10, 11, 22, 24, 105, 110, 153; as response to trauma, 54–55, 70, 85; same-sex families, 130, 147; siblings, 43–44, 57–59, 62, 72, 75, 83, 93–98, 203n75; stability of, 73–74; writing as creation of, 128–29
Kormer, Vladimir. *See* Altaev, O.
Kornblatt, Judith, 137
Kozlov, Denis, 106
Kristeva, Julia, 58
Kuklin, Lev, 43
The Kukotskii Case (*Kazus Kukotskogo*): abortion discussed in, 38, 50–52, 55, 59, 74, 75, 81, 88, 175; adoptions in, 19–20, 35, 38, 74, 81, 88, 175; aging in, 55–56; alcoholism, 88, 144; catatonia in, 52, 65, 74, 175; changes in Soviet gene pool discussed in, 121, 206n53; corporeality in, 62, 197n79; on demographic crisis in USSR, 8; disintegration of marriage, 35–36, 38–40, 50–51, 55, 74, 80, 88, 144, 175; family in, 35, 38–40, 50–51, 74, 81–82, 144, 200n21; illness in, 19–20, 52, 65, 74, 175; intelligentsia values in, 36, 119–20, 144; male authority in, 35, 36, 37, 38, 41, 50, 52, 55, 74, 88; maternal roles in, 40, 80–82; medicalization of women's bodies, 36, 37, 38, 41, 54–56; memory loss depicted, 39, 40, 52, 58, 59, 82; preservation of personality, 144, 146; reproductive rights discussed in, xiii, xix, 38, 50, 52, 81, 88; right to speak, 38, 39, 41, 52, 59, 111; Russian Booker Prize for, 8, 179n2; sexuality in, 62, 64, 110, 197n79; Stalin's funeral described in, 120; worldview in, 37, 38–39, 40, 55. *See also* Stalinism
Kuprin, Aleksandr, 12
Kuzmin, Mikhail, 124

labor camps, 118, 119. *See also* Gulag
"The Ladder" ("Pristavnaia lestnitsa"), 65
Lanoux, Andrea: on abortion, 38; the body in Russian culture, 33–34; on gender and gender roles, 65, 80
"Last Supper" (painting), 78, 163–64, 214n95
Layton, Susan, 152
Leninism, 28, 36, 48, 51, 93, 104, 144, 145, 211n48; Civil War, 51, 73, 98, 143; Communism, 18, 90–91, 105, 145, 160; Marxism, 28, 104, 145
lesbians, 149–50, 168, 170
Leskov, Nikolai, 12
Levantovskaya, Margarita, 5, 26, 146, 160
"Lialia's Home" ("Lialin dom"), xiii, xvii, 42, 58–59, 64, 198n85
The Liberty Sisters (*Sestrichki Liberti*), 20–21, 147–48, 197n74
Likhachev, Dmitrii, 31, 102–3, 104, 114, 135
Limonov, Eduard, 3, 23, 124, 147, 153
Linton, Simi, 43
Lipovetsky, Mark, xii, 18, 30, 105, 127, 170
literature: in Brezhnev era, 18, 34; censorship, xx, 22, 156, 170; history's relation to, 15, 18, 28, 31, 69–70, 108–9, 117–18, 125, 139–40, 167, 170; intelligentsia views of, 10, 11, 18, 22, 24, 105, 153; *samizdat* literature, 107, 110, 112, 124, 128, 171, 173; value of, 10, 11, 22–24, 90, 105, 128–29, 153. *See also* intertexts and intertextuality; readers and reading; *zhenskaia proza*
Litovskaia, Mariia, 153
Little Terrible (*Malen'kaia Groznaia*) (Petrushevskaia), 195n47
Little Vera (*Malen'kaia Vera*) (Pichul), 34
Livers, Keith, 43
Lolita (Nabokov), 148
"Lucky" ("Schastlivye"), xv, xx

Luzhkov, Iurii, 139
Lysenko, Trofim, 143

Maletskii, Iurii, 138
Mandel'shtam, Osip, 16
"March 1953" ("Vtorogo marta togo zhe goda"), xiii, 54-55, 59-60, 92-93
marriage: abandonment in, 41, 42; of the disabled, 46, 87; disintegration of, 35-36, 38-40, 50-51, 55, 74, 80, 88, 144, 175; eroticism, 53, 57, 59, 61-62, 63, 64-65, 196n56, 198n85; infidelity, 57, 58; same-sex partnerships, 35, 130, 147; violence and, 65, 150. *See also The Kukotskii Case; Medea and Her Children;* sexuality; *zhenskaia proza*
Marxism, 28, 104, 145
Mary Magdelene, 41
masculinity: eroticism, 53, 57, 59, 61-62, 63, 64-65, 196n56, 198n85; fears of emasculation in post-Soviet era, 70; in film, 34, 35, 54, 71, 131, 193n6; male authority, 35-39, 41, 50, 52, 74, 87, 88; male physique, 34, 35, 42, 114, 193n6; sexuality, xvi-xvii, 19, 35, 62-63, 65-66; Stalinist representations of, xxii, 33-34, 98, 114, 136, 193n6; transgendered characters, 47-48, 195n39; virility, 35, 71. *See also* homosexuality; sexuality; *zhenskaia proza*
Master and Margarita (Bulgakov), xxi
materinstvo. See mothers and motherhood
Mayakovsky, Vladimir, 15
meaningful existence. *See bytie*
Medea and Her Children (Medeia i ee deti): Anna Karenina as intertext for, 14; *byt* in, 157, 158-59; Crimea, 5, 25, 68, 72-73, 85, 142-43, 151, 168, 212n64; death in, 52-53, 72-73, 78, 119, 161-62; family in, xiv-xv, 14, 16, 29, 72-73, 79, 89, 93, 175, 199n17; gatherings in, 52-53, 78, 161-62; kindness in, 49, 51, 79, 93, 98, 123, 142-43, 157; and kinship, 72-73, 79, 111, 161, 167, 175; marital relations in, 49, 57, 72-73, 83-84, 96, 97, 161-62; Moscow as focal point in, 143; motherhood in, 83-84, 87, 93, 96-97, 155, 175; publication of, 8, 16; religious identity in, 50, 72, 73, 157, 161-62; sexuality in, 57, 110-11, 175, 198n85; sibling relations in, 57, 72, 75, 83, 93, 96-98, 203n75

Medvedev era, 22, 35, 79-80, 88, 120, 134-35
memoirs. *See Childhood 45-53: There Will Be Happiness Tomorrow; Discarded Relics*
Men', Aleksandr, 27, 137, 138, 159
Men'shov, Vladimir, 70, 106
Mikhail Khodorkovsky: Articles, Dialogues, Interviews (Stat'i, dialogi, interv'iu), xviii, xix, 133-35
Mir (Belarus), 140
morality: compromises of, xviii, 115, 122, 124, 126, 129, 155-56, 205n41, 207n65
Morson, Gary Saul, 14, 15, 27, 159
Moscow, 3, 18, 19, 107-8, 143, 204n21
Moscow Does Not Believe in Tears (Moskva slezam ne verit) (Men'shov), 70, 106
"Moscow-Podrezkovo, 1992," 117
Moscow to the End of the Line (Moskva-Petushki) (Erofeev), 118
Mother Ioanna, 163, 164
Mother of God (*bogoroditsa*), 41, 61
Mother Russia, 80
mothers and motherhood: biologization of, 35-37; childbirth, 8, 29, 34, 36, 38-40, 58-59, 80, 83-84, 153, 175; childlessness, 3, 55-56, 58, 83, 84, 175; in family of affinity, 80, 86-87; grandmothers, 54, 57, 91, 124-25; imagination, 84, 85, 86; sacred images of, 41, 61, 80, 158; surrogacy, 83; upbringing, 91-92, 202n62. *See also* the body; *The Kukotskii Case; Medea and Her Children*
Mulvey, Laura, 61
music, xv, xvi, 17, 53, 104, 107, 126, 127, 148
Muslims, 132, 140, 142-43, 151-52, 159, 160, 212n69; Chechens and Chechnya, 14, 71, 151, 168, 212n64
"My Favorite Arab" ("Moi Liubimyi arab"), 160
My Grandson Veniamin (Moi vnuk Veniamin), 54-55, 141, 175
My Past and Thoughts (Byloe i dumy) (Herzen), 111

Nabokov, Vladimir, 16-17, 24, 26, 148
narod (common people): behavior of, 115, 117, 121-23, 127; coup, 116; culture of, 29, 117, 119; genetic decay precipitated by, 121-22;

narod (*continued*)
  insect analogy for, 122, 123; intelligentsia tensions with, 27–28, 61, 105, 112, 116–20, 123, 139, 145, 153, 167, 192nn84–85, 206n43; intertexts depicting, 117–18; Jewish tensions with, 112, 205n32; Russian Orthodox Church, 138; Stalin's funeral and, 120; values of, 118–19, 120–23, 157, 213n80
National Bolsheviks. *See* Limonov, Eduard
naturalism, xvii, xx, 48–49
Nazis: Bobruisk massacre, 54–55, 175; escape from, 77, 118, 140, 162, 211n48; fascism, 44, 54–55, 70, 98, 112, 145, 153. *See also* Holocaust
neosentimentalism, 15, 16, 33, 180n6
New Russians, xxii, 33–34, 35, 98, 114, 136
New World (*Novyi Mir*), 8, 102–3
New York, 8, 26, 42, 78, 162, 176
Nichiporuk, Petr, 211n48
Number One or In the Gardens of Other Possibilities (*Nomer Odin, ili V sadakh drugikh vozmozhnostei*) (Petrushevskaia), 19, 189n52

On the Bright Side of the Street (*Na solnechnoi storone ulitsy*) (Rubina), 24
O'Reilly, Andrea, 80
"Orlov-Sokolovs" ("Orlovy-Sokolovy"), xx
Orthodoxy (Russian): conversion to, 31, 137, 138, 157, 164; degradation of the flesh, 46; folklore, 119; holy fools in, 30, 46–48, 176, 195nn35–36, 195n39; marriage and, 41–42; moderate tendencies of, 136–37; Pussy Riot, 168, 170; Putin's relations with, 28, 139, 157; responsibility of, 137–38; Russianness and, 132; saints' lives, 119; tolerance in, 137, 168; Ulitskaya's criticism of, 94, 118, 132, 137–38; values of, 157
orthopraxis, 156–58, 164
Orwell, George, 110
Our Crowd (*Svoi krug*) (Petrushevskaia), 70, 87, 189n53
Our Family and Others' (*Sem'ia u nas i u drugikh*) (Timenchik), 130
Oushakine, Serguei: on the demographic crisis, 213n70; on kinship, 69, 71, 84–85; patriotism of despair, 29, 30, 34, 57
"The Overcoat" ("Shinel'") (Gogol), 65

Palei, Marina, 52, 62
Palestinians. *See* Arabs
Panfilov, Oleg, 208n5
Paperno, Irina, 28, 103, 109, 111, 128, 136–37
"Paper Victory" ("Bumazhnaia pobeda"), 201n55
Papkova, Irina, 136, 137
Parfenov, Leonid, 134
Pasternak, Boris: on artistic inspiration, 126–27; and *byt*, 126, 207n67; *Childhood of Luvers*, 122; *Doctor Zhivago*, xi, xiv, 17, 109, 125–27, 173, 207n66; and intertexts for *The Big Green Tent*, xi, xiv, 15, 17, 109, 122, 124–27, 175, 207n66; kinship of positive characters used by, 11; as modernist, 17; moral compromise and atonement of, 207n65; and Moscow, 204n21; sincerity of post-1953 intelligentsia, 17; Ulitskaya influenced by, xiv, 4, 10, 14, 63, 122, 125–26
patriotism of despair. *See* Oushakine, Serguei
Peculiarities of the National Hunt (*Osobennosti natsional'noi okhoty*), 34
Pelevin, Viktor, xii, xx, 105
People of Our Tsar (*Liudi nashego tsaria*), 12, 87, 108
perestroika: coup, 116; family during, 70, 98; ideology conceived as paternal curse, 89–90; images of the body during, 34, 40–41, 62; literature affected by, 21, 167; older generation and, 54; Russian diaspora, 26; sexuality, 62, 147; the Thaw emulated by, 106; Ulitskaya's publications during, 8, 20–21, 26, 30; *zhenskaia proza*, 21. *See also* *The Funeral Party*
person-idea (*chelovek-ideia*), 144
Petrushevskaia, Liudmila: ailing body in works of, 49–50, 195n47; *byt*, 19; on family, 70, 74, 81, 189n53; on feminism, 21; on gay men, 20; on the intelligentsia, 22; missing father in works of, 87; Moscow text, 18; style of, xx–xxi, 19, 30, 189n52; violence in works of, 19, 34, 52, 66, 189n53
philanthropy, 133, 170
photography, xvii, 61, 85
Pirogov, Lev, 40
Platonov, Andrei, 47
Podnieks, Elizabeth, 80

Poet: A Book of Memories: Natal'ia Gorbanevskaia (*Poetka: Kniga pamiati: Natal'ia Gorbanevskaia*), 169, 215n10
poets and poetry, 13, 15–16, 102, 103, 110, 112, 118, 120, 123–24, 127
Pomerantsev, Vladimir, 4, 18
"Poor, Happy Kolyvanova" ("Bednaia, schastlivaia Kolyvanova"), 65
Poor Relatives (*Bednye rodstvenniki*), xx
Popkin, Cathy, xxii–xxiii
Popper, Karl, 154
pravo golosa. See right to speak
prevarication, 85–86, 87
Prilepin, Zakhar, xii
Prokhanov, Aleksandr, 28, 131, 153
Prokhorov Foundation, 136
publitsistika (journalistic works), 4, 18, 147, 165, 170, 174. See also *Discarded Relics*
Pugachev, Emel'ian, 117
Pushkin, Alexander: *The Captain's Daughter*, 117; *Eugene Onegin*, 63, 116, 202n61; influence on Ulitskaya, xx, xxi, 14, 15, 47, 63; poetry of, 124; Romantic organicism, 126
Pussy Riot, 168, 170
Putin, Vladimir: authoritarianism of, 4, 23, 69, 100, 131; book market under, 22; characters identified with, 167; cult of celebrity and, 5; Great Family, 31, 167; history, importance under, xii, xiii, 106, 168; homosexuality attacked by, 35, 181n23; ideology of, 68–69, 106, 112, 131–32, 143, 167–69; intelligentsia under, xviii–xix, 120, 170; Khodorkovsky's opposition to, 133–35; kinship under, 71, 79–80, 85; Medvedev era, 22, 35, 79–80, 88, 120, 134–35; opposition to, 23, 100, 101, 133–34, 168, 170; prisoner releases, 168; reelection of, 18; relations with Russian Orthodox Church, 28, 139, 157; stroll for freedom, xix, 23, 100, 101; virility of, 35, 71; writers and, xviii–xix, 15, 168, 169, 171, 182n34. See also Crimea

queerness. See homosexuality

Radio Liberty (*Radio Svoboda*), 68, 72, 183n3
Radishchev, Aleksandr, 33
rape, 51, 62, 63, 122, 150

Rasputin, Valentin, 28, 115
readers and reading: children's literature project, 4, 8, 101, 130–32, 133, 208nn1–2; transmission of tolerance, 136; education, 18, 102, 109, 111–12, 133, 153, 164; Good Book initiative, 29, 136; illiteracy, 152–53; importance of books, 10, 22, 110, 164, 186n22; intelligentsia on, 10, 11, 22, 24, 105, 110, 153; kinship of, 10, 11, 22, 24, 105, 109–10, 153; *narod*, 117; readership for Ulitskaya's works, 26–27; sexuality constructed by, 63; Sonechka and, 63, 76, 176; value of, xxii–xxiii, 10, 11, 22–23, 24, 128–29, 136
Red Pinkerton, 22
Red Square protest against invasion of Czechoslovakia, 120
religion. See Islam; Jews; Judaism; Muslims; Orthodoxy
religious conversion, 31, 77, 84, 137–39, 141–42, 157, 164
religious extremism, 77, 138, 139–40, 142, 151–53
Remizova, Mariia, 200n23
Repentance (*Pokaianie*), 70
Rep'eva, Ekaterina, 145
The Return (*Vozvrashchenie*) (Zviagintsev), 71
Richter, Sviatoslav, xvi
right to speak (*pravo golosa*), 38, 39, 41, 52, 111
Robski, Oksana, 35
Rovenskaia, Tat'iana, 83
Rubina, Dina, 24
Rufeisen, Oswald. See *Daniel Stein, Interpreter*
Russia. See Bolsheviks and Bolshevism; history; intelligentsia; Leninism; readers and reading; Stalinism
Russian Ark (*Russkii kovcheg*) (Sokurov), 128
Russian Jam (*Russkoe varen'e*), xxii, 98, 114, 115, 117, 176
Russian Orthodox Church. See Orthodoxy
Russophone diaspora, 26, 42, 52–53, 78, 138, 141, 162
Rutten, Ellen, 33, 126, 156
Rybakov, Anatolii, 210n33
Ryzhova, Svetlana, 132, 209n22

Sadur, Nina, 19
Said, Edward, 25, 152
saint's life (*zhitie*), 119

Sakharov, Andrei, 9, 27, 136
same-sex families, 130, 147
samizdat (underground) literature, 107, 110, 112, 124, 128, 171, 173
Savkina, Irina, 16, 69, 74, 206n53
Scott, Walter, 180n10
Second World War. *See* Great Patriotic War
sentimentalism. *See* neosentimentalism
Sergeenko, Andrei, 157
Seven Saints from Briukho (*Semero sviatykh iz derevni Briukho*), 47-48, 51, 137, 176
sexuality: and the aging female body, 57; constructed by reading, 63; corporeality, 53, 57-58, 62, 64, 65; discussions of sex during Stalinism, 60; eroticism, 53, 57, 59, 61-62, 63, 64-65, 196n56, 198n85; euphemisms in describing, xx-xxi; flight sensation and, 65, 198n85; gatherings and, 53; homosexuality, 20, 34, 35, 148, 149, 151; male sexuality, xvi-xvii, 35, 61-63, 65-66, 122; menstruation, xiii, 60, 122; of Muslim men, 151-52; older men and younger women, xvi-xvii, 61-62, 66, 122; rape, 51, 62, 63, 122; self-awareness, 59-61, 197n76; sexual discovery, 60-61, 62, 64, 110, 122; transgendered characters, 47-48, 195n39; violence, 151-52; *zhenskaia proza* on, 18-19
Shafranskaia, E. F., 161
Shalamov, Varlam, 10
Shengeli, Georgii, 204n21
shestidesiatniki (1960s intelligentsia), xviii-xix, 17-18, 23, 78, 106, 108, 114, 116, 156, 169
Shimes, Gershon, 77
Sincerely Yours, Shurik (*Iskrenne vash Shurik*): awards for, 179n2; critics on, 33; depiction of upbringing, 91-92, 202n62; disabled body, 44, 176; Gogol's "The Overcoat" as intertext for, 65; inaction portrayed in, 104; intelligentsia ethics, 92; kinship in, 91-92, 176; moral compromise, xviii, 88, 115-16, 124, 128, 155-56, 182n31, 205n41, 207n65, 208n74; paternal role in, 88; relations with women, xvii, 44, 64, 65, 92, 176; sexuality and lack of sincerity, 155; state neglect of the disabled, 44
sincerity (*iskrennost'*): ailing body, 29, 30-31, 48-50, 53; consumerism as opposed to, 5-6, 9, 18, 27, 105, 156, 160, 168-69, 184n9, 204n14; corporeal sincerity, xv, 29-33, 50, 52, 57-59, 64, 66, 74, 76-77, 80, 89, 155; in documentary genres, 169-70; *intelligenty* on, 4, 17, 18, 43, 85, 102, 106, 108, 111-12, 126, 146, 159, 167; kinship, 71, 73, 86-88; moral compromise, xviii, 88, 115-16, 122, 124, 126, 128, 129, 155-56, 182n31, 205n41, 207n65, 208n74; new sincerity, 4, 64, 183n4; preservation of personality, 4, 146; prevarication, 85-86, 87; and religious belief, 139
"Singing Masha" ("Pevchaia Masha"), 41, 42
Siniavskii, Andrei, xviii, 46, 119, 124; trial of, 29, 127-28, 134, 182n31
sisters, 43-44, 57, 72, 75, 83, 93, 95
skaz, 19, 109
Skomp, Elizabeth, 189n54
Slavnikova, Ol'ga, 196n56
Slezkine, Yuri, 25
smatterers (*obrazovanshchina*), 103-4
Snyder, Timothy, 141
Sof'ia Petrovna (Chukovskaia), 195n48
"So It Is Written" ("Tak napisano"), 140, 213n81
Sokurov, Aleksandr, 128
Solzhenitsyn, Aleksandr: on cancer, 50; corruption of intelligentsia, 128; cult of sincerity, 18; ethical equivocation in works of, 156; *Gulag Archipelago*, 18, 107; influence of, 9, 17, 107, 137; on kinship, 71; literature as documentation, 108; Matryona as positive character, 54, 57; prison literature of, 134; smatterers, 103-4; Ulitskaya influenced by, 17, 18, 24, 27, 71
"Someone Else's Children" ("Chuzhie deti"), 59, 94
Somov, Konstantin, xvi
Sonechka: artistic talents in, 61, 127, 161, 180n18; corporeal insincerity in, xv, 64, 75-76, 176; corporeality, 167; euphemism in, 182n42; family in, xv, 63, 75, 76, 161, 176; intertextual references in, 12, 14, 76; reading imagery in, 63, 76, 176; sexual liaisons in, xvi, xvii, 62-63, 64, 66, 75-76, 122, 175-77, 176-77; stage adaptation of, 12, 186n28; Stalinism resisted in, 61, 145
Sorokin, Vladimir, xii, xx, 105, 147, 181n27
space program (Soviet), 28-29

Spasokukotskii, Sergei, 51
Stagnation era. *See* Brezhnev era
Stalin, Joseph: death of, xiii, 55, 60, 120, 173; as Father of the Peoples, 70, 76, 90, 173; intertextual references to, 15
Stalinism: the body and, 40, 43-44, 46, 50-51, 70, 76, 144, 195n47; Bolsheviks and Bolshevism, 48, 51, 93, 144; *byt* during, 169, 173; collectivization, 56, 70, 121; communal apartments, 66, 90, 117, 120, 144, 173, 206n45; deportation of Chechens and Tatars, 72, 142-43, 151; the disabled in, 46-47, 60, 76-77; in film, 70; illness, 51-52, 90, 195n47; intelligentsia under, xviii, 36, 106, 107, 114, 124; kinship under, 46-47, 60, 70, 76-77, 81-82, 93, 99, 143; Marxism, 28, 104, 145; nostalgia for, 29, 169; opportunism under, 46-47, 60, 76-77, 104, 173; oppression under, 16, 18, 23-24, 51-52, 73, 120, 213n77; population control during, 36, 38, 50-52, 70; revisionist history of, 28-29; sincerity and, 4, 18; surviving, 7, 36, 54-55, 61, 92, 146; Young Pioneers, 46-47, 76-77, 141
state patronage, 46-47, 60, 76-77, 104, 114
Stephens, Robert, 15-16
Stishova, Elena, xiv-xv, 180n17
The Story of Antwerp the Sparrow, Mikheev the Cat, Vasia the Aloe Plant, and the Centipede Mar'ia Semenovna and Her Children (*Istoriia pro vorob'ia Antverpena, kota Mikheeva, stoletnika Vasiu i sorokonozhku Mar'iu Semenovnu s sem'ei*), 132
stroll for freedom (Moscow, 2012), xix, 23, 100, 101
Strugatskii, Boris, xix
Strukov, Vlad, 5
suicide: infidelity as cause of, 20-21, 79; intertextual references to, 14, 86; Masha (*Medea and Her Children*), 79, 93, 161; of Mikha (*The Big Green Tent*), 13, 127, 149; Mon'ka ("Cabiria from the Bypass"), 61-62
"Summer in the City" ("Letom v gorode") (Grekova), 70
surrogate fathers, 87, 88-89, 90, 91-92
Sutcliffe, Benjamin, 5

Tarkovsky, Andrei, 180n17
Tatars, 72, 118, 142-43, 151, 211n48

telesnost' (corporeality). *See* corporeality
"A Terrifying Story on the Road" ("Strashnaia dorozhnaia istoriia"), 65
test stroll. *See* stroll for freedom
Thaw era: assessment of, 106; "Babii Iar" (Evtushenko), 135-36; family during, 70; intellectual expression during, 123-24, 126, 176, 204n22; Khrushchev era, 34, 70, 106-7; physicality, evocations of, 34; *shestidesiatniki*, xviii-xix, 17-18, 23, 78, 106, 108, 114, 116, 156, 169; urban intellectual culture after, 17
theater hostage crisis (Moscow, 2002), 151-52
thinking class. *See* intelligentsia
Three Girls in Blue (*Tri devushki v golubom*) (Petrushevskaia), xxii
Timenchik, Vera, 130, 147
The Time: Night (*Vremia noch'*) (Petrushevskaia), 87, 91, 189n53
Timina, Svetlana, 79, 143
Toker, Leona, 203n6
tolerance (*tolerantnost'*): authoritarianism and, 4, 23, 69, 100, 131, 133; benevolence contrasted with, 135; charitable projects promoting, 29; Chechens and Chechnya, 14, 71, 151, 168, 212n64; in children's literature, 4, 8, 101, 130-32, 168, 208nn1-2; depictions of moral compromise, 115, 124, 154-56, 205n41, 207n65; the handicapped (irregular) body, 29-30, 43, 44-48, 60, 76-77, 87, 176, 195n39; hybridity, xvi-xvii, 57, 145, 158-59, 160-62; intelligentsia, 45, 135, 136, 154, 159, 167; kindness as, 50-51, 79, 93, 98, 119, 123, 142-43, 157; kinship, 29, 52-53, 68-69, 71, 73, 78, 142, 162; limits of, 147-53, 156; literature as extension of reality, 136; nondenominational spirituality, xv-xvi, 25, 32, 138-39, 158-59, 162-64, 167; personal responsibility as connected to, 111-12, 120-21, 128, 131, 133-34, 144-45, 166; religious tolerance, 31, 91, 135, 136-37, 159-60; as part of Russianness, 135-36; translation and, 25; violence, 131; xenophobia, 26, 29, 32, 112, 113, 117, 131-32, 153, 205n32, 208n5. *See also* family of affinity; Jews; Muslims
Tolokonnikova, Nadezhda, 168
Tolstaia, Tat'iana, 22

Tolstoy, Leo: *Anna Karenina*, 14, 86, 180n12; philosophy of the ordinary, 159; Ulitskaya influenced by, 4, 14
transgendered characters, 47-48, 195n39
translation and translators, 24-25, 141, 146-47, 160. *See also Daniel Stein, Interpreter*
trauma, 39, 40, 43-44, 52, 55, 57-59. *See also* history; Holocaust; Stalinism
Trifonov, Iurii: the body in works of, 34, 50; on *byt*, 108; critique of Stalin, 50, 108; *The Exchange (Obmen)*, 34; on family, 74; on the intelligentsia, 17-18, 156; literature as documentation, 107, 108; nostalgia in works of, 108; problem of compromise in works of, 156; Ulitskaya influenced by, 17, 27, 50, 107, 213n77
Tsiporkina, Inessa, 95-96
Turgenev, Ivan, 75
twins, 43, 58, 59, 62, 94-95, 96

Ukraine. *See* Crimea; Putin, Vladimir
Ulitskaya, Ludmila, 7, *101*, *134*; awards received by, 8, 19, 179n2; biography of, xxii, 6-8, 26, 49, 50, 53; charitable projects of, 20, 29, 136, 168; children's literature project of, 4, 8, 101, 130-32, 133, 208nn1-2; commercial work of, 11, 205n41; connections (*sviazi*) in works of, xiv; conversion to Russian Orthodoxy, 31, 137, 138, 157; critics on, xii-xiii, 5, 13-16, 21, 23, 26, 48, 138, 141, 180n6, 202n61; on ending her career, 169-70, 215n9; feminism, xii, 21, 174; gender differences and, xii, xii-xiii, 179n5, 180n10; genetics background of, 48, 68, 80, 143; Gorbanevskaia and, 120-21, 206n55; interviews with, xii-xiii, 68, 72, 151-52, 169, 183n3, 198n3, 215n5; Jewish heritage of, 24, 26, 31, 160; Khanty-Mansiisk visit, 130-31, 132, 208nn1-2; Khodorkovsky correspondence, xviii, xix, 133-35, 170, 174; limits of tolerance and, 147-53, 156; literary influences on, xiv, 4, 10, 14, 16-18, 63, 122, 125-26; literary style of, xiii-xvii, xx-xxii, 4, 17-18, 44, 97, 171, 188n46; Moscow text, 18, 107; on Petrushevskaia's prose, 19, 189n52; political activism of, 23, 100, 101, 120, 168, 170; popularity of, xii, xxi, 23, 26-27, 147, 169, 179n5;

publitsistika, 4, 18, 147, 165, 170, 174; rejection of unitary truth, 145-46; Russianness defined by, 135-36; and *shestidesiatniki*, 17-18; *zhenskaia proza* as problematic inheritance for, 18-19
underground literature. *See samizdat* literature
upbringing (*vospitanie*), 91-92, 93, 202n62

Vasilenko, Svetlana, 195nn36-37
Venttsel', Elena (I. Grekova). *See* Grekova, I.
Viazemskii, Petr, 124
village prose (*derevenskaia proza*), 54, 57, 73, 199n17
Vojvodić, Jasmina, 17
Voloshin, Maksimilian, 11
vospitanie. See upbringing

Wachtel, Andrew, 11, 14, 23, 25, 31, 94, 100, 129
wakes. *See* death
Wanner, Adrian, 24
A Week Like Any Other (Nedelia kak nedelia) (Baranskaia), 85
Well-Tempered Clavier (Bach), 127
What Is to Be Done? (Chto delat'?) (Chernyshevsky), 16, 97
Wilde, Oscar, xvi
Winter Notes on Summer Impressions (Zimnie zametki o letnikh vpechatleniiakh) (Dostoevsky), xxii
A Woman for All (Zhenshchina dlia vsekh), 11, 119
women. *See* the body; *byt*; sexuality; Stalinism; *zhenskaia proza*
Women's Lies (Skvoznaia liniia), 85-86
women's prose (*zhenskaia proza*). *See zhenskaia proza*
"Worm-Eaten Sonny" ("Chervivyi synok") (Sadur), 19
"The Writer's Daughter" ("Pisatel'skaia doch'"), 90, 104, 155
A Writer's Diary (Dnevnik pisatelia) (Dostoevsky), xxii

xenophobia, 26, 29, 32, 112, 113, 117, 131-32, 153, 205n32, 208n5

Yeltsin, Boris: capitalism and, 98; *chernukha*, xvii, xx, 34, 50, 59, 167, 181n28, 197n74;

economic crises under, 171; intelligentsia's decline and, 9, 115, 116, 171, 205n41; patriotism of despair, 34; *shestidesiatniki*, 106, 114, 171; trauma and, 116, 117, 131; *zhenskaia proza*, 21

younger generation, immaturity of, 28–29, 145, 173

Young Pioneers, 46–47, 76–77, 140, 141

Yurchak, Alexei, 109

zhenskaia proza (women's prose): attack on beauty, 20–21, 40–41, 56; communal apartment neighbors in, 117; corporeality in, 34, 50; crisis in works of, 19, 21–22, 34, 56; critiquing male authority, 35, 38, 50, 87; on gender roles, 19, 20, 21, 80, 93, 95; illness in, 19–20, 48–49, 52; impact of psychological trauma, 55, 57–58; sexuality in, 19, 20, 59–62, 65–66, 148–50; Trifonov's influence on, 108; Ulitskaya and, 21, 23, 69, 168; on violence, 19, 34, 56. *See also* Petrushevskaia, Liudmila

Zherebkina, Irina, 51–52, 199n20

Zhirinovsky, Vladimir, 115

zhitie. *See* saint's life

Ziolkowski, Margaret, 102

Zolotonosov, Mikhail, xii, 13–14, 15, 33, 180n6

Zubok, Vladislav, 114, 124, 153

Zviagintsev, Andrei, 71

CPSIA information can be obtained
at www.ICGtesting.com
Printed in the USA
LVHW021841300322
714843LV00003B/270